'[...] as officer, as [...] pris[...] [...] and as a Polish Unde[r]ground activist and courier, [i]s beyon[d] remarkable. In a world today where words such as "courage" and "heroism" have been so overused – applied freely from sports to entertainment to politics – as to be rendered practically meaningless, Jan Karski was the rare human being who embodied both' David Harris, Huffington Post

'Karski's exploration of the moral fog in which he and his colleagues operated resembles scenes tantalisingly directed by Hitchcock . . . Karski's account of the systematic brutality of the Nazi regime is literally chilling' Peter Conrad, *Observer*

'Truly staggering . . . an extraordinary testament to Man's inhumanity to Man, and the even more remarkable courage required to resist it' Ben MacIntyre, *The Times*

'It tells with great passion, fluency and the pace of an adventure story how Karski became qualified to be not just a messenger, but one of utter integrity' Andro Linklater, *Spectator*

'A Boy's Own tale of disguise. In one escape Karski leaps from a moving prison train; in another he swaps uniforms with a fellow inmate; in a third he is sprung from the Gestapo's clutches . . . This eye-witness testimony from a war that was still raging while Karski was writing is imbued with a passion that subsequent memoirs can rarely match' Stefan Wagstyl, *Financial Times*

'His is not a story of conventional heroism. It is a morally grave resistance in which any attack or escape is likely to cause the deaths of comrades or civilians . . . Karski provides an astonishing insight into the operation of the secret Polish state . . . His story deserves not just revival but reflection . . . Karski's electrifying words still speak only too eloquently for themselves' Marek Kohn, *Independent*

'The might-have-beens of history are never more heart-rending than when applied to the story of this impossibly heroic young Pole, and first-rate literary and historical figure: Jan Karski' Andrew Roberts

Jan Karski was born 24 June 1914 in Łódź, Poland. He received a Master's degree in Law and Diplomatic Science in 1935 and then served in various diplomatic posts in Germany, Switzerland, and Great Britain.

At the outbreak of the Second World War in 1939, he became a POW of the Red Army. Two months later he escaped and returned to occupied Poland, joining the Underground Polish Army and repeatedly crossing enemy lines as a courier. In November 1942, he delivered an impassioned plea on behalf of Poland's Jews to top Allied officials in London, and later told President Franklin D. Roosevelt about the extermination of the Jews in Europe.

In 1954, Jan Karski became a citizen of the United States, and, over time, a successful academic. After the fall of communism, Karski's wartime role was officially acknowledged in Poland. He died in Washington, DC, in 2000.

Andrew Roberts' *Masters and Commanders* was one of the most acclaimed, best-selling history books of 2008. His previous books include *Salisbury: Victorian Titan* (1999), which won the Wolfson History Prize and the James Stern Silver Pen Award for Non-Fiction, and *Hitler and Churchill: Secrets of Leadership* (2003), which coincided with four-part BBC2 history series. He is one of Britain's most prominent journalists and broadcasters.

JAN KARSKI

Story of a Secret State

My Report to the World

With an afterword by ANDREW ROBERTS

PENGUIN BOOKS

PENGUIN CLASSICS

Published by the Penguin Group
Penguin Books Ltd, 80 Strand, London WC2R ORL, England
Penguin Group (USA) Inc., 375 Hudson Street, New York, New York 10014, USA
Penguin Group (Canada), 90 Eglinton Avenue East, Suite 700, Toronto, Ontario, Canada M4P 2Y3
(a division of Pearson Penguin Canada Inc.)
Penguin Ireland, 25 St Stephen's Green, Dublin 2, Ireland (a division of Penguin Books Ltd)
Penguin Group (Australia), 250 Camberwell Road, Camberwell, Victoria 3124, Australia
(a division of Pearson Australia Group Pty Ltd)
Penguin Books India Pvt Ltd, 11 Community Centre, Panchsheel Park, New Delhi – 110 017, India
Penguin Group (NZ), 67 Apollo Drive, Rosedale, Auckland 0632, New Zealand
(a division of Pearson New Zealand Ltd)
Penguin Books (South Africa) (Pty) Ltd, 24 Sturdee Avenue, Rosebank, Johannesburg 2196, So

Penguin Books Ltd, Registered Offices: 80 Strand, London WC2R ORL, England

www.penguin.com

uth Africa

First published in the United States of America by Houghton Mifflin 1944
First published in Penguin Classics 2011
This edition published in Penguin Classics 2012

002

Copyright © Jan Karski Institute and Robert Laffont, S. A., Paris, 2010
Translation of new material copyright © Sandra Smith, 2011
Afterword copyright © Andrew Roberts, 2012
All rights reserved

The moral right of the author, the translator, and the author of the afterword has been asserted

Set in 11.16/13.71 pt Dante MT Std
Typeset by Jouve (UK), Milton Keynes
Printed in England by Clays Ltd, St Ives plc

ISBN: 978-0-141-19667-1

www.greenpenguin.co.uk

Penguin Books is committed to a sustainable
future for our business, our readers and our planet.
This book is made from Forest Stewardship
Council™ certified paper.

ALWAYS LEARNING

PEARSON

Contents

Note on the Text

The present volume follows the text of the original 1944 US edition of *Story of a Secret State*, supplemented with translations of additional material provided by the author in 1999 for the Polish edition. These have never before appeared in English. In the introduction to the 1999 edition, Jan Karski explained these additions: 'When I wrote this book in 1944, I faithfully and honestly reported what I remembered. But certain circumstances at that time imposed limits on what could be published.'[1]

Preface by Jan Karski[1]

I do not pretend to have given an exhaustive picture of the Polish Underground, its organization and its activities. Because of our methods, I believe there is no one today who could give an all-embracing recital. This would be possible only some years after the war with the aid of information yet to be gathered and checked. This book is a purely personal story, my story. I have tried to recall everything I experienced, to tell all about my own activities and to recount the deeds of all those with whom I had actual contact.

Poland's underground state, to which I belonged, was under the authority of the Polish Government in London. I know that, besides this organization, there were other elements carrying on their activities under the direction or the influence of Moscow. Because of my sincere intention to describe only my personal experiences, their activities could not properly be included in this book.

Being the first active member of the Polish Underground in the fortunate position to publish some aspects of its story, I hope that it will encourage others to relate their experiences and that out of such narratives the free peoples all over the world will be able to form an objective opinion as to how the Polish people reacted during the years of German conquest.

J. K., 1944

Story of a Secret State

I

Defeat

On the night of 23 August 1939, I attended a particularly gay party. It was given by the son of the Portuguese Minister in Warsaw, Mr Susa de Mendes. He was about twenty-five, my age, and the two of us were good friends. He was the fortunate brother of five charming and beautiful sisters. I saw one of them frequently and was looking forward with keen anticipation to meeting her again that night.

I had not been back in Poland long. After my graduation from the University of Lwow in 1935 and the traditional year in the army, I went abroad, to Switzerland, Germany, and then to England pursuing researches in the highly interesting and erudite subject of demography. After three years spent in the great libraries of Europe, working at my thesis, improving my knowledge of French, German, and English, and familiarizing myself with the customs of those nations, the death of my father recalled me to Warsaw.

Although demography – the science and statistics of populations – was, and has remained, my favorite subject, it was slowly becoming apparent that I had little or no aptitude for scientific writing. I dawdled and lingered in the completion of my doctor's thesis and most of my work was rejected as unacceptable. This was the only cloud – and one that disturbed me little – in my otherwise clear and sunny prospect.

The atmosphere of the party was carefree, festive, and in some respects almost lyrical in mood. The huge drawing room of the Legation was adorned in elegant if somewhat romantic style. The wallpaper was a cool shade of blue and contrasted with the dark, severe Italian furniture. The lights were subdued and everywhere were ornate vases of long-stemmed flowers that added their scent to the perfumes of the gayly dressed women. The company was congenial and soon cheerful and excited discussions spread about the room. I remember some of the topics: a heated defense of the beauties of the Warsaw botanical gardens against the alleged superiority of rival spots in Europe; exchanges of opinions on the merits of the revival of the famous play, *Madame Sans-Gêne*; bits of scandal and the usual sorties of wit when someone discovered that my good friends, Stefan Leczewski and Mlle Marcelle Galopin, had vanished from the room – a custom of theirs. Politics were hardly touched.

We drank wine and danced interminably, mostly the airy, mobile European dances, first a waltz, then a tango, then a figured waltz. Later, Helene Susa de Mendes and her brother demonstrated the intricacies of the Portuguese tango.

During the course of the evening I made a number of appointments for the following week. I finally succeeded in convincing Miss de Mendes that I was indispensable as a guide to Warsaw. I made a luncheon and a dinner appointment with two friends, Mr Leczewski and Mr Mazur. I promised to meet Miss Obromska the next Sunday and later had to excuse myself when I recollected that it was my aunt's birthday. I was to telephone Mlle Galopin to arrange the time of our next riding hour.

The party ended late. The farewells were lengthy, and outside, various groups continued to take leave of each other and to make appointments and arrangements for the balance of the week. I came home tired but so full of intoxicating plans that it was difficult to fall asleep.

It seemed my eyes had hardly closed when there was a loud hammering at the front door. I dragged myself out of bed and began to walk down the steps, breaking into an angry run as the hammering increased in volume. I yanked open the door. An impatient, surly policeman standing on the steps handed me a slip of red paper, grunted unintelligibly and turned away.

It was a secret mobilization order. It informed me that I was to leave Warsaw within four hours and to join my regiment. I was a second lieutenant in the artillery and my detachment was to be quartered at Oswiecim,[1] directly on the Polish–German border. Something in the manner of the presentation of the order, or possibly the hour at which it arrived, or the fact that it threw so many of my plans into confusion, made me feel suddenly very serious and even grim.

I woke up my brother and sister-in-law. They were not at all impressed or alarmed and made me feel a little foolish because of the grave air I had assumed.

While I dressed and prepared myself we discussed the situation. It was obviously only a very limited mobilization, we concluded. A handful of us were being called to the colors simply to impress the country with the necessity of being prepared. They cautioned me against burdening myself with too many supplies. My sister-in-law protested when I wanted to include a few suits of winter underwear.

'You aren't going to Siberia,' she said, looking at me as if I were a romantic schoolboy. 'We'll have you on our hands again within a month.'

I brightened up. It might even turn out to be fun. I remembered that Oswiecim was situated in the middle of an expanse of fine, open country. I was an enthusiastic horseback rider and I relished the notion of galloping about in uniform on a superb army horse. I carefully packed away my best patent-leather shoes. I began to feel more and more as though I were going to a smart military parade. I completed my preparations in a mood that was almost hilarious. I remarked to my brother that it was too bad that they could not use any old men at the moment. He called me names and threatened to wrestle me and take some of the cockiness out of my hide. His wife had to admonish us both to stop behaving like children and I had to complete my preparations in a hurry because so much time had been wasted.

When I got to the railway depot it looked as though every man in Warsaw were there. I quickly realized that the mobilization was 'secret' only in the sense that there were no public announcements or posters. Hundreds of thousands of men must have been called. I remembered a rumor I had heard about two or three days before to the effect that the government had wanted to order a complete mobilization in the face of the German threat but had been prevented by warnings from the representatives of France and England. Hitler was not to be 'provoked.' At that time, Europe was still counting on appeasement and reconciliation. Permission for a 'secret' mobilization was finally and reluctantly conceded to the Polish Government in the face of the nearly naked German preparations for attack.

This I learned later. At the moment, the memory of the rumor disturbed me as little as when I first heard it. Everywhere about me thousands of civilians were swarming to the trains, each carrying an easily recognizable military 'locker.' Among them were hundreds of spruce, animated reserve officers, some of whom waved to each other and called out to friends as they, too, hustled to the train. I gazed about for a familiar face and, seeing none, made my way to the train.

I had to almost force my way in. The cars were packed; every seat was occupied. The corridors were jammed with standing men and even the lavatories were crowded. Everyone looked full of energy, enthusiastic and even exhilarated. The reserve officers were trim and confident, the mood of the civilians a trifle less exuberant as though many of them did not care to have their business or work interrupted by such an expedition, however painless it appeared. The engine chugged and the train began to crawl forward slowly to the usual comments of 'We're moving, we're moving!' which finally rose to a full-throated exultant shout of pure, meaningless excitement as we cleared the station and sped onward.

During the journey, I became increasingly impressed with the seriousness of the occasion. I still did not have the remotest inkling of how close actual warfare was but I could see that this was obviously no pleasure jaunt but a full-dress mobilization. At each station new cars were added which absorbed fresh crowds, now composed chiefly of peasants. They were a little more businesslike and seemed to consider the probability of actual warfare somewhat more realistically. The village boys in particular stepped into the cars with what seemed to us to amount to a parody of quiet, adult determination and steadfast enterprise. Everyone, however, still seemed eager and confident. Even if by now the tone was a more settled one of 'there's work to be done,' the mood was still far from dismal. Except, of course, for the women – wives, sisters and mothers – who thronged every platform like so many wailing Niobes, wringing their hands, hugging their men, and trying to withhold the departure if it were only for another second. The boys, ashamed, would tear themselves firmly away from their mothers' arms.

'Let me go, Mother,' I remember hearing a boy of about twenty call out loudly at one of the stations. 'Soon you can come and visit me in Berlin.'

With the long stops at every station to hook on cars and take on passengers, the journey to Oswiecim took nearly twice as long as it should have. By the time we reached the camp it was well into the night and the heat, congestion, and fatigue from the long hours on our feet had wilted the fresh spirits with which we had begun. After a fairly good dinner, considering the hour at which we arrived, we revived somewhat and I went to the officers' quarters in the company of a group of officers with whom I had become more or less familiar at the mess. I did not find all the officers of our division. Two batteries of the horse artillery had already been sent to the frontier. Only the third battery and a reserve were still in the camp.

As we strolled toward the barracks, we tended to avoid any weighty subjects and confined ourselves to topics of more immediate moment.

Second Lieutenant Pietrzak, a student at the Cracow University, remarked that he was half-dead from exhaustion. Like myself, he had been to a ball the previous night. It had been, he gave us to understand, a very magnificent and glamorous gathering. His success with the ladies had been unbelievable; he had actually had to resort to Machiavellian subterfuges to avoid becoming involved with a number of importunate belles. At any rate, he was a few doors away from the entrance to his house when he noticed a policeman ascending the steps. Terrified, he shrank back and wondered which event in his reckless existence had attracted the notice of the law. He then drew for our benefit a comic picture of the panicky interval he had spent waiting for the policeman to withdraw, his guilty tiptoed entrance into the house and his mingled consternation and relief when he found that his presence was desired merely at an army camp and not in the court of law.

The entire story was promptly disbelieved and admired by everybody present. It gave rise to a similar series of anecdotes about the previous night, although of a more plausible variety. The remarks of relatives and wives were cited, we informed each other about our backgrounds and interests and began to form bonds of friendships that were destined to last but a few short days.

Pietrzak, the young man who told the first story, became my constant companion. He came from an affluent family and his occupation, as nearly as I could discover, consisted of something nebulous in the world of finance. Like myself, he was extremely fond of horses and books and this, coupled with his inordinate urge to tell anecdotes, made him an ideal companion for me during the next few days. The anecdotes, I later discovered, were compounded from the same odd and invariant formula of a core of truth surrounded by comic exaggerations and downright inventions.

I had the opportunity of listening to many of them in the pleasant Officers' Club at Oswiecim. Army routine and drill were more than usually severe and caused considerable grumbling but did not exhaust us sufficiently to mar our leisurely evenings and even left enough free time for Pietrzak and myself to indulge our desire for excursions on horseback into the beautiful surrounding country, under the brilliant and cloudless sky of the Polish summer.

It is difficult to explain why, but, in the evenings at the Club, by almost mutual consent, we tended to shy off any political topic that seemed likely to prove either too controversial or too weighty. When we did, at length, launch upon a consideration of the present position and the possibilities that were in store for us, our opinions tended to confirm each other and finally congealed into a uniform optimism that served admirably to protect us from doubt, fear, and the need to think clearly about the complex changes that were taking place in the structure of European politics with a rapidity that we could not and did not want to understand. I know that in myself there was an inertia of thought that simply would not let my mind make any effort to grasp at this frightful novelty. My whole past and present mode of existence would have been too deeply threatened.

There were, too, the remarks my brother had made during the hours immediately after the mobilization. My brother, who was my senior by nearly a score of years, held an important government position and had belonged, as far back as I could remember, to the 'well-informed circles.'[2] The citations which Pietrzak made from his father, who had even more authoritative channels of information, amplified and confirmed the analysis given by my brother. Others joined in with gleanings from relatives, friends, and their personal deductions. The entire compilation, when sifted down, tended to leave us with the conclusion that our mobilization was simply the Polish riposte to the Nazi war of nerves. Germany was weak and Hitler was bluffing. When he saw that Poland was strong, united, and prepared, he would back down quickly and we should all go home. If not, the farcical little fanatic would be taught a severe lesson by Poland and, if necessary, by England and France.

One evening our Major said:

'England and France are not needed this time. We can finish this alone.'

Pietrzak remarked dryly:

'Yes, sir, we are strong, but . . . well, but . . . it is always nice to be in good company.'

On the night of 1 September, around 5.00 a.m., while the soldiers of our Mounted Artillery Division tranquilly slept, the Luftwaffe roared through the short distance to Oswiecim undetected and, perched above our camp, proceeded to rain a blazing shower of incendiaries on the entire region. At the same hour, hundreds of the powerful and modern German tanks crossed the frontier and hurled a tremendous barrage of shells into the flaming ruins.

The extent of the death, destruction, and disorganization this combined fire caused in three short hours was incredible. By the time our wits were sufficiently collected even to survey the situation, it was apparent that we were in no position to offer any serious resistance. Nevertheless, a few batteries, by some miracle, managed to hold together long enough to hurl some shots in the direction of the tanks. By noon, two batteries of our artillery had ceased to exist.

The barracks were almost completely in ruins and the railroad station had been leveled. When it became apparent that we were incapable of any serious resistance, the retreat, if such it could be called, began. Our reserve battery received orders to leave Oswiecim in formation and to take our guns, supplies, and ammunition in the direction of Cracow. As we marched through the streets of Oswiecim toward the railroad, to our complete astonishment and dismay, the inhabitants began firing at us from the windows. They were Polish citizens of German descent, the Nazi Fifth Column, who were, in this fashion, announcing their new allegiance. Most of our men instantly wanted to attack and set fire to every suspect house but were restrained by the superior officers. Such actions would have disrupted our march, which was exactly what the Fifth Column wanted. Moreover, loyal, patriotic Polish people also lived in these houses.[3]

When we reached the railroad, we were compelled to wait while the track was being repaired. We sat down under the blazing sun and gazed back at the burning buildings, the hysterical population, and the treacherous windows of Oswiecim until the train was ready. We boarded it in weary, disgusted silence and began crawling eastward – toward Cracow.

During the night, the train was held up by innumerable delays. We slept fitfully, and in our waking moments cursed, speculated on what had happened, and expressed our unanimous desire for an early and more favorable opportunity to do battle. Early the next day a dozen or so Heinkels appeared to bomb and strafe the train for nearly an hour. More than half the cars were hit and most of their occupants were killed or wounded. My car was untouched. The survivors left the wreckage of the train and without bothering to organize or form ranks proceeded on foot in an easterly direction.

We were now no longer an army, a detachment, or a battery, but individuals wandering collectively toward some wholly indefinite goal. We found the highways jammed with hundreds of thousands of refugees, soldiers looking for their commands, and others just drifting with the tide. This mass of humanity continued to move slowly eastward for two weeks. I found myself with a group that still constituted a recognizable military fragment. We kept hoping to find a new base of resistance where we could stop and fight. Each time we found one that looked at all suitable, an order to continue marching would somehow filter through the mob to our captain, who would shrug his shoulders and point wearily to the east.

Bad news followed us like vultures feeding on the remnants of our confidence: the Germans had occupied Poznan, then Lodz, Kielce, Cracow. Frequent strafings reiterated that whatever planes or anti-aircraft had been ours had vanished. The smoking, abandoned ruins of towns, railroad junctions, villages, and cities added to our bitter knowledge.

After fifteen days of marching – fatigued, sweating, bewildered, and resentful – on 18 September we approached the city of Tarnopol.[4]

The road to Tarnopol was so hot and our feet and shoes were in such poor condition from nearly four days of continuous marching that the hard surface of the road caused too much pain to be borne for long. Most of us preferred to walk along the soft sides, even though it meant proceeding more slowly.

As we went along in this fashion, in no particular haste, since we hardly knew our purpose in walking at all, I noticed the increase in noise and the movement of individuals from group to group that generally betokened the arrival of an important item of news or some startling rumor. I had been walking with a group of eight medical officers ever since I had stopped one of them a few miles back to obtain some bandage for a blister on my heel. We all realized that something was up.

'I'll find out what it's all about,' said one of them, a youthful-appearing captain at whom everybody marveled because of the neat exterior he managed to preserve. 'Perhaps it will be good news for a change.'

'Sure,' someone answered ironically, 'maybe Hitler has decided to surrender to us.'

'Well, we'll soon know,' the captain answered and walked toward a company of infantrymen who had paused about twenty yards behind us and were talking excitedly.

We decided to wait under the skimpy shade of an old, parched tree until our self-appointed messenger returned. He was back in a few minutes, breathless and unable to contain himself, breaking into speech a few paces before he reached us.

'The Russians have crossed the border,' he shouted to us. 'The Russians have crossed the border.'

We surrounded him and deluged him with questions. How reliable was the information?

Someone had heard it from a civilian who had a radio.

What did it mean? Had they declared war on us, too? Do they come as friends or as enemies?

He did not know for certain, but, in his opinion . . .

He was politely told that his opinion was not of interest at the moment. We wanted facts.

Well, according to what he had heard, a Russian radio broadcast from somewhere inside Poland had been picked up. A long series of announcements had been made in Russian, Polish, and Ukrainian telling the Polish people not to regard the Russian soldiers who had crossed their borders as enemies but as liberators. They were coming to 'protect the Ukrainian and White Ruthenian population.'

'Protection' was an ominous word. We all remembered that Spain, Austria, and Czechoslovakia were under 'protection.' From whom were we to be protected? Were the Russians going to fight the Germans if it proved necessary? Had the Ribbentrop–Molotov pact been denounced?

He did not quite know. He had asked the infantrymen and they apparently did not know either. As far as he could make out, the radio statement had contained no definite information on these points. The announcement had, however, contained references to our 'Ukrainian and White Ruthenian brothers' and the urgent necessity

for a union of all Slavic peoples had been stressed.[5] Besides, it was
no use standing here in the broiling sun and speculating about it.
The intelligent thing to do was to march to Tarnopol as fast as we
could and find out more definitely.

There was nothing we could do but agree to this suggestion. The
outskirts of Tarnopol were some ten miles away. By exerting ourselves, we could make it in a few hours. We resumed our weary
march with a little more energy. We now had, at least, something to
look forward to, a motive to urge us ahead. It made us almost happy
to have a definite reason to march. As we walked, we continued to
wonder and speculate, almost forgetting the heat and our misery in
having something to talk about besides the probable extent of the
territory Germany had already conquered.

Before we arrived in Tarnopol we had our answers. About two
miles before the town proper we heard a loud hubbub. What sounded
like a speech was being delivered through a loudspeaker at some distance from us. A bend in the road made its source invisible and the
words were so distorted that we could not make out their purport.
We sensed that something important was occurring and, tired as we
were, broke into a trot.

After the bend was a long, straight stretch of road. The two hundred or so yards directly in front of us were deserted; the straggling
groups that we had been accustomed to see in front of us had all
merged into a single, stationary horde standing far down the road.
From near this knot of men the voice continued its resonant, unintelligible address. Behind the men we could see a long file of military
trucks and tanks on the road, but we could not tell of what nationality they were.

The men behind us had likewise been infected by the excitement
and some of them, running even more rapidly, had passed us. As they
did, one of them, evidently gifted with the eyes of a hawk, shouted:

'The Russians, the Russians . . . I can see the hammer and sickle.'

We did not need the evidence of our own eyes to confirm his
statement. We now understood that the voice we were hearing was
speaking Polish, Polish with not so much an accent as the sing-song

intonation we familiarly associate with a Russian speaking our language. We could distinguish, however, only an occasional word and as we came closer the voice ceased altogether. It was followed by silence and then a hum. The Polish soldiers grouped around what we now saw to be a Russian sound-truck and began to discuss what they had heard.

We joined them breathlessly, panting and asking questions. We saw now the hammer and sickle, painted conspicuously in red on many of the Russian tanks and trucks. The trucks were crammed with Russian soldiers, formidably armed. We gathered that the voice in the truck had substantially confirmed what we had heard previously in the rumor of the broadcast. The voice had also appealed to the men gathered in a crowd around the truck to join the Russians as brothers. Everyone was giving his opinion about what should be done when we were all silenced by an impatient voice thundering through a megaphone from one of the Soviet tanks:

'Hey, you,' it addressed us familiarly and collectively, 'are you or are you not with us? We aren't going to stand here in the middle of the road the whole day waiting for you to make up your minds. There's nothing to be frightened about. We are Slavs like yourselves, not Germans. We are not your enemies. I am the commander of this detachment. Send some officers to me as your spokesmen.'

A confused buzz ensued on the Polish side, as a hundred different opinions and comments were promptly put forth. The soldiers, on the whole, were gloomy and hostile to the proposal, the officers uncertain and apparently dissatisfied with everything, including themselves. I was myself completely at a loss and, what with the combined exertion and excitement, my heart was pounding so furiously that I could barely manage to gasp out replies to the one or two questions I was asked when someone mistook my silence for disagreement.

At this point, some of the officers must have decided that we would have more bargaining power if we had a semblance of military organization. Non-coms began to circulate among the soldiers, trying to assemble them into formations. This was completely futile, as we were by now little better than a mob, a motley conglomeration of officers, men, and non-coms, no dozen of which seemed to come from the same unit or detachment. Many of the soldiers were unarmed and there were no machine guns or artillery. The indecision continued and threatened to prolong itself indefinitely.

Among the many officers were two colonels. They had been conversing for some time and had now decided upon a plan of action. They beckoned authoritatively to others of the senior officers who came to join them. They held a whispered conference. At length, portentously, a captain detached himself from the group, plucked from his pocket a none-too-clean white handkerchief, and, waving it over his head, walked gingerly toward the Soviet tanks.

The crowd watched him as if he had been a figure in a play, an actor crossing a stage at some moment of fateful climax. No one moved or stirred. We watched him in choked silence until a Red Army officer appeared among the tanks. The two officers met halfway and saluted each other briskly. They appeared to be conversing politely with each other. The Soviet officer gestured in the direction of the tank from which the commander had spoken and they walked off toward it together. There was a slight exhalation of relief from the crowd at even this perfunctory display of friendliness.

Nevertheless, we were still by no means calm. We had gone through two and a half weeks of as much emotional and mental discomfiture as any man can stand. Physically, we had emerged comparatively unscathed. But the blitz had derailed our minds and emotions, bewildered, stunned, confused, and frustrated us to the point where we hardly knew what was happening. And if we were uninjured, by and large, we were utterly exhausted, completely without energy.

The Polish officer was gone for about fifteen minutes. During this interval, we did nothing but wait with limp, nervous, dazed apprehension. The events that were passing before us were so unreal, so wholly unlike anything we had ever experienced or imagined that we did not dare even to discuss them with each other any more. This fevered silence was finally broken by a strong, determined voice, speaking without an accent through the megaphone of the Soviet commander's tank.

'Officers, non-commissioned officers, and soldiers,' it began, in the style of a general addressing his men before a battle, 'this is Captain Wielszorski speaking. Ten minutes ago you saw me leave to confer with the Soviet officer. Now I have grave news for you.'

The voice paused. We braced ourselves for a shock. It came.

Up to now the voice had been slow and impressive. Now it increased in speed and volume, sweeping us along with it.

'The Soviet Army crossed the frontier to join us in the struggle against the Germans, the deadly enemies of the Slavs and of the entire human race. We cannot wait for orders from the Polish High Command. There is no longer a Polish High Command nor a Polish Government. We must unite with the Soviet forces. Commander Plaskow demands that we join his detachment immediately, after surrendering our arms. These will be returned to us later. I inform all officers within hearing of these facts and order all non-commissioned officers and soldiers to comply with the request of Commander Plaskow. Death to Germany! Long live Poland and the Soviet Union!'

The reaction to this speech was utter, paralyzed silence. Events had moved completely beyond our comprehension, deprived us of all volition. We stood there in a dumb trance. Not a whisper, hardly even a sound of movement could be heard. I felt as though I had been bewitched, I had the same sensation of dreamy suffocation I had experienced once when I had been put under ether.

The spell was broken by the sound of a single sob from somewhere down front. For a second I thought it was a hallucination. Then it was repeated, a rasping, desperate sobbing that seemed to tear the throat from which it issued. It increased in violence, became racked and choking, then caught itself, changed into shrill, hysterical speech:

'Brothers, this is the fourth partition of Poland. May God have mercy on me.'

The sound of the revolver shot that followed spread dismay and confusion everywhere. Everyone attempted to crowd closer to the spot from which the shot had come. News traveled like lightning. It was a non-commissioned officer who had committed suicide. He had put the bullet through his brain and had died instantly. No one knew his name, company, or anything about him.

No one was quite up to explaining or interpreting this terrifying act. It inspired no further outbreaks of a similar nature, but caused a sudden vocal frenzy. Everybody began to talk all at once like the audience in a theater the minute after the last curtain falls. The pandemonium was increased by officers who ran from man to man, urging them to lay down their weapons, arguing with those who refused, and, here and there, tugging at a rifle someone was loath to relinquish.

Again a message in Polish with a sing-song intonation issued from the megaphone of the tank of the commander.

'Polish soldiers and officers! You are to pile your arms in front of the white hut surrounded by larch trees – on the left side of the road. All the arms in your possession, machine guns, rifles, and hand weapons. Officers may retain their swords. Soldiers must surrender their bayonets and belts. Any attempt to conceal weapons will be considered treason.'

As one man, we turned our eyes on the white hut surrounded by larch trees, to the left of the road. It shone in the sun, about thirty steps away from us. Among the larch trees on either side of the hut we saw now a row of glinting machine guns trained on us. We hesitated, uncertain of what to do next, no one willing to take the initiative, until the two colonels stepped determinedly forward, unsheathed their revolvers, and dropped them almost in the doorway of the hut.

They were followed by two captains, who did likewise. The first move had been made. One by one the officers came forward and followed the path of their predecessors, the soldiers gazing at them incredulously. I took my turn as if hypnotized, unable to convince myself that all this was really happening. When I got to the hut, I was surprised at the size of the pile of revolvers. I pulled out my own, regretfully thinking of the care I had expended on it and the little use it had been. It was still sleek and smart-looking. I dropped it and returned, feeling empty-handed and without possessions.

After the officers got through, the soldiers shuffled sullenly forward and added their weapons to the pile which had grown to quite a respectable size. We had more arms than I had imagined. To my surprise, I saw some soldiers carrying machine guns and then, in the distance, three pairs of heavy artillery horses pulling a field gun. I still cannot imagine how or why it got there.

After the last gun and bayonet had been dropped wearily into the now immense heap, we were surprised to see two platoons of Soviet soldiers jump down from the trucks and rush along each side of the road in a skirmishing formation, keeping turned on us the light machine guns they carried.

Through the megaphone the order came to us to line up in good order, facing toward Tarnopol. As we complied, a section of the tanks now directly in front of us opened their motors and deftly shot off the road, proceeded along the side till they had come to the end of our line and took up a position in back of us, their guns all pointing in our direction. The guns of the tanks in front of us now swung around till they, likewise, were leveled at us. Slowly at first, then at regulation marching speed, the whole procession moved in the direction of Tarnopol.

We were prisoners of the Red Army. I, myself, strangely, had not even had an opportunity to fight the Germans.

2

Prisoner in Russia

It was dusk when we entered the city of Tarnopol. The rumbling tanks in front guided us to the railroad depot. In the streets, the local population was out in great numbers, mostly women, old men, and children, to watch us being taken off. They stared at us in resignation and made no demonstration of any kind. More than two thousand Polish men who, less than a month before, had left their homes to drive the Germans back to Berlin, were now being marched off to a nameless destination, surrounded by Soviet guns.

We had been slogging along apathetically but now, in the presence of an audience, we became more conscious of the rôle we had been playing and the sorry figures we cut. I began for the first time to think of escape. Glancing at my companions, I realized that many of them had the same thought. Eyes were no longer cast down, they now shifted from side to side as if seeking, in the line of Soviet gunners that filed at our side, a loophole through which they might escape into the crowd that lined the streets.

We walked in the gutter, about ten abreast in irregular lines. I was on the left side of my line, the third man from the end. At approximately every fifth line of men, a Soviet soldier walked, a light machine gun cradled in his arms. Many of them kept their eyes straight ahead, turning them toward us only occasionally for a quick check. Others contrived to walk half-sideways, keeping one eye on us almost constantly. I saw that I had the misfortune to be on a fifth line. An alert guard was at the end of it and even as I twisted my head slightly to look at him and measure my chances, he seemed to be watching me, personally.

Almost at the same moment, I detected a shadowy movement

that set my heart pounding and made me hold my breath in suspense. The end man in the fourth line ahead of me had slipped deftly from the line, passing only a yard or two in back of the guard nearest him who continued, unobservantly, to march directly forward, and had disappeared so rapidly into the crowd that even my anxious gaze could no longer detect him. The guard at the end of my line, more concerned with the men at his side, had apparently noticed nothing. As this audacious soldier had left his place, the man to his right, apparently forewarned, edged over to fill the empty space. Those to his right adjusted themselves to follow suit and, soon, since the lines were in any case irregular, everything was as before.

The whole proceeding took but a tense moment. I sensed, by an indefinable change in their bearing, that the men about me had likewise been following this little drama with bated breath. The man on my right, a short, stocky peasant of stolid countenance, was, I felt sure, gazing out of the corner of his eye at the place that had just been vacated. As it became clear that the operation was completely successful, and as the first thrill of excitement subsided in me a trifle, I felt I wanted confirmation or at least someone to share the elation that welled up in me. Inclining my head slightly to the right I whispered in the softest tones I could manage:

'Did you see that?'

A barely perceptible nod was my answer. Turning away from this cautious soul I saw that the guard at the end of the line had swung almost at right angles to our line of march and seemed to be glaring angrily at me. I didn't have a chance. Not only was he alert, but he had chosen me for a special object of attention. He held his weapon in readiness for instant use and I realized it would be foolhardy to chance his willingness to press the trigger.

As we walked along in the dusk I continued to cast about for a favorable opportunity to escape but without success. By now my imagination had been so aroused that I thought I could see furtive shadows slipping from the line everywhere. Some of these elusive figures were indubitably real but in the deepening darkness I could be sure of nothing. The rumble of the tanks, the glinting of the guns in the moonlight, and the strain of peering into the shadows, all contrived to make me feel like a participant in some eerie game. Each time I thought I saw a successful escape I felt a secret thrill of triumph and glanced stealthily at the guard as though I were involved in a clever plot of which he was the sole victim. When I saw the railroad station looming toward us a short distance away I had to acknowledge that whatever the fate of these poor devils was to be I was destined to share it.

In the resigned faces of the people of Tarnopol I felt a tragic knowledge I could not quite understand, but which touched me deeply. They knew that the Polish state was crushed. More accurately than all the 'intelligentsia' of Warsaw, than my friends with connections, than my highly educated fellow-officers, they knew what was happening, that Poland had fallen. They crowded close to our lines to help those of her sons, who could still struggle to raise her, to escape.

As we neared the end of our sad, puzzled march I saw that some of the women were inconspicuously carrying civilian garments. One audacious, middle-aged woman actually handed a coat to a soldier who had contrived to get past the guards, who by this time, in the main, had considerably relaxed their vigilance. Watching her, a sob of pride and admiration welled up in my heart. Reaching into my pocket, I took out my wallet containing my money and papers and a gold watch that my father had given me. Facing forward to avert suspicion, I tossed them with my left hand into the crowd. I would probably have no further use for them and it was little enough to do for the good people of Tarnopol. I still kept some money, a ring, and a gold medallion. An instant later we were crowding into the dim, shabby railroad station.

Once inside the station, the urge to escape and the possibility of doing so vanished simultaneously, and with them the buoyancy of spirit that had kept us erect in the march through Tarnopol. In the foul-smelling and fearfully overcrowded station, we felt the full weight of the physical fatigue and defeated hopes of the past few weeks. As soon as they entered the room, the men wearily sat or lay down on benches, steps, or the bare floor, and dropped into exhausted slumber. I sat down on the floor and, propping my head against a bench on which three other officers were already snoring fitfully, fell into a tired, restless sleep.

Two or three hours later I woke up, aware of acute discomfort amounting almost to pain. My limbs were cramped and where I had distributed my weight unfortunately stung from lack of circulation. A smell like a barnyard assailed my nostrils – the perspiration, dirt, and breath of more than two thousand men in a comparatively small hall – men sprawled everywhere in every conceivable posture, stirring, groaning, snoring, muttering. Every bone in my body ached. I was thirsty, hungry, and felt utterly wretched, wretched about the past, the present, and a future I could not foresee.

The three men on the bench sat up and were now holding a whispered conversation. One of them had apparently been indulging in speculation of the kind that had been so common in the last few days, speculation as to the actual situation of the Polish Army and the likelihood of its conducting a successful resistance everywhere but in the place the speculator happened to be. A serious-looking mild-voiced lieutenant was answering him:

'They told us the truth,' he said, with quiet weariness. 'There is no longer a Polish Army. How can there be? If we weren't able even to put up a show of resistance against the German tanks and planes, why should you think that the rest of the army was so much better equipped than we were?'

'We had nothing to organize,' the pessimistic one continued, 'nothing that could stand up to their planes and tanks. You can't win a war nowadays by courage. You need planes and tanks. Have you seen anything of our air force? They must have a thousand planes to our one and the same thing happened to the rest of our army that happened to us. We haven't had a message from the High Command in days. Why? Because there is no longer a High Command.'

'Bah!' the third one broke in. 'You're too gloomy. Just because we ran into a little bad luck doesn't mean anything. We're out of touch with the rest of the army and I shouldn't be surprised if we heard from them soon. We'll be back in the front lines before you know it and the Germans will be driven out of Poland faster than they came in.'

'Well,' the gloomy one said, 'if it makes you sleep any better to think we're winning, go ahead. I won't try to disillusion you further.'

The firm, quiet tone of the officer carried a lot of conviction. At first I found myself agreeing with him, but then the gloomy picture he painted repelled me so that I refused to concede to him even a glimmer of accuracy. The whole Polish Army smashed in less than three weeks! It was fantastic. The Germans were no magicians, whatever else they were. Besides Warsaw fought, and there was news that there was fighting in different points of Poland. I stretched myself and rubbed my legs to restore the circulation. The three officers had gone back to sleep again. I did likewise.

In the morning we were brought to complete alert wakefulness by the arrival of a long train of freight cars. The Russian guards began to urge the soldiers forward into the train. There was no examination of papers, no attempt to organize, arrange, or check identity. The number of men entering a car was counted off and when the total reached sixty, that car was considered closed. It was evidently to be a long journey for one Soviet officer instructed us to fill every available vessel with water from the station faucets. While this was taking place fresh detachments of Polish prisoners arrived, causing a great deal of confusion and turmoil. During this period, I learned later, many successful attempts at escape took place, the men slipping out of the lightly guarded parts of the station and, once outside, securing the assistance of the civilian population of Tarnopol, particularly the unforgettable women.

I was installed in one of the first of more than sixty freight cars that were drawn up alongside the station. I sat in my car for two hours while the rest were being filled. In the center of the car was a small iron stove and next to it a few pounds of coal. Evidently we were going quite far north, to much colder regions. A pound of dried fish and a pound and a half of bread were distributed to each of us.

The trip was an eternity – four days and four nights. We sat or lay prone in the crowded cattle car while the train rattled and jounced into increasingly cold territory. There was little to do but finger our aches and brood on our misfortunes, or try to flex our bodies after the cold nights that were scarcely darker than the gray days. So small an incident as the lighting and care of the stove was an event in the bleak monotony.

Each day the train stopped for half an hour. Sixty portions of black bread and dry fish would be shoved into the car. After they had been distributed equally and partly eaten, we would take advantage of the fifteen minutes allotted to us to leave the train. Getting down, we would inhale draughts of fresh air and walk about energetically, delighting in the free movement of our cramped legs and bodies. We also were given a chance to look at the local population.

On the second day of the journey we noticed that they looked and dressed differently and were speaking a foreign language. The last vestige of uncertainty was eliminated – we were well within the Russian border. Small groups of Russians – mostly women and children again, our permanent audience – stood about and eyed us with undemonstrative but not unfriendly curiosity. We hesitated to approach them but, finally, a few of us tentatively walked closer. They did not shrink but watched us calmly, some even smiling. They then offered us water and a few of the women gave us cigarettes – deeply appreciated treasures. It was evident that other prisoners must have passed this way, otherwise they could hardly have been so well-prepared for our advent.

At another stop we had an opportunity to understand their attitude toward us more fully. Two or three of our officers could speak fluent Russian and they served as interpreters and intermediaries. To one of them, a tall, erect man of about thirty, somewhat disheveled, but still obviously an officer, a young, roughly dressed, and sober-faced woman gave a tin of water. He expressed his gratitude and then added ardently, 'You are our friends. Together we will fight and defeat the German barbarians.'

She backed away and stiffened: 'You!' she said contemptuously, 'you Polish, fascist lords! Here in Russia you will learn how to work. Here you will be strong enough to work but too weak to oppress the poor.'

The incident was like a dash of cold water. Henceforward we were more circumspect and less open, aware of the great gulf of misunderstanding between our two countries, so close in geography, origin, and language, but so vastly separated by divergent histories and political systems. In particular we understood that we, the officers, were the especial target of whatever deposit of bitterness the changing relations of our two countries had left in Russia. To them we were idle 'aristocrats,' quite beyond redemption.

On the fifth day the train stopped at an unusual hour. We knew that, at last, we had reached a destination of some sort. The doors were unlocked and guards on the outside ordered us to step down and line up, eight in a row. We jumped out and found ourselves near a poor little village not large enough to have a proper building for its railroad station. It had only a platform to serve the purpose. A few small scattered houses constituted the entire village.

We lined up, shivering in the raw, autumnal wind. It was a dismal, gray day, without sun, without color of any kind. At some distance from us loitered a few specimens of the local population – poor, suspicious, hostile 'moujiks.' The men about me shivered and made themselves as small as possible in the remnants of their light summer uniforms. Many had caught colds and they sneezed, snuffled, and coughed continuously. They looked almost too weak to stand the buffets of the wind. Their faces were pale and downcast. As though it had been the most precious of treasures, each one of us clutched a little ragged bundle holding a few indispensable items: a shirt, socks, a bottle, a spoon, a penknife. On the train we had kicked them about carelessly. Now we handled them as though they contained the rarest provisions. They were all we had left in the world.

From the moment we got down from the freight cars and throughout my entire stay in Russia there was only one important thought and one important word in my consciousness: 'Escape.' I felt homesick, lost, abandoned by Providence, and absolutely determined to

get back to Poland, to help the army that I pictured, despite everything, as still in active combat, revenging itself for that first fearful
bombardment at Oswiecim.

The order to march was given. Grinding slowly uphill over the
bleak terrain, we discussed our situation. The older men, as usual,
showed more fortitude and endured their lot with a dignified fatal-
ism. We, the younger, complained, whined, cursed, plotted rebellion,
and considered our chances for escape.

The march lasted several hours, our spirits sinking slowly away
from the heightened state our talk of rebellion and escape had
induced. Here, for the first time, we felt the full weight of our misfortunes, how far we had traveled from our normal state of existence
in only three short weeks. Till then I had not felt how completely
cut off I was from everything that mattered to me, friends, family –
all my hopes. Now every single incident, every step seemed to
emphasize and magnify this separation. Bending down to adjust
my laces, I would glance at the bitter incongruity of my ridiculous
patent-leather shoes on the harsh Russian soil. Thirsty, I would try
and force some saliva through my parched throat and find myself
recalling the cool wine served at the Portuguese Legation ball and
then the music, the friendly gay atmosphere, the beautiful de Mendes
girls . . .

What a change in twenty days!

The guards at the rear of the line called a halt. Glancing about me,
I saw that we were in a vast, clear area partially surrounded by dense
timber. In the center of the clearing was a group of buildings that
had obviously once been a monastery – a church, a dwelling place,
and wooden shacks that had probably served as barns and storehouses. Through a megaphone, in sing-song Polish, instructions
were given us as to our new order of existence. Guards separated us
into groups and guided us to the quarters we were to occupy.

At the very outset the Russians made it plain that our previous
rank was to serve as the index to our present lot – in reverse. The
ordinary soldiers fared best for they were to live in the stone buildings left over from the monastery and church. The officers were

assigned to the huge wooden barns which had been converted into a kind of barracks – four hundred to each of the ten barracks. Different treatment was reserved for captured policemen, and for officers in the reserves who were judges, attorneys, or high-ranking officials in civilian life. The loudspeaker described them as 'all those who had oppressed the Polish Communists and laboring classes.' The other prisoners had to erect special wooden huts for them in the yard of the monastery.[1]

To us was also assigned the most arduous labor. We, the officers, cut wood in the forest, and loaded it into the trains.

Such as it was, however, I spent little time thinking of the rights and wrongs, the justice or injustice of my lot. I did not contemplate remaining in it long. While I did I adapted myself as best I could and even found some aspects of it salutary. The 'work is no disgrace' principle so popular in Russia was inculcated in us, the 'degenerate Polish aristocracy,' by special means.

The Bolsheviks prepared food for us in huge, heavy iron kettles. The cleaning of those kettles was a hard, sordid task. It required real physical effort of a kind both irksome and fatiguing, since the ponderous kettles had to be turned and maneuvered while the food-remnants were scraped off. The aftermath of a short period of this labor was invariably an aching back, sore bruised hands, and broken fingernails.

An announcement was made to us that Soviet soldiers had no time to clean kettles and that we would have to do this chore ourselves. Volunteer kettle-cleaners, however, would receive as remuneration permission to eat the remnants of food clinging to the sides of the kettle. In our officers' barracks, there were altogether three candidates for this chore and I was one of them. It was an unpleasant and grimy job, to be sure, but for the six weeks of my stay, I had more food than the others. I even found a queer satisfaction in the performance of this task, the demonstration to myself that I could, if necessary, perform menial work as easily and cheerfully as the next one.

With a fellow-prisoner, Lieutenant Kurpios, an impatient but resourceful young man who would have been willing to risk a head-on assault on the Russian guards if he thought it offered a chance of success, I spent nearly every spare moment scheming and going over every possible means of escape. To get out of the camp would not have been too difficult, but we were balked by the impossibility of getting aboard a train. The station was a few hours' walk away and we were almost certain to be caught by the time we got there. Moreover, the trains were too well guarded. To attempt to make our way over the cold, unfriendly country in our uniforms and without knowing the language offered insuperable difficulties. Nevertheless, we were on the verge of attempting one of these hazardous possibilities. Then the lieutenant informed me of a simpler plan.

One day after our meal as I was on the way to do my daily work, I was stopped by a tap on my shoulder. It was my young friend, breathing hard and flushed with excitement.

'I have an idea,' he whispered conspiratorially into my ear. 'A good idea. I think it will work.'

I stopped in my tracks.

'What is it?' I whispered back; then, noticing a Russian guard about thirty paces off gazing at us suspiciously, I continued to walk and changed my tone.

'Calm down,' I said, trying to appear more normal. 'You look as though you were plotting to blow up the camp.' And I pointed surreptitiously to the guard.

He understood and fell in beside me. To all appearances we were merely two prisoners strolling casually to the barracks.

There was, he told me, an exchange of prisoners due to take place soon, according to the terms of the Ribbentrop–Molotov pact. One of the provisions of the pact was that there were to be exchanges of prisoners of war who held no higher rank than that of private. The Germans were to turn over to Russia all Ukrainians and White Russians. The Russians were to release to Germany all Poles of German descent as well as Poles born in territories which had been incorporated into the Third Reich by virtue of the fact that they were 'old Germanic Territory.'[2]

After he had informed me of all these provisions, which he had memorized with the care and accuracy of a jurist, he grinned from ear to ear, snapped his fingers triumphantly, and remained provokingly silent.

'Wonderful!' I said ironically. 'A week from now I shall be in Warsaw on my way to a ball. All I have to do is demote myself to a private, get reborn, convince the Russians of these facts, and escape the clutches of the Gestapo. It's all so simple I can't see how I failed to think of it myself.'

'Karski, Karski!' he wailed sympathetically, shaking his head. 'I'm afraid you are losing your mental powers. We shall have to get you out of here in a hurry.'

'There may be something in all this that we can use. Exactly which are the territories that have been incorporated into the Third Reich? Is Lodz included?'

'It is,' he said. 'So that part is simple. You have some proof of birth?'

'Yes, I've got a birth record, a little frayed, but in good order.' I had kept my birth certificate and an army record tucked away in my cap. 'How about you?'

'My birthplace has not had the good fortune to be incorporated into the Reich. But I'll get around that somehow. Let's dispose of one case at a time. The next thing for you to do is to become a private and that should be easy. I don't see how you ever became an officer in the first place.'

'I can't see how I can pass for a private. The uniform is impossible to disguise. I have no other. Do you expect me to steal one?'

'No, borrow one. Find some private who cannot or does not intend to be exchanged, and if he has any patriotism or humanity in him, you ought to be able to persuade him to trade uniforms with you. Do it while you are out chopping wood in the forest; then you go back to his barrack, and there it is, done.'

It appeared to be an almost flawless method – at least for getting out of Russia. The Russian guards never checked by name or investigated papers. They tallied groups of men only by a rough count.

If I could find a willing private – and I felt sure I would – the trading of uniforms and my remaining in his place would never be detected. I would take my chances on what happened once I was back in Poland. I could have shouted for joy, so certain was I of succeeding ultimately in getting to wherever the Polish Army was fighting.

'Now how about you? You will have to get a document proving you were born in German-incorporated territory. Not many will want to give one up now. What shall we do about that?'

'There is only one thing to do,' he said, 'I must either get a document or try to convince the authorities without one.'

I waved my hand protestingly. 'It is unfair . . .'

'Please,' he said firmly, 'let's not act like schoolboys. I know what you are thinking. If you have to go without me, you must do so. The best thing you can do for me is, once you get your uniform, to walk into the office and demand to be sent to the Germans. Then, notice the attitude of the officer – if he scrutinizes papers carefully, and so forth. Then I'll know what to do.'

We were nearing the barracks. I had to turn aside to enter the crude kitchen and he had to go to his quarters and then to the forest.

'I'll get to work on a private immediately,' I said anxiously, still trying to make amends for my sensation of guilt at having things so easy. 'Maybe I'll have real news for you by evening.'

He smiled and waved his hand.

Inside the kitchen I rushed to work by the side of a big Ukrainian peasant somewhat older than myself but with whom I was on very good terms. He sensed my excitement immediately and asked me what I was boiling over with. I told him that I needed his help and that it was very important, explaining the entire procedure while we clawed the food from the sides of the kettles. He was delighted with the idea and agreed almost immediately. He himself did not trust the German offer and would not accept it, even if he were able, but he was, on the other hand, only too anxious to help me. We ought to do it that very afternoon when both privates and officers would be in the forest, chopping wood. Thus it was settled.

In the afternoon as we went to the woods I took good care to join the group of officers nearest to the privates issuing from the church. We were lightly guarded, the Russians realizing that if anyone did succeed in escaping from the camp, it would be impossible for him to get very far. As we entered the forest, I saw that my Ukrainian friend, Paradysz, had managed to be in the group of privates nearest me; we were some twenty yards away from each other with no one between us. When we passed a tree that was conspicuous for its size, the Ukrainian pointed significantly at it. I nodded in agreement.

Another thirty yards and we had reached the section I was supposed to work in. I took my axe and swung at a fallen tree-trunk in front of me, then raised it in the air as if for another blow, and surveyed the scene. The only guard at all near was at least a hundred yards away and in front of me. I dropped the axe and ran on tiptoe back to the tree which my friend had indicated. I found him waiting, already three-quarters stripped. I dropped down beside him and began to tear off my uniform.

'I can't tell you how much I appreciate this,' I said, embarrassed, tugging off my shirt and jacket.

'Save your breath,' he said, smiling. 'And don't worry. I won't have to go live with your officers. You just put on my uniform and come with me. When they count us at the church entrance, I'll hang back a little and you go in. I'll slip by the guards a little later. Since I have papers and can prove I'm a private, I'll just tear off the insignia and be able to use your uniform.'

'Fine,' I said, 'though we officers aren't such a bad lot.'

'I never said you were.'

'And thanks again.'

We put the finishing touches to our dress. The peasant tore off the insignia and quickly buried it under a rock. We dashed back to where we had been working. I worked like a madman, swinging my axe furiously to release the pent-up excitement inside me. When it came time to halt, I walked toward my left and inconspicuously joined the group of privates. They had been prepared for my arrival and asked no questions. At the church door the guards merely called us off by number. My friend went around to the back and climbed through a narrow window that was left unguarded. Everything had gone off perfectly. I was now a private.

Immediately on rising the following day, I walked up to a guard and asked for permission to speak to the chief officer of the camp. He asked me my purpose and when I informed him in broken Russian of my desire to be returned to the Germans, he scowled, said nothing, and motioned me to follow him. He ushered me into one of the official rooms in the church.

A sandy-haired, middle-aged officer sat at a desk writing. When I came into the room, he looked up, yawned, stretched himself, glanced down at his papers and then asked me,

'Who are you and what do you want?'

'Private Karski, formerly a laborer, born in Lodz.' I paused.

'And what do you wish?'

'To go back to the *Vaterland*, sir.'

'Very well. I will make a note of it.' He seemed about to dismiss me, then changed his mind and added rather negligently, I thought, 'Do you have any proof of your identity?'

I showed him my birth certificate. He glanced at it hastily, seized a sheet of paper, wrote something on it, and tossed it wearily back into its place. He yawned, stretched again, and rubbed his eyes. I must have been grinning at these antics for suddenly he stopped, glared at me, compressed his lips, and snapped, 'Well, well, what are you waiting for?'

I was guided back to the barracks. I had to fight to keep my countenance composed and suppress my inward exultation. In the afternoon I sought out Lieutenant Kurpios in the woods and described what had occurred. Then I added: 'It should be easy to convince him without papers. I don't think they are too anxious to keep anyone entitled to the transfer.'

He nodded in agreement. 'Nevertheless,' he continued, 'I'll spend a few days trying to get some papers. It does not pay to take unnecessary risks.'

'I wish you could come with me.'

'I will, if I can get by in time. If not, we will meet in Warsaw. You had better go now. If I don't see you again, goodbye and good luck.'

'Try to come with me. Good luck to you and be careful.'

I never saw him again. The next morning I was retracing the route I had taken six weeks before with a transport of two thousand soldiers being sent to the Germans in exchange for a similar number of Ukrainians and White Russians. I learned from a man who had been in a later exchange of prisoners that Kurpios had been with him. I was never able to obtain any subsequent news about him.

3

Exchange and Escape

The exchange of prisoners took place near Przemysl,[1] a town on the Russian–German border established by the Ribbentrop–Molotov pact. We reached our destination at dawn and were promptly lined up, twelve men to a line, in an open field on the outskirts of the town. It was a cold, windy day at the beginning of November. An intermittent drizzle began at dawn and kept up all day.

Our clothes by now were the merest collection of rags and patches, the remnants of our flimsy and long-suffering summer uniforms. Everyone had assembled strange fabrics to protect himself against the weather. During the five hours' wait in this unsheltered and muddy field, many men sat down and covered themselves with mats made of reeds and tied together with pieces of string. I had brought along no such utilitarian equipment and found that the moisture and the discomfort of sitting down were hardly worth the alleviation of the strain on my legs.

The Russian soldiers that guarded us were, as usual, lenient enough within the limits of military discipline. I never saw a Russian guard strike or curse at a prisoner no matter how enraged he might become. The worst threat they ever employed was the standard: 'Quiet, or you'll be sent to Siberia!' They knew that Siberia had been a Polish bugaboo for generations.

Many of the Russian soldiers tried to hold conversations with the Polish prisoners. I walked from group to group, trying to pick up information on our present circumstances and future destiny. The conversations suffered from linguistic difficulties and I did not learn much. All the Russian guards echoed a single sentiment. They were offended by our voluntary applications to be placed under German control and they were busy informing the men of the consequences of this foolish act. Frequently they repeated a remark which, after a while, rang in my head like a proverb or a slogan: *U nahs wsyoh harashoh, Germantsam huzheh budiet* – ('Everything is all right here – with us; with the Germans it will be worse').

When a prisoner asked what the Germans would do to them, the answer was always identical:

'Our commanders told the Germans to let you go free. The Germans agreed to it but added that you will have to work very hard, and they will see to it that you sweat.'

Like the rest of the prisoners I felt trapped. Most of us were glad to leave the Soviet prison camps, but all of us feared the Germans like the plague. I was likewise afraid of living under German domination but I never allowed myself to forget that I was going to escape to join the Polish Army. I was still convinced that there were at least active partisan detachments still in existence and struggling valiantly.[2]

The sudden rumble of a military auto put an end to our leisure. We jumped into our original formation as the car skidded to a stop a few yards from our lines. It contained a chauffeur, two Soviet officers and two German officers. Each politely offered to let the other walk ahead. The two Soviet officers finally ended up triumphantly half a step behind. This exquisite graciousness was a special display of officers' breeding for the benefit of the prisoners and was not lost on anyone.

I heard a venomous hissing to my left.

'How polite the — are to each other! May they all rot in hell!'

The remark was dangerously audible. I kicked the speaker in the shins without looking at him. The officers promenaded slowly past us without issuing commands of any kind. No military discipline applied to us, it was obvious. We were merely rag-wrapped, exchangeable serfs. The German officers gazed at us with arrogant and rapacious self-assurance. Once, one of the German officers pointed to a barefooted prisoner, covered with a mat, hairy, dirty, and shivering in the cold, and made some derisive remark to the other three. It must have been tremendously funny, for all four broke into shouts of raucous laughter.

When they had passed by, I turned to look at my indignant neighbor. He was young, slightly over twenty, I guessed, about my own size, with long, dark hair and a pale, emaciated face from which two large, black eyes bulged forth. His uniform hung loosely on his sticklike body. He was without a cap.

'Be careful,' I murmured to him, 'or you'll find yourself in front of a firing squad.'

'I don't care any more,' he answered in angry tones, his eyes full of humiliation and grief. 'Life is too complicated and the world too sordid.'

I was surprised to hear him speak good, pure Polish. The other soldiers all spoke peasant dialects or city slang. I could see that his morale was dangerously low and that he was in a bad psychological condition.

'Let's stick together,' I said to him after a moment.

'All right, sir.'

I smiled. No one had called me 'sir' in weeks. The current habit was to use first names or nicknames with curses for additional titles.

After the inspection we were marched two or three miles to a bridge over a vast muddy river.[3] At the other end of the bridge, as though a mirror had been set in the landscape, appeared an identical motley horde. It was, however, guarded by Germans. As we saw them, we realized that a new stage had begun in our existence. Now we were definitely about to pass under German control. We strained our eyes anxiously to see what the German guards on the other side of the bridge looked like. The four officers split into two pairs; the Germans crossing to their side of the bridge and standing in position, the Russians taking a similar stand where they were.

At length, guards on either side began to form a group of men. One of the guards on the German side of the bridge called out a number. The guard on our side verified it while the two groups waited expectantly. Then they were released and propelled forward. Both groups walked slowly and uncertainly. When they passed each other in the middle an odd, and what would in other circumstances have been an immensely ludicrous incident, happened.

The exchange prisoners had, in most cases, volunteered for the privilege and now that it was actually occurring they felt uncertain, regretful, envious of, and malicious toward, each other. As the first group of White Russians and Ukrainians shambled toward the group advancing from our side, this worry expressed itself in jeers of disdain at each other's expense. A huge Ukrainian began it by shouting in a rough voice:

'Look at the fools; they don't know what they are letting themselves in for.'

His formidable appearance restrained the Poles for a moment and then someone mustered enough courage to reply.

'Don't worry about us. We know what we are doing. We don't envy you, either.'[4]

On the other side of the bridge the Germans promptly assembled us into neat formations. One of the officers who had reviewed us made us a speech which was translated for our benefit. We would be treated well, we were assured, given work and food. As we were marched toward the trains, the German non-coms kept adding to and confirming these promises.

Before we were hustled onto the train, we were each allowed a split second to snatch a drink at the well and fill our canteens and water bottles. Once we were inside the train the guards threw a few loaves of black bread and some jars of artificial honey in to us, at the same time shouting to us that these constituted our sole provender for the next two days. We were sixty men to a car. The loaves were counted. There were only thirty. We divided them equally by pairing off and breaking each loaf in half.

The journey lasted almost exactly forty-eight hours. Most of the soldiers on the train were engaged in discussing their prospects. The vast majority had accepted the German promise of freedom at face value and felt dubious only about working and living conditions under German domination. Some pointed out that we could not possibly be freed since the Polish–German conflict had not yet come to a conclusion. Where they obtained their apparently 'authentic information' on this score was a complete mystery to me but, nevertheless, since I was only too willing to be convinced, their resolute confidence cheered me up a bit.

Under these collective illusions we left the train at Radom, a town in western Poland. This time the Germans lined us up with a great deal of gruff shouting. The officers that took command of us were harsh and issued disguised threats instead of promises. These were disturbing but did not alter our fundamental convictions. The belief that we were going to be freed had effectively prevented the slightest attempt at escape ever since Przemysl and continued to function now, as we marched under a light guard to the distribution camp at Radom. As we marched along, dazed and bedraggled, we began to doubt and conjecture for the first time.

Our conjectures were confirmed when we first saw the formidable barbed-wire fences of this huge, dismal camp. Again we were drawn up in the center of the camp and a speech was made assuring us that we would ultimately be released and put to work. In the meantime, though, any infraction of camp discipline would meet with swift and severe punishment. Anyone who attempted to escape would be instantly shot.

This threat had the immediate effect on me of making me consider it extremely urgent to escape as soon as possible. I reasoned that the only motive they could have for such sharp warnings was the intention of keeping us prisoners and under severe conditions. Glancing about me, I could see that escape was next to impossible. Radom was well-guarded, the barbed wire fence difficult to circumvent, and sentries placed at advantageous points commanded a good view of the terrain.

The next few days at Radom introduced me to a species of mentality and a new type of moral code, if it can be called such, so alien as to be ununderstandable. For the first time I encountered brutality and inhumanity of proportions completely out of the realm of anything I had previously experienced, and that actually made me revise my conception of the range of what could occur in the world I inhabited.

Living conditions were unspeakable. We drew what nutriment we could from a watery slop which was issued twice daily and which was so vile to the taste that many of the men, including myself, could not bring themselves to swallow it. To this was added a daily ration of about twenty grams of stale bread. We were housed in an old ramshackle structure so dilapidated as to be hardly recognizable as once having been a military barracks. Here, we slept on hard, bare ground thinly strewn with straw that had obviously not been changed since the war began.

We received neither blankets nor overcoats nor any protection whatsoever against the inclement, damp November weather. Medical treatment was non-existent. Here I learned how common and lightly regarded death could be. There had been, I learned, and continued to be, during my stay, many fatalities that could easily have been prevented – deaths from cold, hunger, exposure, and from physical abuse – the aftermath of imaginary or real violations of camp discipline.

But what shocked me most at Radom were not merely the living conditions and the brutality of our captors, but the apparently unmotivated character of both. These seemed to be occasioned not by any desire to inculcate discipline or obedience or to forestall attempts at escape. Nor were they designed merely to humiliate, degrade, and weaken us, though this was, in some degree, what was accomplished. It seemed rather all to be part of some unheard of, brutal code to which the guards and officials adhered with casual conformity for its own sake.

No order or remark was addressed to us without the inevitable prefix of 'Polish swine.' The guards seemed to be continually on the alert for an opportunity to deliver a kick in the stomach or to smash in a face. Anything that could by the remotest construction be called insubordination or lack of discipline, the most trifling oversight or inattention, brought an instantaneous and painful retribution. During my short stay I saw at least six men riddled by bullets, who had either been trying, or looked as though they had been trying, to clamber over the barbed wire.

I had formed an acquaintance with three men on the train and when we arrived at Radom we remained together. When, during the first sleepless night, we discovered that we shared a common desire and determination to escape at the earliest opportunity, our association solidified into a kind of definite corporative status, a mutual pool of talents, possessions, and knowledge.

Two of them were peasants, even-tempered, reliable, and courageous fellows who had not been demoralized in the slightest by our misfortunes. The third was one of the memorable individuals I have encountered not infrequently in this war, whose mere presence had illuminated and made bearable what would otherwise have been periods of hopeless gloom.

His name was Franek Maciag and he had been a mechanic in the nearby town of Kielce before the war. He was a robust, thickset man of about thirty, with a mop of wild, kinky black hair that had the strength and consistency of iron and was a constant subject of jokes. He was a clever and competent man, confident of our ability to outwit the Germans for whom he had a burning hatred and contempt. He had managed to retain, in a large part, what proved to be a priceless, natural fund of warmth and gaiety.

When we took inventory of our mutual resources, we discovered that we had quite a collection of useful objects. The peasants had managed to save and keep intact several pairs of socks and leggings. One had kept in excellent condition a mess kit which had belonged to his father in the First World War. Franek turned up a shaving set, a penknife, and a hundred zloty sewn into his underwear. This was good news for we had learned from the railroad men at Lublin that the Polish currency was still in circulation though at a somewhat reduced value. I had a golden medal around my neck and two hundred zloty in the sole of my shoe.

I found the innate fortitude and practical sense of these three men immensely heartening and helpful. In turn, they, realizing that I had some education and a knowledge of German, counted on a certain amount of inventiveness and leadership from me. I think that they must have guessed that I was an officer in disguise but they made no attempt to question me. Early in our association Franek gave me the name of 'professor,' and 'professor' I remained.

Our little corporation proved to be a very satisfactory arrangement indeed. The first day Franek undertook to give me a sorely needed shave. My skin had always been sensitive and was now covered with a variety of blemishes as a result of the combined effects of beard, dirt, exposure, and poor health. The shave was a salutary form of torture. It took nearly an hour and I endured it only by gritting my teeth, listening to Franek's jokes, and by the presence of these men in front of whom I did not wish to exhibit any weakness or inability to withstand pain.

We arranged, too, that one of us would call for the food rations of all four, thus eliminating many trips to the 'kitchen' which was frequently visited by a German non-com with a thick whip which he wielded with terrible effect on the pretext of keeping order or on no pretext at all. He was also the one who had the duty of seeing that we woke up on time, a function which he performed with the aid of his whip and the additional inducement of his heavy, hob-nailed boots. We assisted each other also in the foraging of food that began on the third day of our stay.

The camp was on the outskirts of the town and we noticed that some invisible hand or hands constantly threw paper-wrapped bundles over the barbed wire at unpredictable intervals.

These packages contained mostly bread and fruit and, less frequently, pieces of bacon, money, and even a few pairs of old, but still serviceable and literally priceless, shoes. The news spread like wildfire over the camp and every day crowds of men could be seen, avidly scouring the bushes near the wire fence for these treasures.

I must admit that I displayed considerable ingenuity in these searches. I discovered that packages would be thrown with the greatest frequency into a place where only the exchange prisoners could come and not the prisoners of war. It was a spot covered with bushes behind our latrines. I came here as often as I could and finally was rewarded by discovering a package. I opened it and found it to contain a piece of bread smeared with lard, a pinch of salt in a separate paper, and a bottle of vile-smelling liquid, the purpose of which I could not fathom.

I brought the package proudly to the other men. Franek opened the enigmatic bottle and shouted for joy. It was a medicine for lice and scabies, worth its weight in gold. Our bodies, our hair, our clothes, and our cots were infested with lice and other vermin. Franek divided it, doling it out with hair-line accuracy, cautiously avoiding spilling a single drop. It was powerful and alleviated our condition considerably, though it made us smell even worse than formerly.

In the course of the next three days I picked up three more packages near the toilet and established contact with our thoughtful benefactor. We tore off a piece of paper from one of the packages and with the remnant of a pencil I scrawled a message:

'Could you supply us with civilian clothing? Four of us here will risk anything to escape.'

The next day at dawn I rushed to the spot and scoured the bushes. I had almost given up when I stumbled on a package. It contained more food and a note:

'Cannot supply clothing because I would be seen. You are leaving the camp in a few days for forced labor. Try to escape when you are on your way.'

I took the food and note to my companions. We pored over the words of the message and decided to hold ourselves in readiness.

Five days later we were awakened even earlier than usual. The non-com laid about with his whip and kicked at our limbs and ribs with extra ferocity. In the gray mournful light we were herded together and without a word of explanation were marched off to the nearby railroad station. During the march my companions and I whispered to each other feverishly. Our lines were closely guarded and we could see no opportunity for breaking from the ranks or sneaking away. We decided to wait, reasoning that the train ride offered a much more reasonable chance of success.

A long line of freight cars were waiting at the station. Prodding us with rifle-butts and shouting at us 'Polish swine' to hurry, the guards loaded us rapidly into the train, sixty or sixty-five of us to a car. Inside we found ourselves in what, by its odor and construction, had obviously been used in normal times for the transportation of cattle. It was about fifty feet long, ten feet wide, and eight feet high. Except for the door the only sources of light were four small windows set at about eye level.

In the center of each car a tub of water had been placed. A moment after we were all inside, a sergeant entered accompanied by a guard carrying some loaves of dry bread. The sergeant stationed himself at the door with drawn pistol while the bread was distributed. The guard then joined him with his pistol likewise in readiness. The sergeant glanced about and gestured with his pistol for everyone to settle down and be quiet. He then scowled and spoke to us in rapid, gruff, broken Polish.

'Attention. You are all going to be taken to a place where you will be freed and allowed to work. You have nothing to fear if you behave yourself. The train is well-guarded. You will be shot if you attempt to escape. You will be allowed to leave the train for fifteen minutes every six hours. Anyone who creates a disturbance or fouls the cars will be shot.'

He glared menacingly at us as though he expected a challenge. He backed out of the door and descended to the station. The guard aped his challenging glare and followed suit. The door slammed shut from the outside and we heard the clang of an iron bar dropping into place, locking us in. We heard similar slams and clangs as similar speeches and exits occurred in the other cars. Outside we heard an indistinguishable series of yelled orders and then the train began to move, grinding slowly and jarringly away from Radom.

The train edged forward uncertainly, stopping frequently, and never attaining full speed except for short intervals. Inside it was hot, stuffy, and malodorous, the lingering traces of the cattle mingling with the perspiration of our stifling, unwashed bodies. I held a whispered, excited consultation with my three companions.

'It is now or never,' I said to them, 'if we don't escape from the train, we are liable to remain German pushers for the rest of the war.'

They agreed with me and made suggestions as to the time and

place. One of the peasants argued that it would be best to try to sneak away during one of the fifteen-minute stops we had been promised. We overruled him, pointing out that we should be closely guarded during these intervals. It was decided that we would wait for nightfall. We should be near the forests around Kielce and it would be difficult to jump through the window. I told him that I remembered a trick from my childhood. Three men would hold a fourth in position and half-push, half-throw him out of the window.

One of the peasants said that we should need the assistance of the other men in the car for this purpose. Franek pointed out that, in any case, we should and must obtain the consent of the other men in the car. They would be likely to suffer punishment for our actions and, besides, if they decided to oppose our escape, it would be all up with us. He turned to me and said meaningfully:

'You will have to convince them. Tell them who you are and why you want to escape. Make a speech to them.'

I hesitated for a fraction of a second and then consented. My rôle in the affair was such that I could not refuse this request. Besides, I was not unpracticed at oratory. As a youth, to be a great orator had been my chief ambition. I had practiced arduously and tried to learn the tricks of all the idols of European politics and diplomacy. At the Collegium Maximum, in the Lwow University in 1934, I had carried off several prizes and I remembered in particular one night of real triumph.

'I had better equal or surpass that performance,' I thought to myself, gazing around at the hard indifferent faces of the men in the car.

Our plan was ready. We sat around restlessly, convulsed with excitement, waiting for nightfall and the sight of the forests of Kielce. Franek got up frequently to gaze out of the window. After one of a number of these visits, he returned hurriedly, stumbling over the legs of a man in his way.

'Now,' he whispered breathlessly. 'We shall soon be in a perfect place. Make your speech.'

I got up, took a deep breath and dug my fingernails into the palms of my hands to help me keep my nerves under control. I raised my voice to a loud oratorical pitch.

'Citizens of Poland,' I shouted, 'I have something to say to you. I am not a private but an officer. I and these three men are going to jump from this train. Not because we value our health or safety, but because we wish to rejoin the Polish Army. The Germans say they have wiped out our army but we know that they are lying. We know that our army is still fighting courageously. Will you do your duty as soldiers and escape with me to continue the fight for our country's sake?'

At my first shout, they had come to startled attention. Many of them had smiled as though I had suddenly gone mad. As I continued they became more serious and I could see that many of them were now determined to oppose our project. I paused. There was a hub-bub of comment, agreement, and objections. A group of seven or eight older men in the back of the car, in particular, were maintaining an unyielding resistance to everything I had urged.

'Why should we help you?' one of them shouted back at me. 'If you escape the Germans will shoot the rest of us. We have nothing to gain by jumping ourselves. The Germans will treat us decently once we are working. If you jump we have everything to lose and nothing to gain.'

A few men rallied to his support. 'Yes, yes,' they shouted, 'don't let them jump. We shall all be shot.'

I have always believed that the best stimulus for oratory is anger. Infuriated by this display, I launched into an inspired tirade in which every demagogic and rhetorical trick I had ever learned came unbidden to my aid. Phrases rolled automatically from my lips. 'We are young men,' I concluded pointedly, referring to the age of the active opposition. 'Most of us are in our twenties. Some are only eighteen. We do not intend to spend our lives as German slaves. They intend to subjugate Poland or destroy the Polish people. They have said so many times. Some day you may go home again. What will your families say, how will your friends act, when they learn that you have helped our enemies?'

There was some whispering opposition left but it diminished rapidly. I still had not convinced most of the prisoners to make the attempt with us but at least they would not impede our escape. Another eight soldiers came forward to join us. Together we shouted down the remnants of the opposition. A few men who were at first unwilling to join us even volunteered to help us get through the windows.

It was now dark enough to take the risk. Besides, it had begun to rain and, although that meant we would be wet and miserable, it also meant there would be fewer guards outside. I explained briefly what we were going to do and we lined up in parties of about eight each at two of the windows. Franek went first. One man took him by the shoulders, another by the knees and a third by the feet, I counted three and they shoved and hurled him through the window. We waited a split second. There was no sound. I looked out of the window but could see Franek nowhere. Either he had run off successfully or was lying on the ground, invisible in the rain and darkness.

The train was now moving rather slowly as the track curved through the forests. We set to work with frenzied activity. Each group picked up a man, wedged him through the window, and flung him out into the darkness. After we had disposed of four more in this fashion, we heard a rifle shot ring out. Then we saw the beam of a powerful searchlight probing along the side of the train.

We paused. I realized instantly that the shot and the beam must have issued from an observation post set up on the roof of a car – probably the last one.

'Keep on till the train stops,' I shouted, 'we must hurry.'

I wondered if the train would be stopped. I hoped the Germans would not think it worthwhile to upset their schedules for a handful of men. Apparently they did not, for the train kept moving. We disposed of four more men and then a volley of rifle shots rang out. We launched two more men out into space through the shots. As one hit the ground, we heard a loud 'Jesus!', followed by a cry of pain. There were only three more men left now, including myself.

It was too late to even consider halting now. The other group threw one of their two remaining men out, while I was carried to the window. Another random shot or two rang out as they pushed me forward and I sailed through the air.

I landed on my feet, the motion of the train and the leap combining to drag me forward and to my left. I stumbled onward a few steps, struggling to regain my balance and then pitched forward on my face. The impact of the ground on my head and body was softened by the thick grass. I was breathless and gasping but unharmed. I still heard shots. I got up and ran for the protective line of trees and crouched behind one, waiting to see if anyone would join me. The shots ceased and the train rattled on into the distance; there would probably be no searching parties.

I waited for nearly a half hour, hoping that some of the others would join me. I wondered how they had fared and thought regretfully of the fact that I had neglected to make any arrangements for a rendezvous with my three friends – Franek in particular, who knew this section of the country well. At length I saw someone edging uncertainly through the trees. I called to him, asking if he had been hurt. He replied in the negative and came to join me. It was a very pale and frightened young soldier of about eighteen, with a slim, boyish body and curly hair. He seemed more fit for a children's school or an orphan asylum than an army.

I realized that he had been searching desperately for someone to offer him advice. I made him sit down and rest for a while, telling him not to worry; that we had safely eluded the Germans and there would be no pursuit. He asked me what I intended to do. I told him that ultimately I intended to go to Warsaw, but that our first urgent requirements were civilian clothes, shelter, and food. He thought that Warsaw might be a haven for him, too, as he had an aunt there. We sat for a while in the darkness discussing plans.

We were in a part of Poland neither of us knew well. We were in uniform, possessed no documents of any kind, and had no idea of conditions about us. We were hungry; weakened by the ordeals of the last few weeks, and in the now heavy downpour had no protection but our threadbare garments. In the circumstances, there was nothing to do but trust to luck. Determining to knock at the door of the first dwelling we came upon, we got up and walked through the wood until we came to a narrow strip of grassless soil that was obviously either a path or a road.

After about three hours of trudging through the rain, we perceived the outlines of a village, and slackened our pace, approaching it cautiously. Tiptoeing quietly up to the first cottage, we found ourselves at a small, typical peasants' dwelling. Hesitantly we stood before the door from under which a dim light issued. As I raised my hand to knock, I felt a tremor of nervousness and apprehension. I rapped on the door with brusque over-emphasis to allay my dread.

'Who is it?' The trembling voice of a peasant reassured me slightly.

'Come out, please,' I replied, attempting to make my voice sound polite but authoritative, 'it is very important.'

The door opened slowly, disclosing a gray-headed old peasant with a grizzled beard. He stood there in his underwear, obviously frightened and cold. A wave of warm air from the interior made me feel almost faint with the urge to enter and bask in it.

'What do you want?' he asked in a tone of mingled indignation and fear.

I ignored the question. I decided to try to play boldly on his feelings.

'Are you or are you not a Pole?' I demanded sternly. 'Answer me.'

'I am a Polish patriot,' he replied with greater composure and celerity than I had anticipated.

'Do you love your country?' I continued undismayed.

'I do.'

'Do you believe in God?'

'Yes, I do.'

The old man evinced considerable impatience at my questions but no longer seemed terrified – merely curious. I proceeded to satisfy his curiosity.

'We are Polish soldiers who have just escaped from the Germans. We are going to join the army and help them save Poland. We are not defeated yet. You must help us and give us civilian clothes.

If you refuse and try to turn us over to the Germans, God will punish you.'

He gazed at me quizzically from under his thick eyebrows. I could not tell if he was amused, impressed, or alarmed.

'Come inside,' he said dryly, 'out of this miserable rain. I will not turn you over to the Germans.'

Inside, we collapsed into two old armchairs that had once been ornate and luxurious but were now tattered and rickety. They looked oddly out of place among the other furniture, a table, a bench, and two plain chairs fashioned crudely from unvarnished pine. An oil lamp threw a weak glow over the room. An old peasant woman with a wrinkled, weather-beaten face and a shawl over her head sat by the battered stove which exuded a magical warmth.

We drew our chairs closer to the stove. Every muscle and bone in my body seemed to melt at once in grateful relaxation. The peasant gestured to his wife.

'These are Polish boys, soldiers, who have escaped from the Germans. They are cold and tired. Give them something to take the chill out of their bones.'

She smiled at us and then bustled about to prepare us some hot milk. When it had come to a boil on the stove, she poured it into two thick cups and handed them to us with a couple of slices of black bread. We ate and drank with relish. When we were finished, I thanked them effusively, hoping to compensate for the harsh tone I had taken outside.

The peasant remained taciturn and noncommittal. 'You go to bed now,' he said unemotionally. 'In the morning, when you are rested, we will talk further.'

He got up, beckoned us to follow him, and opened a door in the back which led into a small, dark room.

'There is only one bed,' he informed us, 'but it is large enough for two. There are blankets on it, if you need them.'

We undressed hastily and crawled under the blankets. It was the first mattress either of us had touched in weeks. It was thin, lumpy and the ticking was coarse and irritating but we did not even notice.

We exchanged congratulations on our comparatively good fortune and dropped off to sleep. During the night I woke up several times. I had the sensation that I was being bitten and stung all over my body. I was too sleepy to do much investigating and as my companion slept and snored in peaceful oblivion, I decided it must be either my imagination or the pimples I had accumulated. It developed that neither were responsible. The bed was infested with fleas. They clung to us in the morning and indeed it was weeks before I was free from them completely.

We woke up by ourselves. It was nearly noon and a bright sun shone cheerfully through the narrow window above our rude bed. Despite the fleas, I felt immensely refreshed and full of hope and buoyancy.

The peasant had evidently heard our movements and he entered abruptly, catching us in the act of slapping and cursing at the fleas.

'There are too many of them for you to catch,' he said and laughed loudly. 'I am sorry we had no better place for you gentlemen, but they will not do you much harm.'

I mumbled that we had slept very well in any case and thanked him for his hospitality.

'There is not much we can do for you,' he said. 'We were poor people before and now, with the Germans here, things are even worse. We will help you and give you what we have but you must hurry. The Germans may come by here at any moment to look for you.'

'You are a good man,' I said.

The old man gave us what must have been his last shred of clothing, two pairs of trousers and two warm, though ragged, old jackets. We put them on and left him our uniforms in exchange. We offered him some of our small stock of zlotys but he steadfastly refused. The peasant's wife gave us another cup of milk and handed us two loaves of black bread.

As we stood near the doorway in our new civilian regalia, clutching our loaves of bread, the peasant inquired if we had any idea where we were and where we were going.

'We should be somewhere near Kielce,' I answered, 'and we are going wherever the Polish Army is fighting against the Germans.'

'Then you are not going anywhere at all,' the old man remarked.

'What do you mean?'

'There is no longer a Polish Army. Soldiers, yes. There are many soldiers. But the Polish Army stopped fighting three weeks ago. Didn't the Germans tell you?'

I froze. The first idea that sprang to mind was that this simple man had allowed himself to be taken in by enemy propaganda.

'Yes, the Germans told us but we do not believe them. They are liars and you should not let them fool you so easily.'

'We are not fooled. Everybody knows there is no longer a Polish Army. They heard it on the radio and read it in the newspapers. We learned it from our neighbors, not the Germans. Warsaw and the coast defended themselves for weeks, but they also had to yield. Now there is no longer even a Poland. The Germans have taken half of our country and the Russians have taken the other half.'

Turning my eyes from the sad, lined face of the peasant I noticed that the shoulders of my companion were quivering. His chest heaved and his face was red and contorted.

'Only God can save us,' the old woman interrupted the silence.

'There is no God,' my companion shouted.

'No, my boy,' she answered quietly. 'There is a God. He alone is left to us.'

I put my arm around his shoulders.

'Don't take it so hard,' I said, 'France and England will come to our aid. They are already giving the Germans a taste of their own medicine.'

I turned to the peasant, my arm still around the boy's shoulder.

'Have you heard any news of France or England?' I asked. 'Do you know what the Allies are doing?'

'I know nothing of the Allies,' he answered. 'I know that they did not help us.'[5]

The wife of the peasant approached the boy and tried to console him.

'You must be brave, young man,' she said. 'It is not the first time this has happened to Poland. The Germans will be driven out again. Have faith and go back home. At least you are alive and well.'

The boy said nothing; the peasant then told us how to find the road to Kielce and then to Warsaw. His wife kissed us both on the cheeks and I almost burst into tears myself as I stooped over to let her face come close to mine. She wished a blessing on us and we left.

We walked slowly toward the main road to Kielce, the boy crying now quietly and steadily. It took us three hours to reach the town – the boy marching with his face set and grim.

He seemed to be unable to answer the questions I addressed to him or control himself sufficiently to respond to anything with more than a nod or a shake of his head. In the town of Kielce, or rather, what was left of it, I saw a nurse wearing the uniform of the Polish Red Cross. I explained the condition of the boy to her as best as I could, informing her that he needed rest and constant care and that he should be watched for an attempt to commit suicide. She reassured me and told me that the shelter of the Red Cross was also open to me. I declined and asked her to direct me to the road to Warsaw. She did so, wished me Godspeed and I continued on my way to Warsaw alone.

4

Devastated Poland

In Kielce I scarcely stopped to rest but hastened immediately to the outskirts of the town and the route which led toward Warsaw. I felt an irresistible urge to rush; to flee toward the capital as if it were an unquestionable haven of refuge; as if it were certain that I would find something there on which I could base my existence and obtain – if not consolation and security – some hint or inkling of how to guide my conduct, which now seemed to be utterly without meaning or direction.

It was now nearing the end of the second week of November 1939. Altogether eleven weeks had elapsed since the night I had been handed the red slip of paper that had served as my passport to war. It was only a little more than two months since I had been awakened by the terrifying crash of the German bombs falling on Oswiecim. Those weeks, I realized, had been largely spent in meeting shock after shock, bracing myself for each successive one. The world I lived in was falling apart around me. I felt like a shipwrecked man in the ocean, who, after being hit by a wave, can do nothing but wait for the onslaught of the next one. To the point of exhaustion.

There was no longer a Poland. And with it had disappeared the whole mode of existence that had previously been mine. I realized now the meaning of some of the reactions I had seen in other men – the officer who had committed suicide at Tarnopol, sensing that life was now meaningless and the world too sordid. I understood now how the boy had felt whom I had just left – still silent and weeping – in Kielce. They had accepted as a fact and felt the destruction of Poland earlier than I had. These men had reacted with more sincerity and humanity because they understood the situation. They were true to who they were. And what about me? Was I being true to myself when I stubbornly persisted in talking, in a senseless way, about the Polish Army, an army that was bound to be still fighting somewhere? Did I really believe what I was saying or was it just bravado to silence my anguish?

Why, in Poland, did defeat have such exceptional significance?

How was Poland different from other countries? How was our nation different from the others? I recalled the classes I had taken and my professors at the Jan-Casimir University of Lwow, and the discussions I'd had with my father and brother . . .

In Poland there is a meaning to defeat that perhaps is unknown in countries differently situated. Along with a strong sense of unity as a people, there is present an awareness that a defeat in war entails unique and drastic consequences. Other nations may be oppressed and dominated after losing a war; they may have war reparations imposed on them, or limits on their army, sometimes even their boundaries are changed. But when a Polish soldier was beaten on the battlefield, the specter of total annihilation swooped down upon the entire nation: its neighbors would pillage and divide up its land, and try to destroy its language and culture. That is why, to us, war took on the character of total war.

And that is why, to those who are conscious of how deeply a defeat would affect their personal lives, only two reactions are possible. Either a protective optimism tends to dispel the realization of the true state of affairs – or for others, full knowledge is apt to bring with it a sense of personal annihilation; a state of complete despair that borders on, or enters into, the suicidal. These also, in their own way, 'cancel' out the reality of what has taken place – but by killing themselves. That is what I believe had happened to the man who shot himself at Tarnopol, and to the young boy.

As I walked along I almost deliberately stifled the questions that kept crowding into my consciousness. I did not dare let myself think that Poland as a state had completely, irredeemably, disappeared. I kept constantly before me the notion that Germany would soon be beaten by the Allies, or be forced to withdraw from Poland. And while I knew that all Polish resistance had ceased, nevertheless, I could not bring myself wholly to accept the fact. Irrationally, some part of me continued to believe that something was occurring, at least, in Warsaw, some fragment of Polish activity that had not yet been completely stamped out and extinguished.

I hurried toward Warsaw as fast as I could. During the six days it took me to reach the capital, I wasted little time and took advantage of the most minute opportunity to increase my speed as though I had an urgent appointment to keep and it was of the utmost importance to be punctual. Near Kielce, the roads were deserted but, as I left it some distance behind, I met with refugees swarming to the capital in increasing numbers until, when I finally reached the main highway, I found it to be clogged with traffic and almost impassable.

On foot, and in every conceivable kind of vehicle, men and women of all ages and descriptions were fleeing or returning to their homes. Most of them were, in all probability, former inhabitants of Warsaw – merchants, workers, and professional men. Others were from smaller cities and villages that had become uninhabitable through shelling and bombing. Some were obviously peasants and carried with them the articles they deemed most precious of their few poor belongings. Women carried children in their arms as they walked along with the steady, implacable tread of the hypnotized. Some carried packages of food in their arms, others clothes; one or two even carried books. The carts creaked and sagged under whole households of furniture. I remember noticing the gleaming mahogany and keyboard of a piano in the back of a wagon.

Some, too, were leaving Warsaw to go back to the country and made their way with difficulty against the tide. There were thousands of people along the roads; people of all kinds – uninjured like myself, and who had never had a chance to use their fine-looking but outmoded weapons. There was little fraternization among these refugees; each was too preoccupied with private woes to give much heed to those who passed alongside them. There was little conversation of any kind. All were quiet and looked utterly exhausted.

I found it easy enough to obtain seats on the wagons and carts.

Many of these had emerged from long disuse and were constantly in need of makeshift repairs during the trip. Harnesses were in tatters and the majority of the horses suffered from galls. The knowledge and skill I had acquired were in constant demand and I was a welcome passenger. For my services I received not only transportation but often a night's lodging in a barn or a peasant hut, and food.

Everywhere I found vast areas of devastation left by the Blitzkrieg. Every city, town, and railroad station showed the effects of bombing and shelling. The skeletons of buildings and depots projected stiffly from piles of debris. Whole blocks were cluttered with tangled and inextricable ruins. I saw three empty foundations where a stick of bombs had apparently uprooted three huts as neatly as though they had been carrots. In many of the towns, mass graves had been constructed, where the inhabitants had not had sufficient time to give the dead proper burials before the arrival of the Germans. As I passed, I often found these graves surrounded by groups of kinsfolk and friends praying and placing flowers upon them.

For the last twenty-five miles of the trip, I allowed myself the luxury of a train ride. I had actually earned a little money as a mender of carts and harness and I was very tired. The condition of the railroad was miserable. The Germans had taken every modern locomotive and car for military use in Germany. Those that remained were relics that dated back to before the last war. The windows were broken, the paint peeling, the wheels rusty, and the bodies of the cars dilapidated.

On the train I discreetly questioned one or two of the passengers as to what papers were being demanded by the Germans, where guards were stationed, and what the chances were of being arrested. I was informed that there were guards at the main depots; that the usual papers were required and that they arrested anyone whose papers looked suspicious, or who was carrying large amounts of foodstuffs. I was surprised that people should be arrested for bringing food to cities. Nevertheless, my informants were correct on this score. The policy of starving the major Polish cities had begun.[1] Other arrests, however, had nothing whatsoever to do with papers. If someone looked young and healthy, he might be arrested at any moment and sent to a forced-labor camp. The Germans had no difficulty in detecting an 'error' in one's papers, if, indeed, any pretext was required.

As soon as I had obtained the information I needed, I kept quiet. I felt that since conditions had changed, and since I knew little or nothing of what life was like under German rule, the best policy was to keep to oneself and to be as inconspicuous as one in my circumstances possibly could be. I decided to leave the train at the suburbs, in order to avoid the Germans who would be stationed at the main depot. Many others did the same. I was glad to see that methods of evading German scrutiny were already known.

Warsaw was a shocking ruin of its former self; the disaster that had befallen it exceeded in magnitude my direct anticipation. The gay metropolis had disappeared. The handsome buildings, the theaters, the cafés, the flowers, the cheerful, noisy, familiar Warsaw had vanished as utterly as if it had never existed. I passed through street after street heaped with rubble and debris. The pavements were black and grimy. The inhabitants were worn, tired, and disconsolate. Graves for the dead who could not be taken to a cemetery had been improvised everywhere in parks, public squares, and even on the streets.

At the corner of Marshall and Jerusalem Boulevards, in the heart of Warsaw and close to the Central Railroad Station, the paving stones had been uprooted and a huge mass grave dug for unknown soldiers. It was covered with flowers and surrounded by burning candles. A crowd of mourners knelt beside it, praying. I learned later that this unceasing vigil had been kept up since the burials had taken place three months ago.

During the next few weeks I continued to see the mourners by the side of the grave from dawn to the curfew hours. Gradually the ceremonies that took place ceased to be only a devotion to the dead; they became tokens of political resistance as well. In December, the Nazi Gauleiter for Warsaw, Moder,[2] realized the significance the grave had assumed and ordered the bodies disinterred and buried in a cemetery. But even after this measure, mourners would still come to kneel in prayer at this corner and candles would be lighted as if the spot had been hallowed by a presence the shovels of the Nazi soldiers could not expel.

I stood in silence by the grave for a while and then walked toward my sister's flat. My sister had an apartment in the Praga district nearby.[3] I had always been extremely fond of her, her kindliness, vitality, and good spirits. I had been a frequent visitor there and was on the best of terms with her husband, a man of thirty-eight, an engineer. I hoped fervidly that no harm had come to them and that here at last I could find something from my previous existence that had not been wholly annihilated.

The block in which she lived was comparatively unscathed. The familiar entrance to the house was unchanged. As I was about to enter, I straightened my tie in the automatic way of former times. It occurred to me to think of my appearance. I fingered my beard which was weeks old and matted with dirt; my clothes hung in tatters about my unwashed body. I wondered if I would recognize myself if I were to see myself walking down the street. I decided that I would probably take myself to be a diseased old beggar and pass myself by. This fantasy caused me to laugh loudly.

I ceased laughing abruptly and felt suddenly embarrassed and apprehensive. The house was silent and lifeless. I walked past the other doors rapidly, pushing the disturbing thoughts from my brain. This was my sister's house. It was all over. I was home again. I knocked confidently and waited. There was no answer. I knocked again, a trifle more forcibly.

'Who's there?' The question came in a voice that I recognized to be my sister's, but sounding duller, less responsive than I had expected. I felt it would be unwise to shout my name and for an answer I knocked again softly. There was the sound of slow footsteps approaching and then the door opened and my sister stood in front of me, one hand still on the knob.

I was about to make some sort of demonstration of affection, to take her in my arms or kiss her, but something in her demeanor deterred me.

'It's I – Jan,' I said – though I felt sure she recognized me. 'Don't you know me?'

'Yes. Come in.'

I followed her into the room, chilled and worried by her manner. I glanced nervously around at as much as I could see of the apartment. It seemed unchanged. There was no one else present. I tried to imagine the reason for the coldness of her reception. Her face was expressionless and had aged. The dress she was wearing was plain but serviceable. She said nothing; gave no hint of either welcoming my presence or being annoyed by it.

'I escaped from the Germans about a week ago,' I informed her and continued, anxious to make conversation and elicit some response from her. 'We were on our way from the distribution center at Radom to a forced-labor camp. I jumped off the train at Kielce. It took me a week to reach Warsaw and I came directly here.'

She listened without interest; her face averted from mine. Her body was stiff and upright, as though it were being pulled back by an unremitting effort of will; as though she would droop and collapse. The vitality that had been her most salient characteristic, her ability to react instantaneously to every word and gesture had vanished utterly, making her seem like a stranger to me. Her gaze rested dully on some object across the room – something that was to my right or back. I turned in my chair almost rudely, and saw on the desk against the wall a large mounted photograph of her husband taken more than a decade ago. The face was young, handsome, and illumined by a wide, happy smile. She stared at it fixedly and did not notice my movement.

'What has happened?' I asked anxiously. 'Is anything wrong? Where is Aleksander?'

'He is dead. He was arrested three weeks ago. They questioned him and tortured him. He was finally shot.'

Her voice was calm and deliberate. Sorrow seemed to have dulled her emotions so that she no longer was capable of any fresh grief or

agony. She continued to stare at the picture as if hypnotized. I
understood that she gave me these details to avoid further questions
on my part. I refrained from asking them and sat helplessly silent.
Any speech or even a movement on my part would have been an
intrusion. She wished at all costs to avoid being upset or disturbed
further.

At length she spoke to me again – still without taking her eyes off
the photograph.

'You cannot stay here long. It is too dangerous. The Gestapo
might come; they might hear about you or be looking for you. I am
afraid of them.'

I got up to go. For the first time she turned and looked at me; seemed
to take in my exhaustion – the dirt, the rags, the pallor. Her expression did not change. She turned her eyes back to the photograph.

'You can stay for the night. In the morning you can take some of
his clothes. But then you will have to go.'

She withdrew completely into herself again – took no further
notice of me. I felt like an intrusive visitor. Quietly, on tiptoe, I left
the parlor and walked around the apartment I knew so well. It had
changed little. Without help, evidently, she still managed to keep
the apartment spotlessly clean. I had not noticed before how cold it
was. I remarked to myself that it must be hard to get fuel in Warsaw.
The pantry was completely empty. Apparently she did not have the
strength or will to forage for food. In the bathroom I found a cake of
cheap, strong soap and cleansed myself as well as I could with cold
water. When I was finished, I walked into the foyer and watched her
through the open door that led into the parlor. She sat in the same
rigid position in which I had left her. The profile that was toward me
was pale and immobile. It was as if I had never known her . . . her
grief was something I could not penetrate by sympathy . . . an emotion that made her utterly remote from me; made every action on
my part futile and unwanted.

I went through the foyer and into her husband's den. It was
unchanged – the same leather couch; the same scientific books and
periodicals. I drew out a blanket from a closet and then undressed

carefully, placing my clothes on a chair. On the leather couch, I tossed restlessly for a few moments and then fell into a deep, exhausted slumber.

It was nearly noon when I woke. The light was gray and on the small portion of the windowpane that was not covered by the shade there were streaks of tiny raindrops. My body was heavy with sleep and I still felt tired but acutely conscious of having slept longer than I desired. I forced myself out of bed and, going to the closet, selected a suit of inconspicuous color and cut. In the bureau, I found a shirt and tie. When I dressed, I walked through the foyer. The door of the parlor was closed. I opened it and timidly peered in. My sister was dusting the furniture in the parlor, raising and lowering her arm with tired, methodical care. When she heard the door open, she stopped with a deliberate, unhurried motion and then turned toward me as though she had been expecting me. A faint flicker of expression passed across her face as she took in the clothes I was wearing.

'You will have to leave soon,' she said, without preliminaries. She continued to gaze slightly to the side of me, unwilling to let me enter fully into her consciousness; preserving her grief from intrusion. 'What do you need?'

'Nothing.' I shook my head. 'Is there anything I can do for you, Lili? Can I help you in any way?'

She did not answer my request. She continued as though she had not heard the words. At one time nothing ever seemed to escape her notice; now she had developed the faculty of rejecting anything that did not bear on the one emotion that possessed her wholly.

'You had better shave,' she said calmly. 'When you are through, I will give you some money.'

She turned away from me and picked up the duster. When I had finished, I returned to the parlor. She was sitting on the same chair she had sat in last night opposite the desk and photograph. When I entered, she arose, went to the desk and from a drawer took three rings, a gold watch, and a few bills. She approached me and placed them in my hands.

'I have no use for these things,' she said; 'take them.'

I put them in my pocket. I wanted to thank her but felt inarticulate and uncertain of what to say. She walked to the front door, while I followed, constrained and oppressed. She opened the door and peered out into the hall, scanning the corridor for a suspicious presence. At her side, I placed my hand on her shoulder and, looking intently at her, I repeated: 'Is there nothing at all I can do, Lili?'

She turned toward me and, for the first time, gazed directly into my eyes with a poignant, communicative glance. Silently, she extended her hand toward the doorknob.

When I got outside the rain had ceased; the sky was cloudy and cheerless; the street almost deserted. On the other side a gray-haired woman hurried by, clutching a bundle tightly. Two children – a boy and a girl – sat on a stoop a few doors down – their clothes shabby, their faces pale; their demeanor adult and serious. For no reason, except possibly to avoid the glance of the children, I turned in the other direction and began to walk at random, rapidly, trying to avoid passing close to any of the few pedestrians whom I saw.

After half an hour of haphazard walking about, I stopped at a corner and took cognizance of my whereabouts. It was a neighborhood with which I had formerly been very familiar – now scarcely recognizable, having been severely hit by the bombardment and little or nothing having been done to remedy the damage. About six blocks away lived one of my best friends, whose poor health had kept him out of the army. Amidst so much change, it did not seem likely that I would find him at the same address. Nevertheless, I decided to make the attempt.

5

The Beginning

The name of this young man was Dziepatowski. He had been one of my closest friends for several years, despite the fact that he was three or four years younger than I. When I first met him, I was in my third year at the Lwow University and he was about to be graduated from high school. Everything about Dziepatowski inspired me to respect and admiration. He was a violin student, an extremely talented one; but, unlike most musicians, he had a great love and understanding of the other arts and, because he was so cultured, he embodied the very ideal of Renaissance man.

He came from poor parents; but his determination to make his way by hard work and unsparing self-sacrifice was being rewarded by initial success. The violin was at once an object of passion and idealistic veneration for him – since he regarded his talent as neither an accidental privilege nor a valuable commodity, but a serious responsibility – a divine gift that exacted the utmost effort from him in return. He gave private lessons to less advanced pupils of the school. I would frequently encounter him in the streets, running breathlessly from one lesson to another – too busy to do more than wave his hand at me and run off – his long black hair flying; his violin case held stiffly at a distance from him to keep it from striking against his legs and being damaged. Or he would shout a quick 'Hello there!' from a passing trolley platform.

The money he earned in this fashion was never spent on frivolity – for which, in general, he had little taste – but on the things that were necessary to his ambitions and career – music lessons, books, the advancement of his general education. His austerity and single-hearted purpose frequently brought him into sharp conflicts with his family, teachers, and friends. For, despite a fundamental timidity and modesty that tended to make him shun people and avoid a social life, he had a fierce and intractable conviction of the importance of music and an often irritating respect for his own talent.[1]

Any discussion of music, any joke or sneer at his talent, and the mild, shy Dziepatowski became a raging tiger, snarling at his adversary with incommensurate fury. I remember an occasion when a mutual acquaintance, a brilliant and extremely cynical student of history and politics, attempted to torment Dziepatowski by pointing out his shyness and characterizing his passion for the violin as a weakness, the compensation for his timid character and lack of confidence, especially in his . . . virility. All of this was served up in a 'Freudian concoction' to lend it the appearance of science. Dziepatowski retorted with a vitriolic attack on the personal life of his detractor and proved – by also referring to Freud – that all the female conquests that this fellow liked to brag about were nothing more than the expression of a complex about his manhood and of his total inability to maintain normal, lasting relationships with the fairer sex. The 'Don Juan' friend was stunned into silence and sloped off. He never again spoke a single word to Dziepatowski. He never even acknowledged him any more. The majority of our college friends agreed that he was likable, but too loath to compromise, and quite unapproachable. I never saw him in the company of a young woman. His artistic soul undoubtedly devoted all its emotions to Art with a capital A, and never concerned itself with questions as mundane as flirting with girls.

My friendship with him developed by accident. As a university student, one of my greatest pleasures was my participation in a series of lectures for the peasants of the Lwow provinces which were organized by the well-known 'Polish Association of People's Schools.' The lectures were designed to aid in the general movement to bring about a rapprochement between the intelligentsia and the peasants. For three years, every Sunday would find me in a nearby Polish or Ukrainian village, delivering a rousing lecture on history, Polish literature, hygiene, or the co-operative movement.

To make these lectures a trifle less tedious, the organization sent with me, one day, a high-school boy who was to reward with some violin music those who remained to the end. The affair was a tremendous success. Dziepatowski played well and was, moreover, tall and attractive. When he played, his air of utter absorption in his work – and his long hair, pale face, and dark, mobile eyes – made a devastating impression on the village girls.

The ovation he received made my routine round of applause seem perfunctory. I was much too engrossed in the fate of these lectures to be jealous and I made an agreement with him to make frequent such joint expeditions. He was to attract people to my lectures with his music. The project succeeded wonderfully. After the lectures, people would dance to his music and the whole proceeding took on a much gayer air. Dziepatowski was much more popular than I, but, as the halls were always crowded, I was perfectly content.

At the end of these meetings, we would both feel very happy. Riding home together, we held long, animated conversations. We would discuss the importance of our common work, the need for bringing about a greater understanding between the two classes. In Poland, unfortunately, many of the intelligentsia (the term under which we designate the educated class as a whole) knew the peasants only from books and movies.

I came to admire his flexible mind as well as his talent and I was deeply impressed by the integrity and fortitude with which he struggled against the handicaps of poverty and a delicate, perpetually ailing physique. When I was abroad, we wrote to each other frequently. I learned that he had moved to Warsaw and was pursuing his career with his usual ardor. We had begun to take up the threads of our friendship once more when the war broke out. I felt sure that Dziepatowski was one person in whom, if he were still alive and at home, I would find attitudes and feelings similar to my own. I was not disappointed.

The welcome he gave me was cordial, if restrained by the time and circumstances. I could see that he was deeply pleased to see me alive and free, and was genuinely concerned at the poor health my gaunt figure and bad complexion indicated. He, too, had changed considerably, though by no means for the worse. He was less shy and less arrogant. His delicate, boyish face was still thin but with more manly, determined lines. Poland's defeat had saddened him but he did not seem at all heartbroken or despondent.

When I asked him how conditions were in Warsaw, he smiled wryly.

'They are not so bad as some people think,' he replied in a tone that struck me as curious, enigmatic.

'But everything seems so horrible,' I protested. 'It is no longer the same city. We no longer have a country. I can't blame people for being gloomy or pessimistic.'

'You talk as though Poland were the only country in the war,' he said, a note of indignation in his voice. 'You seem to think the last battle has been fought. You should know better than that. We have to be courageous and think of the future; not moan about the present.'

He was obviously disturbed by my pessimism. I reasoned that my tone had made him feel that, whatever way of life he had adopted, it was open to censure – the life of a man who had not been affected severely by the war. I decided to take a new tack.

'Of course,' I said, 'I know that the Allies will win the war sooner or later but, meanwhile, we have to live here. Conditions and the inability to do anything affect people. It is only natural.'

He scrutinized me very carefully as I made this remark. He leaned forward intently, his chin cupped in his hand and stared at me while I was speaking. He appeared to be satisfied with what he discovered, for he sank back in his armchair, relaxed, and ran his fingers through his hair. Then he inclined his body toward me and looked into my eyes significantly. 'Jan,' he said, lowering his voice slightly and speaking very slowly, 'not every Pole has resigned himself to fate.'

The words were underscored by some hidden meaning, had implications I could not grasp. I waited for him to add something to his statement, but he sat back quietly, running his hands through his hair as if absorbed in the task. I marveled at the inner security and confidence he exuded. Everyone else in Warsaw who I had seen behaved as though their last resource was gone. They had given up attempting to control events; had despaired and let themselves drift. Dziepatowski was evidently occupied in some way that gave him satisfaction, but I could not for the life of me imagine what it was.

I sensed that he expected something of me but was completely at a loss as to how to fulfill his expectations. I puzzled so long that finally I decided in exasperation to ask him bluntly:

'What have you been doing all this time? You seem to derive some satisfaction from whatever is keeping you busy.'

'I keep my spirits up; I fight to prevent myself from becoming demoralized.'

It was a deliberately evasive answer. It was no use prying any further. Whatever his secret was, he would either confide in me when he was ready or guard it carefully. I watched his long agile fingers that never ceased their activity. In a corner of the room I noticed a huge pile of music neatly stacked on the floor and, nearly hidden behind it, his violin stand. The violin case itself was nowhere to be seen.

'How is your work coming along?' I inquired. 'Are you still taking lessons?'

He shook his head sadly. 'No, I practice a little but that is about all.'

'You are foolish; you should keep up your work. If not, you will lose everything that you have worked so hard for . . .'

'I know it, but I have no time; no money. Besides, I no longer feel that it is so important . . . not now, at any rate.'

The change in Dziepatowski had been even more complete than I had thought. I could remember when it would have been worth my life to utter a thought such as he had just spoken. In the past he had infected me with his own belief that his talent created an obligation on his part. I was now outraged at his neglect. He prevented my expressing my sentiments, however, by standing suddenly, leaning over me, and placing a hand protectively on my shoulder.

'You must not interpret wrongly what I have been saying. Conditions here in Warsaw are bad, very bad. A man like yourself – young, healthy – is in constant danger. You can be picked up at any moment and sent to a forced-labor camp. You must be very careful. Avoid visiting your family. If the Gestapo learned about your escape it would mean the concentration camp. They may be searching for you already.'

'I can't see how that could happen.'

'They have ways of knowing. You must be careful. Have you any plans?'

'None whatsoever.'

'Do you have any papers? Do you have money?'

I gave him a brief summary of my possessions. He turned away and walked a few steps toward the window, plucking meditatively at his lower lip with a bent index finger. He came to a decision and indicated it by shoving both his hands deep into his pockets.

'What you need are new papers. Would you have the nerve to live under a false name?'

'I could manage it, I suppose. It would not take much nerve. But what makes you think it is so easy to obtain false papers?'

'They can be obtained,' he said, tersely.

'Possibly – but can I obtain them?' I asked, trying to press him, make him reveal himself more fully. 'Shall I have to pay much?'

'You ask too many questions, Jan.' He had perceived my maneuver. 'In times like these it is not healthy to be so inquisitive. You will pay whatever they ask.'

Still obtuse, I inquired who *they* were. He did not even deign to reply. I began to understand what he wanted. A mystery was involved which I had to take on faith. I was to accept what he offered without confirmation – have confidence in him. I decided to follow all his suggestions. There was no alternative. Ever since I had left the peasants' hut I had swung about like an unmoored ship without direction or destination. Since I had been talking with Dziepatowski I felt my will becoming active again, forming inarticulate resolutions. I had the utmost trust in his integrity and courage.

'What do you think I ought to do then?' I made it clear by my tone that I was no longer prying; that I was now merely asking for advice.

'You will need a place to live, first of all.' He strode quickly to the desk in the far corner of the room, snatched paper and pencil from one of the compartments, and scribbled briskly. I watched him, smiling to myself. How efficient he had become. I had always indulgently thought of him as a dreamer.

He handed me the paper and proceeded to instruct me in what apparently was to be my new mode of life.

'Read this paper, memorize it, and destroy it. You are going to have a new name. Call yourself Kucharski. The apartment I am sending you to is owned by the wife of a former bank employee who was in the army and is now a prisoner. She is a reliable woman, but be cautious with her; in fact, be cautious in general. You will have to get used to a new skin – so don't give yourself away. Your safety depends on this . . . and so does mine!'

Both the manner and the content of what he was saying aroused my curiosity till I could hardly contain myself. A thousand questions came to my lips. He cut them off by taking out his watch and glancing at it.

'It is very late and I have a lot of work to do.' I wondered what kind of work he meant. 'You will have to leave. Go to the apartment. Sell a ring and get some supplies – bread, bacon, brandy. Keep a lot of supplies in the apartment and go out as little as possible. I will come to see you in a few days and bring you a complete set of new documents. Goodbye and don't worry. Your landlady will not ask you for your papers, until I have brought them.'

Although I did not know it at the time, this was my initiation into the Polish underground organization. There was nothing extraordinary about it; nothing at all romantic. It required no decision on my part; no spurt of courage or adventure. It came about as the result of a simple visit to a good friend, dictated largely by my despair, gloom, and the feeling of being utterly at loose ends.

When I left I had not the slightest idea of what had occurred. The depression that had taken complete possession of me at my sister's house had not been dismissed, but at least an inkling had been given to me that the future held something. The definiteness in Dziepatowski's manner, the purposeful way in which he expressed himself and moved about the room had given an intimation that, in the immediate future, a similar aim or function might materialize for me.

At the address Dziepatowski had given to me, I found a decent, though by no means luxurious, three-room apartment. It was occupied by a woman of about thirty-five years of age and her twelve-year-old son. They both appeared to be pleasant and kindly. Mrs Nowak had, at one time, obviously been a handsome and probably an elegant woman. Her features were still good but her face was careworn and pinched and her forehead knitted in a perpetual frown of anxiety at the difficulties of her existence. Zygmus, her son, on whom her eyes were constantly fixed with a troubled tenderness that indicated an all-consuming devotion, was a tall, delicate boy with the features of his mother. He was exceptionally mature for his age.

They both welcomed me cordially; but the mother did so with a lack of energy and the boy with a shyness that made it easy for me to avoid becoming entangled in any exchange of confidences. This was wholly desirable, as Dziepatowski had left me in a quandary as to how I should behave. He had neglected to supply me with anything but my alias. I had no idea what profession or character the 'new skin' I was promised would be expected to cover.

My room was a pleasant chamber of decent size but sparsely furnished, bare and colorless except for a cheap, unframed reproduction of a Raphael Madonna and a threadbare piece of red fabric that had been thrown across the back of the single uncomfortable wooden armchair in a pitiful attempt at decoration. After I had made my arrangements and had also given her money to procure me the supplies Dziepatowski had mentioned, I found it easy to withdraw from the lackadaisical conversation we were holding, and pretending to be more fatigued than was actually the case, retired to my room.

Two days later, a bulky letter arrived from Dziepatowski. Toward noon, Mrs Nowak knocked at my door to tell me I had a visitor. He was a very young man, eighteen years old at the very most. 'Are you Mr Kucharski?'

'Yes.'

'This is for you. Goodbye.'

I nervously opened the envelope. Inside were the documents for 'Kucharski.' According to the information, I was born in Luki; had not served in the army because of poor health and was, at present, a teacher in a primary school. This was a fortunate choice as this class was, at this time, treated better than other professionals, as long as they did not prove refractory to German commands.

The letter also contained a message from Dziepatowski. It included an address where I was to go for a specially prepared photograph for my identity card and the information that he would not be able to see me for two or three weeks.

The photographer was installed in the back of an inconspicuous dry-goods store in the poorer neighborhood of Warsaw. He seemed to know all about me. His job was to prepare a picture of me which resembled me sufficiently to be claimed as mine, but in which the features were so vague that I could disown it if the need should arise.

He was a bold, spry little man who hardly replied to my few remarks. His deliberate taciturnity was not lost on me and I remained quiet while he concentrated on the task of turning out what proved to be a miniature masterpiece of photographic ambiguity. When it was finished he handed it to me with a pleased smile. I glanced at it and marveled aloud at his skill.

'It's incredible,' I said. 'It makes me feel as though I had met myself before but can't quite remember where.'

He chuckled, whipped off the eyeshade he wore to examine his production more closely, nodded in an approving, objective fashion, and agreed with me.

'It is good, very good. One of my best, in fact.'

'They are diabolically clever,' I continued, hoping he would relax sufficiently to loosen his tongue. 'Do you make many of them?'

He roared with laughter at this artful remark and slapped his sides.

'You, too, are diabolically clever, young man! That was a good question, ha, ha! You must come back sometime and ask me more questions. I am very busy right now. Good day. Ha, ha!'

His laughter still continued as I departed. It was obvious now that Dziepatowski was involved in some kind of organization or had friends who were in on some secret, but I could not quite fathom its nature. I had read a great deal about Polish underground activities against Tsarist Russia prior to the First World War but it never occurred to me to connect my knowledge with what was happening. Nevertheless, I derived a certain comfort from having a legal front and an interest in the future that I sorely needed.

The next two weeks were still far from pleasant. Time hung heavily on my hands. I read a little of the unprepossessing library of my landlady, smoked, or loafed idly about the apartment. The relations between the three of us became more friendly but she was always too busy or too tired to be sociable. There was no point in my seeking employment since it would have been complicated and, besides, I figured that the rings and the watch would tide me over for a few months.

On the whole, I was still firmly convinced that the war would be over by then and that the victorious Allies would come to free Poland. This was, on the whole, the opinion of most of the populace and even, as I learned later, of the majority of the underground leaders. This optimism did not serve, however, to lighten my gloom. Everywhere about me I saw chaos, ruins, despair, and indescribable poverty. German arrogance and German terror affected everyone with nervousness and depression.

After two weeks of this chafing existence, I was delighted to see Dziepatowski. He was very cheerful – almost gay. After a few questions about my health and behavior in the last two weeks he sat down, stretched out his legs, lit a cigarette, and inquired casually if there was anyone in the next room. When I informed him that the apartment was empty, he smiled at me and said: 'You know, Jan, I have trapped you.'

I smiled back at him a little nervously. 'Really? It is a comfortable little trap.'

'I don't mean the apartment.' He crushed out his cigarette, rose, and, advancing to where I was standing, put his hand on my arm in a friendly, confidential fashion while he delivered a little lecture.

'Jan, I am going to talk to you because I know you to be an honorable, courageous man and a good Pole. You are now a member of the Underground. I brought you in and you have accepted our documents and assistance. The organization tries to play square, however, and you have the option of devoting your services to it or returning to normal life.'

He paused for a moment and ran his fingers through his hair in the familiar gesture, then, gripping my arm more firmly, continued:

'I must also tell you that if you should turn informer or make any attempt to betray us, you will be shot. Have I made myself clear?'

Listening to him, my spirits soared. This was what I had been waiting for – a task, an occupation – something to take me out of the morbid vacuum in which I had been living. I wanted to hug him, but so as not to seem too over-excited, like some romantic boy scout, I replied with a calm that I was far from feeling.

'I thought that there might be an underground organization somewhere. I know we had them before the last war. But I did not expect to run across it so quickly and get into it so easily. You know I escaped from the Russians and Germans with only one thought in mind – to rejoin the army.'

'Well, you are already in the army.'

'Good. You know how I feel. I want to do what I can.'

'In a little while you will get an opportunity to do something.'

We talked about various things for a while and he left shortly after. Two days later he dropped in again but only stayed a minute.

'It will be difficult to find me in my room for the next few days. Come and visit me at my cousin's house. I will be there most of the time. Only make sure you don't become jealous of my beautiful new home.' He spoke gayly and the last remark was obviously a joke. He gave me the address of his 'beautiful new home' and left.

I went to this address the very next day. It was located in the heart of Warsaw, between Moniuszko, Swietokrzyska, and Jasna Streets – not far from the American Consulate. Before the war, this section was the center for department stores, book stores, and exclusive shops of all kinds. Once the building had been a modern, expensive, and well-kept three-story apartment house; now it was a heap of ruins – piles of stone, timber, and splintered furniture all jumbled together. Sections of wall had remained standing with jagged outlines leaning over at odd angles. A fairly large fragment of the back wall and a third of the entrance remained standing as samples of its former magnificence. The house number had been inscribed on a small post that had miraculously survived.

As nearly as I could judge, a bomb had struck squarely on the center of the roof and had bitten down to a considerable depth before it exploded, blasting everything to bits but the cellars and foundations.

In addition, a huge chimney in comparatively good condition leaned against the broken back wall. On it the names of the present subterranean tenants had been listed in chalk. There were fifteen of them.

The writing had been smudged slightly and I had to scan the names carefully to find the one I wanted. Under the list was an arrow pointing to the new entrance. I followed it and came to a blackened door. Opening it, I found myself at the top of a wrecked staircase, down which I groped my way in the darkness. I could not see any door or entrance.

'Is anybody here?' I called loudly, but without confidence.

A door creaked almost under my feet and I saw the hazy yellow gleam of a kerosene lamp.

'Whom do you want to see?' a feminine voice inquired.

I gave her the name. A bare arm protruded from the door and motioned me ahead.

'Two doors down and to your left,' its owner directed me. I went ahead feeling my way along the wall in the darkness. I had to run my hand over the first door to make sure I had passed one. When I finally knocked, the door was opened at once and I was taken by the arm and yanked inside.

'Come in; don't be frightened,' I heard Dziepatowski say amusedly. I entered; he laughed at the look of relief on my face.

'Let's go into the other . . .' he said jovially, ' . . . we call them rooms – Lord knows why . . .'

I followed him meekly, recoiling from the fearful smell of this hole – the stench of rotting potatoes, long-stagnant water, and other unrecognizable ingredients. It had at one time been a storage bin for potatoes, old clothes, and odds and ends. In the 'other room,' there was a small, grated window at street level.

Dziepatowski lit a kerosene lamp. I was surprised at the display of neatness it revealed. The room was furnished with remnants but in perfect order, and the walls had a bright new coat of whitewash. Alongside the wall opposite me was a broken, tilted cot, carefully draped with a blanket. In the corner to my left was an iron stove and on the wall above it were shelves on which were systematically arranged some cheap old pots, glasses, and silverware. To my right was a table covered with a coarse, clean white cloth.

Dziepatowski was quite alone here. He watched me glance at the surroundings, following the impression they were making on me.

'The house was completely ruined in the bombing,' he informed me; 'the chimney and cellars are about all that was left. The chimney is unfortunately useless but the cellars are excellent for my purposes. Apartments in Warsaw are scarce now – more than thirty-five percent of the buildings are unusable. These are my headquarters. Perfect, isn't it?' I murmured a vague disagreement.

'You still have much to learn,' he said. 'This place is ideal for a number of reasons. Just because it is in the heart of Warsaw and looks the way it does, the Gestapo do not find it suspicious or worth investigating. My cousin works in a tobacco factory all day and lets me use her apartment. Here I keep my papers, work, and talk with people. Nobody around here knows me and that, too, is important. You do not understand how vital all these factors are; how necessary it is to be constantly on the alert.'

I remained with Dziepatowski until far into the night. He told me many things about the Underground – a strange world in which I was destined to live during the following years.

I didn't try to get him to say anything else. I had learned that asking questions did not in any way guarantee getting answers.

6

Transformation

Dziepatowski was one person who, indeed, had the right to lecture me as if I were a schoolboy. I was full of admiration for him. He was the first authority figure for me during this time of war. My admiration would take on the status of hero-worship when I found out what he did. His assignment was to carry out the sentences of death on members of the Gestapo who had been condemned by the underground authorities. I learned this only after he was dead.

In June 1940, he received the order to kill Schneider, an agent of the Gestapo. After trailing him for a few days he caught up with him in a public washroom and shot him dead.

Not long after, Dziepatowski was arrested in the street. More than likely, he had been recognized by someone else using the public washroom, which wouldn't have been difficult, given his long artist's hair. He was interrogated by the Gestapo and subjected to appalling tortures, but did not reveal a single secret. Finally he was executed. He was signally honored by the Germans, who went to the length of putting up public posters which informed all of Warsaw that 'a death sentence was carried out on a Polish bandit convicted of having committed an attack for purposes of robbery on a German functionary.'

Everyone knew the truth.

As far as the Germans were concerned, it was merely 'one Polish bandit' less. But many of them were still left and their number was increasing all during 1940.

During the next few months and later, I became aware of the curious, tragic, and paradoxical situation prevailing in Poland. It developed that in many respects it was a good deal better, even in selfish terms, to be a member of the underground organization than to work for the civil authorities, which required one to be totally loyal, or at least 'neutral' toward the authorities of the occupation. An underground man, except for the risk of being caught, with all that capture by the Gestapo entailed, enjoyed considerable advantages over the rest of the population.

He had the protection of the organization and its efficient machinery at his disposal. He could secure good personal documents and obtain certificates of fictitious employment in German enterprises. He usually received a little money, had a number of addresses to retreat to, homes where he could always find a little food, a bed, and a place to hide from Gestapo raids on streets, even whole districts.

Furthermore, he had the peace of mind resulting from the knowledge that he was serving a good cause. He had the dignity of having remained independent and true to his beliefs, while the turncoat was faced with universal contempt from those he attempted to join, from those he betrayed, and even from his own mind.

No one at all stands behind him who knuckles under. He has neither security in his work, his life, or his liberty. He is constantly at the mercy of German terrorism and exposed to the menace of what the Germans call 'collective responsibility' – the most brutal affliction of the occupied countries. By this is meant the theory that an entire community is responsible for the acts of the individuals in it and must suffer redress for their 'crimes' if the perpetrators cannot be caught.

What frequently happened in Poland was that the members of the Underground who derailed trains, blew up storehouses, set fire to railway cars, and committed other acts of sabotage, went scot-free. The local population would then become the victims of German terrorism and revenge. In December 1939, for instance, two Germans were killed in the lobby of the Warsaw Café Club. They had possessed considerable information about the Underground and had various contacts with informers and spies.

The sentence was carried out by order of the underground

authorities. Those assigned to the task escaped. The Germans, however, arrested and subsequently shot two hundred Poles who had no connection with the incident and merely happened to live in the vicinity of the café. Two hundred innocent people were murdered because of this one act.[1] To abandon our activities because of these cruel tactics would have meant, of course, allowing the Germans to attain completely their objectives.

By using such evil tactics, the Germans believed they could force the Underground to give up its armed fight. In spite of so many innocent victims, in spite of the suffering and misery of their families, we did not allow ourselves to be intimidated. There was no question of letting them feel they were safe in Poland.

In June 1940, the Germans staged a man hunt in the streets of Warsaw and seized about twenty thousand people who were taken to three large police stations where they were searched, questioned, and had their documents verified.[2] All males under forty were sent as forced labor to Germany. All girls between seventeen and twenty-five were shipped to East Prussia for farm labor. All those whose documents were not in perfect order, who could not give a satisfactory account of their ancestry, employment, and political sympathies, or could not clear themselves of charges made against them, were sent to concentration camps. More than four thousand men and five hundred women were sent to the concentration camp at Oswiecim where they were beyond all succor.[3]

We later learned that about one hundred members of the Underground were caught in this raid. They were, without a single exception, promptly released. Every one of those had his documents in perfect order, could prove his occupation and supply a satisfactory account of his personal history. Every one had ready answers to every question that was asked of him and impressed the police by his clear, straightforward, and unhesitating manner.

All this is necessary as background to understand the exact situation of the men working in the Underground in Poland. Life as a member of the Underground had many compensations, which more than counterbalanced what certain members had to endure.

For the few miserable collaborators who wanted to enrich themselves on the fall of their country, there was no envy. They, too, lived in constant fear – fear of everything and on all sides. The Germans had only very limited confidence in these new converts: collaboration is always accompanied by reciprocal mistrust and betrayals often occurred. Besides, the collaborator had the hatred of every Pole and the enmity of the Underground to contend with. The collaborators found themselves between the devil and the deep blue sea.[4]

One thing, however, against which I would like to guard is giving the mistaken impression that all those who did not actively resist the Germans are in a class with those who betrayed Poland. Many Polish citizens who were not members of the Underground were, nevertheless, courageous, honest people who were limited by circumstances to the rôle that they played. That rôle often resulted in great suffering and great sacrifice; sufferings akin to the kind I have mentioned and the sacrifice of never hindering and often aiding the work we did.

The woman who was my landlady in Warsaw is typical of this class of people. Strictly speaking, she was not a member of the underground movement. For one thing, it is not so easy to become one as might be imagined. The underground organization demanded that its members fulfill certain physical qualifications and that they be relatively unencumbered and free to perform the tasks assigned to them. For a bachelor, like myself, it is comparatively easy to devote all one's time and energy to the movement; to live at any address and under any conditions. Many who had families could neither participate in this wholly unsettled mode of existence nor endure the prospect of German punishment and reprisals on themselves or on those who were associated with and dependent on them.

Mrs Nowak had, in any case, enough to do merely to keep herself and her son Zygmus alive. She spent whole days in Warsaw hunting for a bargain in bread or a pinch of margarine for the child, and other days taking long, arduous hikes into the country in search of flour, cereal, or a piece of bacon. In the early stages of the war, she had sold nearly every article of value to pay for food for the two of them.

Later she began to buy tobacco from the peasants and, with the help of Zygmus, manufactured cigarettes and sold them to her friends and stores in what were, of course, 'black market' transactions.

In addition to these activities were many toilsome hours of cooking, cleaning, chopping wood, boxes, and her own furniture, when necessary, for fuel – besides looking after the welfare and education of her son – problems which were a constant anxiety and torment to her.

'After a day's work,' she once told me, 'I fall asleep as though I had been drugged. The only things that can disturb me are nightmares, loud voices in the street, a bell ringing, or heavy steps on the stairs. Often one of these wakes me and I jump to my feet – my blood running cold and my heart beating wildly. Then I am frightened. You cannot imagine how frightened I am at times like these. I stand next to my bed, rooted to the spot, listening, waiting for the Gestapo to come and separate me from my boy. No matter what happens I want my husband to find his son if he returns from the camp. He is such a good, smart boy. My husband loved him so . . .'

At first I did not tell her anything of the truth about myself and the work I was doing. I reasoned that it was better for her not to know and not to worry. Often our work required us to expose these poor landladies to dangers of which they were unaware. But, short of stopping our work, there was no way to avoid this and we, too, took our risks.

One evening I came home in a state of utter dejection and weariness. Mrs Nowak had just finished pressing some clothes and had a free moment. She invited me to sit down at the kitchen table near which, in front of the fire, Zygmus sat doing his lessons. She made me a cup of ersatz tea which I began drinking with relish. Then, with a charming smile, a smile of prewar Polish hospitality that seemed absolutely radiant to me at the moment, she spread some marmalade on a piece of bread and offered it to me.

When I was through we began to talk. We talked about Warsaw and the war and the Germans for a while and then, as is only natural when people are under a strain such as hers, she began to unburden herself, telling me about the struggle to keep herself and her son alive, her anxious nights, her fears for her husband, her hope that whatever happened to her he would find Zygmus in sound condition. At length, as often happens, the revelation of so many woes at once brought them all into a single, overmastering emotion. She began to cry. Young Zygmus was startled and frightened. His delicate face became pale and he ran to her and put his arms around her.

They sat clasped in each other's arms crying as though their hearts were breaking, both thin and pale, sad and helpless. I felt very sorry for them and guilty of being an additional threat to them. I decided, although I was aware that it was not prudent, to tell her the truth about myself. I sent the boy to bed, telling him I had to talk to his mother about something private.

'I have not finished my writing lesson,' he said, obediently. 'May I lie in bed and read? Mama will call me back when you are through, won't you, Mama?'

She accompanied the boy to his room. Through the open door I could see her bend over the bed and kiss him before she returned.

'And now,' she asked, with a knowing, conspiratorial smile, 'what do you have to tell me?'

'I know that what I am doing is against the discipline of the organization to which I belong. Nevertheless, I think you ought to know. I want to warn you that my presence in this house is dangerous to you. I am working in the underground movement. This is my official address. Papers, secret press and radio bulletins are brought here for me and I must often keep them for a few days. Naturally, this places you and Zygmus in jeopardy. I did not intend to tell you at all, but a moment ago, looking at you together, I decided that it would be best for me to move out.'

Smiling gently, she got up from her chair, advanced toward me, and extended her hand. Then she said almost gaily:

'Thank you. Thank you very much.'

Then she walked into the room where the boy was and I heard her say:

'Zygmus, come and join us. He is not telling any secrets.'

Zygmus gave a cry of joy and came running back into the kitchen. He sat down quietly at his table and continued his lesson. His mother sat down beside him and told him to stop writing.

'There is something I want you to hear,' she said. 'Mr Kucharski has just informed me that he wants to move out because he hates to expose us to danger. He works in the Underground fighting for our freedom and for your father to come home. He is afraid that if the Germans find him and arrest him they will hurt us, too. Tell me, Zygmus, what shall we tell him?'

There was a moment of embarrassed silence. I was taken aback. I began to feel that I had been foolish to unmask myself so completely before this weak woman and her child. Zygmus seemed to be perplexed, gazing back and forth from my face to his mother's as though attempting to find out what was being demanded of him. On the mother's face was an exultant expression. Her gaze rested on the boy in proud and confident expectation.

'Well, Zygmus, what shall we say?' She smiled at him.

Zygmus got up, came over to me, and placed his small, moist hand in mine.

'Please don't be afraid for us,' he said, his blue eyes wide and candid. 'Don't move. We knew that you were fighting the Germans. Mother tells me everything. She knows that I can keep a secret.'

His eyes shone and his hand trembled in mine when he added:

'Even if they beat me, I will not say a word. Stay with us, please, Mr Kucharski.'

I must have looked puzzled or undecided, for the boy with a sudden, odd gesture withdrew his hand and began stroking my hair with it to soothe me and make me frown less. The mother smiled.

'You should have no misgivings now. Do not worry about Zygmus. He will never talk. He spends nearly all his time with me and, in any case, he would never endanger us by silly talking. Children grow up fast in wartime.'

I said nothing.

'You must stay here,' she added. 'It soothes my conscience. By letting you live here, I feel as if I, too, am doing what I can for Poland . . . It is not much, but it is all that I can do, and I am grateful to you for giving me the opportunity.'

I got up.

'Thank you both for your kindness and your good hearts,' I said. 'You and your son. I want you to know that I really feel at home here, as if I were with my own family.'

7

Initiation

After I had familiarized myself with underground methods, routine, and discipline, I received the order for my first mission. I was to go to Poznan on an errand, the full details of which I was never able to disclose. In general terms, I was to meet a certain member of the Underground who held an important civil service position before the war and to consult with him on the availability of many of the men under him for underground work. Due to the nature of his work, this official had very extensive contacts among the Germans, as did his former employees. What he knew together with his potential contacts were of vital importance to the Underground.

A perfect pretext was arranged for my trip. The daughter of the man I was to see pretended to be my fiancée. Poznan was in that section of Poland which had been incorporated into the Reich. The inhabitants of this district had the opportunity of becoming full-fledged German citizens.[1] My 'fiancée' was one of these and had, in addition, the advantage of a German name. I used a German alias, too, for the occasion. She had applied to the Gestapo for permission to let me visit her. She assumed responsibility for me and informed them that she was anxious to make me conscious of my German origin and blood. Consent was promptly given and my mission was executed easily, under German auspices.

I reached Poznan without any difficulties. It was a city I had known rather well in prewar days. Poznan is about two hundred miles west of Warsaw. It is one of the oldest cities in Poland and regarded by many as the cradle of the Polish nation, especially when, many centuries ago, Poland was emerging as one of the most powerful monarchies in Europe. The population of the entire province is as purely Polish as in any other district in Poland. For more than one hundred and fifty years, the city and surrounding country had successfully resisted a series of forceful attempts at Germanization.

Frederick the Great had instituted one such campaign. Polish boys were carried off to Germany and were forced to become Prussian dragoons. He did everything possible to spread German influence and culture throughout the province, but to no avail. Later, Bismarck established a policy, the purpose of which was to take away the property of the Polish farmers and to make German serfs of them. After the death of Bismarck, intermittent efforts were made to Prussianize Poznan. They all failed. In 1918, when Poland regained its independence, every vestige of German influence disappeared completely and the true Polish character of the inhabitants emerged, almost without a blemish.

I thought about these things as I walked through the streets of Poznan. The city with the finest historical tradition in all Poland was now, to all appearances, a typical German community. Every sign on stores and banks and institutions was in German. The street names were in German. German newspapers were being hawked on the corners. All I could hear spoken was German, often, true enough, German with an accent, or German spoken grudgingly and sometimes with a deliberate twist and inflection through which the Polish character of the speaker could be discerned, but I do not remember hearing a single word spoken publicly in any other language.

I learned later that Poles who had refused to become Germanized had been expelled from many sections of the city. There were many districts, especially in the center of the city, from which every single Pole had been driven. They were not permitted even to pass through many of the streets. They could live and move around freely only in the suburbs. German merchants and colonists in tens of thousands had been imported to populate 'this essentially German city.' Hitler banners were to be seen everywhere and the stores all displayed large portraits of the Führer and his satellites.

As I took all this in and watched innumerable German soldiers goose-stepping stiffly and, it seemed to me, contemptuously along the pavements, I felt a spasm of anger and frustration. It occurred to me that even impartial people might believe, from seeing what I saw, if they were not told the truth, that Poznan really was an 'essentially German city.' Even I could hardly believe that it was the same city I had known before the war, so thoroughly had its face been remodeled in a few short months.

In order better to disguise myself, for the duration of the mission I was given papers in the name of a genuine Pole of German origin who was living in Warsaw; a month earlier, he had managed to get to France while his family had slipped out of the capital. I memorized all the information pertinent to my 'family.' And so I became – let's call me Andrzej Vogst. I went to Helena's house – let's call her Siebert – who was responsible for my mission to Poznan and, generally, to Germany.

If the Gestapo had attempted to check up on this Vogst, they would have had a great deal of difficulty in discovering the hoax. Naturally, Vogst appeared on the local parish registers and was consistently listed. His apartment was being used by some distant relatives who knew him very well and who knew how to react in case they were interrogated. It was to this same address that his 'fiancée' wrote to him from Poznan. Vogst worked for a company that supplied equipment to hairdressers' salons . . . in turn he would buy hair from them, a valuable commodity in wartime. He possessed all the necessary documents authorizing him to travel throughout the entire General Government area.[2]

All this Vosgt needed to complete his happiness was to get to Poznan and the affectionate insistence of his 'fiancée' that he was German. This also was perfectly believable since his grandfather actually was a German; he had married into a middle-class family in Warsaw who had completely transformed him into a Pole. Clearly, my mission had been meticulously prepared in order to reduce the risks to . . . zero. This was not the work of amateurs.

I arrived at my destination and met my 'fiancée.' She was a dark, pretty girl, so gentle and soft-voiced that I could hardly believe that she was, as I had been told, one of the most courageous and able workers in the Underground. As I had some time to wait before the arrival of the individual whom I had to see in order to execute my mission, we sat down in a large room rather comfortably furnished in an old-fashioned style. At first we discussed my trip and then I told her all I could about the latest events in Warsaw. She then proceeded to enlighten me on the situation in Poznan.

All the intelligentsia and every Pole who owned property had been expelled from the city. The same operation had taken place in every part of the district that the Germans had incorporated into the Reich. The only Poles who had been allowed to remain were those who had registered as Germans or those whom the Germans allowed to survive as outcasts. The humiliation of this latter group exceeded all limits. A Pole who had refused to register as a German had to doff his hat before anyone whose uniform or insignia indicated that he was a German. If a German passed by, a Pole had to step off the sidewalk. A Pole could not travel by automobile or trolley and was even forbidden to own a bicycle. He had been placed completely outside the protection of the law and all his property, movable or immovable, was at the disposal of the German authorities.

She told me all these facts in a controlled voice as though she were reciting a historical incident from which she, personally, remained apart. Many members of the Underground had learned this detached, impersonal way of considering problems very close to them. They had found that the best approach to a problem was to attack it impersonally, no matter how deep or bitter their feelings, to carry out plans as coolly as a surgeon at an operating table. I tried to take the same tone, although I was still a novice, and what I had already seen in Poznan produced a state of mind that was far from either cool or scientific.

When she had completed this detailed description of local conditions I asked her how, in her opinion, we would ever be able to change all that.

'There is only one way,' she replied, and went on to outline a solution which was not so much her personal response as the objective approach to the problem.

'The moment the Germans are defeated, a ruthless mass terror must be organized against the people who invaded our land and made us suffer. The "imported" Germans must be expelled from the vicinity by the same methods by which they were settled here – by force and ruthless extermination. The problem of de-Germanizing Poznan and other parts of Poland will become insoluble if we agree to any compromise, to plebiscites, repayment of damages, exchanges of property. The factual conditions which the Germans have succeeded in creating and which they will undoubtedly amplify in the near future, can be destroyed only by means of a ruthless mass terror.'

Calculated and controlled as her words were, I could detect a genuine passion for her country and an implacable hatred for the Germans. She remained quite calm and only her quivering lips betrayed what she was thinking and feeling . . . It occurred to me that it was remarkable that so independent a spirit had ever been able to bring itself to undergo, even nominally and for the purposes to which she was putting it, the stigma and humiliation of having accepted German citizenship.

'May I ask you,' I inquired cautiously, 'what is the reason you registered to become Germanized, even if the registration was only a formality? Couldn't you have refrained from doing so and still have continued working for the cause?'

'It would have been absolutely impossible,' she said, indicating that if there had been any other solution she would have chosen it. 'You see, you are under the General Government and your methods are, therefore, entirely different from ours. You can escape the Gestapo by other methods. We cannot. Here in our province, Poles in general and the educated people in particular do not "legally exist." That was the only way in which we could remain and work where we are.'

'Did many Polish patriots register as Germans?'

'I want to be frank with you. The answer is no, unfortunately. Even my father is hiding in the country, because he does not want to register as "*Volksdeutsch.*" It would lead him to political collaboration with the Germans which he wants to avoid at all costs. By being so patriotic and independent, many of those who refused to register are doing our cause a disservice. Any sense of loyalty and honor should be suppressed when it is a case of fighting against Nazi methods. Polish citizens of German descent betrayed Poland in a body. That is why, whatever the future of Poland may be, we cannot allow any Germans to live here. They are loyal only to Germany. We have seen that. One or two miserable Polish traitors joined them. The mass of patriotic Poles, almost without exception, stubbornly refused to register. Because of this, we shall soon see a total purge of the Polish population in this province. At all costs we must not allow ourselves to be deported, even if we have to become *Volksdeutsche* or *Reichsdeutsche* in order to remain.'

I could see the truth in her remarks and began to concede in my own mind to her opinions. Though I noticed she had a grudging admiration for the independent spirits who had, at a great cost, stubbornly refused to become Germans, nevertheless, she made me realize that it would have been wiser if those, in particular, who were equipped to do our work, had yielded. She noticed the change in my opinion.

'Do you understand, now, what it means? In two months of occupation, the Germans have already transferred more than four hundred thousand Poles from the incorporated province to the General Government.'

'How do they do it? What is the deportation procedure?'

'Nothing very complicated. Middle-class people who have not registered are imprisoned without warning. Peasants, workers, and artisans receive a sudden notice to be ready to evacuate their homes within two hours. They are permitted to take ten pounds of food and linen. Their homes must be cleaned, and put in good order for their German successors and all their possessions must be abandoned to the new tenants. Police have often ordered children of peasants to make bouquets of flowers and place them on tables and thresholds. These are to serve as symbols of their welcome to the arriving German colonists.'

Our conversation ended then, for her father, whom I had come to see, arrived. He confirmed the general picture and analysis she had given of the situation. We withdrew and discussed alone the questions I had been instructed by my superiors to ask him. Roughly, what I learned from him and what I conveyed back to my superiors in Warsaw was that the men we inquired about would be available for underground work only if they were transferred out of the provinces incorporated into the Reich to the central district controlled by the General Government.

When I reached Warsaw I conveyed this information to the organization and returned to my former dwelling.

Mrs Nowak was pleased to see me, and both she and Zygmus gazed at me with admiration as though I had just come from the battle lines. There had really been very little danger, but nevertheless, I felt that I was now really in the organization, and no longer merely an apprentice.

8

Borecki

It was only after my return from Poznan that I really began to know and understand the underground movement at all well. Dziepatowski had introduced me to a few other members whom I got to know. I continued to drift about. My efforts to find the work most suited to me bore little fruit and induced only haphazard and desultory assignments. The partial cause of this was the general condition of the underground movement at this period, the end of 1939. It had not as yet become at all like the complex, highly organized body into which it finally evolved. At this adolescent stage of its existence, there was no dominant single power, but there were, instead, a number of groups, organizations, and centers of resistance. They were either isolated from each other or connected only loosely, in the hit-or-miss fashion of people who have interests in common but have not found an effective means of expressing their common desires or making them pull together.

As a matter of fact, anybody who had some imagination, a little ambition and initiative, and a great deal of courage could, and often did, start an outfit of his own. The names as well as the aims of some of these heterogeneous and short-lived undertakings were often utterly fantastic. There were 'The Avengers,' 'The Gory Hand,' 'God's Judgment.' Their programs ranged from a kind of black-hand terrorism through political programs to a revival of all-embracing religion. Poles are particularly susceptible to this kind of secret atmosphere and there were excellent opportunities for it to grow. Many of the men who founded these inspired cliques hoped that the war would end soon and that their group would play an important rôle in the reconstruction of the Polish state.

In this chaotic welter, however, there were more stable elements present and principles of unification were beginning to operate. The more stable elements in the picture were the political parties which the German occupation had by no means disintegrated. The principles of unification were both external and internal, a strengthening of the relations between the underground movement in Poland and the government which had been functioning in France under the leadership of General Sikorski[1] and an increasing rapprochement between the political parties themselves in the face of the common threat. The second organization which emerged was military. Its first purpose was to unite all the scattered remnants of the army into a single, strong body.

It was through one of the political parties, the National Party, that I received my second mission. It was arranged for me to go to Lwow, perform a number of functions there, and afterwards make an attempt to reach France and contact the Polish Government in Paris and Angers. Orders had come from General Sikorski and the Polish Government for all young Poles to try to escape to France. These orders applied particularly to pilots, mechanics, sailors, and artillery men, the last category being the one to which I belonged. If I reached France, I would be performing a double task: obeying this order and carrying out an underground assignment.

At this period, the parties in Poland and the government in France were seeking to strengthen their connections. The government needed the support of the people in occupied Poland. The people's only representatives, which were those parties that were the main factors in underground resistance, needed the support of the government and wished to have their opinions expressed in the inter-Allied councils. The only organ which could express them was the government-in-exile.

Thanks to the emissaries traveling between occupied Poland and France, rules of co-operation were established. Each one of the principal political parties had to appoint its representatives to the government-in-exile in Angers. They could be existing members of the Sikorski cabinet, or party leaders or activists who had already managed to get to France. It was in this way that the main political movements – the National Party, the Peasant Party, the Socialist Party, and the Christian Labor Party – were able to have the possibility of influencing the government. In occupied Poland, these same parties formed a coalition. By means of this coalition, the government-in-exile could see that, in turn, its influence would be assured on internal matters, which strengthened its position in the eyes of the Allies: the government-in-exile was not a mere façade but an organization that could control, from a distance, events happening in occupied Poland.

In Warsaw, a partial understanding between the political parties had been in existence since the memorable days of the defense of the capital in September 1939. Despite their diverging views, the political organizations had distinguished themselves notably by the great discipline, devotion, and indefatigability they had shown in assisting the defenders of the capital.

The objective of my Lwow mission included the furthering of an analogous understanding between the parties in Lwow and the establishment of the closest possible union between the organizations in the two cities. Besides, I was to inform the leaders in Lwow of the conditions prevailing under German occupation and, after having thoroughly familiarized myself with the conditions in the Lwow area under the Soviets, I was to proceed to France and report to the Polish Government.

I received my instructions from Mr Borecki, one of the most eminent organizers of the Underground. In the first years of Poland's independence he had occupied a high position in the Ministry of the Interior. He was removed by the regime which came to power after the Pilsudski coup d'état in May 1926. From then on he had belonged to the opposition. He carried on an extensive law practice with remarkable versatility and was known to expend considerable energy in scientific research.

I had had no acquaintance with him before the war. I was surprised to learn that he was still living in his own apartment house and using his own name. He was a tall, thin man of about sixty. He must have received a flattering account of me, for he greeted me with hearty cordiality. As a precaution, a piece of newspaper was used to establish my identity. I carried a torn fragment of this piece in a sealed envelope. He had the other fragment. The two fragments were supposed to fit together. When I handed him my envelope, he took it without a word and disappeared into the next room to perform the matching operation. He returned after a short while, smiled, and said:

'I am glad to welcome you. Everything is in perfect order and I know the purpose of your mission. You are going to Lwow and then to France.'

I nodded my assent. He asked me to be seated with a geniality that seemed to imply that it would be well for us to behave like two normal human beings for a moment or two before launching into our tangled business. His wife and children, he told me, had been sent to the country. He lived alone and displayed considerable delight in his ability to look after himself. He made some tea, poured out two cups, and served me some crackers. I bit into one and noticed that it was far from fresh.

'I have started housekeeping at a rather advanced age,' he informed me, partially by way of amused apology. 'Of course, the training my mother gave me has made it easier. When I was a boy I had to do everything for myself. I learned how to shine my own shoes, press my pants, and sew on buttons at an early age. I also had the good luck to be a Boy Scout.'

He stopped for a moment as if recalling the activities of an earlier day.

'Forty-five years ago, that was,' he added. 'That was when I learned my cooking. Thanks to my mother and the Boy Scouts, I can take care of myself while my family is away. And I am glad they are away. At least if I get caught, I will be the only victim.'

Borecki was one of those men who gives a casual visitor the sense of being completely at ease and on terms of great familiarity with his host.

'May I remark,' I ventured, 'that you neglected to learn how to make a fire in the stove?'

'It is not nice of you to say that,' he replied in mild reproach, 'and you are quite wrong. You feel cold here and it is good for you to feel cold. You will have to get used to it. The occupation may last several winters. The war will be a long one and coal will be scarce.'

It was indeed very cold in his apartment. I noticed for the first time that he was wearing his overcoat and that it had not occurred to me to take off my own. I knew a great deal more about Borecki than he knew about me. I had heard much about his zealous underground activity, his attempts to get in touch with the government and his indefatigable efforts to organize Polish resistance.

'Don't you think,' I asked him, 'that it is rash for you to live under your own name?'

He shrugged.

'Nowadays it is difficult to define what is and what is not rash. In my circumstances, living under an alias in Warsaw, where, after all, I am known by a great many people, would be rather dangerous. I have had to adapt myself to methods different from those used by my colleagues. I rarely stay at the place which is my registered address. I live and work in houses where I am not recognized.'

'How much good does that do?' I asked. 'If the Gestapo should even suspect that you are connected with the Underground, they will have you trailed.'

'Yes, you are quite right. But I have taken counter-measures. I am regularly shadowed by my own men. If they should find out that I am being trailed, then I shall have to adopt an alias.'

'It will be too late if you are arrested then and there in the street.'

'True. But then, at least, I can hope for enough time to eat my candy.'

He extended a long, bony, white hand. On the middle finger gleamed a signet ring of unusual design. He touched a spring on it with a finger of his left hand. The ruby lid snapped back revealing a tiny compartment filled with white powder.

'I've read about devices like that in books about the Medicis and the Borgias, but I never expected to see one in Warsaw except in the movies.'

'There is nothing at all surprising about it,' he replied calmly. 'It simply proves that man remains unchanged. Similar needs dictate similar measures. There are always the hunted and the hunters – the ones that hate humanity and aim to rule the world. I can see that you have not been in underground work long.'

'You are right. I got in only recently – I am proud of being in it but, I must confess, this kind of work does not exactly suit me.'

'And what exactly does suit you?' he inquired with benign irony. 'What did you want to do before the war? What was your occupation?'

'I wanted to do scientific work. Demography and the history of diplomacy attracted me most. Although I did not succeed in completing my doctorate thesis, I still would prefer to devote my time to tranquil, scientific studies.'

'That's fine,' he snapped. 'Just wait till they invent a rocket that will carry you to the moon. That's the place for tranquil, scientific studies. God has not ordained that Poles should have tranquillity. We have to stay at home in Europe, endure these vicissitudes, and fight for a peaceful and studious life in the future. God has placed us in a fearful spot. We are on the most troubled of continents between powerful and rapacious neighbors. We have been forced to fight for our very existence through the centuries. No sooner do we come into our own than we are attacked and despoiled. A curse seems to hover over Poland's destiny. But what can we do? We must fight if we want to exist. It is as if the Creator had purposely added to our woes by filling us with an ineradicable love of our country, our people, our soil, and our freedom.'

He seemed to be gazing at me with dislike and suspicion as though I were for the moment the representative of Poland's enemies. He turned away from me abruptly and paced up and down the room, his hands clasping and unclasping nervously behind his back. When he stopped and sat down again, he was composed and businesslike. His air became brisk and efficient and he proceeded to issue instructions on my forthcoming trip.

He spoke with meticulous exactitude and his manner was stern, with the distant detachment of an official speaking to a minor subordinate.

Yet at the same time, there was paternal good will in the way he looked at me and frowned now and then – something of the feigned severity of a father lecturing to a son. From time to time he stopped, and we sipped the tea which had become quite cold.

'To begin with,' he said forcefully, 'remember that a great deal depends on you. You must report as much of this conversation as possible to the people you will see in Lwow, then to the government in France, and then to any others whom it becomes necessary to inform. The main thing to be made clear is that our cause is not lost so long as we maintain our national continuity, the legal and moral aspects of a state, and a will to fight. That is our purpose – to maintain the continuity of the Polish state which, merely by accident, had to descend into the Underground. Since we are in it, we must reproduce all the offices and institutions of a state. It must have authority over our people and make it impossible for a traitor to arise in Poland. We will not permit any competition on Polish territory. The Sikorski government in Angers must defend us and our rights during this war and be responsible to us. These are the basic conditions, our only hope for an efficacious struggle against the enemy.'

He paused meditatively, then resumed his outline with added emphasis:

'Let me summarize the main points. First, we do not admit and refuse to recognize the existence of any legal or political occupation. The presence of a German regime in Poland is artificial and fortuitous. Second, the Polish state continues its existence unchanged, except in form. Its location in the Underground is wholly accidental and without legal significance. Third, we cannot tolerate the existence of any Polish Government co-operating with the occupants. If any traitors appear, we will kill them.'

A faint smile played about the corners of his lips. With a trace of cynicism, he added,

'It is harder to kill a German on Polish territory than it is to kill a Pole.'

It was not so much cynicism as the result of long years of experience and a realistic knowledge of circumstances. Borecki combined an intense devotion to his beliefs with a shrewd appraisal of the hazards that lay in his way. At every new stage in the conversation, he would visibly pause to measure the effect his words had on me, weighing me constantly in the scales of his ripened judgment.

'The government is abroad, safe and free,' he resumed. 'They must use that safety and freedom to defend our rights and interests. Not only against our enemies but in our relations with our friends. Remember, the main job of fighting the Germans is being done here, by us. It will be done to the limit, to the last drop of our blood, if I may quote our national anthem. In return, we guarantee our loyalty and total support.'

Borecki stood up and walked about, chafing his hands. I noticed that they were blue from the cold. I had been cold myself till Borecki's fervid analysis of the situation had made me forget it. I gazed at him, a thin, stooping old man, pale, sickly and with little physical endurance. The power of conviction, the indomitable will and belief contained in that frail, moribund body were something at which to marvel.

I asked him if it were feasible to organize so enormous and complicated an apparatus while the German terror raged. My question provoked a shrug:

'How can anybody know if it is feasible?' he answered. 'We simply must make the attempt. The Underground must be more than a mere reaction to the oppression of the occupants. It must be the official continuation of the Polish state. Political life must function and in an atmosphere of absolute freedom.

'Yes,' he repeated, noticing my amazement, 'an atmosphere of absolute freedom.'

'But how can you speak of freedom? The Germans do not tolerate the existence of a single political party.'

'Naturally. The Germans don't tolerate anything and we don't intend to ask them. We ignore them. Their presence cannot be allowed to change or restrain us one iota. We will have to act secretly. What I mean is freedom within the framework of the underground movement. Every political party must enjoy civic freedom in the underground state. On conditions, that is. The party must be pledged to fight the occupants and to work for a democratic Poland. It must also recognize the legality of the Polish Government and the authority of the incipient underground state.'

'But,' I objected, 'the net result is likely to be that each group will fight the Germans individually. Our forces will be disrupted and weakened.'

'Not quite. The activities of the Underground will be co-ordinated and divided into three basic sections. There will be an underground administration to protect the population against the Germans, record German crimes against the day of reckoning, and prepare the framework of an administration for the first period of independ-ence. Then there will be untrammeled freedom in political life, and every political group will be free to wage the struggle against the occupation. And now here is what is really the main point—'

He spoke more slowly now and emphasized his words by tapping the table with a bent index finger.

'The Underground must have an army. All military action against the enemy must be subordinated to a supreme military command. The army must be representative, based on a realistic estimate of social and political factors. Every group that belongs to it will have its right to stay in touch with its party. But to the military command must be given supreme control over all centers of the organization.'

My face must have revealed some doubt as to the success of this audacious and elaborate plan, for Borecki hastened to reassure me.

'Don't worry, young man, we all know that this is a complicated and far-reaching plan, but we all know how necessary its execution is, too. This war may take strange turns yet. Our work may set a precedent for underground organizations elsewhere, just as we have set a precedent for armed resistance against the violence of German occupation. In any case, the Polish political parties in the German-occupied areas have already agreed to this plan. The same must be done under the Russian occupation. The Polish Government in Angers must also submit to it. This is, of course, only the broad outline of the plan. Its technique and details will not be told to you. Someone else will carry them to Paris and Angers. We trust, too, that you will not become excessively interested in the solution of the problem.'

He was standing near me when he made this last remark. He bent over, patted my shoulder, and smiled, leaning his face so close to me that I could feel his breath upon me:

'This does not mean a lack of confidence in you. In our circumstances, knowing too much constitutes the gravest of dangers. Many of us, and I among them, are bowed under the burden of knowing too much. But that is inevitable.'

He straightened up as though to disprove his own contention and stood gazing at me, idly fingering his ring. At length, he sat down, turned up the collar of his overcoat, crossed his legs, and said:

'Let us discuss the concrete details of your trip.'

We proceeded to do so for some time, Borecki showing himself as apt a master of underground wiles as he was of the twists and turns of high politics and organizational tactics. The basic plan of my trip was quite simple. I would have in my possession a statement from a Warsaw factory that I was going to work in one of its branches in a town near the Russo–German border. The document was authentic, precluded all danger, and was absolutely indispensable because the Germans frequently searched and investigated train passengers. To travel further than a hundred miles one also had to have permission from the Germans.

Near the border I was to contact a man who would smuggle me across the line. He was part of a cell of the Jewish Underground which was collaborating with us. The main task of this cell was to bring Jews from Germany into Russian-occupied territory where they were safer. I would probably proceed with a group of these fugitives across the line and be guided to the nearest railroad station where I would take a train for Lwow. The Russians, we had been informed, did not stage mass investigations of train passengers. In Lwow I would report to a given address and make myself known by a password.

After we had thoroughly discussed these details, Borecki cast a shrewd, penetrating glance at me.

'I have told you what we expect from you and you must know what you can expect from us. If you should be arrested by the Germans before you meet the guide, do not expect anything from us. We will be unable to help you and you will have to rely on your own wits. If you should be apprehended after you have contacted the guide, you will be more fortunate. We will probably be informed of the time and place of your arrest and will do what we can. But even then you will have to be very patient. If you are arrested by Soviet police it should be simple for you to extricate yourself. Tell them you are fleeing from German-occupied territory and prefer to live under Soviet rule. This explanation has been working very well.'

'I don't think anyone could ask for more careful planning,' I remarked; 'every possibility seems to have been foreseen.'

'In times like these it is impossible to foresee everything,' he answered shaking his head. 'We do what we can. We all have to trust to luck to a certain extent.'

Our leavetaking was cordial and hearty. He escorted me to the door and as I was walking to the stairs, an impulse made me turn around and gaze back. He was still standing in the doorway, stoop-shouldered and tired, watching me impassively and toying with the gleaming ring. We waved to each other and I descended the stairway.

Borecki's foresight had been well-nigh perfect. My trip to Lwow went off without incident. Before six months had elapsed the Underground was organized exactly to the specifications of this capable and experienced executive. The only thing he had not foreseen was his own fate. Neither his methods of personal safety, his bodyguard or his potassium cyanide 'candy' proved of any avail.

Toward the end of February 1940, Borecki was caught by the Gestapo. He was unable to swallow his poison. He was dragged off to jail and submitted to the most atrocious Nazi tortures. He was beaten for days on end. Nearly every bone in his body was systematically and scientifically broken. His back was a mass of bloody tatters from an endless succession of blows administered with iron rods. The gaunt, ailing old man never lost control of himself, never divulged a single secret. In the end, he was shot.

The Nazi newspapers later announced that a Polish adventurer and bandit had been sentenced to death by a court-martial because of his disloyalty toward the German Reich!

9

Contact Between Cells

For the first time since I had escaped from Radom, I now felt that I was performing a worthwhile task. I carefully memorized the statement from the factory and held myself in readiness to be able to respond to questioning.

The train arrived at my destination without even one of the routine inspections taking place. Both the documents and my psychological preparation were wasted. At the station I hired a little peasant cart to take me the eight miles or so to the little village, almost on the Russo-German border. On the outskirts of the village I spotted the whitewashed cottage, with its barn topped with a stork's nest, where I was meant to meet the guide who was to take the group of Jews across the border. I had found the house easily. Its location had been minutely described to me and I had memorized it with great care. I knocked on the door.

At first there was no answer and I felt a twinge of uneasiness. I walked around to the side and listened at the window. There was silence. The window was too misty for me to see through. By dint of much straining, I was able to raise it about an inch. I heard the quiet snore of someone sleeping soundly. Returning to the door, reassured, I knocked loudly. A tall, ruddy-faced young man appeared, his clothes in disarray, rubbing his eyes.

'I must have been asleep,' he apologized. 'Who are you?'

I explained. He had been notified of my impending arrival and accepted me readily. I was to be included in a party of Jews which he would guide across the border within three days. He had completed dozens of such expeditions without a mishap and was very cool and unruffled for a young man engaged in so hazardous an enterprise.

While I talked he slipped into a short heavy coat and, taking me by the arm, piloted me out-of-doors.

'Come,' he said, 'we have no time to lose. You will have to find a place to stay in the village. I must show you the spot where we are to meet.'

He shambled along, still sleepy, pausing occasionally to stretch and yawn. It was about two and a half miles to the rendezvous for the border crossings. He took little notice of me. To make conversation I asked him why he was so sleepy. He answered good-naturedly enough, telling me that he had been up all night conducting a party through, and had already had his sleep interrupted several times during the day to show members of the next group the appointed spot. I intimated that there ought to be a better system than for him to march back and forth all day. He grunted in agreement, but added that nobody had thought of any other.

At length we passed a stream and came to a clearing near a mill.

'This is it,' he said wearily, as though he had made the exact remark on an endless number of occasions. 'You are to be here three days from now at six o'clock punctually. We don't wait for anybody.'

'I'll be on time,' I answered. 'Where do you suggest I stay in the meanwhile?'

'There is a quiet little inn at the far end of the village. You can't miss it. It is the only one. Take a good look around before you go, there won't be anyone to guide you back here.'

Obediently I glanced at the trees, the road, the mill, and the little stream. He waited for my eyes to complete a full circle, and then we set off, walking with long, heavy strides toward his hut. At one time, he seemed to be lurching about and I noticed that his eyes were almost shut. I nudged him. He responded with surprising alacrity.

'Is anything wrong?' he asked.

'No, but you were asleep and staggering. I thought you might stumble and hurt yourself.'

'Hurt myself? Here?' he glanced contemptuously at the inoffensive dirt road. 'Not if I were drunk and blindfolded.'

When we came to the path that led to his hut, he simply marched off without saying a word. I waved to him and he brought up his arm in answer, rounding off the gesture by stifling a yawn with his hand.

The inn was easy to find and the lodging surprisingly comfortable. The innkeeper, a little, wrinkled old peasant, asked no questions and quietly raised his charges in proportion to his suspicions. I passed the three days doing my best to appear inconspicuous, feigning illness and staying in my room. I arrived at the appointed clearing slightly ahead of schedule but many of the others were already there.

It was almost dark. The moon was luminous and full, exposing everyone in the clearing to my view. I could see that there were many of all ages, old men and women, two women with babies in their arms, and a few young men and girls. They were all escaping Jews. It seemed as if they sensed what the future held in store for them, that soon the pitiless extermination of the Jews would start.

They carried a variety of bundles, bags, and suitcases, and some even held pillows and blankets in their arms. They were divided into groups and some formed family units. One old couple had come with four daughters, two of whom had brought their husbands with them, and these eight individuals seemed to form a little detachment of their own. Since it would be necessary to walk about thirteen miles through forest and field, the guide, although it was not really an arduous journey, was supposed to refuse to include babies and any debilitated people.

Apparently this rule was not stringently observed, for when the guide arrived, he contented himself with delivering a formal reprimand to the mothers and demanding that they quiet their offspring immediately since the children both had begun to cry loudly enough to be heard for miles. The two mothers were standing close together, and a number of the older women approached them to offer advice. The two mothers held the babies in their arms and rocked them to and fro, whispering gently to them. At last the babies fell asleep and we set out.

The guide walked on ahead with large, rapid strides, glancing neither to right nor left and occasionally whirling around to hush the party when the conversation became loud. It was, however, hard to imagine the presence of any eavesdroppers. It was cold and the dark silhouettes of the leafless trees made the whole scene lonely and desolate.

Our path wound through forests, fields, paths, patches of mud, and little streams in rapid succession. Often it seemed as though the guide must surely have lost his way, but his steady, unhesitating tread deterred all questioning. When a cloud passed across the moon, it plunged us into pitch darkness and we stumbled forward, clinging to each other desperately, holding onto coattails, falling, bruising hands and knees, scratching our faces, and getting well splattered with mud.

When the moon came out again I saw the two mothers clearly. Emaciated, their hair disheveled by the wind and the low branches, their faces bruised by the sharp twigs, they were holding on with one hand to the coattails of two men who preceded them while they hugged the babies tightly to their breasts with their free hands. We had one hand free to part branches and keep our balance by clutching for support. They had no protection against the large rocks with which the path was strewn, the thorns, the tree roots on which they frequently stumbled.

We always knew when they stumbled. Alarmed, we would hear the babies begin to whimper, and everyone would become tense with fear and anticipation. Each time the mothers would find some new resource of tenderness by which to still them. The guide would stop frequently and make us wait while he reconnoitered the path ahead. He would return gesturing for us to hurry and follow him. The path he followed was tortuous and inaccessible to Soviet and German guards who were unfamiliar with the terrain.

In any case, his prudence was beneficial and the precautions did no harm. We emerged from the forest and found ourselves in the middle of the road. The guide called back to us softly, in a voice that expressed great relief and joy:

'People, we are on the other side of the border. You can rest easy, now.'

We wearily flung ourselves down on the wet ground under the trees by the side of the road. Our guide divided us into three groups and took each group separately into the village.

While he was away with the first two groups which comprised mostly women and the older men, the rest of us waited, huddled together and shivering at the edge of the forest. We spoke little and tried to arrange our disordered attire. Our guard breathed a deep sigh of relief as he returned and piloted us toward the village.

'Well, that's one more bunch safely done with,' he announced, walking on ahead.

'How long have you been acting as a guide?' I asked him, partly to dispel the bleak silence that hung over us like a pall.

'Since about a week after Warsaw fell.'

'Do you expect to continue for long?'

'Until Warsaw is taken back again.'

In the village we separated. I was left at a Jewish hostel with four other men and a woman from our group. The host, a nimble, 'all-knowing' old man, welcomed us with a running fire of sprightly remarks, designed, no doubt, to take the edge off our gloom. He immediately informed us of the latest world news. Hitler's end was undoubtedly close at hand. All of Holland had been flooded and a whole German army had been drowned. A coup was being engineered inside Germany and Hitler would be assassinated in short order. Russia and Germany, he told us, were mortal enemies and would soon come to blows. After we had been heartened by this charming picture of the present and the future, he treated us to glasses of hot tea at his expense and then offered us some vodka at 'prewar prices.'

We spent half a day in this hostel, mostly listening to our loquacious host. In the afternoon we left, walking one by one to the railroad station to which the innkeeper's daughter directed us. It was a distance of about three miles and on the way we frequently passed Soviet patrols. We passed them in silence and hailed the militia by stretching out our arms and clenching our fists in the Communist salute in order to avoid suspicion.

The station was besieged by hundreds of anxious, noisy, and gesticulating people. No more tickets could be obtained at the window, but the black market was doing a flourishing business. Within a few minutes the innkeeper's daughter bought six tickets to Lwow. The next train to Lwow was due to arrive shortly and was actually present almost at the scheduled time. The trip itself was uneventful. There were no inspections. I managed to fall asleep and arrived in Lwow feeling somewhat refreshed.

Lwow station, which I knew very well, greeted me with banners in Russian and Soviet flags. I proceeded directly to the house of a professor whose pupil I had once been. He was still living under his own name and in the small, unpretentious house he had always occupied. He answered my ring promptly but gazed at me in suspicious silence.

'Greetings from Antoine,' I said, uttering each syllable of the password slowly and significantly, 'I have a personal message for you.'

He blinked at me warily, said nothing, and gestured to me to enter. I began to understand that I was apt to have a difficult time convincing the people in Lwow of my status. The underground liaison system, at that time, was still imperfect, chaotic, and so uncertain that members of the Underground were in a constant state of alarm and distrust. The professor, for all his unimposing and eccentric appearance, was known to be an intrepid and able underground leader. Evidently he had good reasons to take every possible precaution against showing his hand prematurely. It was even possible that another courier might have arrived before me and changed the password.

It was extremely important to convince him of my authenticity, for he was the leading figure in the civil Lwow Underground and consequently indispensable in the task of carrying out the new plan. One of the reasons, perhaps, that he had been able to accomplish so much was just this extreme caution and the advantage of his innocent and unimpressive exterior.

He was a small, thin, birdlike man, gray-haired, wistful in expression, with narrow, incessantly blinking eyes of a curious hazel color. The muscles on his face rarely moved and his head itself seemed to be fixed rigidly into the high, stiff, old-fashioned collar he wore. A gaudy bow tie of the kind which has the knot already tied, and is fastened by a hook at the back, added to his quaint appearance. This bow tie kept him in a state of constant agitation, for it was always undoing itself and threatening to fall off, or wriggling up over his collar in a most undignified fashion. Nearly all the time I spent with him, my attention was distracted by his fidgety hand which was perpetually at the back of his neck, replacing the hook in the eyelet, or yanking at the elastic.

'Professor,' I began, 'I have just come from Warsaw. The Underground there . . .'

He had been gazing at me with pretended indifference while I began to speak. At the word 'Underground,' he edged away from me, assumed an expression of utter blankness, walked absent-mindedly to the window and stood there, gazing outside and fidgeting with his bow tie as though he had completely forgotten that I was in the room.

'. . . have instructed me to inform you of the new plan,' I continued lamely with no better success than before.

I ceased and pondered for a moment. Then I advanced to the window and tapped him on the shoulder. He turned around sharply and glared at me angrily.

'Don't you recognize one of your former pupils?' I asked, smiling. 'Don't you remember telling me to come back and look you up, when I was about to go abroad in 1935? Surely this is not the kind of reception you meant me to have.'

'Yes, yes, I recognize you.' He blinked at me.

I could see that he was still uncertain. He had been very fond of me, but had no way of knowing who or what I was at present. He still looked me over like a scientist trying to complete the classification of an unusual specimen.

'I am very busy now,' he said, without much enthusiasm. 'I must deliver a lecture. If you wish to see me, meet me at the entrance to the park near the university in two hours.'

'I will be waiting for you there. I am sorry that under the circumstances I cannot attend your lecture.'

The faint smile was repeated. I had obviously succeeded in breaking through some of the icy suspicion I had first encountered, but he still could not allow himself to be won over on the strength of a previous acquaintance. He needed time to think it over. Meanwhile, in case I had been a spy, he had skillfully managed to avoid betraying himself by even the slightest slip. At the threshold we separated since I had decided that it would be useless to try to talk with him till he had reached a decision about me.

I decided to spend the interval looking up a friend of mine in Lwow. I was so anxious to see him that I did not know what excited me more about going to Lwow – the political importance of my mission or the opportunity of again seeing Jerzy Jur.[1]

Jerzy was about three years younger than myself, a handsome fellow and the son of a Lwow physician. He was smooth-skinned (we had teased him at the university about his lack of a beard), with blue eyes and blond hair. He had always dressed immaculately and in the best of taste. I had first met him at the university and later we had served our year in the army in the same artillery battery. At the university, his cleverness and his scholastic ability had kept him at the head of the class, despite a feverish interest in politics which was rare even for Poland, where boys and girls of sixteen or seventeen are apt to engage in full-scale political activity.

He was the kind of person who is often called a maniac or a fanatic as long as he is unsuccessful. Jerzy was an unusually intense and persistent exponent of democracy. In high school as well as at the university, he had never missed an opportunity to deliver a speech about his beliefs. No democratic school publication ever appeared without carrying one of his articles.

All this, of course, dismayed his parents, who would have preferred their son to prepare more conventionally for his career. I remember one occasion when his mother reproached him for his political activities. He answered her jokingly.

'That's my temperament,' he said. 'Would you prefer, Mother, to have me spend my spare time running after girls?'

The question acted like a sedative. His mother feared nothing so much as the possibility that he would fall into the trap set by a flirt. She knew him to be of an amorous disposition, and this, coupled with his good looks and his youth, made her feel that any alternative was worthwhile as long as it kept him from the greatest danger. Jerzy obtained her consent to continue with his 'social work' after school.

'What she doesn't know,' Jerzy informed me later when we were alone discussing his mother's fears, 'is that I manage to find time for both.'

The outcome of his 'social work' was not always for the best. In 1938, during a period of academic riots, he was beaten by his political enemies and had to spend several weeks in the hospital. In continental Europe, unfortunately, political disputes are not always settled by democratic methods.

Now as I was on my way to see him, many of the scenes of our comradeship in the army came to my mind and I wondered if we could resume the friendship that had been ours. I knew he was living at his former address and I had high hopes of persuading him to accompany me to France.

When I came to his house, I knocked as if I had been on my way home from the university and had just dropped in to see my friend. An elderly lady, whom I had never seen before, answered the door.

'May I see Jerzy?' I asked.

'He is not here,' she answered, 'Jerzy has gone to stay with his aunt for two or three weeks.'

'May I see his parents?'

'No, they have left, too.'

'Where did they go?'

'I really don't know.'

I asked no more questions. It was quite clear. Jerzy's parents had been deported to Russia.

'My name is Jan Karski,' I said. 'May I return in two weeks to see Jerzy?'

'Oh, yes, I heard Jerzy speak of you,' she said with a restrained smile; 'I am another aunt of Jerzy's. If you wish to come back, do so by all means. Of course, in these times, it is not always advisable to wait for those who have left to stay two weeks with their aunt.'

The meaning was plain. Jerzy was either in hiding or abroad. Nearly three months later, in Hungary, I learned that he had escaped to France at the head of a group of ten friends. They had left, one might say, in military formation. They carried an amazing quantity of arms, revolvers, hand grenades, and dismantled machine guns. Miraculously they succeeded in reaching the Carpathian Mountains, reassembling their arms, crossing the frontier, and finally presenting themselves at a Polish post as a fully equipped military detachment. The entire exploit created a sensation.

Later his path crossed mine several times, as he continued along the dangerous route of the underground couriers executing special missions, which involved the crossing and recrossing of all the battle lines of Europe twice in the incredibly short space of twelve months. When I did finally meet him again, I found him sobered and saddened by his experiences, but with the same irrepressible belief in the future and the same craving for social justice, freedom, and order.

I met the professor at the park near the older and smaller of the two Lwow University buildings. The building of this institution was humble compared to the other which was housed in a palace built in the eighteenth century during the Austrian occupation. It would have been interesting to go and hear a lecture, but I was following the cautious principle of speaking to and having contact with as few people as possible.

I loitered near the entrance gazing at the old oaks and the mellow light of the lamps which had just been lit, with something of nostalgia and a certain bitterness. Many of the lamps had been broken and many were not functioning.

The professor greeted me with a decisive, if nervous, cordiality that made it obvious he had decided to risk acknowledging his position.

We sat down on one of the benches. I began to explain the plans and desires of the Polish authorities in Warsaw. He was in instant sympathy with most of the ideas, even anticipating some of the details of the plans. He was, in fact, quite ready to co-operate in the realization of the system of organization that Borecki had outlined to me. He had been thinking along these lines himself. There seemed to be some holding back on his part, the nature and the cause of which I made an unsuccessful effort to have him reveal. Instead of explaining his hesitations, he questioned me closely about the prevailing conditions in Warsaw, the strength of our organization and the methods it employed.

He listened attentively, constantly interrupting me to ask questions on some minute point which he evidently needed to complete whatever analysis he was making. At the end of my long recital, he said:

'There is one thing you must understand and tell the men in Warsaw,' he began. 'Conditions here are very different, indeed. For one thing, the Gestapo and the GPU are two entirely different organizations. The men of the Russian secret police are more clever and better trained. Their police methods are superior. They are less crude and more scientific and systematic. Many of the ruses and practices which work well in Warsaw will not do at all in Lwow. Very often the various branches of the Underground cannot take the risk of contacting each other because of the difficulty of eluding the GPU agents and even knowing who they are.'

'I had not realized things were so difficult here.'

'No. But they are really two different worlds.'

He was now poised, self-assured, and spoke with a calm, modulated voice. Every question he had asked me had revealed an unusual insight. His whole conversation indicated a resourcefulness, an ability to calculate shrewdly, a level-headed tenacity that was difficult to associate with the short birdlike figure in the ridiculously long jacket and the unmanageable bow tie of the afternoon. I wondered how much of this costume was deliberately deceptive, and although I remembered that he had had much the same manner in the days when I had been his pupil, it seemed to me now that it was either consciously or unconsciously exaggerated for protective purposes.

'However,' he continued, 'I would like you to inform Mr Borecki and the others in Warsaw that I am in complete accord with their principles. I will do my utmost to help carry out their plan. They must, however, understand our difficulties, do their best to help us, and be tolerant of our shortcomings.'

I told him that I was certain they would understand and that together we would be able to work out methods of overcoming the obstacles. We sat for a long while in the gathering blackness, after the official part of our discussion was over, talking of old times.

At length, the professor rose.

'I must go now,' he said. 'I am sorry I cannot invite you to my house, but it would be much too hazardous. I suggest you stay at the Napoleon Hotel. Be inconspicuous. Talk to as few people as possible and attract as little attention as you can. You still know your way about Lwow?'

'As well as I know any place. I should like to meet you again, sir.'

'Good. Meet me in the park tomorrow about the same time. Goodnight.'

The next day I decided to see the other major figure of the Underground on whom the success of my mission depended. He was the owner of a clothing store in the center of the business district of Lwow and was the head of the military division of the Lwow Underground. I entered the store and found him quite alone. He was dark-skinned and black-mustached and his eyes were watchful beneath his bushy brows.

'Good afternoon,' he greeted me. 'What can I do for you?'

'Greetings from Antoine,' I said softly, for although the store itself was empty, there very well might be someone within earshot. 'I have a personal message for you.'

Again a suspicious glance. I remembered what the professor had told me about the efficacy of the Russian police. I racked my brains for some formula to convince him of the authenticity of my mission. It occurred to me to wonder how I in turn could be sure of the identity of my customer. This curiosity was soon satisfied.

'Come into the back room,' he said curtly, scrutinizing my face as though he hoped to decipher a puzzle which confronted him in my features. I went willingly, convinced that I, at least, had the right man, for no one but a member of the Underground would have taken me into the back room of an empty store.

In the merchandise-crowded back room, he faced me expectantly.

'I am from Warsaw,' I said. 'I have information to give you from Mr Borecki . . .'

'I never heard of him,' he snapped. 'I don't know anybody in Warsaw except one or two relatives.'

'Look. My name is Jan Karski. I was sent here as a courier to improve the relations between the Lwow and Warsaw organizations, to inform you of the new plans for reorganization.'

I saw him measuring me carefully. I reasoned that he probably had not heard my name and that though he might have been forewarned of my coming, he had no way of being certain that I was the man I asserted myself to be. His hesitation lasted only a split second.

'I never heard of you and I have no connections whatsoever with anybody in Warsaw.'

I was nonplussed. There were no further devices which struck me as affording an opportunity of breaking down his reserve. He, meanwhile, had completely regained his self-possession and apparently considered the entire incident closed. For he had decided to behave with complete nonchalance and add the final touch to his pretense.

'Is there anything else I can do for you?' he inquired with an air of puzzled innocence.

There was nothing further to be done. When I met the professor later in the day, I described what had occurred. He informed me that in Lwow, it was quite useless to press a man once he had made up his mind not to talk. Usually he had good grounds for maintaining his silence and could not afford to risk going by intuition. Many a man had fallen into the clutches of the police by trusting his ability to read human nature too far. Unless a man had adequate proof of someone's identity he would be foolish to take even the slightest risk of making the wrong person his confidant.

He also informed me that the message and information I had brought would be given the widest possible circulation in the Lwow Underground. He asked me about my immediate plans. I informed him that my instructions were to try to reach the government in France, via the Rumanian border.

'It is not very feasible at the present,' he said dryly. 'The Rumanian border is among the most efficiently guarded places in all Europe.'

'There usually is some way of eluding the most watchful guards,' I replied.

'Human guards, yes,' he answered, 'but the Rumanian border is guarded by a cordon of police dogs. I happen to know that it is nearly impossible to slip through. My advice to you is to return to Warsaw and try to go by some other route. You would only waste your time and risk your neck for nothing.'

I agreed with him. Police dogs are one of the most efficient media known for this kind of work. I lingered in Lwow for a few days, explaining more of the details of the reorganization plan, and familiarizing myself with the problems of the Underground in Lwow, and then returned to Warsaw using the same channel as previously.

10

Mission to France

It was near the end of January when I took the train from Warsaw to Zakopane, the official 'starting point' of my route to France. Zakopane is a village about five miles before the Polish–Czech border in the foothills of the Tatra Mountains, which are the highest peaks of the Carpathian Range. It was rather well-known as a resort for winter vacationists. The surrounding country afforded unusually good territory for ski enthusiasts.

In a cabin on the outskirts of the village, I met my guide and the two other young men who were to accompany us across the border as far as Kosice, a Czech city which had been incorporated into Hungary after the partition of Czechoslovakia in 1939.

We were to pretend to be a simple skiing party. In the cabin I changed into a ski-suit which I had brought along for the purpose. My guide was a tall, sturdy young man who had formerly been a skiing instructor. The other members of our party were also excellent skiers. One of them was a lieutenant who was on his way to France to join the army, carrying out the order issued by General Sikorski. The other, Prince Pozyna, was a graceful, self-possessed youth in his early twenties on his way to resume his interrupted career in the Polish air force.

At dawn the next day we set out through the Slovakian mountains. It was cold when we started, and the snow was purple in the half-light, becoming pink and then dazzling white as the winter sun rose behind us. We were all dressed in the customary ski outfits and I felt a sense of luxury in the close-fitting, woolen pullover and the thick socks and well-made substantial boots. We carried provisions in our knapsacks, as we planned not to stop at any of the established points during our four-day trip. Our supplies were ample – we had chocolate, sausage, bread, liquor, and a few extra pairs of socks.

We began in high spirits, with a sense of exhilaration as though we were about to go on an excursion in normal times rather than a serious and possibly dangerous adventure. The lieutenant started to tell us some anecdotes of former skiing trips he had taken. Pozyna sniffed the air and commented enthusiastically upon its quality as though it had been specially uncorked for our benefit. The guide seemed a trifle bored by the whole affair and warned us to restrain ourselves, to slacken our headlong pace and conserve our energy, as we had a long trip ahead of us.

But he did not succeed in dampening our spirits. The weather was perfect during the trip. The white slopes glittering in the sun, the bracing pine-scented air, the sense of freedom and bodily movement after the confined, skulking existence we had been leading, made us feel as though we had just burst out of bondage. We passed the border without incident or difficulty early the first day, merely skiing across. As we progressed deeper into the mountains over unknown and unfrequented trails all thought of prudence or caution vanished utterly. We rarely ever saw and never spoke to another human being.

We would clamber up a long slope, our skis crunching into virgin snow, the fatigue of the ascent accumulating until we reached a pinnacle and released our pent-up desire for speed in the giddy glide of a long descent, which felt as though every resistance had been removed from our path. Then our guide would insist upon a rest. We would find a large rock for shelter against the wind and nestle close to it, the dry snowflakes swirling about us and stinging our faces. We would gulp brandy from the bottles and devour chunks of bread and sausage. The liquor penetrated and warmed every part of my body. Stimulated by the heady air and our exertions, our appetites imparted an incomparable flavor to the coarse victuals. Nothing before or since has ever tasted quite so good.

We passed our nights in mountain caves or crude dugouts made by the shepherds. We would sleep through nearly the entire night and resume our progress a little after dawn. Sunrise and sunset invariably brought a winter carnival of color, revealing splendors visible only at that altitude.

Our guide continued to eye us askance, curbing our exuberance. Once, after we had ascended to the top of a ridge, Pozyna exclaimed enthusiastically, pointing to the scene spread out before us. The guide leaned on his sticks in a posture of complete indifference and pretended to suppress a yawn of weariness.

'Oh, come, now,' Pozyna said, 'it can't be that bad. Aren't you enjoying yourself the least bit?'

He looked at us with a smile:

'You gentlemen constitute my thirty-first group of clients. All sizes, shapes, ages, and conditions. Every possible variety of mood. Some in raptures like yourselves, some groaning with fatigue and complaining. Some just indifferent and anxious to get over with it. I have always liked these mountains and I'm still fond of skiing. But I have had enough for a while, I think.'

We gave up attempting to cajole him into a better humor. We expressed our emotions only to each other. The lieutenant was of an amiable, if serious, disposition. Pozyna was ebullient and elated, a gay, good-looking boy, but not without a certain temperamental self-assurance and steadiness that prevented him from becoming too flippant. He had only one serious weakness – women. He talked about them frequently, the ones he had known and the ones he would have liked to meet and anticipated meeting. The only topics he preferred to this one were flying and his hatred of the Germans.

On one occasion, climbing on a high snowy ledge, we saw minute colored figures moving far down below us near a group of tiny huts. Pozyna made us all stop while he pointed at them and cried:

'Let me go down there for a while. There's a nice girl among them. I can sense it . . .'

We laughed at him and continued on our way. He offered no resistance but I think he was quite serious.

On the Hungarian frontier our party split up, Pozyna and the lieutenant proceeding on to France by a different route than mine, while the guide returned to Zakopane. Pozyna got through to France and later to England where he achieved his greatest desire: joining the RAF. He shot down many German planes and bombed German cities. About two years later, I read the name of Stanislaw Pozyna listed among those 'missing in action.'

Along the border between Slovakia and Hungary the organization had established many 'points' as places for meeting, for the arrangement of transportation, to facilitate the exodus of young Poles to the army in France, and to provide contacts for the couriers. There were a considerable number of these points and they operated with relative ease. The Hungarian officials were apparently not at all anxious to interfere with their industrious activities or, if they were, did not expend sufficient energy to hamper them seriously.

My two young friends proceeded to a station where they were to await their turn to be sent on to France. I went to the city of Kosice, where an agent of the Polish Underground lived, whose address and password had been given to me before the trip. He was well supplied and had good connections. I arrived there shortly before noon. Two hours later, having eaten a good lunch, cleaned up and changed into civilian clothes, I was seated in a powerful car, with the agent and a competent chauffeur, on my way to Budapest.

Kosice is in the southern foothills of the mountains. After we had been driving a little while the country leveled off into a flat, open plain. We passed by a succession of small farms resting peacefully under a blanket of snow, and orchards of pear and apple trees with gray leafless branches bending under crackling burdens of ice. There must have been something strained or wary about my expression for my companion took the trouble to inform me that I could relax and be comfortable for a while. There was nothing to fear, he told me, since the Hungarian police never stopped or inspected cars. In the improbable event of any difficulty, he would be ready and able to get me out of it.

I attempted to follow his advice, leaned back, and lit a cigarette. My relaxation brought in its wake a series of discoveries – I was suffering from a variety of minor physical aches which I had been too preoccupied to notice until then. My throat was so sore and inflamed that I had to stop smoking and shortly afterwards I began to cough and sneeze violently. My hands were chapped, irritated in appearance, and bleeding slightly in several places. Worst of all were my feet which soon began to ache intolerably. I removed my shoes and socks for an examination. My ankles and feet were swollen and sensitive to the slightest touch.

My companion followed my explorations with interest and some amusement. When I was through probing and groaning, he remarked dryly:

'Skiing is a fine sport.'

'I didn't notice anything until a moment ago,' I said ruefully.

'No one ever does,' he replied without much concern, 'but don't let it disturb you. It is a small penalty to pay for a pleasant trip. Besides, there are excellent hospitals in Budapest and you will receive good treatment.'

'Really? Won't it be risky?'

'Hardly. We have a well-organized point in Budapest. You will be supplied with all the necessary papers and you will be able to move about quite freely.'

We arrived in Budapest after a journey of about eight hours. It was shortly after nightfall and the streets of Budapest were a gay, brightly lit contrast to the capital I had left behind. We stopped at the house of a man who was the most important contact in Hungary between the Polish Government in France and the Underground in Warsaw, the director of the Hungarian link in the liaison system. He lived in a quiet, residential section and, fortunately, there was no one about. I found it nearly impossible to put on my shoes and I had to carry them in my hand while I hobbled up the steps. My companion stayed only long enough to introduce me and clear up a few routine matters. I looked nothing like a hero, but rather more like the 'Good Soldier Svejk.'

The 'director,' as he was called – a lean-faced, brisk, and efficient man – had some ointment and bandages brought to me, questioned me while the medication went on and then showed me to my bedroom, after assuring me that I would be in a hospital tomorrow and have time for a look around Budapest afterwards. My cold kept me awake most of the night and I got up late the next afternoon. The swelling of my feet and ankles had abated enough for me to put on my shoes, although with considerable pain. After I had had a substantial breakfast, the director called me into his room and gave me my papers. Among them was a document proving that I had been in Budapest since the beginning of the war and had been a patient in the hospital. There was also a card which indicated that I was a registered, bona fide Polish refugee.

He informed me that a passport to France would be obtained for me shortly, as well as railroad accommodations. In the interim I would go to the Budapest hospital for treatment, and during whatever time was left I would be at perfect liberty, within the limits of ordinary discretion. I spent three days in the hospital and emerged, cured of my cold, with my extremities reduced to normal size and almost completely healed.

I remained in the city four more days, making the rounds sometimes in the company of two of the director's assistants and sometimes alone. Budapest had always been one of the world's most elegant and exciting capitals. The war had served only to increase its hectic charm and to add a variety of uniforms to its elegance. I went to the famous Hungarian baths on the Marguerite Island in the Danube River, which put me in excellent condition. We visited a few of the smart cafés and attended a performance in the Opera House. The existence I had come from was so radically different that I could not adjust myself quickly enough to draw much delight from the luxury and smartness. I felt clumsy, badly dressed, and out of place. Besides, my mind sped restlessly ahead to France and to me the most exciting moment of the day invariably occurred when I met the director and asked if things were ready for my departure.

Everywhere in Budapest I encountered manifestations of the widespread sympathy felt by the Hungarians for their unfortunate Polish neighbors. One day, speaking in German, I was attempting to get directions for a certain address from a cab driver. An elderly couple passing by overheard me. The gentleman approached me, apologized for intruding, and asked me if I were Polish. When I answered affirmatively he offered to drive me to my destination. In the car he spoke with great sympathy about the plight of Poland and the courage of its inhabitants. He invited me to dinner, but I was compelled to decline.

Once when I was sitting with one of my companions in a popular café we were overheard speaking Polish. Before I quite knew what was happening we were surrounded by a little group who assured us of Hungary's sympathy, offered to buy us drinks, and insisted on paying our bill. Numerous incidents of this nature surprised and delighted me and made my short stay in Budapest a pleasant one. At the end of a week I received my passport and railroad ticket.

From Budapest, I took the Simplon–Orient Express route through Yugoslavia to Milan, a ride of some sixteen hours. I left the imposing railroad station erected by the fascists and hurried to inspect the famous cathedral, which for some mysterious reason has always been, for us Poles, one of the most highly revered and venerated buildings in the world. Then, a short train ride brought me to Modane on the Franco-Italian border.

At Modane I first encountered the atmosphere of suspicion and harassed caution that surrounded all the activities of the Polish Government in France. It was due to the constant menace of German espionage. Their spies and agents had filtered into France in droves and placed themselves in strategic positions from which it was difficult to oust them. The Polish Government had organized in Modane an intelligence office to scrutinize every individual arriving from Poland in order to prevent German spies from smuggling themselves into France under the guise of Polish refugees or underground agents. Several of these individuals had already been caught and most of their methods were known to us.

In Hungary and in every place where they could contact Polish refugees, the German spies would buy, cajole, and trick their passport from them. Mostly they would work on simple peasants. They would offer them a fantastic price for their passports, provide them with transportation back to Poland, and assure them that once they returned to their native land, they would be given back their farm possessions and receive grants of land. When the duped refugees actually did return to Poland, they were usually sent either to forced-labor camps or were compelled to work for the Germans under conditions that amounted to slavery.

At the headquarters of our organization in Modane I contacted a man whom I had been told to ask for by name. He took me to a Polish officer in uniform who examined my documents and questioned me. I was not allowed to answer him in full as my mission was important, secret, and I was forbidden to mention it to anyone but Prime Minister General Sikorski. He then asked me for the name of the man in Budapest who had supplied me with my papers and passports. When I gave him the name of the 'director' in Budapest, he asked me to wait and left the room. A few minutes later I was shown into the private office of his superior who welcomed me cordially and without circumspection. Since he had received by wireless a detailed description of me, he knew everything about me. He also had an order to arrange for my entry into France. He was a tall, long-legged man with fair receding hair and a manner that was an odd mixture of confidence, nervousness, and calm.

I was impressed by the cool way in which he scrutinized my credentials and the definiteness of his decision that I was genuinely what I was supposed to be. In the Underground one frequently encounters an individual who absolutely refuses to accept one for what one is, like the head of the military division in Lwow. Even when one finally gains the credence of an individual, there is often a clinging vestige of uncertainty, an unexpressed doubt, for forgery and espionage know no limits.

'Of course,' he said to me finally, 'you understand that we have a great deal to contend with from German spies. They're everywhere in France.'

'I didn't know that. How did such a state of affairs ever come about?'

'Well, it's a long story. They are not particularly clever but they are well-organized, persistent, and unscrupulous. We do our best to combat them and root them out, but like weeds, they grow back again. Our organization isn't large enough to take care of them all, so be careful. Don't give yourself away to anyone till you're absolutely sure of your man.'

'I won't. Don't the French do anything about this?'

'Of course,' he said in a resigned tone, 'they take measures but not very strenuous ones. Remember the war hasn't yet reached a serious stage here. You're not in Poland any longer. It takes a defeat like ours to make people understand and learn how to cope with German methods.'

He reached into a drawer, took out a generous bundle of franc notes, and tossed them to me.

'These are for your expenses in Paris. You're entitled to liberal treatment. But don't go charging full tilt into Paris as you are. It would be perfectly obvious to a spy that you're on a mission of some importance. Pretend to be an ordinary refugee coming to join the army. After you get to Paris go to our army camp and register as a soldier.'

I followed his instructions. In the train from Modane to Paris, a journey of about ten hours, I was in a first-class compartment with six other passengers. I surveyed them carefully. There was an elderly lady, who kept to herself, and industriously turned the pages of a copy of the *Figaro*. There were two men, evidently French and traveling together on business. They talked at random about business, politics, their friends, the war. The other three were like myself, young Poles on their way to our camp to join the army. They, too, had obviously been cautioned, as they talked very little and confined themselves to trivialities when they did.

I listened carefully to all five for a trace of a German accent, a false intonation, or any inconsistency in what they were saying. At times I thought I detected a slip in the conversation of the two Frenchmen. Then I changed my mind. There was no way to know. Besides, there could be Frenchmen in the employ of the Germans. The Poles looked genuine and I would have sworn that they were natives of my country. But still they might be Poles of German descent like the treacherous inhabitants of Oswiecim. To avoid all chances of becoming involved in a conversation, I closed my eyes and pretended to be sound asleep.

Bessières, our army camp, was to the north of Paris, just outside of the city. A Polish camp there served for the reception of refugees and as an induction center for the army. I followed the normal procedure, registering as an applicant for the army and remained overnight as though I intended to stay. The next morning I took a cab into Paris. From the first public telephone booth I could find I called Kulakowski, the private secretary of General Sikorski.

'I come from home,' I told him. 'I have some matters to talk over with your chief.'

That was the most I dared to say on a public telephone. Kulakowski told me to come to his office in the Polish Embassy in the rue Talleyrand near the Invalides. When I got there, he greeted me uncertainly and then had me sit down while he called Professor Kot.[1] Kot was one of the leaders of the Polish Peasant Party and held the post of Minister of the Interior in the cabinet of the Polish government-in-exile. Kulakowski described me over the telephone and asked for instructions. Kot apparently had been expecting me, for Kulakowski gave me additional funds, told me to take a room anywhere I chose in Paris, and to report to Kot at the building of the Ministry of the Interior in Angers on the following day.

'I have to go back to Bessières first,' I told him. 'I left my overcoat and suitcase there.'

'You didn't leave anything important or revealing in the suitcase, did you?' he asked.

'Of course not.'

'Good. Then don't bother about them. Get new ones. We cannot let you go back to Bessières. There might be German spies there. They are trying to infiltrate into our ranks by every conceivable method. All Paris is infested with them.'

'So I heard. And Angers?'

'There is danger there, too. You must be very careful. Now go over to the St Germain area and find yourself a little hotel. Buy your ticket for Angers in advance. Good luck.'

I left and took a cab to the boulevard St Germain. There I registered at a good but very quiet hotel. I had the rest of the day and night to myself and I determined to enjoy it as best I could. The menace of the spies was disturbing, but only when I was actually on business. Though the caution and warning of the men I had met had affected me to such a degree that I constantly felt like turning around to see if I were being followed, and had induced me to examine my hotel room carefully for a possible site for eavesdroppers, nevertheless, I knew and could relish the fact that here at least I was free from the dangers of Warsaw.

It was altogether only two and a half weeks since I had left Warsaw and I was still possessed by the tension and alertness that never wholly left a member of the Underground. It is difficult to describe this feeling of being constantly on the *qui vive* even when one is most relaxed and confident. No one could ever tell when a leak might occur, when someone who had been caught might have cracked under torture, so that one's identity and the address to which one was going might, at any moment, become known to the Gestapo.

In Paris this fear was unknown. Nor could I, when I left my hotel and went to the boulevards for a stroll, notice a trace of any kind of fear or any other of the ravages of war in the people who passed by. Although it was a gray, wintry day, with skies that threatened rain and even drizzled intermittently, the boulevards were crowded with a gay, well-dressed throng, even more cosmopolitan in appearance than in peacetime. Soldiers and officers in the uniform of the colonial troops with crimson capes would cut a swathe of color through the crowd like that left by the passing of a tropical bird of brilliant plumage.

This was Paris during the period of the 'phony war,' the *drôle de guerre* soon to come to an abrupt end. On the place de l'Opéra, traffic was at a maximum. Swarms of the nimble French taxis maneuvered dexterously through civilian and military vehicles apparently unaffected by gas rationing. Horns honked as vigorously as ever in the peculiar brassy Parisian symphony. In the Café de la Paix it was hard to find a seat. Conversation seemed unusually lively, and guests sat about sipping coffee, beer, and vermouth with delectation. Even in this weather, the terraces of the café were crowded with animated groups sitting about the famous, cheerfully glowing street braziers. Flirtations at various stages were progressing.

I spent the rest of the afternoon on a shopping spree, then treated myself to a luxurious dinner and wandered restlessly about the boulevards and cafés for a while without much happening. I returned to my hotel with an armful of French newspapers. Most of their contents were familiar to me and I fell asleep early.

In the morning I dressed in my new clothes and left for Angers. Angers was a typical French city of about eighty-five thousand inhabitants, situated on the Loire, about a four-hour train ride to the southwest of Paris. The streets and buildings were well-kept and modestly prosperous. It had the customary pleasant city square. The French Government had designated it as the seat for the Polish Government. It was a quieter and more convenient place to work than crowded, noisy wartime Paris. The French had granted us the status of extra-territoriality and the Polish cabinet enjoyed all the privileges of full State sovereignty. Thus foreign ambassadors and ministers to Poland resided officially at Angers. (I was amused by one diplomat whom I heard complaining bitterly at having to live in such a provincial community after the splendors of Warsaw.)

When I arrived, I had no difficulty in finding the government's headquarters. A middle-aged Frenchman gave me directions, adding that the city was proud to welcome the authorities of that 'ill-fated Poland so treacherously attacked.' I went to Kot's office in the Ministry of the Interior. His secretary was polite and cautious. He informed me that he was sure Kot would prefer to meet me outside his office. He checked my credentials and arranged for me to meet Kot for lunch at a nearby hotel. When I arrived at the appointed place Kot was already there.

He was a short, gray-haired man, quiet, precise in his habits and movements, and inclined to be pedantic in speech. We introduced ourselves and after we were seated Kot remarked that I looked more like a Parisian banker coming from a banquet than an emissary from starved Poland.

'I don't suppose it was very enjoyable walking around Warsaw in wrinkled trousers and torn socks, was it?' he asked.

I informed him that there were a great many misconceptions current as to how we lived in Poland.

'I've managed to mend my own socks and press my pants by keeping them under a mattress at night,' I said. 'Most of us manage to look fairly presentable.'

Kot eyed me shrewdly.

'In spite of all your passwords, papers, and evidence as to your identity, it is my duty to be careful. I might find you trustworthy, but I must assure myself absolutely that you are the man I am expecting.'

'What further assurance do you wish, sir?' I asked.

'Tell me all about yourself, who you are, what you did both now and before the war. Tell me about the people you work with.'

We launched into a long discussion, chiefly about the people I knew in the Underground. In this way Kot was able at once to satisfy his doubts about me and his insatiable curiosity about people. His method of questioning and his comments marked him at once as intelligent, well-informed, and shrewd.

We, or rather, Kot, continued to discuss Polish personalities for a long time. It was indeed one of his distinctive features to analyze events and situations not so much by the problems they presented as by the character of the personalities involved. His ability to understand people was considerable.

When it came time to discuss the Underground in detail, Kot told me that it would be more advisable for me to write down my oral report so that his records would be in perfect order. He would have a secretary and a machine sent to my hotel in Paris.

'In your report, do not write down any personal names or the names of political organizations. Dictate them to my secretary who will put them in code.'

I spent most of the next six days in Paris working on this report. After I was through, I called Sikorski's secretary again for an appointment. Kulakowski requested me to come to our embassy to meet him.

I went with considerable excitement. Sikorski was highly regarded in Poland. He was the kind of man whom Poles call a 'European,' a man of broad culture. He was a great general, a convinced liberal and democratic statesman who, during the Pilsudski regime, was strongly in opposition. After the catastrophic defeat of Poland, we put all our hopes in him.

In the anteroom of Sikorski's office in the embassy, I was astounded to meet Jerzy Jur, my friend from Lwow. We greeted each other with delight. He told me about his escape and then we both became embarrassed as the conversation turned to what our present occupations were. Neither one of us was allowed to discuss our status and so, amusingly enough, we had to fence with each other. Later, we realized that we were both going to Poland, but unfortunately we could not discuss it. We exchanged addresses, however, and I went in to see General Sikorski.

Sikorski was a man of about sixty, tall and upright in bearing. He appeared to be in excellent health. His manner was polished and his gestures had become slightly Gallicized. During the period of his opposition to Pilsudski, he had spent many years in France, becoming deeply attached to her. Since the First World War he had been particularly close to the French General Staff and many leading French military men held him in high esteem as a strategist.

He permitted me only a very brief conversation in his office and told me to meet him in the Café Weber for lunch on the following day.

We met in the restaurant lobby; a secluded table had been reserved for us. We sat down and I ordered a drink. Sikorski excused himself.

'Lieutenant Karski, permit me, please, not to join you in drinking,' he said with an apologetic smile, 'I am too often compelled to drink at diplomatic banquets and I am usually sick afterwards.'

He was extremely polite and affable, inquired a good deal about myself and my past, and listened to my responses with attentive and sympathetic interest. We discussed the military situation. Sikorski granted that the German Army was formidable but had faith in the ultimate victory of France. He refused to risk an opinion on the probable time of the conclusion of the war.

'Whatever my private opinion is,' he said, 'the organization ought to count on a long war and act accordingly, to be on the safe side. I insist that you pass this on, Lieutenant. We must be under no illusions.'

During the ensuing conversation, I realized how this man looked at the future.

'This is not only a war of independence for us. We do not want merely to re-establish the prewar status quo. We cannot revive mechanically a past which was, to some degree, the cause of what has happened. Remind them of this over there, and let them not forget that we are fighting not only for an independent Poland but for a new democratic state assuring to all her citizens political and social freedom and progress. Unfortunately, our prewar rulers thought that Poland should develop, not according to democratic ideals, but through the so-called "strong hand" system. This was contrary to our tradition and national spirit. It cannot be revived and the men responsible for it cannot come to power again. Postwar Poland must be built up by the free political parties, the professional unions, by men of knowledge, experience, and good will and not by any privileged group.

'I know,' he continued, 'that many of my compatriots still do not understand my language. But you and your friends, the Polish youth, will understand me. I rely mainly on you. Let us finish first our job with Germany – then a hard task of reconstruction awaits us.'

At the end of the lunch, he suggested a second meeting in a hotel at Angers. There I outlined the viewpoint of the underground leaders on the need for a unified organization and what its structure should be. Sikorski concurred almost wholly. He expressed an opinion similar to Borecki's.

'The movement,' he said, 'must not be confined merely to the function of resistance but must take shape as an actual state. All the apparatus of a state must be created and maintained at all costs, no matter how crude it is.'

Furthermore, he pointed out that the army must be unified into a whole rather than exist as an aggregate of atomic bodies, and stressed that the military had to be integrated completely into the social and political structure.

'It cannot be allowed to remain distant or isolated. The liaison must be complete and conditions of mutual responsibility must be made to prevail,' he insisted, laying his finger unerringly on the weak spot.

An image came to my mind of the scowling, beetle-browed countenance of the military leader in Lwow and my nod of agreement was unusually emphatic.

'But the army,' General Sikorski went on, 'shall never be allowed to interfere in political life. We have had enough of that. It must be the armed force of the people, animated by the ideal to serve the people, and not to rule them, not to lead them.'

I brought up one of the thorniest questions the Underground had to face.

'How literally should we interpret our principle of "non-collaboration"?' I asked. 'Sometimes it may be valuable for us to have our men infiltrate into the German organizations. Can we do that?'

Sikorski's reply was wholly characteristic.

'The Poles in Paris,' he said with a touch of irony, 'live very well. We eat good food, sleep in comfortable quarters, and have few personal worries. We can't tell the suffering and starving people in Poland what to do. I would not dream of attempting to impose my will. It would be immoral. The function of the government in France is merely to take care of their interests abroad. If they want my suggestions on the matter, I would say that any collaboration is unfavorable to our international political status. They shall do whatever they judge necessary. As long as we are abroad, we cannot issue orders to the Polish people. Our task is to fight the Germans. But please tell them to remember our history and our traditions. Tell them that we here are sure they will choose the right way.'

On the subject of a delegate of the government who would be the chief of the underground administration and the link between the Underground as a whole and the government in France, Sikorski again stressed that what the Poles inside Poland wanted was of primary importance.

'If any individual has the support of the people in Poland and they desire him as our delegate,' he said, 'then he shall have our support, no matter what his political convictions are.'

At the conclusion of the interview, Sikorski made it clear to me that the task of the Underground and the government in this war was not only to continue the Polish state but to develop and improve it.

The next day I ran into Kot in the Café de la Paix. I gathered that he frequented the place with his customary regularity. In Cracow, he had visited a certain café with such mechanical regularity that his students had nicknamed it the Café Kot. We discussed my conversation with General Sikorski. Kot was in complete agreement with the proposals. He ventured the opinion, however, that Poland would be occupied for a long time and that the Underground must prepare for a long struggle. He then suggested that I get in touch with General Sosnkowski, the chief of the Military Underground, for a conference.[2]

I called Sosnkowski's adjutant, who arranged a meeting in a modest bistro. Sosnkowski is a tall, tough, military type of a man, about sixty-five years of age. He has unusually piercing blue eyes beneath bushy eyebrows. He was Pilsudski's chief of staff when Pilsudski organized the underground forces against our oppressors before the First World War. His old training had never deserted him and he still had conspiracy in the very marrow of his bones.

The first thing he did was to snap out a reprimand for calling his adjutant so freely. Didn't I know that telephones could be tapped? I accepted the rebuff without answering. He asked me about general conditions in Poland and offered little or no suggestion while I recited the social and civil problems. His métier was military affairs. His opinion was also that Poland would be occupied for a long time. He told me that it was highly important for the Polish people to realize that this was not an ordinary war and that when it was over, all life would be changed and modified.

Altogether I spent about six weeks in Paris. During the rest of the time I put in long stretches of work, preparing reports and reviewing instructions to take back with me. My scanty leisure was spent going out and making the rounds with Jerzy Jur. Before I left I had a last meeting with Kot. He told me the names of all the important figures in the Underground whom I should be sure to see. He was very cordial and added:

'Traditionally, I should compel you to swear that you will not betray us. But if you are wicked enough to turn traitor, you are wicked enough to break an oath. So let us simply shake hands. Good luck, Karski.'

On the trip back to Poland I retraced my footsteps. The only difference was that I traveled under another name and with another set of papers. I took the Simplon–Orient Express through Yugoslavia to Budapest. I spent two days there and, as a favor to the contact man, I agreed to carry a knapsack full of money into Poland, in place of the less important functionary to whom such tasks were usually assigned. This was by no means a small favor, the knapsack full of Polish banknotes weighing over forty pounds. With my other equipment it proved a considerable burden. I went by car to Kosice where I met the same guide who took me over the mountains. It was an uneventful journey. This time, however, we went by foot, as the snow had begun to melt.

II

The Underground State

It was near the end of April 1940 when I arrived back in Poland, carrying with me the most momentous order of the Polish Government to the Underground. It acknowledged the idea of unification of all underground groups into one underground state and it became known as the 'Doctrine of the Polish Underground.' When, after stopping at a 'point' near the frontier for a few days, I finally arrived in Cracow and contacted the authorities of the Underground, I discovered that the foundations had already been laid for the carrying out of this task, although its completion required some time.

In Cracow, my initiation into the 'mechanism' of the Underground took place and I was able to realize, for the first time, the high level which the organization had already reached, the intricacy of the conspiratorial apparatus and the methods devised to elude detection. I was never left alone for a single moment. It became apparent to me after a few days in Cracow that every movement I made, nearly every word I spoke, and even the food I had eaten, was known to my superiors. Each time I returned home, I found someone at my door who exchanged passwords with me and departed. And if no one was there waiting for me, I had to get away immediately – at all costs I wasn't to go in.

On one occasion, it had been arranged that at 9.45 a.m. I was to meet in front of my door an elderly gray-haired lady carrying a blue umbrella and a basket of potatoes. Early that morning I decided to go to Mass, which ended about 9.30. I returned and found the lady waiting at my door. We went to our destination. The next evening a liaison man called to inform me that the Underground was charging me with sleeping away from my residence or of being in contact with people unknown to the organization. The woman had reported that instead of coming out of the house, I had returned to it.

The awareness that I was continually being spied upon jarred on my nerves. I asked the authorities why it was being done. They informed me that they were not as yet sure of my prudence. Besides, in case I had any trouble or was arrested by the Gestapo, they had to know immediately and be ready to take the necessary measures. Thus was treated a courier who had returned with extremely important instructions – even if he had a high opinion of himself.

Conditions in Cracow had changed considerably during my four and a half months' absence. The first few conversations had made me conscious of the fact that the consolidation of the Underground had practically been achieved. The movement had crystallized into two major organizations: the coalition of the four largest political parties, the Peasant, the Socialist, the Christian Labor, and the National Party; and the official military organization which had been recognized by the government as a military unit enjoying equal rights with the Polish Army in France.

The coalition was actually endeavoring to create a third branch, namely, that of the Chief Delegate and of the provincial delegates of the government. The function of this branch was, in the name of the government, and with the collaboration of the political and social forces in the Underground, to organize the economic, political, and juridical administration of Poland through the Underground.

One of the most important needs was to obtain agreement upon the person of the future Chief Delegate and provincial delegates.

The instructions I brought to Poland upon this point were simple and clear. The government would approve any candidate for the position of Chief Delegate or one of the provincial delegates chosen by unanimous consent of the political parties. The government was not interested in the personality of the candidate, nor his political affiliations, nor would it become involved in settling questions of party representation. The government would confirm the appointment of any individual who possessed enough authority and the

confidence of the population of Poland. Purely in an advisory capacity, the government had suggested the name of Mr Borecki.

One of the first things I heard when I returned to Poland was
news of Borecki's arrest. He and many others had paid with their
lives for the success thus far obtained in organizing the Polish underground state, a task which Borecki and his friends were among the
first to undertake.

The leader of the Christian Labor Party, Teka, had also been shot.
He had been one of the most active political leaders in the country,
having been instrumental in bringing about among the various parties an understanding which was of enormous importance.

The most important topic of the hour in Cracow was, naturally,
the beginning of large-scale Franco-German hostilities. Most of the
leaders in Cracow believed this to mean the hastening of Allied victory and felt convinced that the war would be short. I persisted in
the opinion shared by the government that it would be a long war.

While I was in Cracow, I lived with a man who had been my
friend in prewar days, Joseph Cyna.[1] He was a leader of the Socialist
party and a first-rate newspaper man. Under thirty-five years of age,
he was a man of wide knowledge and broad political views. Moreover, he was sober and realistic in his conduct and appraisals. The
special talent which made him invaluable for underground work
was his ability to avoid attracting attention to himself or his activities. Every excursion he made, every conversation he had, was
somehow given the appearance of a pastime or a light social affair.
Among the many leaders I met he was the only one who seemed to
realize that relying on France's strength was a fatal error.

'The Germans,' he told me, 'are forging ahead rapidly. The outlook would have been more favorable if the Allies had started the
offensive. The mere fact that the Germans began active hostilities
indicates that they had the means to do so. The fact that the Allies
did not undertake an offensive on land, sea, and air is proof that
they could not afford it. In any war, strategically and tactically, the
attacker always has the advantage.'

I stayed with him for about three days. He was living in the suburbs under an alias and working in one of the few co-operative stores the Germans had spared. The address of his house was the one in which he had registered and his living quarters were on the second floor. As a precautionary measure, he slept on the ground floor, in the apartment of his contact woman.

'Should the Germans come to arrest me,' he explained, 'they would look for me on the second floor. Naturally they wouldn't find me but I would know that they were there. In the meantime, I would slip out by this door—' And he took a couple of loose boards out of the floor of the kitchen. This was the entrance to the cellar.

'You see, there is an underground passage which continues beneath three houses and leads to the corner of the next street. I think,' he said with a smile of satisfaction, 'that this gives me a fair chance of escaping.'

When I was about to leave his quarters he said to me casually:

'By the way, you might take these things with you and distribute them in the train or in Warsaw. First, read it yourself. It is our May First Socialist Manifesto.'

'What shall I do with it?' I asked, accepting the package he handed to me.

'Distribute the contents. It is not enough merely to talk. Everyone of us must constantly radiate ideas.'

I read the leaflet and disposed of most of the copies on the train to Warsaw. Its title was: 'Manifesto of the Wolnosc [Liberty] on May Day, 1940.' It was an eloquent summation of the position of the Socialist Party and highly indicative of the conditions of the time:

Poles, we appeal to you – Polish workers, peasants, and intellectuals – in an hour of great distress. We raise our voice in these days of our enslavement. It is the same voice you once heard from Warynaki, Montwill, Okrzeya, for it is the voice of Polish Socialism. In the days of Polish independence, that voice was heard again and again rising to condemn the policies of Poland's despotic rulers. It is the voice of the workers of Warsaw and Gdynia calling each other to fight the invader.

We appeal to you to remember the day of independence and Socialism. May First approaches. On both shores of the Bug River it will be set aside as an official holiday. You are aware that it is not a day for tribute to Stalin and Hitler but a day for concentrated preparation for an intrepid struggle.

Poland has been defeated. The murderous attack of the German Army did not meet with proper resistance.

History has taught the Polish nation a dreadful lesson.

For us, now, the road to freedom leads through the torture chambers of the Gestapo and the GPU, through prison and concentration camps, through mass deportations and mass executions.

Oppressed, persecuted, and despoiled, we are finally grasping the bitter truth. The destiny of our country cannot be entrusted to the representatives of those classes that have shown themselves unable to make Poland great, powerful, and righteous. A Poland of large landowners, capitalists, and bankers cannot exist. Only the people of Poland: the laborers, peasants, and intellectual workers, can build up the country.

In the west, England and France are fighting Germany. The new Polish Army is fighting shoulder to shoulder with our Allies. But we must understand that the destiny of Poland will not be decided on the Maginot or Siegfried Lines. The hour of decision will arrive for Poland when the Polish people themselves grapple with the invader. With stubborn patience we must wait for that hour to come. Our political acumen and wisdom must be sharpened for that hour. Arms must be amassed and our fighters made ready. In the new Poland, power must rest with the people. The new Poland must be, in spirit and substance, the motherland of freedom, justice, and democracy. Laws, backed by the power of the people, must be passed which will establish a new regime – of Socialism.

The new Poland must repair the mistakes of the past. Land must be divided among the peasants without the indemnification of the owners. Social control must be extended over mines, banks, and factories. Freedom of speech, religion, and conscience must be ordained. Schools and universities must be opened to the children of the people. The ordeals of the Jewish people of which we are the daily witness must teach us how to live in harmony with those who suffer the persecution of the common enemy. Despoiled of our own state, we must learn to respect the aspiration to freedom of the Ukrainian and White Ruthenian people.

Having established in a free Poland a government of the people it will be our duty to build up a new Poland of justice, freedom, and prosperity.

In this period of dire oppression, without precedent in the history of Poland and the world at large, we come to arouse your spirit of combat and perseverance.

On this first day of May, let the old revolutionary slogans resound through Poland.

I distributed about one hundred copies of this proclamation, keeping one for myself.

Of the four movements that had made the deepest impression on the Polish consciousness, the Socialist movement had perhaps the richest and most unbroken tradition in the fight for independence. It had achieved a position of great influence among the Polish workers who had been in the van of the struggle for independence. The most courageous, uncompromising, and self-sacrificing fighters came from their ranks. In 1905 they had opened fire on the Tsarist dignitaries and had been mercilessly slaughtered by the Tsarist police. The Polish underground press inherited the tradition of *The Worker*, the Socialist newspaper which before the First World War eluded the Tsarist police and aroused the Polish nation to resist its oppressors.

These workers played a leading rôle in the defense of Warsaw under the leadership of the late Mieczyslaw Niedzialkowski. When Warsaw fell Niedzialkowski not only refused to sign the capitulation; he refused to recognize it as an accomplished fact. When the Germans entered, instead of hiding or trying to escape, he continued to live in his old apartment under his own name. During a Gestapo investigation, Himmler interviewed him privately.

'What do you want from us; what do you expect?' Himmler is authentically reported to have asked.

Niedzialkowski raised his glasses and glanced at him disdainfully.

'From you I neither want nor demand anything. With you I fight.'

Shortly afterwards, Himmler ordered the proud and intractable leader of the workers to be shot.

The Socialist movement was based on Marxist ideology at the time of its inception in the nineteenth century and has not deviated from its point of view. It believed that the means of production should be under government control. It advocated a completely planned and organized national economy, the division of the land among the peasants, and, politically, a parliamentary democracy.

The National movement likewise had deep roots in the life of the people. Its basic idea of 'all for the nation' performed an invaluable function in the struggle of Poland for biologic self-preservation, to outlast all its innumerable tragedies and defeats. This politically strong party gathered recruits from all classes and sections of the nation. It was based on Catholicism, believed in the principles of individualism and in many of the tenets of liberal economy. It stressed individual rights and the necessity for their maintenance. One of the great leaders of this movement was Roman Dmowski, who signed the Versailles Treaty in the name of Poland, after which an independent Poland, for the first time since the eighteenth century, returned to life.

During the years that Poland was under foreign domination, the National Party opened and supported schools, worked to maintain the idea of a Polish state, to reunite the peasants with the land of their forefathers, and to rebuild the economic structure of Poland.

Historically, the Polish Peasant Party was the youngest of the four. One of its major achievements was the organization into political expression of the villages, which include more than sixty percent of the total population. Through centuries, the Polish peasants had remained politically passive, unenlightened, living a primitive life, and wholly without influence on national affairs. The Peasant movement endeavored to bring them to a full consciousness of their rights and the rôle they were called upon to play. Through the activity of this movement hundreds of schools and co-operatives were created.

Like the other two movements, the Peasant Party is firm in its belief in parliamentary democracy. Through it the peasant has been brought to realize that only by democratic and parliamentary institutions can he find his rightful position in a unified national life. This movement also demands the division of the land for the peasants. Another of its fundamental aims is to mitigate the over-congestion of the villages by industrialization and by bringing a portion of the peasantry into city life. One of their leaders, Maciej Rataj, who had been President of the Sejm of the Polish Republic for several years, was murdered by the Germans in 1940.

The fourth, the Christian Labor movement, is likewise democratic in consequence of its ideologic line. It is based chiefly on the Catholic Church. The realization of the doctrines set forth in papal encyclicals, national assigns, and the Catholic faith in general, is the chief aim and major determinant of the content of its program.

These parties had no place in the government that ruled Poland in the years preceding the present war. Interior political conditions did not permit them to take any action or to enter the elections. Those in power at the time held it to be a primal necessity that the structure of Polish politics be in conformity with the 'strong' regimes of its powerful eastern and western neighbors. They held that there was no place in Poland for parliamentary and democratic movements, and kept them out of the government. These in turn reacted by refusing to participate in the electoral system.

Paradoxically, while the Underground was a continuation of the Polish nation, at the same time it broke away from this prewar tradition and returned to the still older traditions of Polish parliamentary democracy. The political parties in the Underground had more power and freedom and were able to increase their activity beyond anything that was possible in prewar Poland.

These four political parties represented the vast majority of the Polish nation in the underground state. Of course there were other organizations, from the extreme right to the left which included the Communists. The majority of these organizations had been non-existent before they took root and flourished in the rich political freedom of the Underground. Conditions being what they were, it was difficult to analyze their scope and influence in the community, or the exact purview of their political programs. A great number of them were purely local in character. Nearly all made their presence felt by printing one or more secret newspapers.

When I arrived in Warsaw I was impressed by the same facts that I had noticed in Cracow. The consolidation of the Underground was proceeding rapidly and the inhabitants of the capital, including those in the highest positions, believed in the invulnerability of France and England. In my conversations I found that everyone firmly believed that the French Army had purposely allowed the present penetration of its soil by the Wehrmacht to give themselves the chance of encircling and destroying it. When I informed them that, while I was in France, no one had even suggested that the French Army had any other intention but that of holding its positions in the Maginot Line, I was called an alarmist.

I remained in Warsaw for about two weeks and then returned to Cracow for additional conferences before departing once more for France.

My chief work was concerned with the creation of a special center in the Underground, the office of the 'plenipotentiary of the government.' The creation of this office was contingent upon the acceptance of two basic principles: first, that no matter what course the war might take, the Poles would never agree to collaborate in any way with the Germans. Quislings were to be eliminated at all costs.[2] The second principle was that the Polish state was to be perpetuated by the underground administration which would be synchronized with the government-in-exile.

The so-called 'stiff attitude toward the occupants' simplified the problem of obtaining the consent of the people to the authority of the underground state. The German occupation was never recognized by the Polish people, and there could be no doubt on this score because, in Poland alone of all the occupied countries, there never appeared anything remotely resembling a legal or pseudo-legal body composed of Poles and collaborating with the Germans. Indeed, in all Poland, not a single political office in the German-controlled administration was ever held by a Pole; not a single head of any province was Polish.

The legal character of the underground state and the authority thus obtained facilitated the problem of dealing with actual or potential Quislings. When the Underground attained the peak of its development, the problem of collaboration was defined in precise terms as, in ordinary circumstances, a civil crime would be defined, and punishment was meted out in accordance with the ability of the Underground to carry out the sentences entailed.

The framework of the Underground was the result of all these circumstances. Once the principle of the continuity of the state was accepted, the necessity for the formation of a delegate of the government became apparent. The residence of the government outside the zone of danger also flowed from this principle of maintenance of continuity. I had earlier been present at innumerable debates in which the question of the location of the government had been thrashed out.

According to the tradition handed down from the Polish insurrections against Tsarist Russia in 1830 and 1863, the place of the government should have been directly within the underground movement. It was realized, however, that such a government would have to be secret and anonymous. Consequently, Poland would have no contact with her Allies and no method of pursuing a foreign policy. If this government were liquidated, moreover, it would be impossible to appoint a new government. Chaos would result. The final factor that determined the decision that the government should remain in exile for the duration was the realization that the Underground required a method for maintaining the technical continuity of the organization. This could be obtained by having the appointment of personnel emanate from a source beyond the danger zone. This system insured orderly continuance of underground activity against any losses suffered as a result of Gestapo encroach-ments. No matter what the rank or eminence of those who became casualties of war inside Poland, they could be replaced by an orderly, legal procedure.

Resolutions were also passed limiting the government's preroga-tive to the appointment of individuals previously sanctioned by the leaders of the Underground. This system was at once reciprocal and flexible. It maintained the power of those closest to the main activities and at the same time had an orderly safety, engendered by the fact that a ruling center existed outside the danger zone, which made possible the elaborate and harmonious development of the Polish underground state.

The greatest difficulty in the path of this development was occa-sioned by the fact that the parties which came to power in the Underground had not participated in the prewar government and had not entered the elections. It was consequently impossible to determine the exact degree of their popular strength and influence. Their estimates of their relative strength and importance in under-ground work naturally conflicted. It was readily apparent that the coalition of the four in the underground state had the support of the vast majority of the Polish people, but it was very often impossible to separate this common achievement into its component parts.

This was complicated by the fact that all four parties, as a result of their prewar experience, were anxious to safeguard their inde-pendence from any administration. From prewar times these parties distrusted the state administration. They did not want the govern-ment to interfere in their internal affairs and were anxious to keep complete control of their parties in their own hands. Steps had to be taken to reassure each party in the Underground that the adminis-tration created in the Underground would not be inimical to its interests and principles. It was of crucial importance for the repre-sentatives whom I met at Cracow and Warsaw to agree on the person who, as the plenipotentiary of the government in the Under-ground, would have very extensive powers.

A successful accord was finally reached on the persons for the chief plenipotentiary and the provincial delegates, though the process was difficult and complicated. Urgent stress was placed on the responsibility of these officers to all the political parties that were to constitute an underground parliament and control the personnel and budget of the administrative branch. A so-called 'political key' was decided upon to apportion the most important administrative posts among the parties. On my return to France, part of my mission was to report to the government there all the points of view of the various parties, the agreements and conditions under which their representatives in France would support Sikorski's government.

The second half of my mission consisted of what I consider to be the most honorable trust I ever received in my life. I was sworn to transmit all the most important secrets, plans, internal affairs, and points of view of *all four* of the political parties to their own representatives in France. In my oath I explicitly promised that I would not transmit any of this material to anyone but the persons designated by each party in Poland, that I would not use my knowledge against any of the parties politically, and that I would never exploit this information to further my personal career. My position amounted to that of a father confessor for each party.[3] As I have said, I regard it as the most honorable appointment I have ever received.

12

Caught by the Gestapo

I remained in Warsaw about two weeks altogether and then received instructions to start out again for France by the same route after stopping at Cracow. Accompanying me was a seventeen-year-old boy, the son of a Warsaw physician. His parents regarded my route as safe and had implored me to take the boy to France, where he would be able to join the Polish Army. I spent about three days in Cracow conferring with the underground authorities and then left for the frontier with the boy and a tiny roll of microfilm on which a message of thirty-eight pages of plans and suggestions for the organization of the Underground was photographed. The film was undeveloped and the text could be obliterated in an instant by exposing it to the light, if the need arose.

As I journeyed to meet my guide, I could not quite analyze certain misgivings I had about the trip. I was to follow a route with which I was thoroughly familiar, and my own experience was to be backed by that of a guide who had an excellent reputation. Nevertheless, there was something ominous in the air. My superiors in Cracow seemed to have been a shade too anxious in their warnings, too solicitous about my safety. Sitting in the train, traveling toward the frontier, I could not help glancing at my youthful charge and brooding about our prospects.

Once I'd reached Zakopane, I had to proceed several miles on foot in order to meet my guide. After I met him, I would be under his care. I would be, so to speak, his responsibility. For it was the rule for the underground authorities in each country to plan in detail the routes of their emissaries. Each courier has his own special route. His appointed guide knows all the intermediary stopping points along this route from the frontier where he takes over to the place where he delivers his man to the underground organization in the neutral country – Hungary, to be specific – beyond the danger zone. Till this point the guide is as if physically attached to his 'patient,' as the courier was often nicknamed in this relationship. He is not supposed to leave his ward for a single moment and the courier is wholly at the mercy of the guide while the latter's responsibility lasts.

When I met my guide, I noticed that he, too, seemed unusually worried about this trip, a trifle gloomy and reluctant. At first I thought it was my imagination, that this mood was merely a projection of my own, but he soon revealed the source of his foreboding. It appeared that his predecessor, who had been due back a week before, had not yet returned. In conversation, he seemed to be hinting at postponing our trip or casting about for some suggestion on my part to delay our starting out.

My mission was much too urgent, however. I gave his suggestions little attention and impatiently insisted on our immediate departure. The boy was with me. It was the end of May 1940. Holland and Belgium had fallen, and the Germans were marching on Paris. Although I believed, with nearly everyone in Warsaw, including the most well-informed, that France would hold and that Germany had over-extended herself in the offensive and would ultimately be crushed as a consequence, nevertheless, I could not help speculating on what the defeat of France would mean. I was by now accustomed to considering remote eventualities, since the improbable frequently materialized in underground work and did so with appalling results. I realized that if France were defeated, I would be left in mid-air somewhere in Europe with a seventeen-year-old boy. The entire liaison system between Poland and the government was based on continental routes. If France collapsed, this system would collapse with it.

The guide, although he never overtly counseled delay, continued to intimate his desire for it and express convictions which augured ill for our success. I continued to react impatiently, urging even greater haste. We had to wait for the weather to clear, however, and passed two days in my guide's cabin in the Carpathians.

On the last night before our departure, my guide went out to the village to make some inquiries. I ate supper in the company of my guide's father, an old but robust mountaineer, and his sister, a spirited girl of about sixteen. She knew all about her brother's activities, was very proud of him, and usually behaved very stoically about his affairs. But this evening she seemed depressed and behaved peculiarly from the moment she arrived.

After the meal, while we were sitting about in a glum, preoccupied silence, she beckoned to the young boy and asked him to go outside with her. This action startled me, but I could think of no valid reason for contradicting her. After about fifteen minutes, during which the old man and I maintained an unbroken silence, mutually embarrassed and scarcely glancing at each other, they returned.

The boy was pale and nervous, visibly struggling to control himself, although his youthful face betrayed his agitation all too plainly. The girl was red-eyed and solemn, her glance fixed timidly on the floor. I expected her father to scold her or at least to question her, but instead he got up from his chair and, to my surprise, led her outside the cabin. I was now thoroughly alarmed.

'What is wrong?' I demanded harshly of the boy. 'What sort of mystery is this? . . . What did she tell you?'

'It's nothing important,' he answered, his lip quivering and his voice almost breaking.

'Don't be foolish,' I said. 'You must tell me. I am responsible for your being here, you know.'

He stammered reluctantly. Bit by bit, I made him reveal their conversation. The girl had informed him that they feared the other guide had been caught by the Gestapo. If this was the case, the route was now extremely perilous. Her brother had warned her not to worry me, but she felt that at least the boy ought to be told and, if possible, prevented from undertaking the trip. She had told him to remain behind in the cabin and that it would not be long before he found another and safer opportunity to cross.

This was enough to bring me to a decision. I went out and confronted the father and daughter who were talking excitedly by the well. They confirmed the boy's story. The girl added that it would be nothing short of criminal to take the boy under such circumstances, since not only would he be in jeopardy but he would hamper us in case of an emergency. I told her that we would discuss the entire matter with her brother when he returned.

My guide entered shortly after this conversation and appeared to be in somewhat better spirits than before. The instant he arrived I confronted him with the facts in the presence of the others. I then informed him that, as far as I could see, it would be wisest to postpone the trip.

At that moment all his doubts disappeared and he became purely and simply the loyal underground agent who had received orders to take me across the border and whose duty was to do so, regardless of dangers.

'Postpone the trip?' He glowered at me. 'Are you mad? Because a couple of silly children jabber wildly, you expect me to cancel our plans?'

Then as his sister began to sniffle, he glared at her.

'Yah! Silly child! That's what you are!'

Despite the fact that I was irritated by this harshness, I nevertheless felt a good deal of sympathy for the guide. Obviously he meant no serious harm, but was torn by a conflict between his nervousness and his sense of responsibility. He was uneasy, distraught.

'Still,' I said, 'if what she says is true, we ought to use our heads. We ought to be careful.'

'Careful?' He repeated the word disdainfully. 'The best thing we can do is to get some sleep. Remember, according to regulations, the moment you report to me, I take over the command. I am responsible for the entire affair and I don't see any sense in arguing further and making ourselves nervous.'

'There happens to be a great deal that requires discussion,' I said, glancing at the boy, who sat nearly doubled up with strain and tension.

'As far as I am concerned, there is nothing further to discuss,' he growled angrily, and then, catching the meaning of my glance, added, 'my orders do not include the boy, so he will have to stay here. As for you, I think you had better get some rest. It is raining now, so we start in three hours. It's safer for us to travel in the rain, and from the way things look, it will keep up for several days.'

I was reluctant to leave the boy, for I had grown quite fond of him. He, too, appeared anxious to continue the trip and proudly resented any imputation that he might not have the necessary courage or stamina. After some heated conversation with him, I persuaded him that it was all for the best. I dozed off for an hour or two and was awakened by my guide.

'Get up,' he said. 'We must leave now.'

I dressed hastily and slung my knapsack on my back. Outside it was pitch-black and the rain slashed at our faces. My eyes were still heavy with sleep and passively I followed my guide. The earth had become a sea of mud and as we churned through it our boots became caked, making each step laborious. Unlike my companion, who advanced along the twisted, uneven path with sure feet, I would stumble often, lose my balance, and, at every other step, lurch heavily into him. Every time this happened, I fully expected him to curse or scowl, but he merely laughed at my clumsiness. He was in high spirits, humming snatches of folk-tunes under his breath, and occasionally turning to me to bless the weather which would relax the vigilance of the guards at the border.

'Pray that this downpour continues,' he called out. 'When it rains, the border guards stay indoors.'

As he had foreseen, we found that the downpour had kept the guards away from their posts and we crossed the border with Slovakia without incident and without trepidation.

The rain continued with intermittent violence for three days. We slogged along without exchanging a word except in case of necessity. The woods were soaked and the tedium of the march was unrelieved by the cheering warmth a fire would have afforded. We stopped occasionally in caves or shepherds' tents to snatch some rest. We would fling ourselves on the hard, damp ground and alternate, one standing watch while the other slept fitfully. When I suggested that we rest at some of the cabins established as stopping points, he refused, muttering:

'We'd better not. I have a feeling that it would be dangerous. Don't you city people have any endurance? Or common sense?'

On the fourth day, the sun broke through the clouds and the day became sticky and muggy. The woods steamed like an African jungle. Our tempers became increasingly irritable. My guide plodded along – stubborn, anxious, and vigilant. I followed him wearily, unable to match his stamina. One craving took entire possession of me – to get my shoes off. My feet had become swollen and each of the heavy hobnailed boots I wore felt like a vise clamped around my ankle and foot.

I bore up as long as I could, not daring to incur the guide's wrath by suggesting a halt. Finally my strength and patience gave out. I tapped him rather diffidently on the shoulder and said:

'I'm sorry, but it is impossible for me to continue this pace. I must get some rest. Isn't there some place we can be put up for the night?'

I was surprised that he did not become furious. Instead, he was mild and understanding. He put his hand benevolently on my shoulder and said:

'I know how tired you are. It hasn't been too easy for me, either. You must realize that we are only fifteen miles from the Hungarian border.'

'If it were at all possible I would try to make it,' I said. 'But fifteen or fifty, it makes no difference to me.'

The thread of his patience snapped.

'You think it makes no difference, eh? Let me tell you,' he said, grinding his teeth in suppressed fury, 'it's damned dangerous stopping over, even for a few hours. The Gestapo are certain to be on the lookout in these parts.'

'I think you are exaggerating the danger. There may be any number of reasons why the other guide did not come back – if that is still worrying you. In any case, even if he has been caught, he may not have talked.'

He eyed me narrowly as if he regretted ever having begun the trip with me.

'Have it your own way,' he shrugged gloomily. 'There is a village stopover where we can put up for the night.'

Then, gazing at me in a sort of mute appeal, he added:

'It will add another three miles to our trip.'

'Don't be so pessimistic.' I laughed weakly, trying to get on some terms of good fellowship with him again. 'You will probably enjoy this rest as much as I will.'

'I don't think so,' he said dourly, 'I won't feel good till we are on our way again.'

We walked along the trail for about a mile in strained silence. I was acutely uncomfortable. As we were about to turn up a path that led to a road, I summoned up enough courage to suggest to him that if he thought it was too dangerous to risk staying in the house, then he could direct me to it and camp nearby until morning, when I would rejoin him.

'You know well enough,' he answered quietly, 'that as soon as we begin this trip, we become one person. Whatever happens, it's my duty to stick with you until we reach Hungary.'

At this moment, although my fatigue made me resent his attitude, I could not help admiring him tremendously. He was obviously acting against his better judgment and his instincts of prudence, doing so with a discipline, a loyalty to the organization, and a resolute calm of which few men would have been capable. We reached the road and tramped over its hard surface for about an hour. The sensation was almost pleasant by contrast to the clinging mire through which we had been laboring like plow horses.

After a bend in the road, we saw the lights of a village evidently quite close to us. My guide stepped off the road and motioned me to join him behind a large oak tree. Resignation and sulkiness were mingled in his voice as he said to me:

'We can't walk into the village looking as we do. It's a small hamlet and we'll be noticed and talked about.'

'What do you think we ought to do?' I was conciliatory, anxious to please.

'Get rid of our knapsacks, shave, clean up, and make ourselves as presentable as we can.'

We searched about for a stream and, after about fifteen minutes, found a small brook. Flattening ourselves out on the bank, we washed and shaved. We scooped up some ground near an easily recognizable tree and buried our knapsacks. I refused to comply with his demand for me to do the same with my briefcase. It contained the important films and, somehow, I felt that I would not be able to rest if I let it get out of reach, even for a moment.

We found the hut, a stopping point for couriers, without any difficulty. Before the guide knocked, he eyed the house, the road, and the clump of trees from which we had just emerged. The door was answered by a short, chunky peasant, a Slovakian of Polish descent, beaming with good nature and a hospitality which expressed itself in a volubility which soon became irksome. I had only one desire – to tear off my clothes and sleep. My guide, however, had other thoughts. Before we could even seat ourselves in front of the roaring fire, he shot a series of questions at the peasant.

'Have you seen Franek? . . . When did you last hear of him? . . . Is there any news?'

'Whoa! Whoa!' the peasant shouted, roaring with laughter. 'You are running away with me.'

Then he scratched his head.

'Now let me see . . . Franek . . .'

The peasant's slow speech exasperated the guide.

'For Heaven's sake, tell me! When was the last time you saw Franek?'

'About three weeks ago, I think,' the peasant drawled.

'Well, what did he have to say?' the guide questioned him impatiently.

'Nothing much. He felt fine. He was on his way back from Hungary. Is anything wrong?'

The guide grimaced at this last naïve question and lapsed into moody silence. Franek, I conjectured, must be the predecessor whose failure to return had so upset my guide. The peasant looked from me to my guide and back again, shook his head in bewilderment and then trudged off to the kitchen, returning with brandy, sausage, bread, and milk. I swallowed a glass of the warming liquor and ate ravenously, although my guide merely picked at the food and sipped abstractedly at the liquor without swallowing much. He was obviously preoccupied with his misgivings. The peasant chatted on until I interrupted him with a request that we be permitted to go to sleep. He acquiesced, showing us, with heavy joviality, to our beds. I flung off my clothes hastily, slid between the cool, inviting sheets, and fell asleep instantly, my hand clutching the precious film under my pillow.

I had not slept for more than three hours when I was awakened by a loud outcry and the smashing impact of a gun butt against the side of my skull. I was stunned, utterly bewildered, and before I could recover my senses, I was jerked roughly out of the bed, onto my feet, by two uniformed Slovakian gendarmes. In the corner of the room stood two grinning German gendarmes. My guide was doubled up with pain and bleeding from the mouth. A sickening thought penetrated my consciousness – the films under my pillow. For a moment I was rooted to the spot, stricken by anxiety. Then, in a frenzied leap, I grabbed the films and flung them into a barrel of water near the stove.

The gendarmes at my side were frozen with fear, thinking, perhaps, that I had hurled a grenade or a bomb. Then, as nothing happened, one of the Germans walked to the barrel, plunged in his hand and fished out the roll of film. The other, a red-faced, thick-necked bull of a man, crashed the back of his heavy hand into my face. As I staggered back, he pounced on me, pulled me forward, and shook me violently from side to side, spitting questions at me.

'Where is your knapsack? – Did you come with anyone else? – Are you hiding anything?'

When I did not answer, he made me reel with repetitions of his previous blow. Across the room, I could see the guide undergoing a similar beating and questioning. At one point, his face streaming with blood, he looked up at the peasant, not in anger or hate, but in deep, resigned sorrow.

'Why did you do it?' he asked reproachfully.

The peasant shook his head inarticulately and blinked painfully as tears ran down his plump, coarse-grained cheeks. I did not believe he was a traitor. The girl's guess had been correct, I realized. Franek, the missing guide, must have been arrested. Under torture, he had probably revealed the complete route and all the stopping points. My guide's forebodings had been warranted. This was the bitter result of his adherence to me out of a sense of duty and loyalty, despite the clarity with which he had foreseen our dangers. I could have wept with shame. How could I have pressured him like that? Why hadn't I kept on going until the end of our journey?

As we were dragged out of the house, I kept shouting to him over and over:

'I am sorry! . . . I am sorry!'

I could see him smile weakly at me as if granting my plea and urging me to keep up my courage and faith. We were separated on the spot and dragged off in opposite directions. I never saw or heard of him again.[1]

13

Torture

I was taken to a prison at the Slovakian military barracks in Presov[1] and cast into a dingy little cell containing nothing but a straw pallet and a slop bucket. The Slovakian gendarmes lounged outside the bars, looking at me without emotion, without curiosity. I wiped the blood from my face and stretched out on the filthy pallet. The beating I had received, the blow of the gun butt, had stunned me.

Possibly they had no room in the ordinary prison at Presov, but it is more likely that they thought I would be more efficiently guarded in a military establishment. There were Slovakian soldiers in the same prison and from time to time I could hear their voices. They were obviously not criminals but were being punished for minor infractions of military discipline. They had some liberties, they could walk around in the prison yard, and could wash and clean themselves in the lavatories.

When my head cleared slightly I sat up, drew my knees up to my chest, and cupped my chin in my hands. An elderly Slovakian had taken the place of the two gendarmes and was gazing at me with a mixture of pity and simplicity that bewildered and even irritated me. For a fleeting moment I wondered if the Gestapo regarded me as an utterly insignificant case, not worth the trouble of Nazi guards. But my hopes were rudely shattered. Two men walked into my cell and yanked me brusquely to my feet. One of them deliberately spat on my bed as if to indicate his contempt, then ordered me to follow his companion.

I was taken to a small office, thick with cigarette smoke, in the Presov police station. It was sparsely furnished. At a square table was a thin, sandy-haired man poring over some papers. Against the walls of the room a few men sat, puffing negligently on cigarettes, talking to one another as if I were not present, as if I were an inanimate or invisible object. Strangely, my eyes were glued to the flakes of dandruff on the thin man's shoulders. I fidgeted about, shifting from one foot to the other, wondering whether the empty chair had been placed at the table for me. At length, the guard behind me bawled above the droning voices:

'Sit down, you dirty swine,' and pushed a huge fist into the small of my back. I stumbled into the chair.

So this was it, I thought – the Gestapo questioning about which I had heard so often. Up till then, the notion I had formed of Gestapo brutality was clear but vaguely unreal. It had never occurred to me that I could become an actual victim. The accounts I had heard of the horrible ordeals of my friends had always somehow remained in the realm of theory, wearing the fugitive aspect of a nightmare. But now it was here. I sat biting my lips in anxiety, clasping and unclasping my moist hands. My mind seemed blocked and powerless.

The thin man shoved the papers to one side and looked at me as if my presence added even more tedium to his irksome routine. He pushed some of the papers on the table toward me.

'Are these your papers?' he asked dryly.

I froze into inarticulateness. Any wrong answer, I felt, would be like a tiny breach in a dike – one false response, and then perhaps a flood. The pale-blue eyes of the man glittered dangerously. His thin lips twisted in a humorless smile.

'You don't like talking to us? . . . We aren't good enough for you?'

The room exploded into violent guffaws. The guard who was at my back leaped on me and squeezed my neck in his grip.

'Answer the inspector, you swine,' he roared. His fingers dug into my neck like claws.

'Yes, they are my papers,' I said. My voice seemed disassociated from my will, as if someone else were speaking through my vocal cords. The inspector bobbed his head up and down with elaborate sarcasm.

'Thank you. It is so good of you to acknowledge my question

with a direct answer. As long as you are in that frame of mind, my friend, you won't mind telling me the entire truth about your connection with the Underground?'

I answered promptly:

'I have no connections with the Underground. You can see by my papers. I am the son of a Lwow teacher.'

My papers were arranged in such a way that I was supposed to be the son of a teacher in Lwow, which was at this time under Russian occupation. The name was true, as were all details in the documents of the teacher's son, who, however, had previously escaped and was now abroad. So even if the Gestapo should try to establish my identity, they could not find out that I was not really the son.

The inspector leered at me sourly.

'I know, I know, isn't that clear from your papers? And for how long have you been the son of a Lwow teacher? Two months? . . . Three months?'

Again from the chairs lining the walls a chorus of titters and guffaws broke forth. Obviously the inspector was the humorist of the local Gestapo and an appreciative claque had gathered for this performance. It was not too bad as yet. I drew some comfort from the fact that the man's ostentatious buffoonery would give me intermittent breathing spells in which to formulate answers and dodge difficulties. I knew I was poor at a rapid-fire cross-examination and dreaded the moment when I would have to improvise quickly.

The inspector pursed his lips, obviously in contemplation of an especially brilliant sally of wit.

'So, you are the son of a teacher at Lwow. That makes you an intelligent man. We like to deal with intelligent men, don't we?'

His eyes roved about the room and, like trained dogs, the men smirked and nodded. He acknowledged his round of applause with the satisfied smile of an actor.

'Tell me, teacher's son,' he drawled, 'have you lived all your life in Lwow?'

'Yes.'

'It's a beautiful city, Lwow, isn't it?'

'Yes.'

'Some day you would like to see it again, wouldn't you?'

I maintained a stolid silence, knowing that any response at all would simply make me appear ridiculous.

'You don't care to answer that question?' the inspector asked softly. 'I'll answer it for you. Yes, you would like to go back. Tell me, why did you leave Lwow?'

The last question was added with exaggerated gentleness. I had been coached in my identity thoroughly and I responded with mechanical alacrity.

'Because of the Soviets. My father didn't want me to stay in Lwow while it was occupied by the Russians.'

He made a sympathetic grimace.

'Your father doesn't like the Russians, but you do?'

'I didn't say that. I do not like them either.'

'You like us better?' His tone was quizzical, sarcastic.

'Well' – I tried to appear puzzled, ingenuous – 'we trusted you more.'

'Trusted us more? You mean you don't any longer? How terrible!'

'It's not that I don't trust the German people . . . It's that I don't understand why I am not believed,' I said, acting confused. 'I merely wanted to get to Switzerland . . . to Geneva . . . to a friend in Geneva.'

He looked at me with mock credulity.

'You liked and trusted us,' he murmured ironically, 'but you wished to escape us? I am not a teacher's son. I don't understand you.'

This man was a buffoon but not without a certain cleverness. He could twist my remarks adroitly. I made an effort to maintain a completely grave and ingenuous expression.

'I am a student,' I said simply. 'War interfered with my studies. I have had enough of all this war; I wanted to go to Switzerland to study.'

'And not by any chance did you want to go to France to join the Polish Army?' he interrupted.

'No. I swear to you I wanted to go to Switzerland to live in peace until the end of the war. I did not want to fight you or anybody else. I wanted to study.'

'Yes, yes, go on,' he simpered. 'You intrigue me.'

Again roars of laughter. He held up his hand in the manner of an entertainer modestly acknowledging his applause but wishing to get on with the show.

'Tell me all,' he continued. 'Your trip must have been very interesting.'

'It wasn't interesting, exactly. My father and I discussed my leaving. Then, one day I crossed the Russian–German frontier and went to Warsaw. I wanted to escape the Russians at any price.'

'That was illegal, you know,' he said primly. 'You shouldn't do things like that.' Then, waving his hand, he added, 'I am sorry to interrupt. Please go on.'

I continued the tale without much heart. It was beginning to sound too pat, too foolish. However, I realized that if I tried to take a new tack it would merely land me in confusion.

'In Warsaw I met by chance a former schoolmate of mine and asked him to help me to go to Geneva. His name is Mika. He lives in Warsaw at 30 Polna Street. He was somewhat mysterious and told me to meet him the next day in a café. When I met him he promised to help me get to Kosice in Hungary if I delivered to a friend of his a film showing the ruins of Warsaw. I agreed and my friend gave me the film, forty-five dollars, and the address of a guide in a town near the frontier. That's all that happened until your men picked me up. It's the truth, I swear it.'

I gave him a false address and a false name in Kosice. But the name of my friend, Mika, in Warsaw, who was supposed to have helped me escape, was a true one. His address was also true. But I knew that my revelations could do him no harm because he had escaped from Poland three months ago.

At the beginning of my recital the inspector had tilted his chair back, clasped his hands behind his head, and closed his eyes as if he were about to hear an exceptionally sweet solo and wanted to enjoy it fully. When I had finished, his eyes opened slowly and his lips spread slightly into a grin of sardonic appreciation.

He looked to the side of the room and gestured to a man with a pad on his knees.

'Did you get the touching story all down, Hans? I don't want a word changed. I want to read it exactly as it is.'

Then his eyes focused on my face and he murmured:

'Neat, very neat. Won't you excuse me if I don't listen to any more? Tomorrow someone else will have the pleasure of hearing it. Your conversation with him will surely be a much more pleasant one.'

Then he turned and with a surprising change of voice growled to the brute behind me:

'Get that lying bastard back to his cell.'

The guard again dug his fingers into my neck and yanked me up. Then he pushed me violently. As I stumbled forward another man pushed me ahead. The other men joined in, each adding his contribution toward keeping me in motion, as if I were a ball with which they were playing. As I reached the door the guard encircled my neck in his heavy hand and flung me, head foremost, out of the door. This little trick nearly broke my neck. Tears of rage and humiliation made my eyes smart, but I managed to look at him impassively, even a trifle disdainfully.

When I arrived at my cell I found that an ingenious device had been rigged up for my benefit. A huge reflector had been fitted to a powerful bulb. The light from it was magnified and diffused over the entire cell, so that there was no escape from the powerful glare.

As I flung myself on my straw pallet the rigid control I had exercised in the office deserted me. My legs were weak and hollow, my muscles trembling with the reactions I had suppressed. I tossed about, trying to shield my eyes from the blinding light that poured from the reflector. It was impossible to order my chaotic thoughts or devise a plan.

I had no illusions that my story had been found credible or that the mildness of my first examination would continue for long. My story had been too pat, too glib, and at the same time, too feeble, to warrant their belief. Yet I knew I would have to stick to it if only to guard against the danger of revealing any important information.

I had to persist in my story as if it were a magical incantation which would prevent me from blurting out the damaging truth. Also, it was a sort of anodyne; it gave me positive relief to know I would not have to cudgel my brains to invent anything new. All night long the phrases of my story ran through my head in a monotonous rhythmic chant.

At dawn the guard who had escorted me on the previous day appeared in my cell. He was unshaven, his uniform unbuttoned and disheveled. Scowling fiercely at me to indicate that I alone was responsible for his being up so early, he jerked his thumb in the direction he wished me to take. I was blue with cold and sleeplessness. My teeth chattered and my knees nearly buckled as I walked.

We went to the room where the preliminary examination had taken place. Some alterations had been made in its furnishings. A small table had been set next to the large one. On it had been placed a sleek new typewriter, some pads and pencils. The chairs that lined the wall of the office had been removed. There were only four men in the room besides myself. Behind the larger table a padded swivel chair in shiny leather was occupied by a new official.

He was the type that one saw in Germany not too infrequently, but that was scarce in the Polish division of the Gestapo. He was an extraordinarily fat man, but his flesh seemed to have been smoothly molded from a single, uniformly rich substance. His fat curved rather than bulged. His face appeared more Slavic in origin than of the vaunted pure Nordic strain. His complexion was olive, his eyes narrow and black. He had high, sharp cheekbones which projected from the thick, soft contours of his cheeks, suggesting that he had been thin in his youth. A strong but closely shaven beard lent a bluish tinge to his heavy jowls.

This large face, from which the black, glossy hair had been brushed severely back and pomaded, with its cruel, pursed lips, made an extraordinary impression of contrasts, of gross power mingling with feminine delicacy and cruelty. A strong odor of pomade and lotions exuded from his person. His hands were, for a person of his bulk, surprisingly slender, the fingers tapering into well-manicured nails. He kept drumming on the table impatiently as he glanced around the room, his small eyes darting to and fro.

The other three were the usual, nondescript Gestapo guards – tall, well-muscled, and neatly uniformed. My blood ran cold as I noted that two of them held rubber truncheons.

'Sit down at this table,' the officer began, 'and tell us the truth. We are not going to harm you if we are not forced to do so. You will sit down opposite me. All the time you must look directly in my eyes. You are not allowed to turn your head or to look away. You must answer all my questions at once. You are not allowed to reflect. I warn you – it will be very bad for you if your replies are contradictory or if you try to think back over your lies to make sure you are telling your story as you told it before.'

These words came mechanically, as though he had said them innumerable times before.

As I sat down, I tried desperately to repress any signs of fear. However, I could feel a muscle in my cheek twitch uncontrollably and I kept licking my dry lips. His eyes passed over me restlessly, examining me thoroughly. I was restive under his inspection and his deliberately prolonged silence. The shifting feet and the heavy breathing of the guards made the room oppressive and tense with expectancy. Finally, heaving his body partially out of his chair like an elegant seal, he placed his elbows with finicky delicacy on the clean part of the table, pressed his fingertips together, and spoke in a subdued but resonant and mellifluous voice.

'I am Inspector Pick,' he said portentously. 'If you haven't heard of me, you can draw some comfort for a short while. I never allow a man to walk or crawl out of here without getting the truth out of him. If I fail, there is usually not enough left of a prisoner to be recognized as a man. I assure you, after a few of our caresses, you will regard death as a luxury. I don't beg you to confess. I don't give a damn if you do or don't. If you are sensible and tell the truth, you will be spared. If you don't, you will be beaten to within an inch of your life. I don't have the slightest respect for heroism. I am utterly unimpressed by the ability of some heroes to absorb an unusual amount of punishment. Now, I am going to begin your questioning. Remember, I don't want any hesitation. You get a fraction of a second to respond to a question. Each time you fail to answer promptly you will receive a painful reminder from the guards.'

This lengthy preamble seemed to exhaust him. Like a deflated balloon he collapsed back into the leather chair and rocked lightly back and forth.

'Do you know a man named Franek?' he purred indolently.

'Franek? . . . Franek? No, I don't think so.' My voice was evasive and shaky.

'I thought you would say that. But we won't give you your reward for your first lie – just yet. Franek was a guide for the Underground. We landed him a few weeks ago and he told everything – the routes, the stopping points. We know about pretty much all of you passing this way. What are you doing and why all this traveling? Do not deny your work in the Underground. It is useless. We expect you to tell everything you know . . . Herr Courier. Do you understand?'

I licked my lips. My throat felt sore and parched. Apparently he either knew or had guessed a great deal. I stared stupidly at him, and in a hollow voice I protested weakly:

'I don't understand you. I am not a courier.'

He nodded to the men behind me and clasped his hands on his stomach. This was the signal for one of the men to rap me sharply behind the ear with the rubber stick. A vivid, agonizing pain shot through my entire body as if a bolt of lightning had gone through me. Of all the beatings I have endured, I never felt anything to equal the instant of sheer pain produced by the impact of the rubber truncheon. It made every muscle in my body wince in sharp agony. It was something like the sensation produced when a dentist's drill strikes a nerve, but infinitely multiplied and spread over the entire nervous system.

A cry broke from me and I flinched away as I saw out of the corner of my eye the other truncheon being raised. The inspector held up his hand, warding off the blow.

'I think we'll give him another chance,' he said with a short laugh.

'He doesn't look like the type that can stand much punishment. Will you talk now?'

'Yes, but you won't believe me,' I mumbled. The pain of this paralyzing blow vanished fairly quickly, leaving only the memory and the sickening anticipation of a repetition. But my fatigue, the lack of food and sleep, the other blows I had received, and the sapping nature of the ordeal combined to make me dizzy and nauseous. I gagged and nearly toppled from my chair. The inquisitor recoiled with refined loathing.

'Get him out of here,' he shrieked at the men. 'Take him to a basin before he throws up all over the place.'

They dragged me from the chair and hustled me to a dingy washroom. I vomited into a smelly urinal, the muscles of my stomach contracting in tormented spasms. When I stood up weakly, one of the men handed me a bottle of brandy. I gulped a mouthful and they snatched it away from me and dragged me back to the chair. I collapsed into it, feeling drained of every ounce of energy, lifeless, and light-headed.

Inspector Pick dabbed at his mouth with a handkerchief.

'How do you feel?' he asked, his face wrinkled with repugnance.

'All right, I guess,' I said weakly.

'Then answer this. Where did you start your journey? Who gave you the papers and the film?'

'I told the other inspector,' I answered. 'I started from Warsaw. My friend, my schoolmate, gave me the film.'

'You insist on repeating this absurd story. You expect us to believe that the films showed only the ruins of Warsaw?'

'That's all it showed. I swear it.'

'Why did you throw it in the water if that was all it showed?'

I hesitated. My one source of strength lay in the fact that the film had been destroyed by the water. Except for the fake documents there was not a shred of material evidence against me.

'Answer me!' His voice, now high-pitched and exasperated, interrupted my reflections. 'Why did you throw it in the water?'

'I don't know,' I said in a timid voice. 'I thought I would protect my friend.'

'You thought it would protect your friend,' he sneered. 'How? Did it have his name written on it?'

'No. It was instinct, I guess, that made me do it.'

'Instinct? You are in the habit of doing things by instinct? You hid your knapsack by instinct, too, I presume?'

'I did not have a knapsack,' I denied this charge indignantly with an air of injured innocence.

'You're a goddamned liar!' one of the guards shouted and then crashed his fist into my mouth. I felt a tooth crack and loosen. Blood oozed out from my lips. I ran my tongue over my lips and then placed it against the loose tooth. Bemusedly I sucked it back and forth, trying to detach it altogether.

The inspector waved the guard away from me. He looked me over coolly, distantly.

'You expect us to believe that you hiked from the border for four days without any food?'

'It is the truth,' I said vehemently. 'Please believe me. We bought food from the peasants on the way.'

'I know you are lying,' he said with peculiar, oily pleasantness. 'We had men stationed at all the stopping points that Franek listed. We caught up with you near Presov. There were no peasants from whom you could have purchased food and you did not stop in any village or we would have caught you. Now, for the last time, where did you hide your knapsack?'

I turned the problem feverishly over in my mind. There was nothing incriminating in my knapsack. But I felt that once I started to change my story I would lose track of it easily, and might reveal something important if I was at a loss for words.

Again the sharp pain rocketed through me without warning as the rubber truncheon landed behind my ear. I slid forward from the edge of the chair, pretending to faint and crumpling to the floor. Inspector Pick's voice seemed to drone far above me like the hum of a distant plane.

'That fainting act won't get you anywhere,' he was saying. 'Those swipes behind the ear have been worked out by our greatest medical authorities. They are painful, I know, but you cannot faint or lose consciousness from them. Theatrical scenes will not change scientific facts.'

These professorial remarks on the effects of the blows, for some reason, evoked a frenzied and sadistic delight in the guards. Above their laughter, the voice of the inspector, shrill, excited, and disdainful, registered on my nerves.

'Get to work on him,' he shouted. 'Leave over just enough of him to be questioned.'

The guards pounced on me and propped me upright against the wall. A veritable barrage of fists thudded and crunched against my face and body. As I sagged, they supported me by holding me under the armpits. With the last remnant of my consciousness, I felt them release me and I collapsed on the floor in an insensible heap. They had overestimated my stamina and had not left over enough to be questioned.

They let me remain in my cell for three days without disturbing me. All my joints ached, my face was puffy and bruised, and the side where I had been kicked was sensitive to the slightest touch. I felt the hopelessness of my situation. I realized that it was obvious to the Gestapo that I was lying. During every hearing there were more and more questions which I could not answer. But I was persuaded that the only thing that could save me was sticking to my story.

The aged Slovakian who brought me food and water would encourage me to eat but I could barely manage to swallow the slop. The second morning he took me to the lavatory where I tried to wash the dried blood from my face. In the lavatory there were several Slovakian soldiers washing and shaving. Suddenly I noticed a used razor blade left on the window sill above the basin where I was washing. Almost automatically, without a clear purpose in my mind and without drawing attention to myself, I snatched it frantically and thrust it into my pocket. Walking to the cell and lying down, I clutched it feverishly. That night I fashioned a frame from a piece of wood that had been lying in the cell and carefully inserted the blade. It was an excellent weapon. I hid it in the mattress, thinking that it would be useful if the torturing were to continue.

At the end of the third day the Gestapo guards entered my cell. I expected the usual torrent of abuse and a beating, but somehow I felt suddenly defiant, almost contemptuous of them. This note of challenge must have been communicated to one of the men.

He scrutinized me and spoke venomously:

'I think you would like another session with us. Maybe you want to show us how tough you are. Well, I hope you get a chance. But today we have to pretty you up for a visit to an SS officer. Don't you feel important?'

Deadened as all my faculties had become, I reacted sharply to this news. I was ready to encourage the feeblest hope in myself, the faintest prospect of life and freedom. Perhaps they believed my story, I thought, or, as I had hoped before, they considered me an unimportant link – scarcely worth bothering about. I became even more cheerful when a barber entered to clean and shave me. While this was being done the guards took my clothes and shoes and brought them back brushed and cleaned.

Nothing dampened my optimism when I entered the office of the Schutz-Staffel man. He dismissed the guards curtly, even with a faint touch of loathing, then offered me a chair with patent graciousness and courtesy. As he walked over to dismiss a crippled soldier who was standing rigidly at attention at the other end of the room, I studied him eagerly, seeking a clue to the strategy I should employ.

I saw an extraordinarily handsome youth, not more than twenty-five, tall, slender, with long blond hair that fell with premeditated charm over his forehead. He had cultivated an attitude of cool, offhand masculinity. At other times, I would have been amused by the minute effort he made to fulfill each detail of this carefully worked-out pose. His uniform was a resplendent affair, meticulously tailored and garnished with ribbons and medals. His superiors had undoubtedly cast him as an archetypical specimen of youthful Prussian Junker[2] and he strained to fulfil his obligations.

He walked toward me with a firmly regimented stride as if his personality had been split, with one part functioning as a harsh taskmaster perpetually observing and grading the behavior of the other.

Something about him fascinated me. This was the genuine article, so authentic a product of Nazi education and Prussian tradition as to be vaguely unreal. Movement in him became incongruous, as if a sculpture of glorified Nazi youth had stepped off its pedestal.

I was utterly amazed when he came close to me, laid a gentle hand on my shoulder with a touch of youthful embarrassment, and said with palpable solicitude:

'Don't be afraid of anything. I am going to see to it that no harm comes to you.'

The candid charm of this speech upset all my expectations and made me slightly clumsy. I stammered out something sounding like surprised thanks.

'Please don't thank me,' he replied. 'I can see that you are not the type of man we usually get here. You have culture and breeding. If you were a born German, you would probably be very much like I am. In a way, it is a pleasure to meet someone like you in this Godforsaken hole of a Slovakian village where there are only fools and lice.'

My brain was working at top speed, trying to fathom the purpose of this new approach. None of my friends who had been caught up in the Gestapo dragnet had ever mentioned an interview even remotely resembling this one. I replied to his speech with extreme wariness, like a man stepping across a field full of holes in the dark.

'May I say,' I said cautiously, 'that you seem to be different from those I have encountered here?'

The response to my remark, which I awaited nervously, consisted only of a frank, direct stare, evincing neither approval nor disapproval. He inclined his head to me and said quietly:

'Will you please come to my room with me?'

For a moment it was as though I had a choice. I accepted the offer and we walked through a musty corridor, the untidiness of which seemed to disturb him, for he kept patting his uniform as if he were removing dust specks. The room to which he conducted me was furnished in old-fashioned Germanic style, apparently redecorated for his special use.

The table was of stout mahogany, severe in design and richly finished. The capacious armchairs and an overstuffed couch were upholstered in maroon with a border fringed in gold. The walls, painted a somber yellowish-brown, had been decorated with huge enlargements of photographs of Baldur von Schirach, the leader of the Nazi youth movement and Heinrich Himmler, the Gestapo chief. On the wall above his desk was suspended an old Germanic sword. I averted my gaze from these portraits to a third somewhat smaller picture of an aristocratic, delicate, middle-aged lady with a young girl whose features and blonde hair clearly resembled those of the man before me. He helped complete my idle speculations.

'They are my mother and sister,' he vouchsafed. 'My father died five years ago.'

There was a moment of constrained silence. Despite his air of self-confident masculinity, he was obviously not a veteran in this branch of Nazi inquisition. He seemed to be floundering about, seeking a proper approach to whatever problem I represented for him. His uncertainty put me at an equal loss. With an air of abrupt determination, assumed, I felt, to cover his confusion, he pointed dramatically at the picture of Schirach.

'Look at him,' he said bitterly, a hurt expression on his face. 'A wonderful-looking man. Isn't that so? Once I worshipped him. I thought I was his favorite . . .'

He ceased talking and paced the floor restlessly. During this war, I have seen many men of impassive, even steely exteriors, who, exceptionally taciturn and reserved on the surface, were yet nearly bursting with the desire to talk about themselves. This lieutenant behaved as if he had been aching for a long time to confide in someone who was not close enough to him to be dangerous. He talked to me in a confidential manner that was inexplicable to me.

I knew that recipients of similar confidences often suffered for the privilege of listening to them. Men like this young lieutenant are usually ashamed later of their sentimental behavior and end by resenting and hating the person who witnessed their weaknesses. There was, however, no conceivable way to stop him. He placed a chair in front of me, sat down, and, leaning forward close to me, plunged into a recital of his life. From time to time, he would get up as the recollection of some incident provoked an intense emotion in him and when this subsided, he would sit down again.

He had been raised in a typical Prussian household. A delicate and sensitive child, he had developed an intense hatred for his stern, tyrannical father who had been contemptuous of his frailty. His mother and sister adored him. After a hard day under his father's strict regimen, they would comfort him and urge him to obey the severe discipline his father imposed. When he was seventeen, he was sent to an *Ordensburg*, one of the famous Nazi colleges, in which the elite of the new order were trained. At that time, before Hitler's rise to power, this *Ordensburg* had been operated secretly.

His eyes blazed fanatically as he told me about the *Ordensburgen*, and his voice became hoarse with emotion as he relived the events of those years. When he was a student in this Germanic 'monastery,' he met Baldur von Schirach, who selected him for his favorite, visited him frequently, and took him for long, intimate walks in the surrounding forests. In his third year at the college, he had been superseded in Schirach's favor by a boy who, as Schirach had told him, sang old Germanic songs more beautifully than he and was, besides, the best discus thrower in the school.

Recounting this incident seemed to reopen an old wound, the pain it gave him causing him involuntarily to shade his eyes as if a powerful light were being flashed into them. The recital came to a sudden end.

'I became an SS officer,' he said, returning to the job at hand, 'and I am proud of the work I am doing. I wanted to see you because you impressed us. I am sure we will come to an understanding. I beg you to believe that I am not going to do anything to harm you personally, nor shall I ask you to betray anybody or to become our agent. The matter I want to talk over with you is of vital importance for the future of Poland.'

At last the purpose of this unusual interview became clear. I was to be converted to the new order by this offspring of purest Nazi breeding. I said nothing, trying desperately to work out an inoffensive response to this implied invitation to confess and confide in him. Although a great deal of his candor and charm had been provided for the purpose of luring me into the fold, I felt sure that this display was not entirely an act contrived solely for my benefit. It had too genuine and passionate a ring.

For an instant I hoped that when his efforts proved fruitless and I failed to succumb to the alluring offers, he might still like or respect me sufficiently to intervene on my behalf. It did not take much reflection to clear my head of this delusion. Apart from the plain psychological fact that he would turn on me all the more venomously because I had been the recipient of his confidences, I realized that he had been thoroughly indoctrinated with the Nazi principles of power and cruelty.

He continued in his former vein of reminiscence, at once candid and boastful.

'You know,' he said, 'the National Socialist Party, at its inception, was based on purely masculine ideals. We have a purely masculine ideology.' Then he added proudly, 'When I went to the *Ordensburg*, I never spoke to a girl and have never gone out with one except in the line of duty. I like to talk frankly, man to man, and I'm sure we'll get on together.'

After this remarkable speech he strode to a chest in the corner of the room, brought out a decanter of brandy, and offered me a drink and cigarettes. In a fresh access of geniality he gave me a drink, lit my cigarette, and pulled his chair closer to me.

'Well, let's get down to business,' he said smilingly. 'First, I ought to tell you – I had your status changed to that of a military prisoner and have issued instructions that you be treated accordingly.'

'Thank you,' I replied.

'Not at all. You aren't, after all, a criminal, and I am positive that after you hear me out you will wish to work with us and not against us.'

I ventured a mild protest.

'I have never worked against you, as you put it. Surely you will believe me when I say that I have nothing to do with the Underground . . .'

He interrupted me and looked a bit grimmer.

'Please don't bother going through that rigamarole. We have conclusive evidence, which I shall soon show you, that you are a courier for the Underground.'

He looked at me, waiting to see if I would continue in my denials. As I maintained silence, he patted me on the knee.

'That's better, old man. Don't make a fool of yourself by denying the obvious.'

Then, shaking his head in genuine bewilderment, he continued:

'I can't for the life of me understand the stubbornness of you Poles at the present time when you are now in a simply hopeless situation. France has fallen, England is bidding for a negotiated peace, America is thousands of miles away.'

His eyes clouded with a faraway look as he sipped his brandy. Then he rhapsodized:

'Very soon the Führer will dictate peace in London. In a few years, he will proclaim the New Order on the steps of the White House in Washington. The new peace will be permanent, not like the lying, hypocritical promises of the Judeo-democratic plutocracies. Pax Germanica, the peace Nietzsche and all the great thinkers and poets who have worked for the New Order dreamed of. I know all the world fears us. They are wrong. We do not want to harm anybody.' Then suddenly changing his tone he continued, 'With the exception of the Jews, of course. They will be exterminated. This is the Führer's will. For the non-German world we want to do justice and we will do justice. For work, bread, and life. For loyalty to the Third Reich, we will permit participation in our new civilization. As you see, our conditions are generous.'

The brandy, the heat of the room, the intense, emotional speech of the lieutenant had fatigued me. I felt drowsy and slightly drunk. I cut into his speech rather rudely.

'I've heard most of that before,' I said. 'What do you want of me?'

If my tone was insolent, he didn't detect it, so wrapped up was he in his glowing visions of the future. He pulled himself together and assumed an air of firmness – the air of the determined realist and administrator in a position of responsibility.

'We wish to be fair to you,' he said. 'We know who and what you are. You are carrying information from the Underground to your leaders in France. But I am not going to ask you to betray your nation, your leaders, or your friends. We do not want to punish them. We want to collaborate with them. We want to be able to contact them to persuade them of the benefits of a thoroughgoing Polish–German collaboration. We will guarantee their safety, on our German word of honor. You yourself shall be the intermediary in making such contacts. If you love your country, you will not reject this proposition. It is your duty to give your leaders an opportunity to discuss the present situation with us. Look at the other occupied countries. In each of them there are men of realistic understanding who have entered into collaboration to the great advantage of themselves and their country. You Poles are a strange exception – unhappily for yourselves. What I am proposing to you is not dishonorable or unworthy.'

He looked at me encouragingly, his face contorted with excitement and supplication, and added solemnly:

'Do you accept my proposal?'

I replied softly, surprised at my own firmness.

'I cannot accept. For two reasons. I don't believe that the results of force can achieve anything but evil. Collaboration can be based only on mutual respect, freedom, and understanding. Besides, even if I found your principles acceptable, there is nothing I could do. You have over-estimated my importance. I know nothing of the Underground or its leaders. Believe me when I tell you that.'

He looked at me with such fanatical savagery and contempt that I felt I had been utterly foolhardy in my response. I could have wavered, temporized with his offers, but the atmosphere of frankness and subtlety influenced me with artless boldness.

'You persist in that stupid comedy?' The lieutenant's voice became controlled, each word was measured and struck home like the lash of a whip. He rang a buzzer alongside his chair. The crippled soldier hobbled in, glanced at me curiously, and then turned to the officer, who said:

'Heinrich, bring me the film and send the Gestapo guards in.'

As the soldier hobbled out the lieutenant walked about the room, muttering to himself and flashing looks of hatred at me that had an actual personal quality. I could see that he despised me, not solely as an intransigent enemy of his country, but as one who showed himself unworthy of collaboration and who had deceived him.

The soldier came into the room, followed by the two Gestapo men. He handed some prints to the lieutenant, who in turn handed them over to me.

'These are enlarged prints of the films you threw into the water. We saved a small portion of them – a small but important portion. Look at them.'

I took the films with trembling hands. For a moment I thought I would go mad with rage and impotence. I recognized the prints as the last three pieces of my Leica film. I understood. The water had not soaked through the entire roll. I looked at the prints. Nothing had been set in code except for the names and places. Everything had been plainly written out, but fortunately, the three pieces they were able to save contained nothing important or dangerous. I must have failed to control my emotions. The man who had given the films to me had had no time or was too careless to put the text into ciphers. My dominant reaction was not fear but rage that I could not denounce him for his carelessness. The officer regarded me searchingly.

'Do you recognize this text?' he asked. 'I am still frank with you. Thirty-five pieces were destroyed. The gendarmes who allowed you to throw this film in the water were sent to the front – I hope they will behave better there than in our services. Now I expect you to tell me what was in the rest of the film.'

I answered in a choked, desperate voice. 'No, I can't. There must be some mistake . . . I must have been misled.'

He became livid with rage.

'You'll never stop that idiotic drivel about your innocence, will you?'

He walked to the corner of the room, reached into the chest, from which he had not long before taken the brandy, and extracted a riding whip.

'A short time ago,' he shouted furiously, 'I spoke to you man to man, as a Pole whom I could respect. Now you are nothing but a dirty, whining coward, a hypocrite, and a fool.'

He slashed the whip across my cheek. The Gestapo men flung themselves on me and drove their fists into me. The world crumbled about me as I received their orgiastic blows.

In my cell, it was without any sense of triumph that I realized I had again survived a Gestapo beating. Lying on the pallet, everything that my body touched contributed to the throbbing pain that spread from head to foot. Running my tongue across my bleeding gums, I felt, without any emotion, that four of my teeth had been knocked out. My face felt inhuman, an ugly, bloody, distorted mask. I realized that another beating would probably kill me and I burned with humiliation and impotent rage.

I knew that I had arrived at the end. That I should never be free again, that I should not survive another beating, and that in order to escape the degradation of betraying my friends while I was half-conscious, the only thing for me to do was to use the razor blade and to take my own life.

I had often wondered what people had in mind when they died for an ideal. I was certain that they were absorbed by great, soaring thoughts about the cause for which they were about to die. I was frankly surprised when I discovered it was not so. I felt only overwhelming hatred and disgust which surpassed even my physical pain.

And I thought of my mother. My childhood, my career, my hopes. I felt a bottomless sorrow that I had to die a wretched, inglorious death, like a crushed insect, miserable and anonymous. Neither my family nor my friends would ever learn what had happened to me and where my body would lie. I had assumed so many aliases that even if the Nazis wished to inform anyone of my death they probably could not track down my real identity.

I lay down on the pallet, awaiting the hour when the Slovak would complete his rounds. Till then my purpose seemed to have formed itself. I had hardly reasoned or reflected, merely acted on the promptings of pain and the desire to escape, to die. I thought of my religious convictions and the undeniable guilt which would be mine. But the memory of the last beating was too vivid. One phrase dominated my mind. *I am disgusted, I am disgusted.*

The guard had finished his rounds. I took out the razor and cut into my right wrist. The pain was not great. Obviously, I hadn't hurt the vein. I tried again, this time lower, this time cutting back and forth as hard as I could. Suddenly the blood streamed like a fountain. I knew I had got it this time. Then, clutching the razor in my bleeding right hand, I cut the vein on the left wrist. This time it was easier. I lay on my bed with my arms outstretched at my sides. The blood spurted out evenly, forming pools beside my legs. In a few minutes I felt I was getting weaker. In a haze I realized that the blood had stopped flowing and that I was still alive. In fear of being unsuccessful, I flung my arms about to make them bleed again. The blood flowed in thick streams. I felt as though I were suffocating and tried to draw breath through my mouth. I became nauseous, retched, and vomited. Then I lost consciousness.

14

The SS Hospital

I have no idea how long I remained unconscious. I returned to my senses only gradually. Blurred impressions began to seep through the dull pain that blanketed me, shutting off the world. At first my consciousness could register only a few painful, physical facts. The inside of my mouth and my tongue were cracked and inflamed and exuded a bitter taste. A monotonous, inescapable ringing troubled my ears. Feebly, I tried to determine the nature of my surroundings, but something held back my effort. My will was impeded by an agency that acted to seal off all new sensations and return me to the oblivion from which I struggled to emerge.

Against this unremitting pressure, this ceaseless urge to let go and fall back into darkness, I forced myself into awareness bit by bit. One thing became clear. I was not in my cell. I was lying on a hard wooden slab and not on the filthy pallet of straw.

My body was rigid, cramped. I tried to twist over on my side. I encountered resistance of some kind. Again I wrenched, with greater violence. I still could not move. My muscles contracted in a sudden panic. I felt sure that I was paralyzed, that some injury to my nerves had affected me so that my body could no longer execute the commands of my brain. Frenzied now, I lashed my body about until I felt something cutting into my flesh in several places. It dawned on me that I was securely tied to a wooden slab. Inappropriately, a grim bit of humor entered my mind. My Nazi captors, it occurred to me, must have credited me with the prowess of one of their own fabled supermen.

This thought was astringent, rejuvenating my will to perceive. I forced my eyes slowly to open and focus on the objects about me. A powerful glare beat down on my eyeballs, making them water and blink. Suspended from the ceiling by a wire, a lamp dangled. It had been shaded in such a way as to concentrate its beams on me, as if I had been spotlighted on a stage.

I felt exposed and humiliated. A face loomed above me, magnified out of all proportion. Then, above a ringing sensation in my ears, I heard a voice speaking Slovakian.

'Don't be frightened. You are in a Slovakian hospital. We are going to make you well. In a moment you will receive a blood transfusion.'

His words registered like an icy shock and I managed to speak.

'I don't want a transfusion. Let me die. I know you don't understand, but please let me die.'

'Be quiet. Everything will be all right.'

I remember praying that I would not come back to life. Death was the consummation of all my desire. I wanted no more of the struggle. All I wanted was the blackness where physical pain did not matter.

The doctor, for I was now able to see that he was garbed in the conventional white gown, moved away, and beyond the spot where he had stood I saw the broad, menacing back of a Slovakian gendarme, hunched over a newspaper. My inspection of the room came to an abrupt end. The doctor moved back into my line of vision and this time I noticed that he was a short, compact man. A sharp instrument jabbed into my leg. I tried to pull away.

'This will do you good,' the doctor said.

I tried to stop them, tear away from their hands and, twisting in a last burst of resistance, I fainted.

When I awoke, I found myself in a small, narrow room with three other patients, all Slovakian. There was a sharp, unpleasant odor of carbolic acid and iodoform. It was late at night, a bright moon illumining the beds and their occupants. My three roommates turned restively in their beds, emitting loud snores. One bald, pinch-faced man groaned occasionally in the throes of a nightmare.

I sat up in my bed, surprised at the absence of pain. Apart from the slight pressure in my temples, my body was steeped in a luxurious torpor. With difficulty, I roused myself to the contemplation of the possibility of another attempt at suicide or of escaping. I glanced about the room. Apparently it had been left unguarded. Then, through the half-open door I noticed the omnipresent blue-uniformed figure of the Slovakian gendarme still bent over his newspaper. Exhausted and discouraged, I let my head fall back on the pillow.

In a rambling, disconnected fashion, I began to speculate on my prospects. There was little hope for me. Even if a chance of escape should present itself, I doubted whether I could muster sufficient strength to take advantage of the opportunity. Soon, it occurred to me, I would probably be facing the Gestapo torturers again. I resolved to make another attempt at suicide. With whatever shred of comfort I could draw from this decision, I fell asleep.

Next morning a cheerful feminine voice awoke me. A nun was standing at my bedside, holding a thermometer. She placed it in my mouth and whispered:

'You understand Slovakian?'

The thermometer between my lips, I mumbled an affirmative. Slovakian is very much like Polish and I understand almost every word.

'Listen carefully,' she said. 'It is better to be here than in prison. We will try to keep you here as long as possible. Do you understand?'

I understood the words but could not quite fathom the purpose behind them. The desire to question her made me remove the thermometer from my mouth. She replaced it sternly, placed her finger on her lips, and shook her head in admonition.

'Now I shall have to take your temperature all over again. You must learn to behave.'

In the next week I made considerable progress toward regaining my health. My general physical condition was much improved, although I could not yet do anything with my hands, even feed myself. Splints held my wrists rigid and the yards and yards of white bandages gave the appearance of white boxing gloves. I remembered the sister's words, however, and pretended a weakness I felt less and less each day.

The days I spent in that Slovakian hospital in Presov were perhaps the strangest of my life. My convalescence inspired mingled emotions in me. A keen exultation and a nearly rapturous sense of returning strength alternated with fits of despondency at the recurring dread of another questioning by the Gestapo. It became increasingly irksome to feign helplessness. I longed to get out of bed, move about, walk, and sit outdoors in the sunshine. It was difficult to repress these normal desires and I was impatient with the constraint of doing so.

Although the Slovakian doctor and nuns were kind to me and exceedingly considerate of my wants and needs, I was wary of conversation. The eternal presence of the Gestapo agents did nothing to inspire a desire on my part for any exchange of confidences. Besides, I believe that I had an unconscious resentment toward the doctor – first of all, that he had seen me in the state of emotional upset the night of the transfusion, and secondly, for his brisk, professional dismissal of my desire to die that night. But as the days passed, I realized that they were sincere in their desire to help me.

To my astonishment, it developed that nearly everyone in the hospital had heard of me. The patients frequently expressed their sympathy by sending little gifts of chocolates and oranges. The Gestapo agents who were assigned to guard my room did little to disturb me. With the complacency of overfed watchdogs, they spent most of their time dozing in chairs propped against a wall in the corridor.

On the fifth day, lying inertly in bed became intolerable. When the sister who had held the thermometer in my mouth the first day appeared, I implored her to bring me a newspaper. She glanced warningly at me but finally consented. She stepped into the corridor to request permission of the guard. He growled his consent and it was not long before she returned with a neatly folded copy of a Slovakian newspaper. I looked at the paper with avid expectancy. The headline, in huge black letters, exploded inside my brain like a bomb. *France Surrenders!* it read.

Word by word, for I could not read Slovakian well enough to

understand a phrase or a sentence in a glance, I read the account beneath the headline. I read it over and over, as if repetition might change what I thought had been a lie of the SS lieutenant. The report was brief. Marshal Pétain had signed an armistice in the Forest of Compiègne. French resistance had completely crumpled. The aged marshal had called on his countrymen for absolute obedience. Collaboration . . . Germany had mastered Western Europe.

It took me a few minutes to read and grasp the facts. And then I knew real despair. For hundreds of years we have been bound by historical and cultural ties that made France, to us Poles, more than a country. France was almost another motherland to us, and we loved her with the same deep, unreasoning love with which we loved Poland. Moreover, we had based the hope for Poland's freedom on a French victory. Now I could see no hope.

Then I realized – the article contained *no* information on the fate of Great Britain. I searched the pages feverishly until I came to the word England. I read further: *England Commits Suicide* . . . Then this really was the end. I finally managed to read the entire line. The whole world changed; I wanted to rise up so that I could kneel to pray because it said: *England Commits Suicide by Continuing to Resist.* I prayed the way all free people were praying those days, I suppose, but with a passion known only by those who have been defeated. I prayed that Churchill be given strength for the trials he was undergoing, for the steadfast and stubborn resistance for Britain's fighting men, that they would never admit defeat, and I prayed for courage for all those who did not rest in this struggle. Everything else became secondary to the prime fact, England had not surrendered, England resisted.

The article contained little additional information. I let the paper slide to the floor and closed my eyes.

Each day, when the doctor came to my room to examine me, I begged him for further news about England. Often he could not talk. The guards were near. But while bending over me, he managed to whisper a few words in my ear. He told me about Dunkirk, about the bombing of England. He told me of the coming German invasion, low civilian morale in England, strife within the British Government. The news was bad and he was pessimistic. England would have to surrender in a few days. Germany is invincible.

But I was not dismayed. I had the feeling that his information had been gleaned from German sources and I knew of Goebbels' ability to twist into the fabric of truth any fancies which suited the Nazis' purpose. I made no comment. I knew England. I had been there in 1937 and 1938. There were things I disliked in their national character – they were stiff and dry, many did not understand continental Europe and did not care to. But they were also stubborn, strong, realistic. A Frenchman or a Pole, with an exaggerated love for the grand gesture, might commit suicide for a lost cause. An Englishman, never. Even Dunkirk, shocking as the news was, could not shake my conviction. I knew that this nation of businessmen, organizers, colonizers, and statesmen had the ability to evaluate their own strength, that they knew where and how to utilize their potentialities. They do not gamble recklessly with a worthless hand. If they still resist, I told myself, it is because they have calculated and seen a chance of winning. I was not interested in their idealism; I had seen idealism too easily crushed by the Nazis. Perhaps it was not just on England, but it was on British common sense alone that I pinned all my hopes.

On the seventh day early in the morning two Gestapo men stamped into my room. One flung a bundle of clothes on my bed and then turned to his companion.

'Help him get dressed – and hurry. I don't feel like hanging around this morgue all day.'

The shorter of the two, a bald, middle-aged, and scrawny individual, swaggered to the bed. I said nothing and lay there with my eyes half-closed, feigning utter exhaustion. His face reddened with anger.

'Get up, you Polish swine!' he roared. 'We know you are faking.'

His roar was heard by the doctor who hurried indignantly into the room.

'What's all this commotion? What do you mean by trying to get him out of bed?' he snapped at them. 'He is a very sick man. He can't be moved.'

'Oh, can't he?' the tall guard lounging in his chair drawled insolently. 'Look, doctor, you take care of your pills. Leave the prisoners to us.'

'But I tell you,' the doctor remonstrated futilely, 'if you take him out of here, he won't last. He must have further treatment.'

The tall one shook his head in mock solicitude, while his companion grinned vacantly.

'I'll write to his mother . . .'

The doctor was livid with suppressed rage. He jerked the clothes from the short one's hand.

'I'll help him dress,' he said curtly. The two Gestapo men sat down and lit cigarettes. While the doctor buttoned my shirt, he whispered in my ear:

'Act as sick as you can. I'll telephone.'

I nodded imperceptibly, signifying my comprehension.

We walked through the dimly lit corridor, the Gestapo men supporting me. My arms were still encased in splints and had to be held stiffly at a distance from my body. As soon as we emerged from the hospital, I pretended to be on the verge of collapse. I staggered and reeled in the blinding sunlight. They put their arms around my body and, swearing under their breath, shoved me into a sleek automobile that was waiting in front of the hospital.

We drove off. The keen air coming through the window revived me. Surreptitiously I drew deep breaths. But each time I felt their eyes upon me, I displayed new symptoms. My acting must have been convincing. The tall one, who dominated the other, commanded the driver to slow down.

'Watch those bumps,' he growled. 'We don't want this bird to have a hemorrhage . . . We must have him in good shape . . .'

He grinned malevolently.

We approached the prison gates. The gray walls loomed up before me, grim, dreadful, and utterly devoid of hope. I cast about wildly for a chance to hurl myself out of the car. Before I could reach a decision the wheels were grinding to a halt. The short one nudged me.

'Get out, darling,' he smirked idiotically. 'You've come home.'

I peered at them as though I had lost all control of my volition and sat there rigid and unresponsive. The tall guard opened the door and stepped out. The other spun me about and pushed me through the door into the arms of his waiting colleague. They dragged me forward to the door of the prison office. As we crossed the threshold I caught a glimpse of one of my former inquisitors, the specialist in urbanity. Then I stumbled deliberately, pretended to collapse, and sagged to the floor in a heap.

The youthful Gestapo official prompted them ironically.

'How long are you going to stare at him? He won't float up to his cell. If it isn't asking too much, would you please install him in his cell and then take him some water?'

Muttering under their breath, they lifted me up. None too gently, they carried me to the cell and deposited me on the bed. One of them fetched some water and splashed it over my face and body. Then they both left. Their heavy footsteps echoed down the corridor. When I could no longer hear them, I turned over on my side and tried to get some sleep.

After tossing restlessly for a while I gave up the attempt and opened my eyes. A series of faint smudges on the wall attracted my attention. As my vision became accustomed to the gray light of the cell, the smudges assumed a definite shape. I was looking at a cross I had drawn with soot in this very cell a little while before I had severed my veins. Under it I had inscribed a line from a poem I remembered vaguely from my childhood:

'My beloved Motherland . . . I love you.'

I repeated these words over and over again to myself, deriving a strange, lulling effect from this incantation, until I drifted off into sleep.

After two or three hours I awoke refreshed, my nerves quieter. Sitting in the cell was the gaunt, kindly Slovakian guard, a round parcel balanced on his knees. He greeted me softly but with great warmth.

'I am happy to see you,' he began and then broke off in confusion. 'I don't know what I am saying, I'm such a clumsy old fool. I mean . . .'

'I know what you mean,' I smiled. 'Thank you, my good friend.'

He unwrapped the parcel and handed me a thick slice of white bread and an apple.

'It is from my wife,' he said.

'Thank her for me.'

'But you eat. You must be hungry.'

He waited with an instinctive courtesy until I had finished eating. Then he shook his head slowly and reminiscently.

'I shall never forget the day I found you in the cell, blood spurting from you like from a hose.'

'Were you the one that found me?' I asked almost reproachfully. 'How did you know what I was doing? It was not the hour of your rounds.'

'I heard you groaning and vomiting,' he explained. 'I looked through the judas and saw you lying all crumpled and covered with blood. You should not do a thing like that,' he added solemnly. 'It is a sin and everyone has some reason to live.'

Our conversation languished, while I thought how easy it was to think philosophically about pain and torture if they happened to someone else. How could one explain that after a certain stage of pain had been reached, death became the aim of insensate longing, the greatest of privileges. I tried to make this clear to him, pointing out in the simplest terms that men really face a combination of intolerable pain and a totally black future. He listened attentively and when I finished he clasped his hands about his knees and rocked back and forth on the stool, pondering my remarks.

'I still believe,' he said at length, 'that it is a sin to try to take one's life. You say the future may be hopeless for a person. But how does one know the future?'

I smiled rather bitterly.

'I know my future. What do you think the Gestapo will do with me after they have finished their questioning?'

'It may not be as bad as you think. Perhaps you won't stay here.'

'They will never permit me to leave.'

He smiled encouragingly.

'I think differently. I heard the doctor from the hospital phoning the prison doctor. From what I heard, he was telling him that you must be sent back or he will take no responsibility.'

I felt a momentary surge of hope but repressed it. I had been disappointed so often.

'What sort of man is the prison doctor?' I asked.

'Don't worry – not a German. He is a Slovakian,' he replied, implying that the mere nationality of the doctor was sufficient guarantee of sympathetic treatment.

The prison doctor came to my cell while the turnkey and I were still in conversation. He had the same short, compact body, the sensitive gray eyes and frank expression of his colleague. He smiled reassuringly at me.

'I understand from Dr Kafka that you are a very sick young man. I shall examine you and report to the authorities on your condition.'

He proceeded to examine me in cursory fashion. However, to any onlooker, it must have appeared thorough. Finally he straightened up and murmured laconically:

'You are in bad shape.' Then he patted me on the shoulder encouragingly and walked briskly out of the cell.

In an hour or so my 'good friends,' the two Gestapo guards, made their appearance. From their sour, disappointed expressions, I knew immediately that I was going back to the hospital. The tall, domineering one was the first to speak:

'So you fooled that idiot of a doctor and now we've got to take you back to the hospital, eh?'

I did not answer.

He continued, with heavy-handed sarcasm:

'Will you walk with us to the car, sir, or would you prefer being carried on our shoulders – like a champion?'

'I prefer walking,' I said coldly, restraining a desire to smash my fist into his sneering face. I could not entirely repress a sneer of my own but felt, a moment later, a shock at my rashness. It had been provocative. The tall Gestapo agent was not without a certain shrewdness. He eyed me evilly, as if calculating the exact degree of defiance that was offered to him. Luckily, the little, scrawny one popped up between us.

'I prefer walking, I prefer walking,' he crowed, mimicking me.

The other directed a look of such contempt and distaste at him that anyone with a thinner skin would have shriveled under it. Then he turned wearily to me.

'Get up,' he growled, 'let's clear out of here.'

My re-entrance into the hospital must have been comic. Flanked by this ludicrously contrasted pair, I walked through the corridor, a grimy, bandaged figure. My reception, however, was exceptionally cordial. As we passed through the corridor, doctors, nurses, and patients smiled in sympathy and signaled their greetings by imperceptible nods of their heads, not daring openly to affront my watchdogs. The tall one's face was red with anger and he glowered at everyone we passed, while the short one added to his rage by vacuously strutting and posturing in front of all.

Despite the heartening evidence of the sympathetic attitude of those about me, the future appeared as black as ever. I realized that with all their good will, I could hardly expect these Slovakians to take any risk in helping me to escape. I could see endless days spent in feigning sickness, in temperature readings, in whispered consolations of doctors and nurses . . .

The routine I had envisaged proved as chafing as I had anticipated until the eleventh day after my re-entrance to this hospital.

On that day, as I was lying somnolently in bed, staring at the listless and obviously bored Nazi guard, a young girl, who was an absolute stranger to me, diffidently entered my room. She was a rather plain girl with blunt, good-natured features, dressed in surprisingly smart street clothes. In her hand she held a bunch of roses. I was taken aback when she spoke to me in German.

'Do you understand German?' she inquired softly.

My reply was sharp and rather hostile.

'Yes. What do you want?'

I could see the Gestapo man begin to stir in his chair and eye her with curiosity, but I could not feel any threat of danger in the situation. I had assumed that this girl had blundered into the wrong room. I was about to stop her, ask her whether she was mistaking me for somebody else, but she spoke hurriedly, shyly:

'I am a German. I have just had an appendicitis operation. All the patients in the hospital have heard about you and sympathize with you. I would like you to have these roses, so that you will not think all Germans are as bad as those you encountered in the war.'

I was aghast. Apparently she had no idea that the man in civilian clothes sitting near my bed was a Gestapo agent. I collected my wits sufficiently to blurt out:

'But I never saw you before . . . I don't know you, never spoke to you. Why do you bother me?'

She looked hurt, puzzled.

'Please don't be so bitter. Learn to forgive. You will be happier.' She put the flowers on the bed and turned to leave. The eyes of the Gestapo man followed her like a cat's.

'Thank you,' I almost shrieked in desperation, 'but I don't know you, I never saw you . . .'

The Gestapo agent rose indolently from his chair, strolled across the room, and barred the door with his outstretched arms.

'That was a lovely speech,' he said. He seized her arm, turned her around, and forced her back to the bed. When she heard him speak in German, she turned pale and began to tremble. I pitied her immensely. I tried to expostulate with the guard:

'She didn't mean any harm. I tell you, I don't know her. You ought to let her go. She is frightened to death – can't you see?'

He looked at me coldly. 'Save your breath. You'll need it later.'

He picked up the bunch of roses and tore them to shreds searching for a hidden message. Then he locked his fingers around the girl's arm and propelled her brutally out of the room.

In less than an hour, a Gestapo official I had never seen before paid me a visit. He was one of the more subtle, polished kind of agent, a type the Gestapo employed to ferret out secrets unobtainable by their ordinary methods. He was a middle-aged man, scholarly in appearance, wearing horn-rimmed glasses and impeccably dressed. His tactics, which had rather more finesse than those of my erstwhile tormentors, were still sufficiently transparent.

He introduced himself in a reserved, dignified fashion, inquired after my health, and offered a few random observations about hospitals, science, society, and the war. Then, almost as if it had slipped out, without purpose or design, he sighed and observed:

'I should think that people with a little experience in politics could devise more ingenious stratagems than the use of a little girl carrying roses.'

He paused for a reply which was not forthcoming.

'I merely meant to comment,' he ignored the rebuff urbanely, 'on the judgment of your colleagues, not to condemn your actions – which is not my function at the present moment. You will be removed from this hospital in two hours.' He calmly watched this remark register on me. I tried to keep my face blank and expressionless. 'Of course,' he said, 'we realize that moving you is very dangerous, possibly fatal. We are not quite the monsters we are made out to be. But what choice do you leave us? Your colleagues obviously know exactly where you are . . .'

He paused, removed his glasses, extracted a handkerchief, and began to polish them in the manner of a man tactfully waiting for someone to put into order his jumbled thoughts before answering a difficult question. I was in a hopeless predicament. Through all the Machiavellian tricks one factor was painfully obvious. He genuinely believed that the girl and the roses were elements in a scheme to set me free. Ironically enough, the one time I could have told the Gestapo the truth, it was certain not to be believed. I shrugged wearily, fatalistically – I was beaten.

'The girl is completely innocent. She is much too naïve to be mixed up . . .'

He interrupted me impatiently.

'Oh, come now, if that's your attitude you'd better get ready to leave.'

The rest of my speech died on my lips.

15

Rescue

Again I was ordered into my clothes and conducted to a car. I had no notion of my destination and I was too miserable even to speculate about it. The Gestapo men took up their positions on either side of me. I sat, sunk in apathy. We rode along in the gathering twilight of the Slovakian mountains. The air was sharp and a trifle chilly. Village after village passed by but I took little notice of them. Only one thought stirred in my mind . . . suicide, an opportunity to leap from the car.

It was just before darkness that a spark of interest quickened in me. I realized with an accelerated beat of my heart that I was gazing at a familiar landmark – a small white house with dark blue shutters. We were over the border, in the south of Poland. In the past, I had spent a happy summer vacation in this very house. We were out of the town of Krynica before my eyes could drink in its features and within an hour we had reached a small town where I had frequently done some work.[1]

It was all I could do to control my excitement and exultation. It was from this very place that I had been sent abroad twice by the Underground. I had an extensive acquaintance here – my liaison agent, my guides lived in this town. Could this be our destination? I dared not even allow myself to wish it. It would be too fortunate, too unreal. And yet, the automobile had slowed down; the chauffeur was picking his way more carefully through the turns and crossings and peering through the side windows as if searching for something. We entered the heart of the town, threading in and out among peasants, cyclists, and pedestrians. When we reached the marketplace, we took a sharp turn to the right, rattled over a narrow side road, and then came to a halt in front of the hospital.

Again a repetition of my entrance into the Presov hospital. The guards flanking me, I tottered up the stairs. I was genuinely sick and weak but I exaggerated my condition. My bandages were soaked in blood which made my acting more impressive. My guards were obliged to carry me to the second floor where they dumped me unceremoniously on a bed.

My accommodations were not so private as they had been at Presov. When the guards had left, I propped myself up on one elbow and studied my roommates. There were five of them, all old, ranging in age, it appeared to me, from seventy to eighty. They all stared back at me in wonderment, seeming to merge into a single vision of matted beards, bald heads, and toothless gums. It was a strange sight but, at that moment, I could not savor its humor. What were the Nazis up to, I wondered. Was this a new piece of psychology on the part of the 'master race'? Perhaps, I reflected, they wanted to make me feel overconfident and betray myself. Then it occurred to me that I might have been taken to this town especially to lure my friends and colleagues into the open. But it did not seem possible that they could know my connections with this place. My mind gnawed anxiously at this problem, but I could reach no definite conclusion.

The muttering of these old men ceased abruptly, as if a gust of wind had blown them out of the room like so many withered leaves. I had been in a hospital long enough to know that this signaled the entrance of the Gestapo. I closed my eyes and writhed feebly on the bed. Alongside my bed, a man and a woman were conversing in Polish and I judged them to be a doctor and a nurse. The guard must have been hovering nearby for the doctor addressed him curtly.

'Isn't it your duty to guard the room from the corridor? You won't do any good by crowding me.'

The guard did not answer and walked away heavily, his footsteps resounding like a cannonade in the oppressive silence.

The doctor bent over me to examine and dress my wounds. As he unwound the clotted and filthy bandages, he fired questions at me in a rapid, anxious whisper.

'Where did they arrest you? . . . May I help you? . . . Shall I let someone know about you?'

The circumstances were not such as to arouse my trust easily. I suspected a trick and answered in aggrieved and injured tones:

'I have no one to send messages to. I am innocent of all these charges. All I wanted to do was to go to Switzerland. Why won't you believe me?'

'Don't be afraid,' he whispered. 'I am not a provocateur. The entire staff – doctors, nurses, and attendants – is all Polish and there is not a single traitor or renegade among us.'

I opened my eyes and stared intently at him. He was extremely young for a doctor and looked as if he were playing a rôle. He had the face of a farm boy, light-skinned, freckled, and topped by a thatch of tousled blond hair. The guileless countenance made me feel like opening my heart in a burst of confidence, but the prudence and caution that had become second nature by this time checked my impulse. I said nothing.

The following morning, a sister (as in Presov, all the nurses were nuns from a nearby convent) entered my ward, nodded at me and without a word, inserted a thermometer between my lips. She watched me impassively, almost woodenly, then removed the thermometer and read it. I gazed anxiously at the mercury. It stopped at 100°. She took the chart in her hand, gravely entered a figure of 103°, and then left the ward. She returned quickly with an elderly man who introduced himself as the head physician. He raised his voice and addressed me harshly.

'Look here, young man,' he snapped. 'You are very sick but you can be cured if you co-operate with us. We can only give you proper medical treatment. If you want to live you must rest and avoid anxiety. If you don't follow my advice –' he shrugged callously, '– we can always use this bed for our townsfolk. Now lie quietly and let me examine you.'

He turned to the nurse and ordered her to remove a tray and bring some ointments and bandages. As she left the room, she stumbled against the guard, scattering the contents of the tray on the floor. He hastened to help her pick them up. While they were engaged in groping about on the floor, the doctor whispered to me.

'Now listen to me . . . As soon as I leave, begin moaning and whining. Shout that you are going to die and that you wish to go to confession. Be brave. We will not abandon you.'

When the nurse returned, he issued crisp, peremptory instructions to her:

'Change his dressings every two hours and see that he doesn't get out of bed. If I am needed, call me. I'll be in my office.'

As he turned on his heel, he barked to me: 'As for you, if you want to live, follow instructions.'

After the nurse changed my bandages, I began to twist about wildly, gradually working up to a series of frenzied, convulsive movements accompanied by loud moans.

I wailed loudly, 'I am going to die – to die, do you hear? . . . I want to be confessed . . . Please, sister, please, speak to the doctor. You are a good Catholic . . . Don't let me die a sinner . . .'

She glanced at me stonily and walked over to consult the young Gestapo man. He was of a different breed than most of the sentinels I had seen. Remarkably, he was without a trace of cynicism. Indeed, his face was noteworthy for its total lack of any positive expression. It was blankly devoid of either intelligence or stupidity, sympathy or cruelty. Sitting, his posture was rigid and unyielding. He never even allowed himself the luxury of tilting his chair. He never read while on duty. He seemed to regard himself as the incarnation of Nazi discipline and prestige. When the sister addressed him, he snapped to attention and stiffly nodded his agreement.

She returned with the head physician, who eyed me with annoyance and distaste. He spoke with loud exasperation.

'Can't you be a man? If you have determined to die, there is nothing we can do about it. Bring him a wheelchair, please, sister.'

I continued to moan and whine. The doctor shouted at me:

'Enough of your moans! You are getting your way. This nun will take you to confession. Have some respect for our other patients – you're not the only sick person here.'

A wheelchair was brought in. The nurse tucked me into a bath-
robe and helped me into it. She wheeled me out of the room, the
Nazi guard marching behind us as if he were on military parade. In
our wake I could hear the feeble clacking of the octogenarian chorus begin again as if a conductor had raised a baton.

The hospital's chapel was on the ground floor. I made my confession to an old, kindly priest, who displayed great sympathy and
concern for me. At the conclusion of my confession, he placed his
hands on my shoulders and said in consolation:

'Do not be afraid, boy. Maintain your faith in God. We are all
aware of your suffering for our beloved Poland. Everyone in this
hospital is anxious to help you.'

My confession left me with a feeling of tranquillity and peace. It
did not endure very long for, during the next few days, I had to concentrate on the task of making myself appear deathly ill. My body
responded to this need. Modern psychiatrists have insisted that the
physical and psychical life of an individual are closely linked. My
own experiences have persuaded me of the truth of this belief. After
a few days of intensive effort, I actually became a very sick man. I
was unable to eat, to lift my arms, to dress unaided, or to walk to the
lavatory. Despite the administration of sedatives, I had a perpetual
headache. Chills and feverish spells alternated and my temperature
was always abnormal.

Consequently I had been granted a concession by the hospital
authorities. I was permitted to be brought to the chapel daily. One day
while I was praying in the chapel, the sister who brought me in the
wheelchair knelt down beside me. I studied her face with its courageous, determined lines and decided to risk everything. I knew that I
could not speak to her while there were other people in the chapel, so
I asked if she would mind waiting for me to finish praying. She said she
would wait. While I sat there in the high-backed wheelchair, I could
hear the faint click of the rosary slipping between her fingers. The
coolness and quiet of the chapel with its familiar, faintly exotic smell
of incense, her calm firmness gave me reassurance. I felt certain I could
trust her. Finally we were alone. I leaned over to whisper to her:

'Sister, I know you are a good woman. But it is important for me to know if you are a good Pole . . .'

She looked me full in the face for a moment and, continuing to tell her rosary, said simply:

'I love Poland.'

But it was not necessary for her to tell me. I had seen her eyes. I spoke rapidly, in a low voice:

'I want to ask you to do something. But before I tell you what it is, I must tell you that it may be dangerous for you. You are free to refuse, of course.'

'Tell me what you want. If I can do it, I will.'

'Thank you,' I said fervently. 'I knew you would say that. Here is what I would like you to do. There is a family in this town by the name of—. They have a daughter, Stefi. Find her and tell her what has happened to me. Tell her Witold sent you.' I gave her the address. Witold was my pseudonym in the Underground.

'Today,' she said quietly.

After I had made this request, I felt a great burden slip from my mind. Not that I expected much to materialize from it, but at least it lightened the feeling of being alone in a hostile world. It gave me a friend whom I could trust completely and in whose character I had confidence. A measure of hope was restored to me.

When I saw the sister again, I looked at her with questioning eyes.

She whispered: 'In a few days, you will be visited by a nun from a convent nearby.'

'A nun? Why should a nun visit me?'

'I don't know. I was told to give you this message.'

'But it doesn't make sense.'

'Have patience.'

I was on tenterhooks for the next two days. I realized that if my friends were going to the lengths of sending a person as innocuous in appearance as a nun to visit me, it meant that some definite plan was already afoot. The third day after this conversation, shortly after noon, the nun arrived. I could hear the rasping breathing and snoring of the old men as they slept in the drowsy afternoon sunshine that filtered into the dingy ward. She moved toward me as if on tiptoe, approaching my bed with short, hesitant steps.

There was a vague familiarity about her delicate, pale face, but I could not place her as I was peeping with one eye, not daring to allow myself a closer scrutiny till she reached the bed. Then recognition was quickly kindled in an instant of excitement and fear. It was the sister of the guide who had been apprehended with me by the Gestapo.[2]

Her voice was girlish but firm as she introduced herself.

'I am a nun from a nearby convent. The German authorities have permitted us to bring cigarettes and food to the prisoners. Is there anything you need?'

I simulated great weakness and murmured inaudibly so that she would have to stoop to hear me. She understood this maneuver and said in a voice distinct enough to be heard by the guard:

'I am sorry, I can't hear you.'

Then stooping over, she whispered, 'Word has been sent to your superiors. Be patient.'

I have learned the technique of speaking without moving my lips.

'What happened to your brother?' I asked her, keeping an eye on the guard. Tears welled up in her eyes.

'We haven't heard from him.'

It was no use attempting to console her with hypocrisies. Losses of that kind cannot be mitigated by cheerful, empty phrases.

'I want you to tell them that I must have some poison. I am sure the Gestapo have brought me here to make me give away the Underground in this vicinity. I can't stand any more torture. The sooner I have the poison, the better. For everyone!' I said, secretly keeping an eye on the guard.

'I understand. Take good care of yourself. I will return in a few days.'

The period till she returned was one of endless suspense. It was like being thirsty and seeing water at a distance which was too great to be reached. Beyond the hospital walls, plans were being formulated for my rescue and I could almost taste liberty and freedom in the offing. It was maddening to be in bed, waiting.

When she finally returned, she brought me fruit and cigarettes and placed them on the shelf next to my bed. Again we employed the stratagems devised during her first visits. I muttered. She stooped, cupping her hand to her ear. Then we would whisper, hurriedly, our words tumbling over each other in our desire to crowd as much information as possible into a short moment. She began to speak with tremulous excitement and I had to stroke her hand surreptitiously to calm her and prevent her from raising her voice.

'They know everything,' she gasped. 'You have been awarded the Cross of Valor.'[3]

She pretended to smooth my pillow and whispered without looking at me: 'I have just put a cyanide pill under your pillow. It kills quickly. I implore you, don't use it unless you are absolutely sure the worst has come.'

I looked at her gratefully.

After her departure, I felt a surge of courage and determination. I was now armed against the worst contingencies. The poison gave me a sense of luxury, a feeling that I had a magic talisman against the eventualities which I had dreaded most – torture and the possibility that I might crack and betray the organization. As soon as I could I went to the lavatory and carefully hid the tiny capsule. She had left me a piece of flesh-colored adhesive for the purpose, the hiding place being the customary one for prisoners – the perineum.

So great was this feeling of security that it served even to quell my disappointment at the fact that the nun had given no intimation of a plan for my escape. Not wishing to appear querulous or demanding, I had stifled the questions that had been on the tip of my tongue all during her visit. However, events soon began to move with a much greater rapidity than I had anticipated.

That evening the young doctor with the fresh, ingenuous face of a country lad, came to give me what I presumed was merely a routine examination. When he was through, he peered quizzically at my face as if trying to read in it my chances for recovery. Then in a normal, semi-humorous tone that left me aghast at his seeming imprudence, he drawled:

'Well, you are going to be set free tonight . . .'

I started as though I had been stung. Sitting bolt upright, I hissed indignantly, 'Are you mad? Don't talk so loud! The guard will hear you. He has left only for a moment – probably to get water or something. For Heaven's sake, watch yourself and be careful.'

He chuckled good-humoredly. 'Don't worry. We have bribed him. He won't come back while I am here. Now listen carefully. Everything has been arranged. At midnight, I will pass this room and light a cigarette. That is your cue. Hop into your clothes and go to the first floor. On one of the window sills you will find a rose. Jump from that sill. Men will be stationed below.'[4]

He paused a moment. 'Is everything clear?'

My heart pounded like a trip-hammer.

'Yes, yes, I understand perfectly.' I repeated his directions in a strained voice.

He grinned and patted me on the shoulder.

'Relax,' he said, 'and don't worry. Good luck!'

He could not have given me advice more impossible to follow. The one thing humanly out of the question for me was to rest or relax. A thousand doubts rose to my mind. I thought feverishly of innumerable precautions and contingencies. Most of my time I spent in scrutinizing the guard who returned to his post shortly afterwards. Could he have merely pretended to accept the bribe in order to set a trap for my comrades? He had appeared to be so thoroughly indoctrinated with the Nazi code. I felt reassured when he turned toward me. There was a faint smirk of greed and self-satisfaction upon his lips, which I interpreted to mean that he was content with his pickings and impatient to begin indulging himself in the wealth he had been promised.

Of course, he did not realize that the money he would receive, the forged papers that he had indubitably been provided with, did not mean that a life of ease was within his grasp. His happy dreams of leisure on a handsome estate would soon go up in smoke. The Underground had bribed hundreds like him before and then had turned the tables by mercilessly 'exploiting' them, as it was termed in underground language, forcing them to co-operate in other schemes by holding over their heads the constant threat of exposure to the Gestapo.

Some time before midnight the guard pretended to drop off into a deep sleep. His head on his chest, he emitted stentorian snores. Precisely as the church clock tolled the hour of midnight, the figure of the doctor appeared in the doorway. He drew a cigarette from his pocket, lit it with slow, conspicuous gestures, and moved on. I gave the ward a cursory inspection. An encouraging medley of snores, breathing, and sleepy groans issued from all sides. I slid out of bed, took off my hospital pajamas and stuffed them under the cover. I transferred the cyanide pill to my hand, ready to swallow it in case of sudden danger. Completely naked, I padded down to the first floor.

Slightly bewildered, I studied the dimly lit corridor. My sense of direction had vanished momentarily and since there were two similar staircases, I could not tell which was the front or the back of the hospital. In this strange dilemma, I felt a draft of cold air on my back. I reasoned that a window had been left open for me as whoever had engineered the scheme would probably realize that I would be unable to open one unaided.

I headed in the direction of the open window. My heart leaped with exultation as I saw the rose, which had been blown from the sill to the floor. I stared for a moment at the inky blackness below, then clambered onto the sill with difficulty and looked down.

'What are you waiting for? Jump!' I heard someone say.

I took a deep breath and jumped. I felt strong arms grip me tightly. Several pairs of hands had caught me before I hit the ground. Someone handed me some trousers, someone else a shirt and jacket, while barking out orders:

'Quickly! Get dressed. We haven't a moment to lose . . . Can you run?'

Half-heartedly, I said yes. Like myself, they were all barefooted. We sped across the lawn until we reached a fence. I had not the faintest idea who my rescuers were or to what underground organization they belonged. We paused at the fence, panting from the sprint.

One of them spoke. 'It will be impossible for you to get over the fence without help. This is what we will do. I'll climb over first. Then our friend will bend down. You get on his back, climb on the fence, and jump. I'll catch you.'

He scrambled neatly over the fence. We performed the operation as he had directed. Then the other member came over. When we were all together, we continued to run, over a muddy field, across two paved roads toward a row of protecting trees. My bare feet began to smart and pain, my ribs ached and I felt a burning, choking sensation in my lungs each time I inhaled. Finally, I stumbled, pitched forward, and collapsed on the ground, gasping for breath.

'I can't make it,' I gasped. 'I am sorry to cause you so much trouble but I must have some rest.'

They did not answer me. One of the men, an unusually tall, burly individual, reached down and flung me over his shoulder as though I had been a bundle of old clothes. I must have lost a great deal of weight for he carried me, without the slightest stagger, into the woods.[5]

When we were well within the comforting darkness, one of the men gave an audible sigh of relief.

'I guess we can rest here a bit,' he suggested to the man on whose shoulder I hung limply.

The latter deposited me on a mound of earth under a tree. I leaned back against the tree, trying to recover my breath and bearings. They lit cigarettes and offered me one, which I waved away speechlessly. After a few puffs, they held a brief monosyllabic conversation, stood up, and threw away the butts, ready to resume the trek.

'Do you think you can walk yet?' the tall, burly one asked me.

'I – I don't think so. Have we far to go?'

Without answering, he bent down again and flipped me over his shoulder. They walked at a steady methodical pace for about fifteen minutes and then emerged from the woods onto what looked like a broad, open field. The moon, which had been obscured by clouds, broke through, illumining a river so that I saw the faint silvery glimmer of water before us.[6] The two men stopped and my carrier set me on my feet. The other placed his fingers in his mouth and emitted a thin, piercing whistle.

From behind the bushes to our right, two men stepped forward – two of the hardiest, toughest-looking individuals I have ever encountered. One of them held a revolver in his hand and the other, a long knife which glinted evilly in the moonlight. As they approached they loosed, in measured, controlled tones, a series of hair-raising curses directed at the Germans. From time to time they remarked caustically that there was 'always trouble with these intellectuals.' They held a brief, inaudible conference with my rescuers and took up positions as guards, while the husky one whom I judged to be the leader of the expedition beckoned me to follow him along the reedy, marshy ground by the side of the river.

We churned through the slush until a man who had apparently been lying prone in the reeds jumped up and confronted us, his face split in a wide grin.

'Good evening, gentlemen,' he greeted us.

Staszek Rosa was standing in front of me.[7] He was a young Socialist from Cracow. He gave the impression that he was a womanizer and rather happy-go-lucky. I never, ever would have thought he had any ties whatsoever with the Underground. Seeing him stunned me to such an extent that I stood dumbfounded. He gave me a friendly pat on the shoulder:

'Congratulations, Jan, on your divorce from the Gestapo. I bet that was one wedding you didn't care for, eh?'

'Thanks, Stas,' I mumbled. 'Where are we going to now?'

Rosa was already pulling out a canoe hidden in the reeds. He squeezed us all into it. Then we moved away from the bank. There were five of us, which was at least two too many for a canoe of that size. The burly man took the oars. I was sitting in front of him, on the left. The current was pulling us toward the middle of the river but we had to get to the other side as quickly as possible. All the rower's efforts were in vain. He was swearing and the canoe started pitching more and more. At one point, I stopped holding onto the sides so as to relax my hands, and fell overboard. The big lad let go of one of the oars and, very calmly, grabbed me by the collar, all the while steering with the other oar. With the help of the others, he pulled me back on board. He was gifted with rare strength and even rarer composure.

I was lying at the bottom of the canoe, soaked to the skin, and shivering with cold. But what a surprise! With me weighing down the bottom of the canoe, it was easier to maneuver it. After an hour of fighting the current, we finally made it to the other side. Numb from the cold, I tried to warm myself up by beating my arms together and hopping from one leg to the other. Staszek hid the canoe in the gorse bushes.

We set off toward the forest. Staszek was obviously trying to get his bearings, for the river's current had pulled us further downstream than anticipated. He finally worked out where we were, and after an hour walking through the forest, we were close to the edge of a village. We could make out a shed in the distance. We headed toward it. Rosa checked that it was indeed the agreed meeting place.

'End of the line! This is where we separate,' said Staszek, as we were saying goodbye. 'You go into the barn. Hide in the hay. And get some sleep. Tomorrow morning, your host will pay his respects. He will see to it that you are well-hidden for a while. Once the Gestapo has stopped looking for you, we'll come back for you.'

I began to express my gratitude for the dangerous task they had undertaken on my behalf. Rosa cut me off, a faint, derisive smile on his thin lips.

'Don't be too grateful to us. We had two orders about you. The first was to do everything in our power to help you escape. The second was to shoot you if we failed. You were lucky . . .'

And after a moment he added: 'Be grateful to the Polish workers – they saved you.'

I gaped at him in dumbfounded amazement.

'Pleasant dreams,' he chuckled, and turned to leave with the other who broke his phlegmatic silence for the first time to bid me farewell. I climbed up into the loft and sank wearily into the soft hay. I was a free man again.

16

The 'Gardener'

It had become necessary to lie low while my pursuers spent their energies in random movements. I learned, without surprise, that a close scrutiny was kept over the railroad station and all roads leading from the town.[1] All trains, vehicles, passengers, and pedestrians were halted and minutely examined. However, nobody was arrested; no reprisals were exacted. The bribed Gestapo agent had evidently become alarmed and had fled. This fortunately led the authorities to conclude that he was the only culprit involved and vigilance was therefore somewhat relaxed. When later I sought to learn his fate, I was informed by organization authorities that he had been thoroughly 'exploited,' but further details were denied me.

I spent three days in that shed. My benefactor was a kindly, grizzled old Polish Socialist who had fought the Tsar under Josef Pilsudski in 1905. It was the military organization of his party, the Polish Socialist Party, which had engineered my escape at the order of the commander of the Polish Underground and thus earned my deepest gratitude. It was curious, I reflected, that these simple, stalwart workers who had saved my life were so completely remote from me. For, despite occasional meetings with them, and reading newspaper accounts of their struggles for better working conditions and political influence, I did not know very much about them. It was ironic that my first close contact with them should have occurred in an affair when my very life was at stake. When I discovered who had saved me I was amused at the recollection of my mother's solemn warning to guard myself against actresses, cards, and radicals.

My host proved to be an expert at camouflage. I was so thoroughly draped with straw, boards, and a variety of agricultural implements that even his wife and children, who made frequent visits to the shed, were completely unaware of my presence. In my weakened and feverish state, the noises, the drone of peasant voices, the variegated sounds of farm and woods, the sunshine filtering through the cracks in the shed made my self-imposed imprisonment most difficult to bear. During the four weeks of prison and hospital treatment that I was forced to endure, the unnatural excitement and tension served to sustain me, but now a reaction was setting in. A feeling of deep fatigue had taken possession of me but I was unable to sleep. I could eat little and was subject to fits of uncontrollable trembling. My host, who visited me at noon and at twilight, with rough tact and gentleness pretended not to notice any signs of my weakness. With utmost solicitude he would urge me to eat, and would dress those of my wounds which had not yet healed.

On the third day, when my confinement had become almost intolerable, the forester arrived with a young man who had been sent by the authorities of the Underground. He appeared to be a typical young Polish officer – slim, alert and with a careless, dashing manner. However, one could sense a determined and steadfast attitude beneath.

In easy, sociable tones, as if he were issuing an invitation to dinner, he notified me to prepare to leave the next day for a small estate in the mountains where I was to remain for a minimum of four months.

'You understand,' he explained in crisp tones, 'the purpose of this order. Apart from the fact that the doctor of the hospital from which you escaped has deemed a total recuperation to be necessary, all your tracks must be completely covered from the Gestapo. You must promise, furthermore, not to engage in any activities which will lead you to any cell of the movement, unless they issue a specific order to that effect. Should you do so, it will be considered a breach of discipline.'

I suppose the finality of his tone rubbed me the wrong way. Somewhat peevishly I flung back at him:

'You sound as if I am under suspicion, as if I've committed a wrong in escaping. Do you think that because I fell into the hands of the Gestapo, I've become rash or cowardly?'

'Don't be a fool.'

'I'm not a fool. I simply don't want to lie around in cold storage. I can still be useful.'

'Of course you can, but not by becoming impatient and undisciplined.'

'Do you call it impatience to realize that much work has to be done and that I am perfectly capable of doing my share?'

I could see the corners of his mouth tighten and his face become grim. He screwed up his eyes.

'Listen, Mister Impatience,' he snapped, 'you know what "no contact upward" means. It's the most basic rule of covert action. And you're not the one who's going to change that.'

The principle of 'no contact upward' was a precautionary measure, adopted in the formation of the Underground. It was originally designed against the infiltration of spies and provocateurs into our cells. The presence of any suspect individual, anyone who might, by the remotest possibility, have been a spy or provocateur presented us with a complicated problem. We could not eliminate all those who were touched by suspicion without causing a complete stoppage of all activity. However, to let them carry on their work without taking any precaution exposed the Underground to the possibility of falling en masse into the hands of the Gestapo. 'No contact upward' was a kind of compromise. The extent of the damage any suspected individual could inflict was limited, since he was denied any contact with his superior officers. However, he could still carry on some of his duties by issuing orders to those inferior in rank. Naturally, if suspicion proved well-founded, the suspect would be eliminated. Thus the work of the Underground could go forward effectively without the constant apprehension that would otherwise have developed. The rule was extended to include the cases of those who had been arrested. Indeed, even further precautions were taken. After each arrest, immediate changes in meeting places were put into effect, the personal papers of all members having had contact with the 'infected' member were altered and that member was ordered to remain in isolation for a certain period of time.

As I reviewed to myself the implicit meanings in this important rule, I could not help but admit to myself that this handsome young liaison officer was perfectly justified in rebuking me severely. My feelings of sheepishness and chagrin must have become apparent in my bearing, for he immediately broke into an infectious grin and explained:

'You know, you've got an underground version of measles. You were in the hands of the Gestapo and as far as we are concerned, you have become tainted.'

He paused while we smiled understandingly at each other. Then he added slyly:

'With the kind aid of a portion of the Gestapo we managed your escape. So for a short time you'll have to submit to a voluntary quarantine. This is a formality, you understand, but a formality that permits no exceptions.'

I began a tentative apology for my conduct but he waved it off humorously.

'Have your baggage ready, my good man; for tomorrow you take a little pleasure trip. You will stay at a small, out-of-the-way estate, far from the cities and the German officials. It's nice there – you'll have a good time.'

My 'little pleasure trip' began the next day at dawn when a rickety old wagon was backed into my shed. I was placed in a barrel which was carefully hoisted into the wagon to the accompaniment of loud wheezes and groans from my host and a bearded farmer, of whom I barely caught a glimpse. Again it seemed to me as if at least half the agricultural produce of Poland was dumped around, above, and under me. A profusion of straw, hay, and vegetables surrounded my cramped and cheerless quarters. I experimented for a while with various positions in the barrel and finally adopted one in which my chin was pressed rigidly against my drawn-up knees, while my arms were locked around my legs. The wagon rattled and creaked on for what seemed an eternity. In a short time, my elbows, knees, and shoulders were a mass of bruises from the bouncing and jostling. Finally, at what I judged to be about noon, a merciful halt was called.

I could hear the farmer jump heavily from his seat to the ground, climb aboard the wagon, and tunnel his way through the choice assortment of vegetables strewn around my compartment. He thumped on the barrel and announced gruffly:

'We're here. You can get out.'

I uncoiled myself from the contorted position I had got into and clambered out. I stood on the loose boards of the wagon, blinking in the sunlight, stretching my arms and working the kinks out of my legs. It took some time for me to get my bearings.

We were in a forest clearing. The trees appeared gigantic after my sojourn in such a cramped and narrow space. The fresh, green grass looked extremely soft and inviting. I kept inhaling deep drafts of clear country air. This was luxury beyond my dreams. The farmer broke in on my trance.

'Don't you think it's about time you got off the wagon to meet the girl who is waiting for you?'

I was startled and spoke sharply to him:

'What girl are you talking about?'

He extended a brown, gnarled finger and pointed in the direction behind me, grunting, 'Turn around and look.'

I turned around and to my amazement saw a young girl standing alongside a carriage. She eyed me with frank curiosity. I jumped rather stiffly and clumsily from the wagon, awkwardly thanked the farmer, whose bearded and wrinkled face was split in a wide, ear-to-ear grin. Feeling a bit silly, I walked over to the girl, and as I did so I tried to collect whatever dignity I could under these circumstances.

I must have cut a sorry figure to her cool, appraising eyes. My trousers were three sizes too big for me and, unconsciously, I had been holding them up with my left hand. My right hand was clenched into a fist which still enclosed the cyanide pill that had been given to me. The jacket I was wearing was so small and tight for me that the sleeves reached just to my elbows. As I wore no shirt, my chest, dripping with perspiration, was completely bare.

For a moment, as I approached her, I felt she was going to burst into irrepressible giggles and I became slightly irritated. However, she contrived to remain solemn and mildly aloof. She seemed, despite, or perhaps because of, her excessive dignity, pert and childlike. She was not beautiful or even pretty, but her slender, lithe figure, the freshness of her skin, and the general air of grace and well-being combined to make her singularly attractive and appealing. She must have felt that I was gazing at her with frank admiration. For a moment, she averted her eyes and stared upward as if searching the trees for the invisible birds that were chirping so merrily.

I was greatly amused to see her composure thus ruffled, and seized the opportunity to parody a deep bow and murmur:

'Mademoiselle, j'ai honte de moi.'

She did not take this amiss, responding instead with a prim curtsy:

'Monsieur, vous êtes excusé.'

The old farmer, who had been watching this tableau as if it had been staged for his benefit, shook his head in wonderment and bellowed his farewell. His voice recalled to her the necessity of being stern and dignified.

'I am instructed,' she began, pedantically, 'to welcome you to my home. My name is Danuta Sawa, the daughter of Walentyna Sawa. We live on an estate nearby. We hope your stay will be pleasant.'

'That is very kind of you, indeed. I am Witold.'

I kept my face unsmiling and somewhat grim. She sensed a note of raillery.

'Oh, how thin you are,' she smiled, 'like a scarecrow. The Germans don't leave us with much substantial food, but we shall have to stuff you with our best strawberries, plums, and pears.'

'Thank you. It is most kind of you.'

A look of annoyance crossed her face suddenly.

'How foolish of me! I almost forgot to give you your legend.'

A 'legend' is the collection of data which composes an underground member's identity. It is furnished to all new members and to all those who find it necessary to change their identity. It consists of a fictional biography and a number of equally fictional dates and places necessary to constitute a new personality. It must be carefully memorized until it becomes a part of one's normal consciousness.

'You are,' she informed me rather archly, 'to be my newly arrived cousin from Cracow. Since you are a rather useless and lazy person, you couldn't hold onto a job. To add to your troubles, you became ill and a doctor ordered you into the country for a long rest. You are a gardener by profession. You will aid the workers in my garden. I have taken the trouble to register you in the *Arbeitsamt*.'

The *Arbeitsamt* is a German agency with which every Polish worker must register. He may be called upon at any time to show his card which contains information as to where and how he is employed. I became rather worried.

'But I know nothing about gardening. It's all I can do to distinguish a tree from a bush. How shall I possibly be able to fool anybody?'

She looked at me in amazement.

'How can one be so insensitive to nature? Well, I suppose you city people are all alike. You needn't fret. We have made preparations for your ignorance. Don't forget, you're an impossible lazybones. You'll spend your time lolling about the house, moaning about your aches and pains, except when you pretend to run after pretty girls.'

I protested.

'I'm a very serious young man,' I said. 'I shall find it difficult to act so flippantly.'

She interrupted me:

'When you arrive, you will make a tour of inspection of our estate. Be sure to let everybody see you – peasants, servants, villagers – everybody, in fact, of importance or significance.'

She looked at me gravely.

'Do you understand?' she added slowly, as if she were coaching a young and backward student.

'I believe if I tax my mind sufficiently, I can manage to understand your instructions. One thing bothers me. Suppose I am asked questions about gardening or farming – I'll be in a terrible fix.'

'I will be your teacher. Every day, before your tour, I am going to

coach you. In case of difficulty, frown and turn to me in annoyance.
Assume at all times an air of boredom and indifference. You understand – act the gentleman.'

'I'm your devoted student,' I assured her. I was enjoying the play-
fulness between us. It had been such a long time since I had had the
occasion to taste humor of any sort. I was touched and grateful to
her for her sensitivity that seemed to recognize this need.

She ran to the carriage and took out a light-colored overcoat
which she handed to me with a smile.

'We didn't know your size. Please put it on. Tomorrow we'll
choose you something nicer.'

I stared at her in surprise.

'Why do you want me to wear that thing? It's so warm. Really,
I'm not suffering from chills.'

'How silly you are,' she retorted. 'It's nothing to do with keeping
you warm; you have to hide what you're wearing – I can't introduce
you to people looking like this!'

I glanced at my oversized trousers, my skimpy jacket, and my
soiled bandages. I shrugged, put on a martyred look and donned
the overcoat she held out for me. We entered the carriage. As soon
as I sat down on the soft velvet seat, a surge of complete weariness
and faintness overcame me. It became difficult for me to pay attention to the remarks of Danuta, my hostess. With a mixture of
amusement and concern, she had been listening to my abortive
efforts to say something witty or interesting. Now she smilingly
interrupted me.

'You needn't bother about being brilliant. Relax and try to get
some rest. Tomorrow you will have plenty of time to shine.'

She folded her hands demurely on her lap and set me an example
by resting her head on the cushion. Suddenly she started up and
called to the driver:

'Pass me the wine, please.'

The surly peasant who was driving us apparently regarded Danuta's association with me with complete disfavor. I could see him
shaking his gray head sullenly, muttering:

'Such goings-on – all this trouble – if only the master were alive . . .'

He handed the bottle to her, his manner critical and refractory. After I drank some of the warm red wine, I felt much better. The lethargy I had sunk into vanished temporarily and I became aware that the road we were traveling on wound its way through a dense forest.

My work in the Underground had completely altered my mental outlook. Whereas formerly I might have remarked only on the beauty of the scenery, I observed that the forest afforded superb concealment for meetings, the passage of couriers and, grimly enough, for assassinations. I reflected that the Gestapo would have its hands full with any group that was well-organized, with proper leadership, and that had the advantage of knowing the terrain. These cold, professional calculations kept me preoccupied until we reached the estate.

Our arrival was greeted by a noisy medley of sounds and bustling activity. No sooner were we out of the carriage, followed by the disapproving glances of the driver, than we were in the midst of a group of peasants who stared openly at me and whispered comments to each other which I was unable to overhear. Danuta, in the meantime, had been surrounded by a horde of peasant children, each trying to outshout the other with his confused and rambling tale. They all tried to kiss her hand, and I marveled that her arm was not wrenched from its socket, so violent was the competition of each child to be the first to reach the hand of his beloved mistress. In addition to this noisy babble of voices were heard the squawking of chickens, the excited barking and yapping of dogs, and, from a distance, the intermittent moos of cows.

By great effort I managed to push my way through the group of children to Danuta's side. Her hair was disheveled, her face flushed, and her clothes rumpled by the children who constantly pressed against her, but she was obviously pleased by the enthusiastic reception. After many stratagems and much cajolery she sent the children off.

I was enabled now to draw my breath and survey my new surroundings from the steps of the broad veranda. Before me was a large, well-kept lawn, in the center of which bloomed luxuriantly a bed of pink and white peonies. A short distance from the house were grouped the outbuildings – stables, cowsheds, and the smithy. The manor house itself, white and glistening in the sunlight, was bordered on three sides by a dense grove of shade trees. Lulled by this tranquil rural scene, I closed my eyes and listened to the pleasant hum of the countryside. Warsaw, the Underground, the Gestapo, seemed remote and unreal.

17

Propaganda from the Country

Inside the Sawa home, on the high, gleaming white walls, hung a miscellaneous collection of photographs and portraits. Small old-fashioned pictures of family groups in the dark tones of an earlier period were interspersed among still older portraits of bearded dignitaries and formidable matrons. There were also modern photographs of more recent members of the family, among which I recognized with some amusement a freckled, gawky Danuta, posed with becoming dignity for her graduation photograph. I stood gazing intrigued at all these.

Danuta was not slow to call attention to my lack of courtesy.

'You see, Mother,' she said, emphasizing the word 'mother' determinedly and nudging me to call attention to the fact that the lady was actually present, 'how badly my cousin has been brought up in the city. He hasn't seen his aunt in ages and he stands there looking at the pictures as if they were a collection of freaks. He doesn't even take the trouble to say "good day." '

This bantering little speech had its effect. I was embarrassed and did not know which to apologize for first – the rude way I had stared at the photographs, or my failure to perceive the entrance of my 'aunt' whom, turning around hurriedly, I now noticed for the first time. My 'aunt' was a woman of sixty, enormously stout and with a surprisingly fresh, ruddy face. Her hair was still a lustrous auburn. She stood there, adding her smile to Danuta's giggle. All I could do was stammer unintelligible excuses.

Danuta turned to her mother.

'The cat must have his tongue,' she mocked.

'Oh, stop teasing the poor boy,' my 'aunt' reproved her and came forward. She smiled to put me at ease. To my surprise, her voice, which I had expected to be deep and resonant, was soft and melodious.

'Pay no attention to Danuta,' she said. 'She is always trying to fluster people. I want you to feel free here, free as you would be in your own home. Danuta informed me that you became our "cousin." I'm very glad to help you – nevertheless, I must say that the world is becoming strange, too strange for me. I've been accustomed to acquiring cousins by birth, not by my daughter's order. But I see that I am too old for this world.'

'You are very kind,' I said. 'I hope I shall not prove a burden.'

'Not at all,' she replied, and then added, 'Oh, dear, how pale and thin you are. We shall have to do something about that. Sit down and rest, and later, after you have had some cold milk and a bite to eat, you can tell us all the news from Cracow.'

I gave her a grateful glance.

'Thank you,' I said. 'I would enjoy some cold milk. It has been a hot day and I was not, as you see, properly dressed for it. I hope everything is well with you.'

A shadow passed across her face.

'Well,' she said, 'things are none too good. The Nazis are not exactly angels, and my dear son, Lucien . . .'

'Sh-sh, mother.'

Of the first three weeks in Danuta's charming home the greater part was spent recuperating from my illness – lying in bed, reading, or idling about the parlor with its creaking floors and gay profusion of flowers, gossiping with the servants, or indolently examining the portraits which had become pleasantly familiar.

Usually I make a special effort to have pleasant relationships and now I was trying even more to develop this characteristic. Thus I had managed to ingratiate myself with the household staff, ensuring their loyalty in a time of stress. Of the entire ménage, the only one who remained resistant to my friendly advances was the ancient driver. He claimed a unique position in the large body of servants because, as he put it, 'he was the driver for the father of the late master.'

On the other hand, the cook was extremely fond of me. She was a solid, big-boned woman who looked quite capable of annihilating an entire Nazi regiment – which she often threatened to do, while brandishing a sharp knife and muttering terrifying curses. She would often secretly slip me juicy tidbits so that I would 'fatten up and not walk around the house looking as thin as a wheat stalk.' Her dietary suggestions were orders I dared not question. They were mysterious formulas designed to bring me back to health in rapid strides.

The chambermaid, the daughter of the cook, selected me as a sort of confidant. She was a pale, sallow girl who was as angular and gaunt as her mother was broad and rounded. From her, I garnered volumes of gossip about the neighboring estates and the village. The household was completed by two kitchenmaids, shy, blonde, and rosy-cheeked, who seldom entered the parlor. To converse with them, an interloper like myself had to tolerate much fluttering, giggling, and pouting.

All the occupants of the house, from the sweet elderly lady, Danuta's mother, to the twittering kitchenmaids, were singularly united in an atmosphere of intense loyalty and mutual confidence. At first I attributed this fact to the patience, tact, and gentleness that emanated from Danuta and her mother. Then it dawned on me that it included something more – an impalpable, fugitive fact which I could not quite put my finger on. It annoyed me to have them cast covert glances about the room when they thought I was not present, or abruptly and confusedly discontinue a discussion when I made an appearance. It seemed to me as if the entire household shared a secret which they could not expose to a stranger.

On some nights I fancied I heard a rattling of the windows that faced the rear garden, followed by indistinct voices. I dismissed this as the product of my overwrought imagination – the imagination of a sick and suspicious person. One night when I was unable to sleep I sat at my window and perceived a girl whom I assumed to be Danuta walking with a man in the garden. I thought nothing of it until at the breakfast table I said casually and jokingly to Danuta:

'Romance is fine in its place, but you shouldn't be out walking late at night. Your feet will get wet and sniffles and romance don't mix.'

I could see confusion and vexation mount in her face. She looked daggers at me.

'What right have you to go peeping and prying?' she retorted brusquely. Then, with a feminine lack of logic, she added, 'Anyhow, I wasn't out last night. You're imagining things'

That annoyed me, so I flashed back:

'Do as you please, flirt with whomever you like. Only don't tell me I've become blind. I made a joke and you got angry . . .'

'I'm sorry. I just don't feel well today. Though you are still mistaken. I was not out last night.'

I shrugged and dropped the matter. It was really none of my business if she chose to hide what might be a budding romance.

The following week all my uneasiness was diverted in activity. I could no longer delay the inspection tours of the estate that were necessary to sustain my rôle as 'the gardener.' It had become imperative for me to fulfill perfectly the requirements of my legend, particularly as I was anxious to get in touch with my liaison officer and obtain some immediate work in the Underground.

I faced the prospect of inspecting the estate with great trepidation. For one thing, natural history was a closed book to me. In school I had passed these courses only by assiduous study. I realized that in order to pass muster as 'the gentleman gardener from Cracow,' it was necessary to compensate for my ignorance by the utilization of stratagem and ingenuity.

We put our heads together – Danuta and I – to plan a campaign for the next day. After prolonged discussion we hit upon the following plan: a rehearsal. We would walk through the part of the estate I was to inspect the next day and Danuta was to coach me on all the necessary observations I was to make.

'Well,' she inquired, 'do you think you will be able to get by as a gardener?'

'Frankly,' I replied hesitantly, 'my memory is none too good when it comes to farming matters. Suppose I get confused and put the remarks in the wrong sequence? For instance, I'll know what to say about cabbage plants but we may be in front of a tomato patch.'

'Mmmm,' she hummed in perplexity. 'That *is* a problem. But let's be methodical. For any difficulty there is always a solution.'

'But I thrive on difficulties,' I interjected, 'and this is what I propose.'

I reached for a notebook and pencil, seized her hand, and, pulling her out of her chair, protesting and laughing, hurried her through the door and into the garden.

It was lovely out of doors – sunny and warm. The pear and linden trees that bordered the house looked tall and graceful and cast deep pools of shadows. We sat down on a bench under one of the pear trees. There we felt relaxed, confidential.

'Before I tell you of my plans for the tours of inspection,' I began, 'I wish to apologize for my remarks at breakfast the other day. I didn't mean . . .'

'Nonsense,' she interrupted in some confusion. 'Please, let's forget it. What brilliant method for the tour have you devised?'

I arose from the bench in the manner of a professor about to begin a lecture.

'In any situation where one is confronted by the seemingly impossible,' I orated, 'it becomes necessary for the individual to take stock of his weaknesses and his strengths. I know nothing about plants, true enough; on the other hand, I know a great deal about organizing information and devising methods to circumvent disaster. Therefore, I shall number the remarks I am going to make and put them into my notebook. At the side of each bed within the garden, I am going to put a corresponding number on a tiny stick. This evening I shall memorize the remarks in order. What do you think of my plan?'

Danuta smiled.

'Genius, pure genius!'

The first inspection was eminently successful. I walked about the estate, with a mixture of arrogance and condescension, throwing off remarks like 'The seeds are none too good this season' – 'I like the arrangement of the rows.' Here and there I praised individual workmen and peasant girls at work in the garden. I became intoxicated with my success and could not resist a dig at Danuta's expense. When my tour was nearly completed I stopped to congratulate some workmen on their efforts.

'Excellent, excellent,' I murmured indolently. 'Too bad there isn't a man around to direct your work. One can see the lack of a man's hand.'

I glanced at Danuta. She was furious, blushing with indignation.

We walked back to the house in high spirits at the success of my 'debut.' As we were about to enter the house she took my arm and said with unexpected seriousness:

'Please, Witold, before we go in, I'd like to tell you something. Will you walk with me to the bench?'

I refrained from joking. We walked over to the bench and sat down. She looked carefully around as if to detect any eavesdroppers. Satisfied that nobody could overhear us, she said:

'You were correct the other day when you mentioned that I was walking in the garden. I was in the company of a member of the Underground whom I believe you know. We felt that you were too ill to be active and believed it would tax your strength too much to undertake any tasks. He will be here tonight. I want you to stay up until he arrives, although I don't know exactly what time that will be.'

She rose from the bench.

'Don't look so sober,' she laughed. 'I could eat a horse, I'm so hungry.' Before I could question her, she tucked her arm under mine and pulled me into the house.

I awaited the arrival of Danuta's guest that evening with the deepest anticipation and some anxiety. I had been on the shelf so long that I felt I was becoming useless, that the faculties which I had developed for work in the Underground had begun to rust.

Dinner that evening was difficult. By common consent, Danuta and I forebore to chide each other. After dessert Danuta, pleading a headache, slipped up to her room. Later, I passed some pleasantries with my 'aunt.' Then I went to my room, placed the armchair in front of the window, and made an effort to read. The heat of the day, the fatiguing walks, the tension I was under, made me drowsy and I dozed off.

Some time past midnight I felt a hand on my shoulder; I awoke startled and a bit hostile. It was Danuta. She whispered gently:

'Wake up, Witold. He is in the garden waiting for us. Come in ten minutes, will you?'

It was obvious they had things to talk about without me. After waiting ten minutes I tiptoed down the stairs out into the garden. I peered about unsuccessfully in the darkness. Suddenly I heard Danuta speaking with someone whose voice sounded familiar. It was a man, but I could not quite recognize who it was. Danuta was weeping, complaining how bad things were. She had no money . . . The Germans were taking all the farm produce . . . What was worse, she worried so much about him.

I was surprised at the change in her. She had always seemed so self-reliant, so gay and full of confidence. The man's voice was trying to reassure her.

I came closer and was astonished to find out that the voice puzzling me was that of the liaison officer who had visited me in the shed where I had stayed after my escape from the hospital. His appearance had not changed. He was still the same lithe, debonair, and polite young officer. He turned to me with an engaging smile.

'How are you, Witold? How has Danuta been treating you? If she acts badly or is impudent, you have my permission to put her over your knee.'

I replied that Danuta was a wicked, cruel girl, but that I had become used to suffering. I added:

'I'd like to congratulate you on your ability to melt into the landscape. I hardly even recognized you at first.'

In underground slang 'to melt into the landscape' means the ability to avoid attracting attention by seeming to become a normal part of an environment. It was a skill that was held in great esteem by the members of the Underground.

'It's nice of you to say so,' he said, looking highly pleased and a trifle embarrassed. 'But really, I came here to discuss your problems, not my abilities.'

He turned to Danuta. 'Bring us some milk and food, will you, please? I'm hungry. Besides, I want to discuss something with Witold.'

Danuta obediently went away without a word. I wondered if he were her husband or perhaps her fiancé but I did not dare ask. There was something mysterious about all this and I knew that he was the one to clear it up.

He lay down on the grass with a weary sigh and put his hands behind his head. I did not want to break the silence. At last he spoke, still looking up into the sky.

'I want to tell you something, Witold,' he began, a trifle embarrassed, I thought. 'You know, you are here in this house alone with Danuta. You realize that she is an honest girl . . .'

'Why are you saying all this?' I asked, genuinely puzzled.

He burst out laughing.

'Oh, never mind. Because I know myself, I suppose – and I have no particular reason to think you might be different.'

Now I tried to joke.

'Why are you so careful about Danuta, if you profess to be such a *roué*? Is she your wife?'

'No. She's my sister.'

I was amazed. So this was Lucien, the brother whom Danuta was so anxious to keep her mother from mentioning. Before I could reply Danuta came back with the food and my strange companion greeted her joyfully:

'Well, my little sister, because you neglected your social duties I was obliged to introduce myself to Witold. Now the situation is clear. But let us get down to business,' he said, beginning to drink his milk. 'How are you feeling now, Witold?'

'It's kind of you to ask,' I said warmly. 'I am much better now than when I arrived here, but I simply must have some work to do. I feel that I am wasting my time. There is no danger for the organization; from all the available evidence, it looks as if the Gestapo have given up the search for me. In any case, my appearance has changed so much, I don't believe they could recognize me.'

Lucien looked at me with that combination of candor and sincerity that was so engaging a trait of his.

'Exactly what sort of work would you like to do?' he inquired.

After considering the problem for a few minutes I answered:

'Taking all factors into account, such as my present physical weakness, and my general experience with journalism and propaganda technique, I should think I'd fit into the propaganda branch.'

I said it without much conviction as I did not particularly relish the notion of operating within propaganda. The deceit, dishonesty, and subtle cruelty one has to practice was not to my taste, but I knew that in contemplating the harm it would do the enemy, I would be able to steel myself to any unpleasantness.

Lucien seemed to read my thoughts.

'You don't really like propaganda, do you?' he said. 'You'll have your answer in a few days.'

After waiting a few days for Lucien, I grew impatient. I paced restlessly about the house, irked by the delay. Danuta's wit irritated me; my replies became curt and snappish. One evening as I sat moodily in the parlor with Danuta, we heard a faint scratching on the window that faced the back of the house. We leaped out of our chairs and ran to the window. I restrained my impatience while Danuta reproved her brother for his indiscretion in coming so early. He patted her head.

'Don't worry, Danuta, dear,' he reassured her. 'I haven't been caught yet, have I?'

She burst into tears.

'You are so careless and headstrong. You don't care what happens to us. You don't even take care of yourself. Some day you will get caught. What will become of us?'

She looked wildly about and then ran out of the room. Lucien became uneasy, uncomfortable. In a burst of fresh confidence, he said:

'This life is killing her. She is a very sensitive girl, and repressing all her feelings, as she has been doing, is not healthy for her. Take care of her, won't you, Witold?'

'I'll do my best, Lucien,' I answered simply.

He shook his head and sighed. Then, rather curtly and abruptly, he changed his tone. His voice took on the precise, impersonal ring of the official.

'Your request for work in the propaganda branch has been accepted by the underground authorities. You will draw up a list of the required equipment and begin activity as soon as you can. Now let us go into another room. I brought you some instructions for your new work.'

We went up to my bedroom and talked over what I was to do. When we finished, he watched my reaction silently for a moment and then smiled at me.

'Good luck, Witold, and make the Nazis sweat.'

The smile somehow seemed to emphasize the strained, worn appearance of his face.

'I'll do my best,' I answered. 'And you had better take care of yourself. Try to get some rest and remember, you can't do everything by yourself.'

Danuta reappeared, red-eyed and obviously ashamed of her outburst. She proceeded to restore a lighter atmosphere to the room.

'You know,' she said, 'I've been counting the silver. There is practically nothing left to count.' She glared menacingly at Lucien. 'Just because you have learned to slip in and out of the house like a thief, you don't have to play your rôle too literally. If you keep it up, between you and the Nazis we won't have a thing left.'

Lucien turned to me as though he were deeply aggrieved.

'You see, Witold, how I'm treated in my own house. She does nothing but insult me. She spends all her time thinking of new ways to injure me. I will leave before she blackens my reputation completely.'

He brushed her cheek with a kiss, clapped me on the shoulder, and left. We stood there a moment watching him disappear through the trees.

'I'm sorry I lost control of myself like that,' Danuta said.

'It's only to be expected – you've been under a strain. We all have to give way to our feelings once in a while. You'd better go to sleep now. I think you are going to be very busy during the next week.'

She smiled at my air of mystery, turned, and went up the stairs.

After my long period of enforced inaction, I took to my duties as a propagandist with exaggerated zest. The very next day I had Danuta scurrying all over the village, scouring every house for city and telephone directories and all sorts of advertising literature.

When Danuta, at length, found time to catch her breath, she asked for an explanation of the endless requests I had been making.

'Not, mind you, that I am inquisitive,' she remarked, 'but if I am going to wear myself out running all over the village, I should like to feel that there is a purpose behind it.'

'My dear girl,' I answered in high spirits, for I felt elated at being active again. 'You are about to witness the birth of an immortal literary masterpiece. In a few moments, I shall begin the composition of an eloquent letter. This letter is going to be received by everyone in the Reich who has a Polish name. Or at least, that is what we shall try to accomplish. We want to remind everyone of Polish origin that, although they are nominally German, Polish blood continues to flow in their veins.'

Danuta interrupted my oratory.

'Calm down, Witold. Don't excite yourself so. If you raise your voice much louder you shan't have to send any letters. Everybody in the Third Reich will have heard you, including the Gestapo.'

I became aware that I had gradually worked myself into a frenzy, pacing the floor and shouting. I sat down, took a deep breath, and continued more soberly:

'Furthermore, in this letter I shall urge the former Poles to study the history of their country. I shall cite some of the worst examples of Gestapo brutality and terror and I shall conclude by attempting to convince them that, despite the ruthless, barbaric methods of Nazi warfare, Germany will indubitably lose the war.'

'And when you finish this masterpiece, to whom and where will it be sent?'

'During the next few days we shall go through all these directories with a fine-tooth comb. We shall pick out every Polish name and compile a directory of our own. Then we shall have this list and copies of the letter delivered to the members of the Underground who work in the part of Poland incorporated into the Reich. They will have the letter copied by the thousands and forwarded to the names we have selected.'

'It is all so simple,' she scoffed. 'And just how are they going to send them – on the wings of hope? By carrier pigeon?'

'Neither. It will be much simpler to use the means which the German Government has established for us. Since the incorporated part of Poland is now considered by the Nazis to be a genuine part of Germany, all we have to do is to address the letters, put stamps on them, and mail them. Letters from one part of the Reich to another are seldom censored.'

Danuta and I set to work. Hardly allowing ourselves any time to relax, we finished the task in a few days. Lucien, who visited us at the completion of this project, was very pleased. He showered me with compliments and provoked Danuta by asking me if she had slowed up my work much.

Nevertheless, despite his apparent good humor and high spirits, I sensed in Lucien a hidden preoccupation and an anxiety. I had seen many men attempt to present one mood to the world while I knew that their inner emotions were entirely opposite. There are minute signs by which this condition can be detected. A faint air of absent-mindedness, a slight delay in responding to a remark, followed by an exaggerated effort to show that nothing had been missed, an overstrained air of attentiveness, are unmistakable symptoms of this mental division. It was quite evident that Lucien had something on his mind besides my letter. His interest was, by turns, a shade too casual and a shade too absorbed in what I had to say. At length I gave it up and decided to try to pin him down.

'You are hardly listening to me, Lucien,' I said. 'You must have something more important on your mind. Tell us about it, if you can.'

He denied that he had been inattentive. He did have something on his mind but it was not really very important.

'Do you know Bulle?' he asked me.

'I think I've heard the name,' I replied, 'but it doesn't mean much to me.'

Danuta cut in.

'So the name of Bulle means nothing to you? How could you help hearing about him? Everybody in the neighborhood knows that beast. That dirty swine . . .'

'Come, Danuta, don't explode. You are snapping at Witold as if he were responsible for Bulle's actions.'

As he turned to me to explain his face was set in hard, tight lines.

'Bulle is a *Volksdeutscher*,' he said, spitting out the word as if it were something foul to the taste; 'one of the worst kind.'

His expression was one of intense contempt. He paused to collect his thoughts and rummaged in his pocket for a cigarette.

The *Volksdeutsche* category to which Bulle belonged had been improvised by the Germans to meet changing conditions. It had a dual purpose: the denationalization of Poland and the lowering of morale. Originally it was confined to that third of Poland which, in the words of Gauleiter Forster,[1] 'had always been German until the Poles had Polonized it by terror and oppression.' Into this territory a 'pure Germanic culture' was to be introduced, the German language, German schools and institutions holding sway to the exclusion of all others. It was decreed that the only persons who would be tolerated in this territory were those individuals who would speak German, send their children to German schools, and serve the *Vaterland* in one capacity or another.

Most of the prewar Germans now hastened to obtain German citizenship papers and to become *Reichsdeutsche*. The overwhelming majority of the Polish population steadfastly refused to accept 'this glorious opportunity to establish solidarity with the Reich.' They continued to speak in Polish and were hopelessly slow at learning German. Faced by the prospect of having their generous offer humiliatingly ignored, the Nazis decided to make some concessions. Any person who had the remotest claim to German blood could, by applying to the proper German racial officials, secure equal food rations, certain privileges, and the boon of citizenship after the war. To the chagrin of the Nazis, only the merest handful of Poles were gathered in by this alluring offer. These were the *Volksdeutsche*. The Nazis made desperate efforts to augment their number, finally abandoning the slightest pretense to racial purity. Almost everybody was offered future German citizenship and concomitant present advantages in the form of special food and clothing rations for nearly any service at all. All the blandishments, the extra rations, and the enticing propaganda served to bring forth only a tiny handful of renegades.

The *Volksdeutsche* were objects of unmitigated contempt. They were regarded either as criminal traitors or weak-kneed, sniveling wretches. Naturally, I was aware of and shared in this universal attitude. Nevertheless, I found Lucien's attitude toward Bulle rather incomprehensible. Danuta's outburst could be interpreted as emotional and far-fetched. It was apparent, however, that Lucien's had much the same tinge of embittered animosity and unbridled hatred tempered only by the discipline and self-control which was the sine qua non of the Underground and without which no underground member could survive for long.

I wanted to know the motives that animated Lucien's hatred of this individual. I wondered if there was in it an element of the purely personal, whether the families were carrying on something in the nature of a private vendetta.

'Why do you hate him so much?' I could not help inquiring. 'Is there anything personal between you? He is, after all, only one of those vermin.'

Lucien's initial gust of anger had subsided. He sat down quietly in the overstuffed armchair, crossed his legs, and lit a cigarette from the packet he had finally extracted. He spoke coolly and calmly.

'The problem of the *Volksdeutsche*, for us, is one which we cannot afford to treat merely with cool disdain. Many of them, it is true, will quail before social ostracism and the disfavor of those who surround them. But some of them are impervious to this kind of pressure. This type is genuinely dangerous and will have to be restrained by more drastic methods. Bulle is one of the worst.'

Danuta clenched her fists and grimaced in uncontrolled indignation.

'The dirty swine should be killed. He is not even an ordinary traitor. He sneaks about buying drinks for the peasants, filling them with the latest bits of filthy Nazi propaganda, and urging them to co-operate with the Germans. Everyone knows that he turns in the names of our members to the Gestapo . . .'

Lucien checked her sharply.

'We have no proof of that.'

'Proof, proof!' She threw up her hands. 'Do you expect a full confession in his best handwriting? Don't pretend to be naïve, my dear brother!'

'We must have proof. We cannot behave like the Nazis and condemn people without evidence. Sooner or later, Bulle will make a slip. When he does, we will take action.'

Danuta remained discontented. Before she could bring herself to retort, Lucien switched the conversation into different channels.

'Well, Witold, now that your first job as a propagandist has been successfully completed, what do you propose to do? Have you any ideas?'

'Yes, I have. It may seem like coincidence, but I have been thinking about the *Volksdeutsche* myself. I would like to devote myself to them for a while and see to it that they get some of the rewards they deserve.'

Danuta's eyes gleamed with pleasure.

'I would like nothing better than to help you, Witold. But how are you going to set about it?'

The answer came from Lucien.

'I imagine our friend is simply going to use the "conscription" method. Am I right, Witold?'

I nodded in agreement.

'We did well with it in Germany and in some Polish districts. I think we can try to do the same thing here.'

The very next day, with Danuta eagerly assisting me, I set to work. Danuta had the task of collecting and collating sets of the names of this traitorous breed, while I called on my literary resources for a new species of composition.

This time, instead of writing appeals to the Polish people to maintain intransigent resistance against Nazi oppression, I was penning letters to the Nazi authorities asserting the most ardent desire to help serve them. This was the method known as 'voluntary enlistment.' Each letter was signed with the name of a *Volksdeutscher* and contained an urgent request from the writer to be allowed to serve his country. They had to be written with considerable variation in order to prevent our fraud from being too apparent. They ran more or less true, however, to the form a Nazi convert would naturally use to his 'masters':

> The Führer has awakened in me the consciousness of the German community. I am at present serving the *Vaterland* as a farmer (or merchant, policeman, etc.). I cannot continue any longer to stand by while my German brothers are heroically dying. I wish to contribute my services to the glorious German Army and herewith solicit the privilege of immediate induction into the Wehrmacht . . . I would consider it a great honour to serve in your army and I hope that my patriotism will be rewarded very quickly by my joining and being sent to the front . . .

When Danuta read the first letter I had written, the eagerness she had displayed for the project suffered a sudden setback. She gazed at me with unusual seriousness, obviously disturbed. I sensed that this trick violated her principles of decency and honor. Despite her hatred for the more traitorous members of the *Volksdeutsche* and her contempt for the merely craven, I could see that she felt it to be somewhat too cruel a trick to play on them.

I had long since become hardened to methods which affronted me at first but which I had finally learned to accept calmly because of their absolute necessity. But Danuta made me feel my initial emotions again. I regarded her sympathetically and said in as soothing a manner as I could manage:

'I know what is going on in your mind, Danuta. You think that perhaps we ought to be above this sort of trickery. But you have to understand our position and how much harm these individuals can do us – even the least of them. We can upset the Nazi schemes only through underhanded tricks like these. Otherwise we haven't a chance in the world against them . . . Besides, these are my orders.'

She appeared to brighten up and interrupted me ironically.

'Witold,' she said sadly, 'you had better confine yourself to letter-writing. Stay away from mind-reading. It just is not your specialty. I happened to be wondering why you address these letters to the central military authorities in Berlin rather than to the local powers-that-be. Is it not a rather roundabout system?'

I was a little annoyed at not being sure of whether she was telling the truth or going to great lengths, as usual, to avoid being labeled feminine, sentimental, and squeamish.

I answered with rather ponderous sarcasm.

'Of course, I could not hope to read your mind. It is much too complex and profound. So much so that it is hard to see how you missed the answer to your own question. These letters are sent to Berlin because the central military committee has not the time to consider each application. From there the appellant is drafted almost automatically. They never bother to consult the local authorities since they have more important things to do than to hold conferences about the drafting of a *Volksdeutscher*. Moreover, the risk of a local authority's consulting one of these draftees and exposing the trick is eliminated.'

Danuta responded to this by a long yawn.

'Witold,' she said in a bored voice, 'when you arrived here you hardly said a word all day. One month of country air and decent food has certainly made you glib. Another month and you will make longer speeches than a Nazi official.'

But she could not repress her curiosity for long. A moment later she was asking what would happen to a *Volksdeutscher* if he refused to go when called and denied sending the letter. I pointed out to her that the victim was usually unaware of the nature of what was happening. He usually thinks that he is enmeshed in the official Nazi conscription machinery. Even if he does suspect a trick, it is too difficult for him to go to the authorities and retract his demand or show unwillingness to serve. Besides, the letter itself is a thousand miles away, securely tucked in a file, beyond his reach.

I had got somewhat more than I bargained for when I asked Lucien for propaganda work. I had not yet fully recovered from my illness and the simple projects I had embarked upon had mushroomed into ambitious efforts that required a considerable expenditure of energy. The nucleus of the program had been simply to contribute some spadework toward sustaining the morale of the Polish population and bringing retribution on the heads of pusillanimous or treacherous collaborators.

But each idea seemed to sprout new ones that could not be neglected without a vital injury to the entire growth. I found myself, with the consent and aid of the Underground, involved in a large-scale production of letters, leaflets, and, finally, of periodicals and newspapers. I had the responsibility of preparing the texts for a wide variety of propagandistic forays. It was at once a delicate and exciting venture into literary and political realms. The lines of each text had to be traced out with minute precision, for nearly all our documents were displayed as the products of secret German organizations, Liberal, Socialist, Catholic, Communist, and even Nazi. It was a cardinal principle of our propaganda technique to issue all our exhortations, proclamations and even news reports under the aegis of a fictional body which espoused the Catholic ethos, the traditions of German parliamentarianism, international labor solidarity, or individual liberty. Each piece had to be written in scrupulous conformity with the tenets of its purported sponsors. After a while, I began to feel like an overworked actor in a poverty-stricken variety company. I was constantly on tenterhooks for a single slip could easily give away the whole thing.

The policy of issuing propaganda under German auspices was attended by increasing success, greater daring and, as a consequence, more ambitious projects that were constantly enlarged in scope. The Underground ultimately established two newspapers that circulated not only in the ranks of the German Army in Poland, but quite widely in the Reich itself. One was a presumptive organ of the German Socialists, the other an ardently nationalist sheet.[2]

In connection with these publications, I might say that it is my conviction that the rumors of a successful and extensive German underground movement may well have sprung solely from our work. I have come to know Nazi Germany rather well from many angles during this war. I have had occasion to travel in the Reich and I have never encountered a trace of any important movement hostile to the Nazi regime. Perhaps the German Government succeeded in putting the entire German resistance into concentration camps. But this would not speak hopefully for a German underground. It is a fact that during my travels to Germany, I could find no trace of an active German underground. I believe that all accounts of such movements are either pure fiction or wishful exaggerations. I know that much of our output, abroad as well as in the Reich, has been assigned wrongly to German sources.

In the midst of all this feverish activity, I had to make intermittent tours of the estate and continue to memorize the elaborate system of numerology I had constructed to help me over my difficulties in dealing with vegetables. The exacting demands of these tours were, however, compensated by my gradual accumulation of a meager agricultural lore and my success in cultivating the esteem and friendship of the local folk. To my surprise, I had succeeded in partially denting even the granite resistance of the ancient driver. Now when he had occasion to ask me the name of some destination he did so in a semi-civilized, though by no means cordial, rumble instead of his former growl.

Nevertheless, even though my fear of giving myself away had lessened, these inspections were a burden when added to my other tasks. The energy I had stored up in three weeks of convalescence was being used up too rapidly. After a hard day, I would feel a peculiar weakness. My body seemed to move itself about without any will or desire on my part. My temper had become short and my patience limited. Danuta frequently urged me to relax and rest for a few days. The cook wagged her head at me and rebuked me for my poor condition as though I had been a pig she was anxious to fatten. With renewed zeal she plied me with all sorts of healthful concoctions and appetizing dishes. Finally, I succumbed to this concerted pressure and my own realization that I was relapsing into illness. I promised that I would do nothing but loaf for a few days and eat everything prepared for me.

I set aside one day each week as a holiday. But the work had now taken such a hold over me that I found it almost impossible to idle. I had to discipline myself into grim and systematic relaxation, force myself to lounge, read, and chat innocuously while my mind was elsewhere. On one such night as I sat restively fingering a book I heard the familiar scratching at the garden window which signaled Lucien's visits. Glad to have an end put to my tedious relaxation, I rushed to greet him. I was brought up short by the presence of a stranger.

He was a short, powerfully built young man. His face was tanned and something youthful about his features contrasted oddly with deep lines that usually come with maturity. His straw-colored hair was clipped and bristling. He wore common farmer's garb and his manner was in general rugged and rustic but by no means naïve or insensitive.

I knew immediately that he was an underground man, by the circumstances of the visit and by the swift, appraising glance he shot about the room. He eyed me with unruffled calm, his attitude unusually alert and self-assured. I glanced inquisitively toward Lucien. Something about the stranger's bearing struck me as completely extraordinary, not at all typical of the person I expected to meet with Lucien. His face was set in hard, unyielding lines, his lips clamped tightly together. He seemed determined, preoccupied, even a trifle cruel.

18

Execution of a Traitor

The three of us gazed at each other without uttering a word. I felt
that it was Lucien's place to break the ice and I decided that if he
were to persist in being rude I would maintain a stubborn silence
myself. It seemed to me that some obscure point of pride was
becoming involved as the silence prolonged itself and became
increasingly oppressive. I had changed my attitude and was about to
let fly some pointed remark, when Lucien, to my complete surprise
and indignation, tugged his young friend's sleeve and withdrew with
him to a corner of the room. They whispered together for a moment
or two and then came forward again. Their strange behavior was
now beginning to infuriate me. As they approached the center of the
room, I advanced to meet them and said harshly:

'If you prefer privacy, Lucien, just let me know and I'll leave you
two gentlemen alone.'

Lucien looked at me in genuine astonishment and then his
expression changed to one of comprehension and finally even to
mild amusement.

'Oh, wait a minute, Witold,' he said apologetically. 'We really did
not mean to be rude. We had some urgent business and I'm afraid I
completely forgot my manners. I'm terribly sorry.'

It was my turn to feel embarrassed. My insistence on good manners had been ridiculous. I had taken offense at a trifle. I muttered
something sheepishly. We both were caught up for a moment in a
little comic orgy of mutual apology. Lucien finally dispelled it.

'I would like you to meet Kostrzewa,' he said in a businesslike
fashion.

Kostrzewa's sober expression vanished instantly and he broke into a cordial, youthful smile, his wide blue eyes candid and friendly. He appeared much less guarded and constrained. Apparently he had now sized me up and had formed an opinion of me.

'I've seen you around the village,' he said easily and sociably. 'I'm very glad to meet you.'

I liked Kostrzewa and found him difficult to pigeonhole. He could appear innocent and guileless, and yet at the same time he was shrewd and determined. He was probably a tough customer in a pinch, I decided, and let it go at that. We all then wasted time demonstrating our ability to socialize and make up for the previous oversights. Kostrzewa made the least effort, letting friendly smiles and nods of agreement be his contribution to the humdrum conversation about the estate and local conditions which engaged Lucien and myself.

My curiosity about the purpose of the visit and Lucien's anxiety finally ended these banalities. Somewhat noncommittally Lucien asked me if I would do him a favor.

'Of course,' I replied. 'What is it?'

'Nothing very special. We wish to settle some petty affair in a few days and we need someone to do sentry duty for us.'

This reserve nettled me. I felt he owed it to me to unbend a bit more.

'Can't you add anything to what you have told me?' I demanded.

'There is really nothing to add. All you have to do is to hide behind a tree and when you see anybody coming, whistle our tune. Will you do it?'

'Of course. What night will it be?'

'We'll let you know in a day or two.'

He turned about abruptly and Kostrzewa followed suit. They disappeared through the window. I watched them, thoroughly irritated with them and myself. I speculated wildly about the nature of the expedition but arrived at no conclusion.

Two days later, Lucien returned without Kostrzewa. I felt that something important was in the wind. Not that Lucien displayed any unnatural emotion or tenseness. He was too well-trained to expose any of the natural effects of an unusual situation. But I had seen too many men in similar states. They always carried themselves with a certain self-conscious ease. The usual inflections of their voices were missing and there was something exceptional in their attitudes, either an unwarranted gravity or an inappropriate nonchalance that gave them away. These nuances invariably communicated the presence of tension to me, though I could not say of what kind. It was as though, after a period of underground training, one became a kind of delicate machine registering the slightest of tremors.

Watching Lucien's vague smile, I felt my heart begin to pound and my palms become damp and hot.

I greeted him coolly.

'Is this the night you want me to do the little favor for you?'

'Yes,' he answered thoughtfully. 'You should put on some galoshes. It will be damp walking in the grass.'

I started up to my room. He stopped me, surveyed me briefly.

'You might put on some dark clothes, too. I don't want you to be conspicuous.'

'Very well. I'll be down in a minute.'

Lucien sat down in the same armchair he always unconsciously chose when he was nervous or strained. I glanced at him as I went up the stairs. The muscles of his jaw worked, his brow was contorted in thought. He held a lit cigarette in his hand without smoking it. I went to my room, changed quickly into dark trousers, slipped on a sweater under my jacket, and returned to the parlor.

Lucien was pacing back and forth.

'That's better,' he said. 'Are you ready?'

I barely had time to nod before he was on his way out, through the back door. I followed him. On the pathway at the back of the house he stopped and put a restraining hand on my shoulder. He pivoted about in a complete circle, casting sharp, searching glances everywhere into the darkness.

Satisfied that we were unobserved, he resumed walking, abruptly, with rapid, intense strides. The air was damp and raw. I pulled up my coat collar and walked silently at his side. We hugged the side of the path, keeping in the obscurity of the tree shadows. After about a half-mile, Lucien turned off the path and cut into the woods. We emerged on a broad, open field and hurried over the thick, moist grass. We were traveling now in a wide arc, I realized, detouring around the village so that we would re-enter the wood along the road through which I had first arrived. We walked through the fields for two miles till the village was at our backs and then re-entered the wood. In the darkness Lucien went ahead rapidly, sure of the locale. I stumbled after him, scratching myself on the thorny bushes and blundering frequently off the narrow path he had chosen into trees, roots, and shrubs. After another tedious and fatiguing mile, Lucien called a halt.

He dropped to the ground behind a thick clump of bushes that had apparently been selected beforehand. It was an excellent vantage point. By sitting up we commanded a clear view of the road, while we were invisible to anyone who passed along. We could not be approached from the rear because the noise of steps through the wood could easily be heard by us. In case of sudden alarm we could retreat and quickly lose ourselves among the trees. I felt sure now that these careful preparations had not been made for a 'petty affair.'

I sat quietly while Lucien peered and roamed about, scanning the road with restless wariness. The aches, fatigue, and cold had begun to affect me. I was annoyed with Lucien's air of mystery and the general lack of any respect or consideration for me. I contained myself as long as I could and then finally burst out:

'Tell me, Lucien, what the devil is the purpose of all this mystery? I don't mind being dragged by you over half of Poland but I would like to have a rough idea of what this is all about. How long am I supposed to sit here? When is it – whatever the devil it is – going to happen?'

I got the same reaction that I had received that night with Kostrzewa. He stared at me in blank amazement.

'What is wrong with you? Are you ill?' he asked me.

'Ill? Me? No, I would merely like to have an inkling of what this is all about; if it is not too much trouble.'

'I have told you before. It is just a petty affair hardly worth explaining.'

'Well, explain it in any case.'

'All right, I shall explain it a little later.'

He resumed his restless walking and peering. I sat and gazed about morosely. What a fool I had been to come out on such a fruitless expedition in my poor state of health. I cursed inwardly. I felt humiliated and balked, but there was nothing I could do. I promised myself revenge later, when all this was over. Lucien sat down beside me for a moment to rest. I began again obstinately to question him.

'You still do not intend to tell me the meaning of all this, do you? Why not? Don't you trust me?'

He frowned and shook his head impatiently.

'That is precisely the case. We do not trust you . . .'

'What?' I jumped to my feet indignantly.

'Sit down, let me finish. Not in the way you think. We know that you are loyal and trustworthy. But you are too intellectual, too tender-hearted to do what we plan to do. We can't afford to take chances. Now sit down and keep still. Silence is imperative.'

I pocketed my pride, sat down grudgingly, and sank into a moody silence. The minutes went by leadenly and painfully. I was about to rise and stretch my cramped legs when Lucien pushed me down, commandingly. Somebody was coming down the road. In the stillness I heard the ringing, stamping sound of a pair of hobnailed boots descending on the gravel with extraordinary force – as though the owner desired to call attention to his presence. I was startled to hear this loud individual commence to whistle the same tune Lucien and I had agreed upon. I glanced inquisitively at Lucien but he remained impervious.

The whistler crunched and stamped his way into our view. In the dim, cloud-obscured moonlight I thought it looked like Kostrzewa but I could not be sure. What was it all about? I cursed myself for being a dull-brained fool. Whoever it was glanced quickly in our direction without, however, slowing down. He continued his noisy progress, his back to me now. I saw that his shoulders were wide and heavy, his figure squat and sturdy.

I stared at Lucien, trying to get some clue to the enigma. He was staring not at the noisy figure but in the direction from which he had come. There was a faint, queer smile on his lips. I stared at the same spot. When my eyes became accustomed to the shadows, I saw the figure of a man scrambling from tree to tree along the side of the road. He was obviously furtively shadowing Kostrzewa, if it was Kostrzewa.

Lucien was breathing hard now, in short, painful gasps. My heart began to pound with excitement. The shadower passed directly across the road from where we were huddled. Lucien nudged me and got up with quick, stealthy movements. We clambered down, obviously following Kostrzewa's shadower. We kept carefully some thirty yards behind him, padding along the soft edge of the road. We hung back for a moment and I lost sight of our quarry. Then there was a wild scuffling noise, the sound of a struggle in the bushes, bodies crashing against snapping twigs and swishing foliage.

Lucien stopped and gripped my shoulder in a spasm of excitement.

'Stay here,' he rasped commandingly. 'If anyone comes, whistle the tune and run for cover.'

He ran down the road and out of my sight. I felt an odd impulse to dash after him, but walked over to the side of the road, disgusted at the rôle I was playing. A bloody fight was going on and I had been assigned the ignominious rôle of a lookout – and a lookout without even a knowledge of what he was doing. I was held in contempt, there was no doubt of it.

About fifteen minutes passed while I crouched by the side of the road, scanning the road and the surrounding country, my ears keyed for the slightest noise of a passerby, my mind occupied in bitter reflections on my treatment, worry and excitement about what was happening up the road.

I saw a tired, spent figure walk slowly up the road. It was Lucien. His face had a ghastly pallor in the eerie light. When he came close, I noticed that his brow was wet with perspiration. His appearance worried me and I felt guilty at the harsh thoughts that had been burning in my brain. I asked him to spend the night at the manor. It was late and the danger would be small. He rejected the suggestion curtly.

'I am not stupid enough for that,' he said sharply, and then, softening, 'I'm sorry, Witold. I did not mean to speak so harshly. I shall be over to the house in a day or two to explain everything.'

We separated glumly, Lucien trudging wearily off through the fields, I taking the path home. I was in low spirits, fatigued, depressed, and eager for bed. When I entered my room, the light suddenly snapped on. I felt a stab of fear and whirled around. It was Danuta. She had apparently been waiting in the dark. I was too weary and drained of all emotion to feel either indignation or sympathy – too fatigued to be either curious or angry. Soberly, anxiously, she questioned me.

'Did anything happen?'

I had a last flare-up of bitterness.

'Was anything supposed to happen?'

She looked hurt but I was in no mood to comfort her.

'You are sure you haven't anything to tell me?' She was almost pleading now.

'Not a thing.'

'Please, I should very much like to know.'

'Know what?'

'What happened tonight, of course.'

'I believe you could tell me what happened tonight,' I said with inexplicable asperity. 'You probably know much more about it than I do.'

'I really don't know. I would not ask you if I did.'

'I am much too tired to solve riddles,' I said cruelly, 'and I would like to go to bed.'

She walked reproachfully out of the room. I felt a faint pang of regret and guilt, dropped wearily on my bed without undressing and fell instantaneously asleep.

I woke up late the next day. I had no desire to see anybody. All the feelings of last night combined into a single, ugly emotion of mixed guilt, fear, rage, and humiliation. I had a horse saddled for me and rode about till it was time for lunch.

Lunch was an oppressive affair. Danuta and I avoided each other's gaze. I ate little and was anxious to finish and leave. In the middle of the meal one of the kitchenmaids burst into the room. She was fairly splitting with excitement, her voice stifled and inarticulate.

'Do you know, do you know,' she stuttered, 'that miserable spy, Bulle, committed suicide last night?'

I walked over to her and put my hands on her shoulders.

'Calm yourself,' I murmured. 'Sit down, speak slowly, and tell us what happened.'

She began to recite by rote, like an embarrassed schoolgirl, slowly, brokenly:

'He hung himself on a tree . . . a woodsman chopping trees found him . . . he left a note . . . wrote that he had had enough of being a rotten Nazi spy . . . he repented of all his crimes . . . he cursed the Germans . . . he asked the villagers to forgive him.'

I listened thunderstruck. I knew instantly that this was connected with my adventure of last night but could not somehow fit the details together. I looked at Danuta for a hint, a clue. If she knew anything she was carrying it off well. She commented coolly with no undue passion:

'I'm glad he repented. It will be a good lesson to the other *Volksdeutscher*.'

Needless to say, the entire village buzzed with the news. The men shook their heads and commented on how far remorse would carry a man. It was a good thing, too, for if Bulle, an agent of the Nazis, who knew their weaknesses, had become disheartened, it indicated an imminent catastrophe for the Nazis. The peasants were simpler in their homilies. They spoke of the rewards of a good conscience and the pangs of the guilty.

The German police were visibly embarrassed by the incident. They hardly knew what to say, they had so much cause for chagrin. I heard one of them remark to an assemblage of skeptical peasants:

'That Bulle was always crazy. We were about to have him committed to an institution.'

A few days passed and I was still no nearer the truth. Danuta and I had become constrained and uncomfortable with each other. I could not judge the extent to which she was informed about her brother's activities. The thought that she, too, might know more than I was the final touch of humiliation. I kept hoping she would tell me what she knew or at least deny that she had any knowledge, but she remained irritatingly close-mouthed.

Finally, Lucien made his appearance. He greeted us blithely, questioned us about the crops, made whimsical allusions to the late Bulle and the excitement in the village. I waited patiently till Danuta left the room for a moment and then I fired point-blank questions at him, the same ones I had asked him before, the same I had been asking myself all week. What was the meaning of all this? Why had Bulle been killed? By whom? Why was I left in the dark?

Lucien prepared to be suave and ironic. He lit a cigarette, raised a supercilious eyebrow.

'Killed?' he murmured. 'I thought he committed suicide . . .'

I spoke roughly. I had absorbed a little too much.

'Come, now. Stop your stupid clowning. I want to know the truth.'

'Very well. But stop shouting. You will know the truth soon enough. Danuta will tell you.'

'Danuta? What has she to do with it? What can she tell me?'

'What has she to do with it? She simply planned it all.'

I was incredulous. I could not conceive of Danuta being involved in the bloody affair. Lucien was looking at me ironically.

'You can't quite believe it, isn't that so? That was one of the reasons we did not want to trust you with the details. You are too delicate, too squeamish for rough work, Witold.'

'I still don't believe it,' I shouted angrily. 'Danuta, Danuta, come here at once.'

I ran to the door and called her. She entered the room, looking so small and gentle that I was touched.

'Danuta, your brother tells me that you planned Bulle's execution. Is that true?'

'Yes, it is.'

She went on to explain the whole story. She had first come to the decision on the night when we talked about the rôle of the *Volksdeutsche*. Something had to be done to quash Bulle's increasing influence among the peasants. She mulled about it for days until a favorable opportunity presented itself. Bulle had confided to one of the maids that he was on the trail of Kostrzewa and that he would soon nab him.

It was a perfect opportunity. They would use Kostrzewa as bait and lure Bulle to his doom. Danuta had procured a specimen of Bulle's handwriting and forged the suicide note. Lucien had acquiesced to the plan now that they had discovered a definite criminal act on Bulle's part. The project had worked itself out and had been executed with greater ease than they had anticipated. I had been called to do my share – a quite important share, she added.

'You need not feel ashamed at not having helped in the hanging. That's a job for a country lad with muscles and a strong stomach.'

I shook my head from side to side, dispelling the last shreds of the mist.

'What beats me is that Lucien asked me, not more than a month ago, to take care of you. You were so weak and lonely . . .'

'Witold,' she said gravely, 'Lucien was telling the truth. Soon this war will be over, we will be out of this hell – a good summer, a few months when we can draw a free breath, and we shall all become normal again. I shall be a weak girl once again.'

She looked at me reproachfully. Her face was sad and earnest. I saw her lips quiver, her eyes become moist. She ran out of the room.

Lucien turned to me and shook his head in disgust.

'You know women like I know Chinese.'

The aftermath of the Bulle affair was tragic.

Lucien had one shortcoming which was as charming as it proved unfortunate. He was inordinately fond of women. Very often, and we all knew it, he used to meet his girl friends and walk with them in the evenings. Probably he did not realize that the time was not suitable for flirtations. When Danuta and I expressed concern, he protested innocently.

'There's really nothing I can do about it. I'm lucky in love, that's all.'

But in other respects, he was very unlucky indeed. One day, as he was escorting a girl home from a neighboring town, he was hailed by a Gestapo officer in an automobile. His first thought was to run but he controlled himself. He approached the car warily and was relieved when the officer merely asked him to help change a flat tire.

Lucien complied and stood mopping his brow, when the officer peremptorily ordered him into the car. It was impossible to determine the officer's reasons for this request. Perhaps there was something suspicious about Lucien's behavior or possibly the officer merely wished to have him about to help carry his heavy luggage. Lucien, at any rate, refused to risk being taken to the Gestapo headquarters. He pretended to enter the car, twisted away, ran behind a clump of bushes, and disappeared.

We were told of these events by the girl he had escorted. When Danuta heard the story she sat rigidly, biting her lips to help her maintain her self-control. We consulted rapidly and I suggested that we go over the house carefully and destroy every incriminating document, then pack up and head for Cracow. Danuta demurred. I insisted on leaving immediately.

'We cannot accomplish anything by staying on here. We shall only make things worse. If Lucien succeeds in escaping, he can join us in Cracow. I do not believe the Gestapo will harm your mother. They will probably think her innocent of any complicity.'

She began to weep softly and nodded assent to my arguments.

We made a rapid investigation of the premises for any incriminating documents, then packed hurriedly. As the entire household staff stood on the veranda, unashamedly weeping and waving

Godspeed to us, we entered the carriage in which I had first arrived at this lovely estate.

The 'ancient,' who was more critical of me than ever before, was about to gather his reins and begin the journey when the last bit of horrible news was brought to us. A young villager sped up on a bicycle to tell us that Lucien had been captured while hiding in the woods. I put my arm consolingly around Danuta's shoulder. She trembled and sobbed wildly.

I shouted to the driver:

'Get started, get started!'

Danuta wrenched herself away from me. She had regained control of herself and spoke quietly.

'Please wait a moment, Witold. The news of Lucien's capture changes everything. I must stay on and face whatever is to come. Someone must take care of the house.'

I began to protest but she put her hand gently on my arm.

'Don't make it any harder for me, Witold. You must leave. There is work that you can do anywhere. I was born and raised here. I would be useless away from this small village. Now please go quickly. Goodbye – and remember us.'

I tore myself away.

I never saw the Sawas again. Months later in Cracow, I heard of their fate. My informants disclosed to me that the entire family had been arrested by the Nazis, tortured, and executed.

19

The Four Branches of the Underground

I worked in Cracow for a period of about seven months – from February to September 1941. The work I did here was quite different from any I had done before. Because I knew languages and something of international affairs, besides having a well-developed memory, I received a new assignment. My duty was to listen to radio reports and to take them to the highest authorities in the Cracow civilian and Military Underground. I was not supposed to listen to Polish broadcasts from London nor to English propaganda, but to those from neutral countries like Turkey, Russia (before Russia, herself, was at war), Sweden, and, if possible, America. My superiors were anxious to have a true and realistic picture of the total military and political situation. In order to provide this, it was essential not to rely solely on broadcasts in English, French, or Polish that came from the Allies' radio stations, whose content, far too like 'propaganda,' needed to be reviewed by using the news and analysis from military and political commentators in neutral countries. If pessimistic or discouraging, my reports were treated as secret material and were used only by our leaders. More often, however, the reports I handed in were used as the basis of foreign news articles in the Cracow underground press.[1]

During this period our work was at its greatest intensity and there was a proportionate increase in the number of arrests. One serious error had been committed in the organization of the Underground at the beginning of the war, which had progressively serious consequences. Most of the members based their calculations on the premise that it would be a short war. The damage and tragedies this erroneous assumption caused were incalculable.

The element of duration makes a vast difference in the intrinsic structure of an underground movement. If, for example, it is based on the assumption of a protracted war, then the entire plan and strategy must be radically different from one organized for a short term only. The main task in a longer war is one of preparation for a single, powerful blow in the distant future. To accomplish this most successfully, small, highly organized, and cleverly concealed units are best. These units must be linked to circles that are like concentric shells of broader organizations that come into being at the climax of the long war. Immediate plans call only for the activity of select individuals, not depending upon each other and not bound together by a single plan. No mass action is contemplated, for the inevitable high losses that attend such action are unwarranted.

An underground movement that anticipates only a brief life aims to produce chaos and to interfere with all the efforts of the usurping administration to establish order. It must operate at the highest possible tension at all times; it seeks the broadest possible range of unified operations; does not lay such a vital stress on secrecy and selectivity, and hopes to succeed more by throwing the enemy into turmoil and confusion than by perfecting its own machinery.

An inaccurate appraisal of the time element can be an absolute disaster. To a certain extent the earlier members of the Polish Underground were victims of such a miscalculation. From 1939 onward, a large number of military and political organizations comprising great masses from all sectors of the population had been functioning. Each one had tried to develop its activity on the broadest possible scale. If the war had ended in 1940, as nearly everyone had expected, then all these forces could have been thrown into the fray at the crucial moment with tremendous effect. As it turned out, the middle of 1940 brought us the disheartening news of the defeat of France and the certain knowledge that an Allied victory, if it were to arrive at all, would be a long time in coming.

The forces had, however, been set in motion and in many cases it was impossible to stop them. The movement sometimes continued to expand with tragic results. A tidal wave of arrests engulfed many of our greatest leaders. This was the period when Rataj, Rybarski, Niedzialkowski, Dabski, and others perished or disappeared. The 'loose organization centers,' as they were called, the individual units not bound to any strong, central entity, were the first and worst sufferers. While they could have done vital work in a short war, their survival was impossible or most difficult in the long run. They succumbed easily to the powerful police machinery of the Gestapo. The last half of the year 1940 and the first half of 1941 were the period of our greatest hardships – the bloody harvest of our overestimating the power of France and Britain.[2]

The hammer-blows inflicted upon us in this period shaped the knowledge of our requirements. It became apparent that if we were to continue large-scale activity and it was indeed impossible to retreat from the work to which we were committed, our survival and success demanded the co-ordinating of many individual units within one single, powerful, large-scale organization. The strong organization, as a unit, could furnish protection against the Gestapo, using pools of man-power and resources which smaller groups could never amass, even proportionately.

The large central organization could develop financial resources and elaborate machinery for manufacturing and obtaining the innumerable documents which are essential to successful underground work. Among these necessary documents were perfect sets of individual identification papers, authentic certificates from the German *Arbeitsamts* (Labor Offices), German identification papers (*Kennkarten*), and separate papers for special occasions. The military groups required adequate explosives and some of the modern equipment that the most adroit little groups would never obtain by themselves. Propaganda and political divisions had to be provided with supplies of paper, printing shops, and specialists of all kinds – writers, printers, and distributors. Once this stage of complexity was reached, a special cadre was needed merely to attend to the harmonious interrelations of all these branches. Liaison workers had to have meeting places, hideouts, warehouses for material, places for files and rendezvous.

Only a large organization could manage to perform the division of labor necessary to make safe and efficient so complete a mechanism. As this central organization crystallized, incorporating the looser units nearest to it, the ones on the periphery were fatally exposed. These became a kind of bloody wall between the Gestapo and the main body. When the Gestapo traced an event to the Underground, they inevitably ran into these groups. This arrested the progress of the investigation and attracted its full fury. They were like the outer suburbs of a besieged city, into which the enemy artillery rarely succeeded in penetrating.

The Gestapo found this situation an endless enigma, and indeed we ourselves were often confused by it. Frequently after a day of mass arrests, the Gestapo would relax under the illusion that the entire movement had been destroyed, broken up, or left powerless. They had merely been roaming in the 'suburbs.' Sometimes an arrested member would get panicky and send us a 'gryps' (any piece of news which a prisoner sends to the organization through the means created for this purpose) which informed us that the Gestapo had penetrated to the innermost recesses of the organization and knew the names of the central authorities.

The prisoner had been questioned about one or two names which he erroneously assumed to be more important than they were. They were usually the leaders of the small, semi-detached groups through which he had been working. In this way the Gestapo would invariably end up in a blind alley just when they thought they had come to the end of the main thoroughfare.

In accordance with the principle that the underground movement was the means through which the Polish state operated inside Poland, the central organization had now been divided into five branches.

The administrative branch was composed of the Chief Delegate of the Government and the Regional Delegates. Under their supervision twelve departments functioned, each one of which had a director who was the counterpart of a Minister of the Polish government-in-exile, now in London, such as the Director of the Interior, Treasury, Education, etc.

The primary duty of this branch was to organize and maintain the autonomous and secret deputy administration of the country. The attitude of 'not noticing the occupant' had prevailed. The Poles had refused any part in the political administration of the German General Government and the edict had been issued that not a single law or decree of this agency was to be obeyed.[3] The result would have been a condition of chaos, and the authority of the Secret Deputy Administration was established to bring control over the country. This administration exercised compulsion on the populace to a much greater degree than the Nazis could with all their brutal measures. In each county, city, and community, there was an official who, invested by the full authority of the state, issued decrees, and contacted the people. These persons were also designated to be ready the instant the country was cleared of the invader, to take over as a complete, democratically chosen administration, fully capable of managing the affairs of the country.

The military branch was organized as a domestic army. The Commander-in-Chief of this army and his regional commanders had all the rights and prerogatives of army commanders with regard to the population of a war zone. They could issue military edicts to guide the behavior of the population, and requisition men for necessary war work. Each soldier in the army had all the rights and duties of a front-line combatant, even including the traditional one that all time spent on the front lines counted double toward all benefits such as veteran's pensions, priority rights, and civil service.

The Commander-in-Chief, although this was not known to the public, was allocated a special power by a decree of the President. He was authorized to call a partial or total mobilization of all Poles the moment the Polish Government, acting in concert with the other Allied governments, gave the order for an open, universal uprising against the German occupants.

The work of the Home Army was divided into two parts: Command included propaganda, political diversions against the occupant, organization for the general uprising, and tasks undertaken in cooperation with the political and administrative branches; the other was devoted to the daily struggle and included sabotage (activity against the German civil and industrial war machine), diversion (direct activity against the German Army, its communications, supplies and transport), military training, etc. In addition, it collaborated with the units that operated in the areas that had been incorporated by force into the Reich and Soviet Union.[4]

The third branch was called the Political Representation and constituted the parliament of the Underground. Each of the four major political parties conducted, on their own initiative, many of their activities within the framework of the Underground. They had the right to engage in autonomous propaganda, political and social activity, and resistance to the occupant. But the representatives of these four parties constituted one official body, and to it were responsible both the Chief Delegate and the Commander-in-Chief of the Army.[5]

It also controlled the finances of the Underground and decided how many representatives each party should have in the Secret Deputy Administration and Offices of the Chief and Regional Delegates. The parties exercised control over the Polish Government in London through their representatives there, who, taken together, constituted the Political Government Coalition.

The fourth branch was called the Directorate of Civilian Resistance and its main function was to bolster up the policy of 'the stiff attitude toward the occupant.' Its members were outstanding scientists, jurists, priests, and social workers. They were to keep Poland clear of traitors and collaborationists, to try those accused of collaboration, sentence them, and see that the sentence was carried out. It had regional branches which functioned like people's tribunals of the type that frequently arise in times of revolution or national upheaval.

It was authorized to pass sentences of either 'infamy' or death. A Pole was sentenced to 'infamy' who did not follow the prescribed 'stiff attitude toward the occupant' and was unable to justify his conduct when asked to do so by us. It meant social ostracism, and was also the basis for criminal proceedings to be held after the war.

Sentences of death were passed on anyone who attempted active aid to the enemy and could be proved to have harmed the activities or personnel of the Underground. The tribunals also had the power to pass sentences of death on exceptionally vicious German office-holders. There was no appeal against the sentences of the tribunals and they were invariably carried out.[6]

In the 'fifth branch' were the loose organizational centers. This branch was an effort to curtail the waste involved in satisfying a desire to give vent to a sense of individuality. An effort was made to co-ordinate the activities of all the political, economic, educational, and religious groups which were active outside the other four branches. Some of them developed aspects which became very important, such as the programs for the continuing clandestine education of primary- and high-school students, as well as instruction at university level. Most of them helped keep up morale, although they lacked the proper technical and financial means to be important factors in resistance. These groups constituted what was called 'the outskirts of the Underground.' Each had one or several printed organs.

This was the picture of the underground state as it existed in the winter of 1940–1941.

Abroad, I was often asked by many prominent statesmen, Polish and otherwise, whether this implacable attitude toward collaboration could be maintained if the war were to be prolonged and the German terror intensified. There was never any doubt in my mind. Besides the will of the Polish people, our organization had perfectly institutionalized Polish hostility to invaders. Any Pole who might undertake to oppose this institution would be quickly liquidated. The Directorate of Civilian Resistance would sentence him to death and that sentence would be carried out by men so hard, so skillful at their work, and so devoted to the organization that their ability to perform these executions was taken for granted throughout Poland. To kill a German general or a high official was difficult – to kill a would-be collaborationist was relatively child's play.

That is why there never was any doubt in my mind that, no matter what course the war took and no matter what sacrifice it involved, this attitude of unyielding resistance would be maintained. As the war progressed, we in Poland came to realize that the extent of the suffering and sacrifice we endured because of this attitude was not always recognized by the outside world. This was a topic for bitter discussion in Poland, for articles in the secret press and queries to the government. Our conduct, we felt, made only too apparent the utter devotion of the Polish nation to the cause of the Allies. All our resources, our life, our very existence as a nation had been pledged to the victory of the democratic powers, and we felt injured by the fact that other countries, less unstinting in their efforts than Poland, willing even to keep up relations with both democracy and fascism, nevertheless 'managed' much better than we did.

20

The Laskowa Apartment

In the Underground, it became a rule not to live in one place too long. It became advisable for me to move from my quarters not only because I had been there for some time, but because a woman in the house had been arrested by the Gestapo. I had not the vaguest idea who she was or why she was arrested, but I thought it best to disappear. I did not register my new address but lived there and returned occasionally to the old one so that I would be seen there. For listening to the radio, I had still a third place.

This was a common underground ruse when one felt that the Gestapo was drawing too close for comfort. When a person became suspect, the Gestapo usually obtained their address from the Registering Office and arrived at night to make the arrest. By keeping in contact with his official apartment and not living there, an underground worker can know when the Gestapo is after him without taking a chance of being caught. This trick saved me. A few nights after I moved, I learned that two members of the Gestapo had called and asked for me by name. It was therefore imperative for me to change my identity again.

During my Cracow existence, my luck followed a consistent pattern. Those with whom I lived were arrested by the Gestapo while I managed to get away. At this stage I took lodgings in one of the co-operative houses tolerated by the Germans, and found employment there as a clerk and librarian. My radio was placed in a room in the apartment of an old woman. I was able to rent the room under the pretense that I was pursuing a side line as a picture dealer and needed the room for storage and to interview my clients.

Tadeusz Kilec was the manager of the co-operative. I used to go to high school with him and had the utmost confidence that, even if he were not a member of the Underground, he would not betray me. He was an unusual person, brilliant and generous. He pursued his beliefs with rare intensity and put them into practice with unselfish consistency and rigor.

After a short while each knew that the other was a member of the Underground. Kilec knew if for no other reason than that he had to register me under an assumed name. I knew that Kilec was in the movement because he was so well-informed about the latest events, knew all the Gestapo methods, and had information that could only have been obtained from underground contacts. Moreover, when one does conspiratorial work for a period, one develops an ability to detect confrères almost by smell.

Nevertheless, for the short time I lived with Kilec, neither one of us revealed or acknowledged his status or questioned the other.

In April he asked for and received permission to visit his family in southern Poland. A few days after he left, news came to us that he had been arrested in Lublin with three other men. The four had been caught loosening the screws in the railroad tracks. A transport of arms and food was due the next day from Russia to the Third Reich and they were attempting to blow it up.

Kilec had been the leader of one of the small, loose underground groups. He and his men were typical victims of independent and comparatively unscientific working methods. They were publicly hanged in the marketplace of Lublin. Their bodies were left on the gallows for two days and two nights as an example to the populace. Posters informed the citizens of Lublin that they had been Polish bandits who had attacked German officials for the purpose of robbing them. Similar punishment would be dealt out to all those who fought against the German community, the poster added, thus making the truth obvious.

The Gestapo came to the co-operative, ransacked the entire house, and questioned the inhabitants. Notice was immediately brought to me in my rooms in a section of the co-operative three doors away. I left most of my possessions behind, skipped out at once, and never returned.

The fate of my good friend Kilec and his comrades depressed me. I had very little money and the organization was in a tight corner. Changing my identity again and securing new papers irked me. In these dispiriting circumstances, a woman whom I knew took me in. She was known as Laskowa, and was the wife of a former Polish diplomat who was in the Polish Army. Immediately before the war, they had been abroad with their son, Jasio. Sensing that war was imminent, they returned to Poland to face it and do their share. Like many others, the war had deprived her of nearly all her possessions.

She was a woman of about forty, but, still youthful in appearance, admitted to being only twenty-eight. Anyone who contradicted her or joked about her age did so at his own risk, for she was capable of delivering a fearful tongue-lashing when she was provoked. She had a five-room apartment and served meals for paying guests in the large dining room. She also made a little money by taking care of a small garden and by selling her few remaining possessions. Most of this revenue was earned by indefatigable labor and it went largely toward the care of her five-year-old boy.

On the subject of Jasio she was absolutely fanatical. No one could even question her on the subject of her devotion to him. For she insisted that he was never to know, never to be allowed to feel for a single moment that there was a war. He had to have everything that had been his in normal times: pretty suits, chocolate, oranges, milk, candy. She worked herself to death to buy these things at unbelievable black-market prices.

Outside of her maternal passion – the most unadjusted to circumstances that I have ever seen – she was efficient, clever, and a fervid worker. Her apartment, because of the fact that she served dinners and therefore the constant flow of people attracted no suspicion, had become a veritable clearing-house for the Underground. Nearly every phase of conspiratorial work was carried on there, often simultaneously.

One day the dining room was filled to overflowing. In one corner, four men were deep in conversation. In another, a group of men and women were busy arranging secret newspapers for out-of-town distribution. In the third corner, three men were busy repacking explosives. At the table I sat with three other men who frequently worked with me.

We had received a few grams of cyanide and were making up pills, for an order had been issued that these should be carried by all men belonging to especially dangerous units. Laskowa was busy distributing minute portions of the cyanide with small apothecary's pincers. A bell rang, announcing the arrival of an expected visitor. In getting up to answer it, she spilled some of the poison on the table. At this very moment, Jasio ran into the room, tried to climb on the table, and got some of the powder on his hand.

Someone else had to answer the door, for Laskowa ran frantically over to the boy, scrubbed his face and hands, removed his suit, and then took him away to scrub him from head to foot. Someone had the temerity to inform her that most of her efforts were superfluous. She silenced him with a glare and went to work, scrubbing the table and the floor around it. Everyone in the room watched her in silent consternation. When she was through, she calmly took up her pincers and began again where she had left off.

Frequent visitors to Laskowa's apartment were Cyna, the journalist and Socialist leader with whom I had stayed when I came to Cracow on my return from France, and Kara, the chief of staff for the district. Their work required the closest co-operation between them, and they met here often. They loaned each other money to pay for material and labor and they borrowed men from each other for the performance of special tasks. If a printer in the military unit were arrested, the Socialists would supply the army with another. If the Socialists had a plan for an attack on a train or a garrison, or had been assigned by the Civil Directorate to execute a sentence on a German official, they borrowed from the army whatever necessary men were obtainable from their own ranks.

My work was in the press bureau of the military unit and required active contact with both of them. Toward Easter of 1941, we began to suspect that our section was in serious danger. One of our distributors was arrested. Some of the liaison women reported that they were being followed and watched. Two of our 'liaison spots' (places where underground press, money, arms, and other material was stored and called for) were raided and, although no members were caught, the material loss was not negligible. It was apparent that either a provocateur had crept into the organization or that the Gestapo was close at our heels. The order of 'no contact upward' was issued for the entire district, but was, unfortunately, too late.

One day Cyna arrived at the apartment, visibly upset. Kara had failed to arrive at an appointment they had made for more than an hour before near the river. Cyna walked up and down the room, smoking furiously, explaining the event to us, conjecturing and reasoning out loud. At length he flung away his cigarette nervously and announced:

'I am going over to Kara's place to see what I can find out.'

Laskowa begged him not to go.

'Don't take the chance,' she said, 'the risk is too great. If we wait a while and have a little patience, the situation will clear up . . .'

'Things may get worse if we wait,' Cyna argued, 'and even if the Gestapo is on our tracks, they certainly won't find Kara's place. I am going. I'll be back in less than two hours.'

Cyna never came back. When the two hours were up, Laskowa and I set to work, packing all the compromising material we could and burning the rest. We placed the unburned material in a suitcase and covered it with vegetables. Then we called in the maid, who naturally knew all the secrets of the house. Laskowa explained that we had to leave. Jasio would be in her care. Each day at 8 a.m., and at four-hour intervals afterwards, she was to take a large china vase and place it on the window sill where it could be seen from the street. If nothing of any consequence had happened, she was to remove the vase after five minutes. If the Gestapo were there, the vase would either not appear at all, or would remain on the sill as long as the house was dangerous.

Laskowa left the house first with the suitcase. I joined her at a street corner a few minutes later and we walked about together for hours trying to decide where to spend the night and where to hide the dynamite-laden suitcase. Laskowa's suggestions and opinions were prudent and sagacious. She did not wish to imperil others. She refused to go to stay with any of her friends or visit any of the meeting places, for she knew she would be highly suspect. As for the suitcase, she came up with a simple, shrewd plan. We would leave it at the checkroom of the railroad station for two days and then send for it, picking out the oldest and most decrepit porter to obtain it for us. If the Germans searched it, he would be the only one caught. They would probably release him and if not – well, one more old man would simply have to be sacrificed for the cause.

Then, after much careful selection and glancing about to see if we were being trailed, we decided to take a room in a small, dingy hotel of very bad repute. The Germans encouraged places like these as part of their campaign to demoralize the populace, particularly the youth. We both tried to behave inconspicuously in the lobby and pretended not to notice the shady-looking inmates. After I had paid for the room, we walked to the staircase and I fancied Laskowa was depressed by our sordid surroundings. I glanced at her with an expression of concern. She took my arm, nudged me in the ribs, and said laughingly:

'Let's go.'

She kept up her spirits remarkably during the next two days, while I went out to check on the vase and learn the news. The vase appeared and disappeared regularly. Cautiously, I got back into contact with the organization and gradually learned the appalling details of the misfortune that had occurred.

The whole thing had begun with the arrest of a liaison man from Silesia. Under indescribable torture, he disclosed the addresses of our meeting places. We were under surveillance for a long period during which no arrests were made. In this way, they discovered the residence of Kara. Fortunately, he had not visited the apartment of Laskowa since the surveillance had begun, and that was how we had been saved.

The day before Cyna had been supposed to meet him, Kara was arrested. The Gestapo, using a world-wide police stratagem, kept him in his apartment and remained with him. During the first day, three liaison women appeared who had had appointments with Kara and came to his apartment to investigate when he failed to turn up. The next day, Cyna fell into the trap in exactly the same way.

The organization used all their resources to get Cyna and Kara out of prison, but failed. The Gestapo were evidently aware that they had caught someone important and took extraordinary precautions. About Cyna's fate, nothing was known to the organization. A 'gryps' had arrived from jail which informed them that Kara had been horribly tortured, both his legs crushed to a pulp, his arms broken, and that he could no longer endure punishment. He asked for poison.

The leadership of the organization sent him two cyanide pills and a message:

> You have been decorated with the order of Virtuti Militari. Cyanide enclosed. We will meet some time, Brother.

On the following day, we heard from the prison again. Kara had been buried in the courtyard of the jail. About Cyna, nothing further was known. Months later I learned that he was in the prison camp at Oswiecim and in comparatively good health. The Gestapo had not discovered who he was.

Laskowa was able to return to her apartment with comparative safety, and resumed her former existence there. As a result of the arrests, the revelations under torture, and the certainty that many of us either were known to the Gestapo or might become so at any moment, it was decided to undertake a thoroughgoing reorganization of all the underground forces in the district. Locations were to be changed, liaison and contact spots rearranged, hiding places moved, the personnel of the units shifted around. Some agents were deployed to other cities. Everything necessary was done to nullify the effects of the German success. This episode was one of the worst defeats we suffered in Cracow during 1941, but still its consequences were not half as damaging as the Gestapo imagined them to be.

I was one of the personnel to be withdrawn from Cracow. It was decided that I was to be transferred to Warsaw to do work of the kind I had started out with in 1939, 'liaison work of the first degree.' I was to become the director of a unit and my tasks consisted chiefly in the maintenance of political contact between the highest underground civilian and military authorities.

The necessity and the importance of liaison work stem from the difficulties and dangers inherent in conspiracy. Its purpose is to avoid the necessity of holding large meetings of the responsible leaders. Liaison offices, to handle all such activity for groups which otherwise would do it less efficiently, are a product of the division-of-labor system possible to a large organization. In our organization, these offices received and forwarded the opinions, requests, decisions, and arguments from the political leaders, the High Command of the Underground Army, the Delegate of the Government and his departmental directors, and the Directorate of the People's Tribunals. The liaison is the communications system which keeps political contact between all branches without the necessity of frequent meetings.

Liaison work demands above all other qualities impartiality, good will, and a straightforward, disinterested approach. Personal opinions and sympathies must be divorced from work and interpretations must be objective and without bias. Violations of this approach can easily cause bitter intrigues, misunderstandings, and hostility of all kinds to disrupt underground unity. I swore above all to do my work with impartiality, loyalty, and good will.

21

Assignment in Lublin

The first problem that confronted me after my return to Warsaw was that of creating a 'legend' adequate to satisfy not only the demands of the Gestapo but to take care of my personal and family relations. It is the better part of wisdom in secret work to allow as few people as possible to become acquainted with facts that could become detrimental, not merely to personal safety, but to the organization. Those in whom one did confide had to be carefully selected and judged not merely from the standpoint of their good intentions and sympathy with our aims but by their ability to carry these out, remain silent, and not give way to carelessness, the temptation to gossip, or the numerous methods of persuasion employed by the Gestapo.

Three of my brothers and a sister were living in the capital. I had not seen or communicated with my sister since I had been to her apartment after the defeat in November 1939. News of her had reached me and I gathered that the condition I had found her in then had become aggravated. Her husband had been wealthy enough and she was still comparatively well-off from a financial point of view. She was, however, utterly broken-hearted and disconsolate. She had completely isolated herself from society and refused to see relatives and members of her family. There was no doubt in my mind that it would be a mistake to go to her.

My eldest brother, Marian, with whom I had stayed on the night before I departed for Oswiecim, was trustworthy and knew nearly everything about me. I had been able to keep in contact with him through intermediaries and had seen him for a short time on my previous visit to Warsaw. My brother had been arrested in the second year of the occupation, and sent to the concentration camp at Oswiecim, which, by a strange twist of fate, had been built in the barracks of my former military unit. Miraculously, he had been set free. Sometimes he talked to me about what being imprisoned there had been like. The Germans had transformed these former barracks into one of the most terrible places on earth. He had told me stories about it, which outdid in horror nearly everything I had ever heard. The guards had been chiefly degenerates, criminals, and homosexuals of all types, deliberately chosen for this purpose. The criminals, in particular, had been spurred on to monstrous cruelties by the promise of clemency for their crimes in direct proportion to their cruelty to the prisoners.[1]

My brother was a man of about forty-eight, well-informed and of wide experience. He held an important position in the Office of the Government's Delegate and knew the inside of the Underground as well or better than I did. Although visiting one's family was somewhat risky, I kept in touch with him while I was in Warsaw. We agreed that it would be best not to let the family know that we had seen each other. He would not reveal to them any of the details of my life since the war and would feign ignorance on the subject.

I had never been particularly close to my second brother, Adam, and decided not to approach him. My third brother, Stephen, a man of about forty-five, was in poor financial circumstances, and was compelled to work hard to get along. I had a great deal of affection for him, and, although I went to see him, planning not to let him know too much about myself, I realized he was not suitable for underground work. He had a daughter of about seventeen, Zosia, whom I liked very much, and a boy of sixteen, Dick, who, my eldest brother informed me, was on the wrong road. His father was unable to influence him, and as the boy was compelled to contribute to supporting the family, he had become involved in some highly dubious undertakings in the black market. I arranged with Stephen and Zosia to conceal from Dick the fact that I was staying permanently in Warsaw.

My greatest problem came from the large number of friends and acquaintances I had accumulated from my prewar days in Warsaw. It was impossible to avoid meeting them on the streets, in public vehicles, restaurants, and nearly everywhere. Social training had a tremendous effect on people, the intensity and depth of which I realized fully during these frequent encounters. It is almost as difficult to be tight-lipped to a smiling friend as it is to remain silent under Gestapo torture. If I recognized someone first, I did my best to sneak away unobserved. If I were hailed and could not get away in time, I cursed inwardly and turned on a mechanical, cheerful smile.

After a while I developed what amounted to a routine designed to extricate myself with a minimum of embarrassment from these situations. In a brisk cheerful fashion, I would say that I was a purchasing agent in a factory near Kielce and came to Warsaw occasionally on business visits. I would throw off one or two quick, polite questions, ignore the answers and any further questions, assure my interlocutor that I was overjoyed to meet him again but too busy to take advantage of my good fortune. Then, I would suggest a meeting at a café later when we would have plenty of time to renew our friendship and talk over the old days. The broken dates that ensued must have earned me many an enemy but it was the only method I could think of to avoid even more drastic consequences.

On the whole, though, the population of Warsaw adapted itself with remarkable facility to the network of conspiracy that had now grown and twined through all the varied life of the city. There were so many people working underground that the rest of the population had begun to accept them as a matter of course, adjusting their habits as people do to the idiosyncrasies of a relative or the secrets of an intimate friend. They learned not to gossip about the doings of their acquaintances or pry into the affairs of an irregular neighbor. They learned not to mention the names of men or women about whose activities they knew nothing.

The number of people in Warsaw who carried false documents or had something to conceal was enormous. When someone met a friend whom he had not seen for a long time, it was highly possible the friend had been in hiding. This was taken for granted and accepted as casually as one might accept a friend's trip to the country. Perhaps too casually. Hiding became the subject of innumerable jokes and witticisms, not only among the Poles but even in the German cabarets. One of the most popular was about the man from Warsaw who sees an old friend of his from Lwow standing at the opposite end of an overcrowded trolley:

'Hello, Wisniewski,' he shouts at the top of his voice, since he is wedged in between the other passengers. 'What are you doing in Warsaw? Don't you live in Lwow any more?'

'Hello, Lesinski,' the other shouts back in a voice equally stentorian. 'It's good to see you. But stop calling me Wisniewski. I happen to be in "hiding."'

Living in constant danger makes one exceptionally alert and sensitive to many things but it also tends to cause a relaxation with respect to daily events that often proves fatal. Some of our wiliest men were caught not because there was a lapse in their ability or shrewdness but simply through failing to take systematic, daily, prosaic precautions. A friend of mine once fell asleep in the Otwock woods near Warsaw. He was awakened by a German patrol, searched, and arrested. In his pockets were some percussion caps and fuses. He worked in a 'diversion cell' and was so used to handling explosives, arms, and poisons that he worried about having them in his pocket no more than an electrician might at having a few pieces of wire.

If danger was a constant specter to underground workers, poverty was even more so: poverty and the malnutrition which had increased in Poland by the deliberate design of the Germans to a point where the health of the entire nation was seriously threatened. To facilitate requisition of the entire agricultural output of Poland, the Germans had forbidden the importation of foodstuffs from the country into the cities. Food cards were issued to urban dwellers for a ration that was not enough to keep anyone alive, much less in good health. The black market was indispensable to perform this function although the prices were far beyond the range most people could afford. Nor could the Underground supply us with even enough to maintain a minimum standard of living.

I received, for instance, four hundred and fifty zloty a month, although the barest subsistence level required the expenditure of a thousand. The prices of even staple articles like bread or potatoes had gone to thirty times as high as they had been in 1939. A kilo of bacon cost fully sixty times as much as it had formerly.

The standard of living became absolutely primitive. The diet of those who fared the worst consisted exclusively of black bread mixed with sawdust. A plate of cereal a day was considered a luxury. During all of 1942, I never tasted butter or sugar. In summer, no one wore socks. Shoes, shirts, and suits of clothes cost small fortunes. Like nearly everyone I knew, I eked out my impossible stipend by selling a few prewar objects which I had managed to retrieve. Nevertheless, we were all hungry nearly all of the time. Everyone fended for himself and did what he could to get by.[2]

Although this poverty and hunger seems incredibly dreadful to me now, and almost inconceivable, I realized that then, painful as they were, poverty and hunger were not quite as bad as they appear retrospectively. For the first time in my life I understood that the sense of poverty is not a result of misery but of the consciousness that one is worse off than others.

Despite my poor resources, I managed to sustain life in Warsaw with the help of a couple of windfalls. I discovered a low-priced, cooperative kitchen. It received contributions: funds from fortunate people, donations of food from those who had an estate or homestead in the country. Here I was able to obtain an occasional plate of soup and a dish consisting of beets, carrots, and two potatoes, flavored with gravy that tasted vaguely like meat.

It occurred to me that as long as I was living under a false identity and my ration card was under an assumed name, there was no reason why the process could not be repeated. With the help of a friend in the organization who worked in the municipal office and my confessor, Father Edmund, who dug up two birth certificates of dead babies, born about twenty-eight years before, I managed to obtain two more sets of fake identity papers and ration cards.

I registered myself at two new addresses and dropped around once in a while, according to a scheme I worked out with the landladies. The advantages of living in triplicate outweighed the annoyances. In case one of my identities was compromised, there were two fresh ones into which I could jump at a moment's notice. The paltry rations of bread, jam, and vegetables were tripled for me, too.

I had no hesitation in doing this since there was not any co-ordinated food plan for the population except the impossible one imposed by the occupants, and everyone was left to his own devices.[3] Any trick that would get someone more food was moral; black-market operations, smuggling, ingenious methods of all kinds for eluding the German starvation program, all thrived.

One of my first tasks in Warsaw was an order to take some material to a political leader hiding in Lublin. I stepped onto the train loaded with a mass of radio bulletins, reports, and secret journals wrapped in a piece of paper to look like a loaf of bread or some other food-package. I carried it ostentatiously on the theory that it aroused less suspicion and could be more easily disposed of in case of emergency.

The trip to Lublin takes about six hours – slightly longer on the dilapidated trains the Germans had allowed to remain in Poland. This one was old, dingy, and noisy. It was unbelievably overcrowded and nearly every passenger on it was engaged in smuggling food. Each seat was taken, the aisles were crammed with people, and the lavatories, the doors of which had been opened wide, were also thronged. I was in the center of a car, surrounded by other standees, bumping into them and the fortunate seated passengers at every lurch and turn.

After three hours of this jolting, stifling journey, the train came to a sudden halt in the middle of an open field, a few miles outside Deblin. Through the window I saw squads of German gendarmes clustering around the train. It was one of the common routine investigations the Gestapo made at unpredictable intervals to check illegal practices which were too widespread to make practicable a concerted effort to halt them. Documents and packages would be examined and questions asked of every passenger.

No one would be allowed to leave until the investigation was over. I saw two gendarmes slowly working their way through the crowd from one end of the car, inspecting papers and packages. Holding my package, I started to move as unobtrusively as I could manage toward the other end of the car. My progress was halted by the sight of two other gendarmes approaching from the other direction. As the jaws of this trap slowly closed in on me, I gazed about for a means of disposing of my bundle.

To drop it on the floor near me would have meant putting all the passengers in the car in jeopardy and the irretrievable loss of the bundle. In the middle of the car was another exit, the door of which had been swung back on its hinges so that it was flat against the wall. I edged over to this exit and leaned against the frame nonchalantly with the bored expression of a man killing time by looking out at the landscape until the investigation was finished. Meanwhile, holding my arm down at my side, I carefully squeezed the package between the door and the wall.

Two of the gendarmes were now quite close to me. I yawned, stretched my arms, and stepped back into place. I produced my papers with confidence, although inwardly I was seething with excitement. My legend had been perfectly prepared and they passed me by quickly without the slightest suspicion. Several other people, however, were arrested and many packages of food confiscated.

A few minutes after the train got under way, having cooled off from the brush with the Gestapo, something that can never be taken calmly no matter how easily one comes off, I headed for the package. At the door an old peasant woman, gray-haired, weather-beaten, and wrinkled, was standing, blocking my way and laughing at me. As I approached she bent down, extricated my package, and handed it to me over the heads of the intervening passengers.

'Here's your package, young man,' she yelled in a voice that sounded like thunder to my horrified ears. 'And it ain't bacon either.'

I was aghast and started to deny owning it. She pressed it on me with an urgency that could not be denied. Frightened both at the notion that someone connected with the Germans might have heard her and that she might raise a greater fuss, I snatched the package, muttered something about 'dealing in currency,' and turned away swiftly to worm my way through the crowd and get into the next car. I was completely out of countenance and felt angered both at myself and the obstreperous female.

A little reflection made my anger at her evaporate. This woman had not the slightest intention of betraying me and had actually been standing near the door to shield me, covering the package with her voluminous skirts and risking her life. It did annoy me, however, to realize that I had concentrated on eluding the Gestapo with such intensity that I had left myself open to danger from differ-ent directions. In avoiding the scrutiny of the investigators, I had behaved with such clumsy obviousness as to put me completely at the mercy of any spectator, even a guileless old woman.

But at the station before Lublin I learned a thing or two about these unsophisticated and candid-looking peasants. The Gestapo had investigated the train with methodical, ruthless efficiency. Every parcel that contained a morsel of food had been confiscated. They had searched everywhere, poking under the benches, standing on tiptoe to peer at the shelves, yanking bags of flour from under the billowing skirts of the peasant women, and even taking slabs of bacon from their brassieres. They had cleaned the food from the train as thoroughly as a horde of locusts.

Yet at the tiny station before Lublin, as if by magic, a swarm of men, women, boys, and girls climbed down from the train, loaded with every variety of bulky, heavy package. I could easily detect loaves of bread, sacks of flour, hams, and sides of bacon. Like a flock of birds, they flew from the train and disappeared quickly into the forest while I rubbed my eyes in amazement and delight. I have never yet understood where and how they concealed those sizable bundles.

Truly, the victims of this war have developed talents equal to their inhuman sufferings. This strangely touching incident made me understand one of the most popular witticisms in Poland:

Question: How could the Allied armies land on the continent in such a way that the Germans would not notice?

Answer: Entrust the Polish black market with the task . . . and rest easy.

I reached Lublin without further incident.

22

Retribution

The German occupation, contrary to the general belief, was not successful, at least not in its policing aspect. The experience of the underground movements, not only in Poland but in all of the occupied countries, has shown that the machinery of repression was powerless against a clandestine body that was well-organized and that benefited from the strong support of the people.

The police and the Gestapo built their reputation on blind and absolute terror, relying on the inhumane treatment of those they arrested, and on the fear they created. Moreover, they did their best to fashion their threatened impact so that it was impossible to predict and defied logic. The average German police officer was most often an uneducated sadist, totally ignorant as well as being a criminal. In 1942, the Gestapo, the Underground estimated, had more than sixty thousand agents in Poland alone, backed by a huge army. Yet they were never able to crush the elaborate organism of resistance we offered them and almost never broke through to its central agencies.

But they did have methods for obstructing the will of the Underground and to some extent weakening its spirit. The most notorious of these methods was the principle of collective responsibility. From September 1939 onwards, the Nazis began massacring hundreds of innocent people in reprisal for their losses. From the very beginning, they established the rules of the game that we were forced to accept. To continue our work despite the application of such a merciless, unutterably cruel measure required a tremendous effort of will to overcome the heartrending knowledge that each act would be followed by the murder of people we knew and loved.

This incredible baseness on the part of Germany will never be forgotten or forgiven. Children will be taught to remember this ignominious principle of collective responsibility. When our hands are freed, we will take every opportunity, avail ourselves of every chance to pay back those murderous hoodlums, the beasts and sadists of the Gestapo, and the German administration in Poland for all they did to us and to the helpless Jewish people. There cannot be a reign of justice in the world unless that band of degenerates pays before the people who endured their outrages.[1]

The principle of collective responsibility inflicted even greater hardships in the rural districts than in cities. The urban leaders never knew exactly who would suffer for one of their acts. If, for example, a Gestapo agent was shot, they might know that every fifth or sixth man in a certain jail or district would be shot. But most often it was not known who would be shot, who would be held responsible. In the provinces, the Germans were more fiendish. In each village and small town, a number of names were posted. These were the names of prominent citizens whom the German administrators had selected to be on 'duty' for a period of three or four months, ready to assume 'collective responsibility.'

These individuals were often the personal friends, the wives, relatives, and families of many of the men in the underground branches that functioned near the town or village. Those in the organization knew that for every act of terror committed, a certain number of hostages would be hung. But there was no alternative. The acts of the Underground simply had to be performed. An order was finally issued arranging the duties of the organizations in the provinces so that acts of terror in a given locality would be committed by members from some other region.

The methods the Germans used to implement their extortion of the agricultural produce were innumerable, but the peasants developed many ways of outwitting them, managing by shrewd devices to save food for themselves and either to turn over to the Germans the most inferior produce or to destroy what they could not salvage. In the latter half of 1942, however, the countryside suffered a new, demoralizing blow.

The Germans issued an order forbidding all marriages unless permission was granted by the authorities. In nearly all cases, permission was withheld on the grounds that the couple were not suited to the program of 'raising the racial standard of the Polish people.' Complementary to this unprecedented edict, another order was issued to the effect that all illegal babies could be 'confiscated' by the authorities and deported to orphanages in the Reich.

When, as a consequence of the first decree, the villagers began to contract secret marriages, the second order was brought into play. The children arriving to these unfortunates were invariably snatched from their parents' arms. Often the mothers attempted to take their infants to another village where they could be hidden. This was rarely successful. The Gestapo employed their resources to track down the mother and tear away the baby as though it had been a puppy. Thousands of Polish children have been irretrievably lost to their parents in this way. No one is even sure exactly what did happen to them.[2]

But the peasants never yielded or knuckled under to the Germans. Amongst others, the Peasants Party did invaluable work in educating and guiding its constituents in their struggle. The repression suffered by people in the countryside contributed to their growing political awareness – the Peasant Party did not hide its desire to see that Poland, in the aftermath of victory, should be re-built with a modified socio-political system.

The 'ten commandments' of resistance issued by the Party became bywords on the tongues and in the hearts of these oppressed people. The underground press printed them; they were distributed in leaflets; the peasants copied them; their children learned them by heart. They were, as a matter of fact, not commandments but practical recommendations concerning the peasants' daily life and daily struggle under the occupation.

1. Fight stubbornly for Poland's independence.
2. In spite of persecution, build up your village organization to hearten the weak and temper the vehement until the hour

comes. That organization should be like a military post! It should sap and continuously weaken the bloody rule of the Germans and overthrow it in proper time.

3. Build up that organization so that it will be able to establish a Poland of the people with the peasant class as her foundation, a Poland without any elite, any cliques or dictatorship, a Poland democratic and law-abiding, with a freely elected parliament and an administration called to power by the people.

4. Demand a righteous social reform, land for the peasant, work for everybody; the country's economy based upon co-operatives; the nationalization of mines and industries.

5. Serve your country honestly, for you are her nourisher. Sabotage the occupant's requisitions. Supply your starving brethren in cities with foods. As a good Christian do not permit any exploitation of your brethren.

6. Be unyielding, cunning, and wise while dealing with the occupant. Be faithful to your organization, keep your word, keep the organization's secrets, defend the nation's dignity.

7. Be merciless to traitors and provocateurs. Condemn servility and social relations with the enemy. Suppress unnecessary prattle and curiosity.

8. Choose as your leaders strong, reliable, tried and tested people, generous and ready for any sacrifice. Do not let yourself be demoralized by the war.

9. Be inexorable in demanding the most severe punishment of the Germans for their bestiality, for their rapaciousness, for their spirit of aggression. Demand that they be crushed.

10. Have faith. Tell your neighbors that though the war may be long and may require tremendous sacrifices, the day of ultimate victory, of truth and justice will come, that an independent, democratic Poland will be re-established.

The rural branches of the Underground displayed a special brand of ferocity and ingenuity all their own.[3] Indeed, in our desperation and outrage against the barbaric methods of the Germans we used devices of which we were almost ashamed, but which we developed as purely rational answers to the appalling German process of exterminating our citizenry. In several cases, for instance, we employed procurers to arrange encounters between German officers and prostitutes whom we knew to have venereal infections. We allowed a great number of criminals to be liberated from penitentiaries in 1939 and encouraged them to resume their former professions of thieving and murdering, with the proviso that they confine their activities to the Germans. Our authorities kept the names, records, and data of every one of them, in order to be able to regain control of them after the war. Of course, they were promised that their sentences would be reduced in proportion to the success of their operations against the Germans.

It is a significant sign of the intensity of the collective hatred against the Germans that not one of these criminals committed a single act against a Pole and that many of them could be trusted to perform one or two of the more bloody requirements of underground action.

The people who did not live under German domination will never be able to gauge the strength of this hatred and will find it difficult to understand that every moral law, convention, or restriction on impulses simply disappeared. Nothing remained but the desperation of an animal caught in a trap. We fought back by every conceivable means in a naked struggle to survive against an enemy determined to destroy us. Poland snarled and clawed back at its oppressors like a wounded cat. I doubt if such a state has existed in large collectivities since the time of Christ.

We developed some real experts in revenge. I remember a man called Jan, who came from the province of Poznan and spoke German fluently. Before the war he traded in pigs. During and after the invasion, the region from which he came endured the most atrocious sufferings under the domination of the Germans. In Warsaw, Jan became one of the many specialists in paying back the Germans with their own coin.

To spread contagious diseases was Jan's favorite activity. He carried on his person an astounding collection of every type of lethal agent. He had an attractive, specially constructed little box in which were housed lice that bore microbes, typhoid-bearing germs, and other diseases. I was so repelled at the notion that I forbore to gather more specific information. His methods, however, were well-known among us.

He would frequent bars, enter into conversation with German soldiers, and drink with them. Drinking was one of Jan's pleasures but he never let it interfere with his main objective. At the appropriate moment he would drop a louse bearing typhoid germs behind the collar of his German friend. He would drop germs into the drinks. He, too, would introduce them to girls who had venereal diseases. He was known to have a number of different methods, which he would utilize according to his convenience or fancy. Not one of the Germans ever escaped lightly with whom the 'walking germ,' as he was known, became acquainted.

We had many proofs of the people's obedience and trust in us. A typical order that was issued to test the discipline and confidence of the Polish people was the one forbidding the reading of German newspapers printed in Polish. The Delegate knew that it would be impossible to forbid completely reading these papers. Curiosity and craving for news are too deep to overcome. The order was limited during some periods to Fridays. On that day, the Polish people were instructed to abstain from purchasing a single copy of Nazi newspapers.

We were soon able to see the results of this order. The Friday editions of the German newspapers had to be drastically curtailed. All over Poland – in Warsaw, Cracow, Lwow, and Wilno – it became known that a person seen buying newspapers on Friday was liable to be hit by a brick as he left the stand. An invisible hand might place a card on his back on which was written: 'This pig patronizes German trash.' On his house the next day, as if by magic, an inscription might appear in indelible paint: 'A fool lives here. A stupid, vile Pole who obeys the German gangsters instead of his own leaders.'

Another simple and clever device to unify and hearten the Polish people and draw them close to the Underground was the order to rename the streets. This order was issued by the Political Represen- tation. It was somewhat romantic and sentimental in spirit, but it proved invaluable in a practical way. Overnight, on the walls, on street corners and lamp posts, inscriptions and placards appeared bearing new names, the names of heroes or statesmen of this war whom the Poles admired: Niedzialkowski Avenue, Rataj Drive, Roosevelt Street, Churchill Boulevard. To use the prewar name or the name the occupants had assigned became an unforgivable crime in patriotic company. When one was with strangers, one could immediately tell which side they were on. If they said 'Roosevelt Street,' one knew that, unless they were provocateurs, one was among one's own kind. If they said 'Debowa Street,' then one had to watch one's tongue. In this way most of the streets in Poland were renamed and the names were accepted by the vast majority of the people.

I saw ample testimony to the success with which the Under- ground maintained the Polish people in a 'rigid attitude' toward the enemy. Frequently I had to draw up reports and circulate them among the leaders on the effects of our instructions.

In the beginning of 1942, the Germans intensified their man hunts. Increasing numbers of men, women, boys, and girls were simply rounded up and sent to labor camps. A Polish gentleman who had been a diplomat in his earlier days, who had studied at Heidelberg, and had many acquaintances in the German aristoc- racy and diplomatic corps, applied to the Delegate for permission to write a memorandum to the central authorities in Berlin. He was courageous enough to describe all the excesses and brutalities of the Germans in Poland. He asked the German Government to put an end to Gestapo excesses and forbid children, pregnant women, and fathers from being sent to labor camps. It was a worthy pro- posal and might have had some chance of success.

I drew up my report from this point of view. All the answers were against granting the request. If he were given permission he would appear to be acting in the name of the Polish nation and the Polish nation did not recognize the right of any German to send a single Pole to a labor camp. The principle of the rigid attitude forbids any collaboration or compromise in the political domain. The project was unanimously vetoed.

Patronage of the movies, theaters, and brothels, which the Germans inaugurated for the purpose of corrupting and demoralizing the Polish people, or reading of German-published books, was, of course, forbidden. In the beginning of 1942, a Polish actress opened her own theater. She had some relations with the Germans and obtained their permission. She did not intend to, and never did, perform any plays that were demoralizing or offensive. As a result, inquiries began to come to the Underground from other actors, many of whom were working in our ranks, as to whether it was permissible to open Polish theaters and what our attitude was.

The answer, backed by a large majority, was:

'The actress in question will either close her theater immediately or be denounced in infamy.'

The decision was based on many reasons. It was pointed out that no Pole could be permitted to relax in a theater while Poland herself suffered, fought, and sacrificed. No Pole could be allowed to forget, even for two hours, what was happening in his country, or to amuse himself. It was forbidden to interrupt the fight and insurrection in permanence against the invader.

In spite of the decision, of which she was notified, the actress kept her theater open. The plays she produced were mostly light, harmless comedies. Soon afterward, she was declared as having committed an infamy and her name was published in all the underground papers. She will be prosecuted for having offended the feelings of the Polish nation. The 'rigid attitude toward the occupant' could not be disregarded by anyone.

In our campaign of revenge and resistance against the Germans, they themselves performed inestimable services for us. German administrators, policemen, officers, and civilians are not so indifferent to worldly goods as a race of 'supermen' were frequently told they ought to be. In occupied countries, the occupants were nothing more than a gang of petty robbers who seemed to have on their minds, besides abusing the local populations, nothing else but money.

The German administration never seemed to be aware of the degree to which we were able to exploit the weaknesses of their agents. Bribery was one of the methods we used to take advantage of their venality. Those who wished, at all costs, to be safe and secure, were tricked by promises that we would protect them after the war in case the Germans succumbed to the Allies. But by far the greatest successes were scored by blackmail. I am afraid that many of us became masters of this fine art.

A German official once sold us some newsprint. His price was outrageous but we paid it cheerfully. He rubbed his hands, expressed his friendship for us and even said something vaguely complimentary about the Polish people. What he did not know was that we had detailed proof, including photographs, of the entire transaction. He was politely requested to render us further services at prices that became steadily reduced as he became involved more deeply. For a long period he supplied us with many useful commodities at what must have been a great loss to him.

An average German soldier, on furlough or convalescing, was often badly in need of money. He longed for good food and liquor, he wanted cigarettes. It was easy for him to sell us a belt, a coat, a blanket, even a revolver or a rifle. Our prices were excellent. After the first operation, the wretch was compelled to supply us with a steady stream of military articles, which he had to steal or buy from his colleagues. He knew it would be an easy affair for us to report the transaction to his superiors if he stopped dealing with us.

Many Germans who were *Treuhändler* (trustees) of estates would attempt to make money on the black market by selling requisitioned grain, furniture, furs, fodder, and nearly anything they could lay hands on without being detected. We had several people whose tasks consisted only of making purchases of this kind. Usually they spoke fluent German. They took whatever the *Treuhändler* had to offer, without bargaining, and disappeared with their purchases. The very same day they would be back with a request for specific articles, at very reduced prices. The *Treuhändler* would hear the request in amazement and often got angry. Then our man would explain.

'You don't understand. I am really doing you a favor. If you shouldn't deliver these things, I might go to your superiors and mention your previous sale. Perhaps you wouldn't like me to do that . . .'

There were moments of intense satisfaction in our work.

I should like to close this chapter by telling about one of the most extraordinary measures taken by us under the German heel. I know of no precedent in any underground organization.

In 1941, the financial condition of the Underground was very poor. The help that came from abroad was insufficient to meet our large expenditures. The Government's Delegate decided to remedy this condition by floating an internal loan. Bonds were to be sold, and when Poland was reborn and the government returned from exile, these certificates would be considered as normal government obligations and would be redeemed with interest. The success of the bond drive that ensued was remarkable proof of the faith of the people in the restoration of their country and their confidence in the authority of the underground state.

The 'bonds' themselves were not very official in appearance. Tens of thousands of small tissuelike scraps of paper bore the following text:

I thank you for the gift of so and so many kilograms of bread, potatoes, coal, etc. I shall do my best to recompense you as soon as possible.

Then came the signature and a secret sign in place of a serial number. The potatoes, bread, coal, etc., served to indicate the amount of money.

The circulation apparatus of the press was used to a large extent in this campaign. People who were not active in the Underground but happened to enjoy public confidence and moral authority were appointed as loan agents. This campaign also served to draw many people into the atmosphere and work of the underground movement. Members of the Underground, and I was among them, were also assigned to the duty of collecting money.

It was a very peculiar bond campaign. The agent went to see people he hardly knew, relying on their good faith, loyalty, discretion, and generosity. He addressed them in the name of an anonymous, secret Government Delegate and unknown state authorities. He could not prove his identity conclusively. I called on about twenty people, many of whom I did not know. Most of them were ordinary middle- or working-class people who were living on what they had stored away from better days. Frequently I was asked:

'Why should I trust you? How do I know who you are? What guarantee do I have that you will not use the money for yourself?'

In answer, I pointed out that I was referred to them by a friend of theirs whom they could trust, emphasized the fact that the Underground was, of course, anonymous, and could not supply addresses. I told them that if they wished I could send them regularly secret newspapers from whichever political party they designated. This was always the best way to persuade them. I concluded simply by giving my word of honor.

Although I had a few disagreeable incidents, it must be stated that out of the twenty people I approached, not one refused to contribute. And I was not particularly deft or skillful in my salesmanship. Of course, some people lowered the amounts I demanded, one person whom I asked for ten thousand zlotys giving me only a hundred. A few bond-buyers, I suppose, contributed out of simple prudence, because the Underground was likely to be the official state after the war. But I felt that the majority gave because they had been touched by what I said and because they were genuinely anxious to help.

The loan was a great success and the sum we got helped us to continue our work. After the liberation, these pledges will surely be redeemed. If they were not, it would be a tremendous abuse of the faith of brave, patriotic people who love their country and made sacrifices for it.[4]

23

The Secret Press

One of the divisions of underground work with which I became thoroughly conversant was the secret press. I had been ordered to turn in a monthly political report for inner use and since this required familiarizing myself with the material in the secret press, a so-called 'sub-report' on this material soon became part of my regular duties. The person to whom I delegated the drawing-up of the sub-report had to read all the important newspapers and periodicals and sort out their most salient and noteworthy features, including polemics, projects, and the expression of viewpoints. From these he culled material for a review of the press which was composed every three days. It served the purpose of keeping the authorities informed on the main political currents in the press and was also a valuable source of information for the government.

I also took a more personal interest in the press. Amateur collecting has always been one of my habits. Before the war I collected old Polish coins, illustrated books on art, and other objects which interested me. During my stay in Warsaw, aware of its historical importance as well as its appeal to me, I amassed what is probably the richest collection of Polish underground material existent – newspapers, pamphlets, and books. At intervals I packed them away in cases and hid them in a safe place. I hope to reclaim them after the war and believe they will be interesting museum material.

The Poles have had thorough, long-standing experience in printing and circulating secret underground newspapers. In this war they have printed and hawked thousands of newspapers, defying the Gestapo as they defied the Tsar's secret police, the famous Okhrana, about thirty-five years before. Then, as under German rule, small portable hand presses were active in Polish towns in the cellars of the workers' dwellings. Other presses, too noisy when working to be placed in basements, were hidden in woods. Kerosene lamps provided light for the editor, who was the reporter, the printer, and the publisher of the underground paper.

One of these anonymous individuals, acting as editor, writer, printer, and publisher, for two years (1899–1901) printed the underground *Robotnik* (*The Worker*) in cellars in the slums at the center of Poland's textile industry – Lodz, the Polish Manchester. Some eighteen years later, he became well-known throughout the world. He was Josef Pilsudski, leader of the revolutionary, anti-Tsarist Polish movement, and later Commander-in-Chief of the Polish armies.

For many years, young Poles, citizens of the already independent Polish Republic, visited the historic cellar in Lodz, at number 19 Wschodnia Street, a narrow, noisy, dark backstreet, where the small hand press, a Bostonka (Boston Press), was shown. (Are there in Boston, Massachusetts, such printing machines? I do not know; but so the history-making old machine was called.) It stood there until the tragic day of 1 September 1939, the day of Hitler's attack on Poland. It is a sacred 'in memoriam' for all Poles – the machine which contributed to their freedom.

The secret press in which I participated did not deal exclusively with internal affairs and party matters. Every paper – daily, weekly, bi-weekly – brings first of all news to its readers. The news of the world was supplied by a large and well-organized chain of secret radio listeners. Risking their lives constantly, young and old, men and women, listened to foreign broadcasts in soundproof cellars, in small huts set up in forests, in attics with faked double roofs. The London BBC, Boston's WRUL, and Columbia's WCBX (New York) were the major sources of information. Every paper had several listening stations, for one could never be sure whether the American and British broadcasts would be heard, or whether one would be able to listen to one at the necessary time. Young boys took the messages to the 'city desk' in the basement or hut in the woods, where the one man serving as editor and printer worked on his hand press or mimeograph. He wrote the editorials; he received messages from 'correspondents' and 'reporters' spread all over the country who transmitted to him by messengers news about what was going on in the country itself.

Special press agencies had been organized by the Government Delegate, the military organization, and the staffs of the large political parties. Through these, Poland received truthful reports of the latest news from the outside world, the battlefronts, and the most important occurrences in the occupied countries. These press services had regular correspondents in neutral and Allied countries.

The correspondence they sent was, of course, in code. Speeches by Churchill and Roosevelt, important interviews with the members of the Polish government-in-exile, and news from the fighting fronts arrived in Poland and were circulated widely within a few hours. The services supplied not only the texts of speeches but comments and explanatory notes. Like regulation press services, they sold copy to the newspapers of the secret press, who elaborated upon the information they bought in their articles. The newspapers, in turn, received funds from sales they made to their readers. The best secret press services were the Military Press Agency, the Agency of the Government Delegate, and the Echo Press Agency.

The newspapers themselves were numerous and heterogeneous in character. Every political group had at least one secret organ and many had several. The influence and circulation of these papers were as diverse as the conflux of political and social opinions of which they were the expressions. The *Information Bulletin*, the semi-official organ of the Underground Army, had a circulation of at least thirty thousand copies and was even greater when one considers the known fact that each copy had a plurality of readers. The circulation numbers of the others were less significant, ranging from one hundred and fifty to fifteen thousand.

How did these papers look? All of them, for understandable reasons, were of small size – from five to six inches wide, seven to ten inches long. They had from four to sixteen pages. The great majority of them were set by hand, some in linotype, some printed on small hand presses, some mimeographed.

These clandestine publications did not all have the approval of the underground authorities. Many of them, even though they were published in good faith, were considered totally surplus to requirements. Some had only a very limited, local readership, others had an irresponsible political tone that spread confusion in the Underground. Some carried opinions based on mysticism, prophesy, and divination. Others did not follow the rules of underground conspiracy and led to arrests and the loss of equipment.

Publishing a successful underground newspaper required men who were thoroughly trained and competent, not merely to produce effective journalism but to make sure that nothing of importance was revealed to the enemy.

The Gestapo, to be sure, had the newspapers minutely scrutinized for any grains of significant information. We took it for granted that all the papers were known to the Gestapo, since it was not hard to obtain them. The editors of many of these papers took pleasure in sending copies directly to Gestapo headquarters in Warsaw, usually with a message:

> We are sending you a copy of our paper to facilitate your research, to let you know what we think of you, and to keep you informed of our plans for you . . .

By and large, the views and tendencies of the secret press were those of the Underground. The Government Delegate had his own official organ, *Rzeczpospolita Polska* (*The Polish Republic*), which expressed the official point of view of the government-in-exile and the underground authorities. In it were published his commands and advice, the speeches of prominent members of the government and the statesmen of the Allied nations, and editorials which expressed the official viewpoint of the Underground. It had a wide circulation and was very influential in molding opinion and conduct. The Government Delegate also published provincial organs from the same viewpoint and serving a similar purpose. Among the most popular were two entitled *Our Eastern Provinces* and *Our Western Provinces* which were especially noteworthy in their treatment of matters of local interest.[1]

Wiadomosci Polskie (Polish News) was the official organ of the Commander of the Home Army. It contained articles devoted to social and military problems. The army also issued the semi-official *Information Bulletin* which stressed current news. The staff of this paper was composed of highly skilled, experienced journalists. Its news, editorial, and make-up departments were all of the highest quality, and it was undoubtedly the most popular secret paper in Poland. The military command also issued *Zolnierz Polski (The Polish Soldier)*, a large part of which was devoted to reminiscences and analysis of the military defeat. It published, too, news of the activities of the Polish Army at home and abroad. *Insurrection* was a special military paper, largely transmitting information for the benefit of army officers on such subjects as street fighting, insurrectionary tactics, and 'diversion.'

The journals of the political parties were in a different class. They expressed the rich multiplicity of political life in the Underground and, taken as a whole, performed immense services in heightening the awareness of the populace and educating them to an understanding of the divergent political trends in the modern world. All shades of opinion could be found, from the extreme right to the extreme left.

The publications of the Socialist Party contained a high level of reporting and a vigorous editorial policy. The chief organ of the party was the WRN, a title formed from the initials of the Polish equivalents of the words 'liberty,' 'equality,' and 'independence.' The *Wies i Miasto (Country and City)* fostered the collaboration and rapprochement of factory and rural workers. *Wolnosc (Freedom)* circulated among the intelligentsia. It had numerous organs worked out to fit their program for different sections of the population and different regions. Many of them were of a local or restricted character, their circulations being accordingly less wide.

The chief organ of the Peasant Party was called *Through Fight to Victory*. They also published a paper for the urban intelligentsia called *Orka*, and others.

The Christian Labor Party, which had suffered the greatest casualties in the underground struggle, frequently changed the names of its newspapers for conspiratorial reasons. Its chief organ during the first period of my underground work was called *Glos Warszawy* (*The Voice of Warsaw*). When I was leaving Poland, their two main papers were called *Zryw* (*The Rising*) and *Narod* (*The Nation*).

The chief organ of the National Democratic Party was *Walka* (*The Fight*). This party also issued a periodical of military and political character called *Narod i Wojsko* (*The Nation and the Army*).

These were, on the whole, the most influential and well-known papers of the country. There were many others, some of them the publications of these same parties but less widely known, and others from the smaller centers.

How were these papers produced?

The printing presses were well-hidden and were kept supplied in many different ways: we used a great deal of imagination. To the secret presses peasants' carts brought paper – newsprint. Hidden beneath cabbages or potatoes were the precious sheets of white, yellow, or even dark brown wrapping paper which was used as newsprint. The paper was mostly taken or bought from the Germans, by using all methods of bribery.

The editor was not always quietly bent over his work at the printing press. Sometimes, for a newspaper man, he had rather unusual tasks to perform. Here is a report taken directly from a Warsaw underground paper, the *Biuletyn Prasowy* (*Press Bulletin*):

The day before yesterday, May 25th, four of our fellow-newspapermen (three men and one woman) were busy writing and setting their paper in the apartment of Mr and Mrs Bruehl, Lwowska Street, Warsaw. Earlier in the day, two Gestapo men came to the house and hid in the Opus Laundry, from where they could observe Bruehl's apartment door. About midnight, the Gestapo men rang the bell.

One of the newspapermen opened the door and the Germans entered the foyer. They ordered our men to stand with arms raised, facing the wall. One of the Gestapo men went to the printing room. There Leon Waclawski, the well-known writer and, since a couple of months ago, editor of one of our papers, took out of his sleeve a hidden revolver and shot the German, killing him with one shot. The other Gestapo man in the foyer shot three times at the man standing against the wall, killed him, and ran away, screaming for help. Two remaining men and the woman had time to leave the house quietly. Leon Waclawski today joined our staff. Today we are proud to print his first article. Unhappily, the printing set in the Bruehls' home was lost. Yesterday, the Gestapo arrested all inhabitants of the house at Lwowska Street.

And here is another story, taken from the Warsaw *Glos Polski* (*Poland's Voice*):

On July 4th, a villa on the fashionable Okrezna Street at Czermiakowi, one of the residential sections of Warsaw, was surrounded by the Gestapo and SS Black Guards, armed with machine guns. The house sheltered one of our printing shops which had to be moved from the Mokotow [another of Warsaw's residential sections] because the editors and printers were apparently being shadowed by the Gestapo. When knocking at the door brought no response, the police threw hand grenades through the windows, blasted the doors, and fired inside several times from the machine guns. Two of our men were killed and two women were seriously wounded. They both died shortly after in a hospital. A few days later, the owner of the villa, Mr Michal Kruk, his wife and two sons, fifteen and seventeen years of age, as well as all tenants of two neighboring houses, were arrested and subsequently shot.

'This case cost 83 persons their lives,' states the paper casually.

The distribution was another problem. We learned much from the experiences of Stanislaw Wojciechowski, Pilsudski's roommate, co-editor, co-printer, and his circulation manager under the Tsarist regime, and later President of Poland in 1922.

He is the creator of the 'three-system' selling of underground papers. This system was used exclusively by us. Every man engaged in the circulation job knew only 'one man behind and one man ahead.' He knew only the man who delivered to him at a secretly fixed place and the man who took the papers from him in another town. When a paper carrier was discovered by the Gestapo, as others had been years before by the Tsarist Okhrana, and submitted to the 'third-degree hearing' in the murder cellars by Himmler's men, he could give only these two names – no more. He did not know any more. This system worked, but only through wholesale circulation. It was different with the hawkers. Here every kind of ruse was practiced.

Newsboys on the streets of Warsaw and Cracow sold the German local papers, *Krakauer Zeitung*, *Warschauer Zeitung*, or the *Ostdeutscher Beobachter* in Poznan, or Adolf Hitler's own *Völkischer Beobachter* in every small and large Polish city. No Pole bought these papers, unless the boy smilingly said to him:

'*Today* you have extraordinary news about German victories . . . Buy it.' And handed him a copy.

The passer-by knew the copy was worth buying, for it was stuffed. Between the pages full of German dispatches describing incredible successes of the swastika-bearing flag, he found a hidden copy of his underground paper.

A butcher would say to a woman customer, while wrapping her steak:

'Put it on ice *immediately* when you reach home, will you?'

And she would know that the paper was wrapped inside.

A more unusual system consisted of putting the papers right into the mailboxes, having them placed under plates in restaurants by waiters, etc. The famous Polish world-record breaker in the 5000-meter race, and 1932 Olympic winner, Janus Kusocinski, was shot by the Gestapo while serving as a waiter in a Warsaw café. He used to put secret newspapers under the patrons' plates.

Never before the war did I understand what tremendous influence poetry may have upon a people fighting for an ideal. There was no underground paper which did not contain some poetry, verses of classic Polish authors or modern poets.[2] The underground press was not only the political and military mouthpiece, but also the medium for culture and religion. I kept one copy of the following article which I dare call a modern version of the Lord's Prayer. It is a blood-dripping, melancholy, and passionate Lord's Prayer of the Polish Underground. It was reprinted in many papers and thousands of boys and girls learned it by heart in secret schools.

OUR FATHER WHO ART IN HEAVEN, look upon the martyred land of Poland.

HALLOWED BE THY NAME in the day of our incessant despair, in these days of our powerless silence.

THY KINGDOM COME, We pray every morning, repeating steadfastly: Thy kingdom come throughout Poland, and may in liberty and sunshine Thy Word of Peace and Love be fulfilled.

THY WILL BE DONE ON EARTH AS IT IS IN HEAVEN. Thy will be done. Yet it cannot be Thy will to have murder and bloody licentiousness rule the world. May it be Thy will that humid prison cells stay empty – that forest pits cease being filled with corpses – that the whip of Satan incarnate in man stop its whizz of terror over our heads. Thy will be done in Heaven and in the air, bringing us light and warmth instead of bombs and fear. Let airplanes be messengers of happiness and not of death. Thy will be done on earth. Lord, look at our land covered with graves, and lighten the path of our sons, brethren and fathers, of the Polish soldiers fighting their way back to Poland. Let the sea return the drowned, the waste spaces of land the buried ones, the sands of the deserts and the snows of Siberia give us back at least the bodies of those we loved.

GIVE US THIS DAY OUR DAILY BREAD . . . Our daily bread is a toil beyond any endurance – it is wandering and migrating and death in dungeons, death that comes from the gun of the firing squad, from tortures in camps, death from starvation, and death on the battlefield. It is the torment of silence while our throats are choking with stifled screams of pain; our daily bread is a forced clenching of our fists and setting of our teeth in the hour that cries for bloody revenge. To this daily bread of ours, Oh, Lord, add force of endurance, patience, and will power that we be silent, lest we burst out before the hour of destiny rings.

AND FORGIVE US OUR TRESPASSES. Forgive us, Oh, Lord, should we be too weak to crush the beast. Strengthen our arm lest it tremble in the hour of revenge. They have sinned against Thee, they have trespassed upon Thine eternal laws. Do not let us sin against Thee with weakness as they sin with criminal debauch.

AND LEAD US NOT INTO TEMPTATION . . . Lead us not into temptation but let traitors and spies among us perish. Do not let money blind the hearts of the rich. Let the replete feed the hungry. Let Poles recognize each other anywhere and at any hour. Let our mouths be silent while the torturer crushes our bones. And lead us not into temptation to forget tomorrow what we are suffering today.

BUT DELIVER US FROM EVIL . . . Deliver us from the evil one, from the foe of our Polish land. Save us, Oh, Lord, from the paths and misery of deportation, from death on land, in air, and in the sea, from treason of our own.

AMEN. Let us again be the hosts on our own soil. Let us rest our hearts with the calm of the sea and the beauty of our mountains. Let us feed the starving crowds in Thy sunshine, Oh, Lord. Let us establish justice in a righteous Poland:

AMEN. Give us freedom, Oh, Lord! Amen.

Besides periodicals, the secret press published books and pamphlets of all kinds. The pamphlets were mostly ideological. The books were chiefly reprints of works the Germans had forbidden – Polish classics, texts for underground education, military works, and prayer books.

The story of the underground press would include endless episodes of ingenuity and heroism. The boldness and enterprise that went into them was exceptional, since it functioned not merely to keep these periodicals alive but to make them in every way a provocation and threat to the Germans, and a symbol of the unyielding attitude of Polish resistance. Energy was directed and dangers risked for the purpose of subjecting the Germans to contempt, and keeping up Polish morale by a defiant refusal to accept the occupation as a reality.

Most of the press was published on common paper and in octavo size for the sake of safety in distribution. At one period, one of the papers suddenly appeared in a bold new format in an issue the size of the London *Times*. This seemed in the circumstances like nothing short of insanity. In their first editorial, the publishers explained themselves:

> We have decided, [ran the editorial] to print our paper in a size generally considered unsuitable for conspirators because we have resolved to take no notice of the bloody scoundrels of Szuch Boulevard [the site of Gestapo headquarters]. We ignore the dangers of the Gestapo and pay no heed to the German occupation. Just as the spirit of a nation cannot be killed, so can neither its courage and contempt for the enemy. The only payment we ask from our readers for the risk we are taking is audacity, a wide circulation, and a bold perusal of our paper, which is being edited contrary to all the rules of conspiracy.

The paper continued to run for some time in this unusual format. Another paper came close to equaling this feat by using an extremely fine grade of paper, a grade that would have been out of the ordinary even in normal times. The proofreading and printing of this publication were also excellent. The editors of this remarkable periodical explained:

> We have no difficulty in obtaining paper from the affable German authorities. The German beasts are corrupt to the core. Anything

can be obtained from them by bribery. We are using this fine quality paper to show the world the infamous venality of the German administration.

The attitude of ignoring the Germans was expressed in many phases of publishing. I remember a pamphlet printed in three colors with artistry and skill that would have been distinguished at any time. These were, in a sense, all superfluous and wasteful efforts, but to us they served a valuable political and morale-building purpose.

The secret press was the means by which the underground state kept in direct contact with the large mass of the population. Through it, the people were constantly kept aware of what was being done so that their morale and hope were kept at a high pitch. For their work to be successful, the underground organizations required the knowledge, too, that the people had faith in them and supported their authority. Testimony to this effect was received in many ways.

24

My 'Conspiratorial Apparatus'

I had at my disposal quite a respectable 'conspiratorial apparatus.' I am using quote marks here intentionally, as a certain amount of explanation seems to me essential. To many people this term is meaningless and even contradictory. They cannot associate 'conspiracy' with 'apparatus.' People whom I met abroad could not imagine how I could hold a normal office in the Underground. The notion of meetings and consultations was impossible to explain. In their vision underground workers met briefly, usually at night, and in dangerous circumstances and eerie surroundings. Illumination for these thrilling scenes was supplied by flickering candles. The conspirators wore masks and spoke in tense whispers. They behaved like a cross between an extraordinarily sagacious detective and a reckless gambler staking his last coin on the turn of a card.

Nothing could be further from the truth. The motion pictures I have seen and the fiction I have read about the Underground in Europe are invariably products of purely sensational imaginations. The kind of work we engaged in had to be done by the simplest, most prosaic methods. Mystery and excitement attract attention and perhaps the greatest law of underground work is: 'Be inconspicuous.' The quality we valued more highly than any other was the ability, as I have said before, to 'melt into the landscape,' to seem humdrum and ordinary.

For the most part, our work was probably less thrilling, less of an adventure, than the work of a carpenter, and was wholly devoid of sensational exploits. Some of our men put in endless hours at 'observation points.' Others had the unglamorous job of calling for and distributing the secret press – dull, heavy, fatiguing work that was dangerous enough in the long run, but certainly unexciting. A great percentage of all our work consisted of nothing more than office routine – precise, detailed, following through of scientific, administrative methods. To execute a raid, to keep a secret press in operation, to run a children's school, or to blow up a train requires extensive preparation, careful analysis, the procuring of information from different sources, and the co-ordination of scattered activities.

My own apparatus was elaborate. I had four well-equipped organization offices; two for meeting places with military and civilian leaders; one for archives; and the last, in which there were two typewriters and the usual office paraphernalia for clerical work. Among my assistants were two women who did mostly typing, two teenage boys who served as my liaison men, and four well-trained and reliable university graduates who had the status of representatives of my department and were entitled to confer with civilian and military leaders.

The two meeting places were large commercial offices. The owners were perfectly aware that we had rented them for work of a 'confidential' nature. We had succeeded in allaying their fears by assuring them that we would never leave anything compromising there, and in addition the agreed rent was three or four times higher than the norm. And besides, they were completely trustworthy people. The fact that the office building in which we were located was visited by numerous business callers and was properly registered with the German authorities, indeed, actually backed by them, was an inestimable advantage to us. A large traffic of people of all varieties added to the camouflage. Everything was normal and there was nothing at all calculated to attract anybody's attention. Yet, after some time, I went to the additional trouble of securing an engagement, in the firm that owned the office, as an advertising agent. This was an excellent pretext for daily calls at the 'office.'

My archives were hidden in a Warsaw restaurant. The art of secreting documents in private apartments, within double walls, double floors, and double drawers, in bathtubs, stoves, commonplace pieces of furniture, and other places, had reached an incredible level of ingenuity. One may even speak of it openly. For if the Germans were to institute a campaign to unearth the buried documents of Poland, they would need a whole army of workers to demolish houses, tear out floors and ceilings, and take them apart inch by inch. They would have to dig up a thousand parks by the roots, rip open hundreds of sewers and gas mains, and split apart thousands of trees.

My personal office was in a private apartment in a prosperous but quiet building in Mokotow, rented from an elderly aristocratic lady who lived in Konstancin, and whose son had been working for a commercial company in Brazil when the war broke out. The apartment had three main rooms as well as a service entrance in the kitchen, which was very important in case it was necessary to make an escape. My own office was in one of the main rooms, large, comfortable, and steam-heated; one of the others was used by the typists. The typewriters were of the noiseless variety, so that they could be used far into the night without complaints. The two women who worked on them were modest in appearance, did not seem particularly interested in what went on about them and attracted no attention whatsoever as they came and went. The dining room was at the disposal of my assistants. The kitchen was used by my liaison agents, who were to have contact only with me.

They were perfectly adapted to underground work. Indeed, I should say that despite the world-wide opinion that women are loquacious and indiscreet, my own experience has led me to believe that women on the whole make better conspiratorial workers than men. There are certain things they cannot do as well, but they make up for this in possessing to a higher degree the fundamental attributes of successful underground workers. They are quicker to perceive danger and less inclined to avoid thinking about misfortunes than men. They are indubitably superior at being inconspicuous and generally display much caution, discretion, and common sense. The average woman who takes up secret political work evinces much more 'underground common sense' than the average man. Men are often prone to exaggeration and bluff, are unwilling to face reality,

and, in most cases, are subconsciously inclined to surround themselves with an air of mystery that sooner or later proves fatal.

My own work was difficult and exacting. Every day I would meet
two or three men who were deep in underground work. Our interviews were carried out with constant knowledge that the Gestapo
might be hovering about. I had to exchange views with them on
scores of topics, explain the attitudes and opinions of other underground leaders, and find out their views, reactions, and decisions to
communicate back again.

To these meetings I often brought a question or an opinion from
the Commander of the Army or the Chief Delegate of the Government. I would have to obtain the maximum amount of information
from my interlocutors to retransmit. The most painful moments, as
far as I was concerned, occurred when an interview had to be interrupted because I was not in possession of all the relevant data. My
interlocutor would usually be furious at having to renew the complicated preparations for another meeting. It would be called 'a lack
of efficiency in the section of political liaison' and I would come in
for severe criticism from my superiors.

Such inefficiency no doubt prevailed during the initial period of
my work. Later, I learned my trade and corrected most of my early
faults. When I was instructed to communicate some 'question' and
to obtain the reactions and viewpoints of all the leaders, I made an
effort to understand it from all angles, grasp the broadest possible
implications of a problem. With all the pros and cons in my mind, I
was able to catalogue the specific viewpoints of individuals more
easily and in making the rounds of the leaders found myself more
fully prepared to explain every doubtful point. As I grew more skillful I was able to see a problem not merely in its entirety but in terms
of all the possible responses it could provoke. I could foresee nearly
all the objections that were eventually made and anticipate questions and observations. This made it much easier to gather all the
elements needed for a full and accurate report.

Some of the problems were thrashed out orally but in the majority of cases I had to prepare reports. These were like any normal

administrative reports, numbered, dated, carefully worded. The title was a definition of a given political question. The substance was a terse, clear summary of the viewpoints of the political leaders. In the conclusion, all the elements of agreement and divergence were summed up and an estimate made of the possibility of reaching unanimity. Sometimes copies of the reports were delivered by my liaison men to each person with whom I had conferred. Names, places, parties, all other important items were always coded or designated by pseudonyms. My department had two special code systems, one for political, the other for military authorities.

If I stated that there was a strong possibility of unanimity and the men who received the reports confirmed my opinion by initialing their copies and returning them, the matter was considered closed and the report was deposited in the archives as testimony and historic document. These reports of mine also became the basis of the monthly and quarterly political accounts which the Polish government-in-exile received from the Underground. If no agreement could be reached on a contemplated step or action, the leaders returned the report stressing that they deemed it necessary to have the country's Political Representation called together for the sake of further discussion, or that their refusal was final.

If requests came for a convocation of the Political Representation, they were forwarded to the director of the office of the Government Delegate. The director had the responsibility of setting a time and place for the meeting. Usually he waited till a group of these unresolved questions accumulated before arranging such a meeting, unless he considered the proposal of vital import. I had nothing more to contribute to the problem and I was not informed of the final outcome.

25

The Liaison Women

During the course of my work in liaison I came to sympathize deeply with the hard-working and suffering liaison women, the chief function of whom was to facilitate contacts between underground workers. They were a vital link in our operations and were in many ways more exposed than those they helped bring together.

One general principle worked for both myself and others engaged in important underground work. Our private dwelling places were kept as free of our secret work as possible. No one was permitted to know my private address except the closest member of my family or my personal 'liaison girl.' Where I slept, no political action was prepared, no interviews were held, and no compromising papers were kept. This enabled us to feel a necessary minimum of security, a freedom from constant fear so that we could sleep without being disturbed. Of course, accidents could and did happen even in these private quarters, but this system reduced them to a minimum.

No one, not even the closest liaison woman, was entitled to know my secret name or the forged document I carried constantly in my pocket. Under conditions of these kinds, communication between members of the Underground was often nearly impossible. The liaison women took care of this problem. If I wanted to contact a political leader whose assumed name I did not know and whose address I could not obtain, I did it by seeking out his liaison woman.

They, on the contrary, were completely exposed. The private apartment of a liaison woman was frequently placed at the disposal of the Underground. She could never be allowed out of sight, had to live where she could be found easily, and was not allowed to change her name or address without permission. As long as she was active, she could not be permitted to go into hiding or get lost to us. To allow this would have meant to break down the contacts between the members and branches of the Underground. A liaison woman and her apartment were always carefully watched by members of a special 'observation department.' If arrested she was unable to betray us, even under torture, because within two or three hours all people in contact with her changed their names and addresses.

She was therefore in constant danger. All the details of her life were known to many people. This itself is undesirable in underground work. She constantly carried compromising documents. Her movements were of a kind that aroused suspicion and her presence was necessary at many imperiled places. The average 'life' of a liaison woman did not exceed a few months.

They were invariably caught by the Gestapo, usually in incriminating circumstances, and treated with bestial cruelty in the Nazi jails. Most of them carried poison and were under orders to use it without hesitation when the need arose. It was almost impossible to get them out of jail and the Underground could not take the risk of their succumbing to torture. It can be said that of all the workers in the Underground their lot was the most severe, their sacrifices the greatest, and their contribution the least rewarded. They were overworked and doomed. They neither held high rank nor received any great honors for their heroism.

Most of the liaison women with whom I had the honor to work endured the common fate of their sisters. One of them was a young girl of about twenty-two or -three. I saw her frequently but knew little about her. She was with us about three months and was a marvelous worker. She was caught by the Gestapo in a trolley car and did not have a chance to get rid of the documents she was carrying or to swallow the poison.

A message, smuggled out of the jail after her first and only interrogation, described her condition. The Gestapo beasts stripped her to the skin and put her on the floor. They tied her legs and hands to hooks and then struck at her sex organs with rubber blackjacks. The message from the prison read: *When they carried her away, the lower half of her body was in shreds.*

There was another woman of about fifty who was with us for a longer period. Before the war she taught French in one of the Warsaw high schools. She associated herself with the Underground almost at its inception. She was poor and lived in a modest little apartment with her husband who was nearly seventy and unable to work. She had placed her home at the disposal of one of the democratic organizations and acted as a liaison woman within it. My contacts with the members of that organization were arranged through her.

The Gestapo caught her red-handed in her own apartment and arrested her husband for good measure. They both were subjected to unspeakable tortures. The husband died during the first 'examination.' Mrs Pawlowska survived two of them although after the second one, she had to be carried back to her cell. She shared the cell with four other women who were arrested at the same time.

The next morning they found her hanging from a beam in the ceiling. She had used her own shirtwaist as a rope, and they had not heard a single noise. Her determination to die had been so inexorable and her indifference to pain so steadfast that she had passed away without a groan, without kicking her legs against the wall in the last spasm before death.

Later I asked a physician whether this was possible. He replied in the negative. A suicide always loses consciousness, he informed me, and when this happens the instinct of self-preservation begins to function. But in this case, as I know beyond doubt, the instinct must have been counteracted by a stronger force.

The liaison women suffered more than the majority of their sex, but the war has worked untold hardships on all the women of Poland.

For the mothers, daughters, and wives of the men in the Underground, misery was their daily lot. If they did not actively participate themselves, then their torment was all the greater because, not having any way of gauging danger or sensing the approach of tragedy, they expected it constantly and never knew a moment's peace. If the wife of an underground man lived under her true name, and her husband was found out, she usually was arrested along with him. Very often, even though she had taken no part in the work, she was tortured and the attempt was made to pry loose from her secrets which they had been unable to get from her husband. Usually the women could not satisfy the Gestapo even had they wanted to, for they simply knew nothing. They died involuntary martyrs, unfortunate women who happened to be the wives of good, courageous men.

It became a generally accepted rule for the wives of at least the leaders to register with the Underground and live under assumed names. They lived as the men did, in concealment, constantly moving about and away from their friends and families, harassed by fear and uncertainty. The worst part of it was that most of them were temperamentally unsuited to this kind of existence. Occasionally they were totally unable to participate in the work and would never have been accepted in the organizations, but, although they had nothing at all heroic or unusual in their make-up as wives, they were forced to share the lives of their husbands.

Many of the other women in Poland led sorrowful existences. The innocent landladies, who harbored members of the Underground and whole cells without knowing it, were frequently dragged off like thin, wailing shadows of the men who were caught by the Gestapo. Pitiful, too, were the girls who served as distributors of the underground press, and rushed about, bulging with the material which they secreted about their persons as well as in their heavy handbags.

This distribution was simple, mechanical work and women were most frequently used because men were apt to become dissatisfied and insist on playing more important rôles. I remember Bronka, a thin, unattractive girl who used to come into my office twice a week, always arriving punctually and almost breathlessly. She was silent and shy, seemed weary of the rabbit-like existence she was forced to lead, and looked frightfully tired and overworked. Possibly she had been caught once by the Gestapo, and, in any case, once in the Underground it was difficult to leave, adjust oneself to a different kind of life, and get a normal job.

Once I asked her why she was so sad and discouraged. She answered reluctantly: 'What do I have to be happy about?'

I felt sorry for her.

'Are things very bad with you?' I asked, almost anticipating a rebuff.

She snapped the answer. 'Just like everyone else. You don't get rich on war.'

She sat down in a chair and relaxed a very little. It occurred to me that she might be hungry. She was terribly thin, her face was pinched, her complexion had an unhealthy greenish tinge. Her eyes were strangely bright in her sallow face, as if from fever.

'Would you have some supper with me?' I asked. 'I have some bread, marmalade, and tomatoes. I am sorry I cannot offer you any hot ersatz. I have no coal to make a fire and I can get hot water only when the landlady is cooking.'

'Thank you,' she replied. 'Could you let me have a glass of water?'

I brought her the water and watched her as she slowly ate the black, hard, tasteless bread smeared with marmalade made of beets. It was strange to see her devour it with intense relish, carefully grinding every morsel to bits and extracting the last drop of flavor from each mouthful before she swallowed it. When she had finished she drank the glass of water. The tomatoes she refused and no amount of pleading would get her to eat one of the two I had. She insisted that I needed them for myself. We talked a bit before she left.

'How long have you been distributing secret press?' I asked her.

'Three years,' she replied promptly.

It was then August of 1942. Her reply came so rapidly because she had been at it since the beginning of the war.

'Haven't you done anything else at all, in those three years?'

'No. Distribution is my specialty. My chief thinks I have exceptional ability to melt into the landscape because I don't look too intelligent.'

We both laughed. Her face underwent a transformation during her brief moment of hilarity. Laughter somehow rounded out her cheeks a little and made her look more normal.

'About how many people do you take care of?' I inquired.

'I have 120 "points" to visit,' she said in a cool, matter-of-fact voice.

I nearly jumped. It was an incredible amount of work. She noted my amazement.

'Yes,' she said. 'I have 120 addresses and I visit each one twice a week.'

'About how many a day?'

'Oh,' she said, 'about forty. It varies. Sometimes I quit a little earlier, when I feel very tired.'

I looked at her pityingly.

'It is time for me to go,' she said, getting up from her chair heavily. 'I have eleven more stops to make today.'

'You must be tired of it,' I said.

'No,' she said, holding onto the word and dragging it out as if uncertain. 'Do you know, though, I keep dreaming of just one thing. I wish the war were over and that I might have a job where I could stay just where I am, in one spot all the time and have people come to me. I would like to be the matron in a ladies' rest room. I really mean it.'

I hardly knew what to say.

'Thanks for the meal,' she called out, going to the door.

And yet Bronka regarded herself as fortunate compared to those women who, as we said, 'had relations with the Germans.' This phrase of shame attached to any woman who merely allowed herself to be seen in the streets with a German, or had a drink with one in a café. These women were surrounded by a scorn and contempt that must have made them utterly miserable. From Bronka I first learned that there are distinctions to be made among this class. Once when I spoke of these women with disgust, she delivered an angry lecture to me about the wickedness of men in general and myself in particular.

'Certainly,' she said, 'there are women living with Germans and they are to be blamed. But among them are many who have not much choice.'

Then she proceeded to tell me about a woman she knew who had been classed by her neighbors as among those who 'had relations with the Germans.' She lived in a moderately well-furnished two-room apartment. Her husband had been in the army and was at the time in a German prison camp. She was an average, middle-class woman with nothing heroic about her and neither more nor less patriotic than the average Polish woman. She subscribed to the secret press and did the normal things that were demanded of her.

A few months before, the Germans had inflicted a tenant upon her, a middle-aged magistrate worker. This in itself was disgraceful, but since she had no place to go, she was compelled to remain. Besides she clung to her few possessions and hoped that if she stayed to watch them, the tenant would be a trifle less quick to pilfer. The German was only too pleased at the idea of letting her stay, for, as Bronka put it, 'these Germans like to be comfortable' and wanted to have the neat, tireless Polish women keeping house, if it could possibly be managed. After he had resided there a short while, he began issuing invitations to the poor woman, to come to a café with him to listen to music, which she refused. Bronka did not know if he did this because he was attracted to her, or whether he was bored and lonely and simply wanted company. Finally, after she had refused for the sixth time, his patience wore out. He informed her that if she did not come to the café with him, he would not only have her thrown out of her house but into a concentration camp.

The woman, as Bronka explained it, had no choice whatsoever.

'What would you expect her to do?' she asked me indignantly, 'she is no Joan of Arc. She is an unfortunate, average woman who wants to live through the war and wait for her husband. The German would have had her arrested. She had no one to whom she could turn. She is not a member of the Underground although she does buy the secret papers, for which she pays. She had no choice. And you men call her by ugly names, and do not even think of her bitter humiliation as she sits in the café. Everyone stares at her in anger and she sits there frightened of them, of the German, and often worried about her purse in which she keeps a secret newspaper. It is not so easy. Women suffer more in this war than men.'

26

Marriage Per Procuram

I had a friend who used the alias of Witek. He was one of the leaders of an organization largely concerned with religion and education.[1] A group of his friends collaborated with him in their chosen task of bolstering up the morale of Polish youth. Besides being the editor of a periodical called *Prawda* (*Truth*), Witek, a man of about thirty-five, talented, courageous, and uncommonly shrewd, was the driving force behind his organization. The inspiration of the organization was a famous woman, one of Poland's greatest living writers, who supplied the spiritual motivation that gave the organization its unusual character, its unique zeal and ardor.[2]

Witek's assistant and liaison woman was a young girl who used the alias of Wanda.[4] They constituted an inseparable, buoyant trio, always gay, hopeful, and indefatigable. Together, they wrote, published, and distributed splendid pamphlets, many of which reached foreign countries and were translated into other languages. The well-known pamphlet *Golgotha*, which described the Oswiecim concentration camp, and was translated into English, was one of them.[3] I used to visit them frequently, if for no other purpose than to inhale the refreshing atmosphere of confidence and vibrant activity that surrounded them.

In the middle of 1942, they were separated. Wanda was arrested accidentally during an inspection. In jail she was beaten and tortured by the Gestapo but divulged nothing. All they had against her were suspicions. They were unable to obtain a scrap of evidence or persuade her to confess. Although they did not take the step of sending her to a concentration camp, they refused to release her and kept her instead in the 'Pawiak' prison of Warsaw.

We established communications with her quickly. Witek and Wanda exchanged weekly letters with each other, which we managed to get smuggled in and out of jail. Witek kept her carefully informed of events outside the jail, and she told him what was happening inside, urging him and all of us to keep up our spirits and courage as though we were under greater duress than she. Then, incredibly, whether it was merely something which they had felt before and these circumstances brought to light or whether it had developed under the emotional strain they were both under, a romance began to grow between them.

Separated by the prison gates, under the influence of their letters, they fell deeply in love with each other. I remember Witek's emotion when he showed me a letter he had received from her. In it, she told him how she had realized her love for him while she was in jail. He was deeply moved and walked around in a state of tense, nervous uncertainty for more than a week, trying to prepare a sincere, adequate reply. As awkwardly and naïvely as a schoolboy, he appeared one day before the writer and myself and with shy questions consulted us, trying to obtain some advice on the difficult letter he had to write.

We teased him a bit and suggested that he accept a dictated letter from the great writer. She would certainly compose a better one than he could. Witek was not amused by our little joke. He went about dazed, but finally plucked up his courage and wrote his answer. He told her that he had always loved her, but had never had the courage to say so. Now at last, she had made it easy for him to reveal his emotions.

Their correspondence continued. I read some of the letters. Hers were always calm, serious, and had an undercurrent of deep emotion. After some time, in a smuggled letter, Witek proposed marriage to her. Of course she could not appear in church for a nuptial ceremony, but Witek had consulted a priest and found out that a marriage 'per procuram' could be arranged. Her consent would suffice for the priest.

It was promptly forthcoming.

I was present at the ceremony. It took place in a little old Warsaw church in the presence of four witnesses. The priest who officiated was a friend of ours. He delivered a brief, eloquent speech that touched on the strangeness of human destiny and seemed to capture perfectly the pathetic beauty of the moment. He reminded us that at one time, the 'per procuram' marriage had been the exclusive privilege of royalty, the spouses being represented by ambassadors in diamond-studded robes and the church hung with the richest, most ornate brocades and tapestries. Gold coins had been tossed to the populace and the streets echoed with cries of 'Long live the King! Long live the Queen!'

'Times have changed,' the priest concluded. 'I am marrying you "per procuram" with permission of the Church, not because you are rich or powerful, but because you are of the poorest, weakest, most wronged, and oppressed.

'This woman is the ambassadress of your wife,' he said and added, turning to the great woman writer, 'and some day you may write, in what I hope will be your most beautiful book, the lives of these people . . .'

'The lives of all of us, Father,' she whispered.

Witek's lips trembled and he turned his face away. After the ceremony, we all had to break up to continue work that could not be delayed. I did not remain in Poland long enough to learn the fate of Wanda and I wonder whether the couple married 'per procuram' were ever united.[5]

Before the war, the works of the writer were translated into many languages, and admired by the entire world. She earned high royalties and received innumerable prizes. Now she would have rejoiced to be able to get one plate of hot soup a day.

She was in every way an exceptional woman. Her good fortune had something miraculous about it. Before the war she had written under a literary name and was known by it to a wide public. Outside her circle of personal friends, few people knew that she was married, and even fewer knew the identity of her husband. From the very beginning she took an active part in the work of the Underground and yet, despite innumerable warnings from her friends, she continued to live in her own house, using her married name. It was pointed out to her that she was in double jeopardy, liable to arrest not merely because of the work she was doing but also because of her fame. Many prominent Poles, to whom no suspicion whatsoever was attached, had already been arrested. She steadfastly refused to change her habits. When we scolded her for acts of unnecessary bravado and lack of prudence, she answered:

'My dears, if God wants me to be arrested, the Huns will catch me no matter how careful I am.'

We stared at each other after this speech and a few of us winked at each other in mutual understanding, but nobody dared to say a word. We all felt that despite her literary genius and her selfless devotion to underground work, she was too naïve for the kind of existence she was called to lead. Providence is no substitute for prudence.

She was soon put to the test. One night two Gestapo officers knocked at the door of her house. She told us later that when she realized who they were, she felt not the slightest tremor of fear. In utter tranquillity, she yielded herself to Providence, trusting that nothing would happen that was not God's will.

The Gestapo men did not wait for her to answer, but opened the door and shouted at her from the threshold.

'What is your name?'

She gave them her married name.

'Give us your passport.'

She retrieved it from her desk and handed it to them. It was in perfect order.

'Who lives here with you?'

'No one. I live alone.'

'We will see. Sit down and be quiet. We are going to investigate your house.'

They proceeded to 'investigate,' looked into closets and under beds, emptied the dressers, knocked at the walls, and turned all the furniture upside down. While this fruitless rummaging was going on, she got up quietly and, without any undue haste or excitement, calmly walked out of the door to the house of a friend a few doors away. They did not notice her departure, and in the street, although it was past curfew, no one accosted her.

The story was the talk of Warsaw. Probably the greatest suffering she endured from the entire incident was the mild teasing to which we subjected her after she had told us about it. For, besides her piety, she had one more unusual trait of character. She never lied and firmly believed that a lie could under no circumstances be justified. The day after the Gestapo visit, when she told the story to a group of us, we subjected this principle of hers to a little test.

'Do you realize that you lied to the Gestapo men about your identity?' someone asked.

She was quite embarrassed and taken aback for a moment.

'Oh, no, I didn't,' she replied anxiously; 'they asked me for my name and I told them the truth. They did not ask me for the name under which I published my books.'

'Very well,' we agreed, hardly knowing whether to laugh or cry at her angelic simplicity. 'But you deceived them. You skipped out from under their noses.'

She answered that triumphantly:

'Not at all. It was my apartment and I have a right to leave it at will. I did not promise them that I would stay in it till they were finished.'

'What? Do you mean to say that if they ordered you to stay and wait for them, you would have obeyed?'

Now she was confused. She wanted so badly to be sure she was right.

'Well,' the answer came slowly, 'I never thought the whole thing out. But I don't think I would have had to stay. As far as we are concerned the orders they give don't exist. Isn't that so? So I would not have had to obey them.'

We stopped the game, a trifle abashed. Her childlike and yet sublime naïveté never failed to amaze us and often put us to shame. The most remarkable aspect of it all was that, despite the handicap of her conscience, she was, all through 1942, the inspiration and the finest flame of Polish underground life. The most eloquent appeals, the most vehement denunciations, the most effective pamphlets and articles in the secret press issued from her pen. Many of them, we all felt certain, would endure permanently as pearls of Polish literature during this war.[6]

27

School – Underground

It had become necessary for me to secure the services of a liaison boy, and I ended up with a boy named Tad Lisowski in a strange way. I had known the Lisowski family before the war. They were then wealthy people who owned an estate and received the rents from two apartment houses in Warsaw. Mrs Lisowski was a small, demure black-haired lady who had the energy of a dynamo. She kept perfect order in a home that was thronged with visitors, held in check her two wild, mischievous children, and attended to the needs of her husband, a gay blade of the cafés, theaters, and gambling centers.

Mrs Lisowski managed the business affairs of the family, attended church sedulously, and found time for extensive social and charitable work. At recurrent intervals, Mr Lisowski would go on a spree and disappear for weeks, leaving the mother alone to cope with the antics of Tad and his younger brother.

After the war started, the finances of the Lisowskis rapidly deteriorated. Their estate in the Kielce district was confiscated. Their apartment houses produced very little; they had lost their jewelry. They were living on the sale of their last few belongings and all Mrs Lisowski could earn in 'trade.' The children, both great admirers of the frivolous, empty-headed father, were left much to their own devices and were rapidly succumbing to the influence of shiftless companions and the insidious German propaganda which aimed at the utter demoralization of Polish youth by encouraging their interest in pornographic books, shows, and movies. Tad, a young friend of his informed me, was a patron of the brothels the Germans had opened to help along their project and, besides, was suspected of theft in his own home.

Tad was but one of the many youths of Poland who constituted a tragic problem to the educational authorities of the Polish Underground. Since our educational facilities were extremely limited, moral and material assistance was extended only to those whose character and patriotism most deserved the advantages. We had to educate, first of all, that section of Polish youth which would provide us with suitable candidates for underground work. We were compelled to ignore those who stood in the greatest need of attention.

Once boys or girls had in any way compromised themselves by yielding to the Nazi blandishments, or if they showed tendencies to irregular habits, the path to underground education became irrevocably closed. This was tragic for them. What made the situation even more pathetic was the fact that the malefactors were invariably shunned by the majority of the young people with whom they had grown up. This naturally tended to perpetuate their vicious habits.

Such, in essence, was the case of Tad. A boy whose outstanding characteristics were his intense pride, high spirits, and affectionate gaiety, he suffered greatly from the coolness and hostility of his former companions. He became defiant and paraded his transgressions openly. His mother became alarmed at his behavior and reproached herself bitterly for her lack of maternal attention. I had admired her from former times when I had been a frequent visitor to the Lisowski household. When, in my presence, she would berate herself for the condition of Tad, I would remonstrate with her.

'It is not your fault,' I pointed out, 'you have to provide a living for a worthless husband and scrape together enough to feed and clothe yourself and your children. It is amazing that you have managed as well as you have.'

Mrs Lisowski, whose hair had become completely gray by this time, and whose figure was now gaunt and shrunken, answered with characteristic spirit:

'I don't care about my husband and myself. The war has destroyed our generation, we don't matter. But I want my children to fight for a new Poland, and build a life in it.'

She looked at me significantly with mute appeal for my help. Mrs Lisowski had known for a long time that I was engaged in underground work and we had, by tacit consent, avoided any reference to the subject. But now she was prepared, if necessary, to take the plunge, her love for Tad overcoming her scruples. She hesitated for a moment, peering into my face as if to see if she could detect traces of irritation or any objection that was forming in my mind. The lack of noticeable opposition in my countenance encouraged her to express herself more boldly.

'You know,' she said, 'I hate to bother you about Tad but I can't help doing it. I know that you are in the Underground . . . please don't become alarmed . . . I will never mention it any more.'

'I am sure that you will not,' I said warmly. 'I have the utmost faith in your loyalty and discretion.'

'Thank you. Jan, I am going to ask a favor of you and I pray that you won't refuse me.'

'If it is about Tad joining the Underground . . .' I began dubiously.

'My family has a tradition, Jan. Members of it have fought in every Polish insurrection. In 1830, my great-grandfather was wounded and exiled to Siberia for seven years. My grandfather fought against Tsarist Russia in the insurrection of 1863. I want that tradition of fighting for liberty to be continued. I know Tad with more than the mere love of a mother. He resembles his father. It is bad, very bad. I want him to be like his grandfather. I am ashamed to talk about this, but I must. At the moment, because of his idleness and his scorn of the other boys, he acts much worse than he really is or desires to be. Give him a chance, Jan. Find a place for him and you won't regret it. He'll live up to your standards. He loves adventure, respects you tremendously, and will carry out your orders to the end. Please, Jan.'

I knew that Mrs Lisowski was not the sort of woman to be put off with vague promises or honeyed words. I responded bluntly:

'I don't believe the authorities will allow me to take Tad. He has a bad record. He has shown himself to be frivolous and irresponsible. Another thing you must understand is that the danger is very great. If he were accepted, a day might come when he would not return to you.'

'We are used to dying for our country in my family,' she said slowly. 'If Tad died, it would break my heart, but I would never repent of sending him to do his duty.'

It was impossible to resist such a plea and such a spirit. I took her hand in mine.

'I'll do all I can for Tad,' I said. 'Send him to me tomorrow at noon. I'll meet him at the Vistula, near the Poniatowski Bridge.'

I met Tad the next day and was rather shocked at his appearance. He was a tall, gangling boy who looked much too old for his age. His face was gaunt and pale, with large black eyes circled by rings of an alarming hue – they looked like bruises.

I am afraid I sounded a bit like a pedant.

'Why don't you take care of yourself?' I said sternly. 'You ought to be ashamed. You look as if you had slept in your clothes for a week.'

He was embarrassed and shuffled his feet uneasily. I relented. He was obviously under a strain.

'Come on, Tad,' I said, a bit less distantly. 'Let's take a walk. I have a lot to talk over with you.'

We strolled about without direction for a long time while I waxed eloquent on the subject of duty to one's family and country. I traced an outline of the bloody history of the Polish struggle against conquerors since the partition of 1795. I stressed the fact that if that resistance had stopped, Poland would never have come to life again as a country. We would have no language or land of our own. It was a serious mistake, I told him, to think that resistance consisted only of offering physical opposition to the conquerors. More important still was the maintenance of our character and spirit against the brutalities and blandishments of our enemies. I told him about the deeds of his grandfather and great-grandfather. I said that I considered him an honest boy and that he would always find in me a trustworthy friend. I stressed the need to serve our cause and the real happiness derived from such service.

I did not spare his feelings. Young men of his kind were the great-est danger to Poland and besmirched our reputation abroad. He listened to me with embarrassed attentiveness, his eyes expressive of the misery I was causing him. When I felt he had had enough, I put my arm around his shoulders.

'Listen, Tad,' I said, 'I'm not going to scold you any more or lec-ture you. I really have a lot of faith in you. I would like you to join the Underground to help us. How do you feel about it?'

Whatever his feelings were they were rendered nearly inarticu-late by this sudden change. He nearly choked with excitement, embarrassment, and eagerness. His eyes blazed with enthusiasm.

'You won't be ashamed of me, I promise you,' he finally gasped. 'Give me the chance.'

I laughed. 'Fine, fine! That's enough business for today. Let's hop in for a swim. But listen – don't say anything to your mother.'

We undressed hastily and swam in the muddy but cool waters of the Vistula until the sun went down. As we were dressing and pre-paring to return to the city, I addressed a command to Tad in a very official tone, impressing him with the fact that he was now very nearly a full-fledged underground worker.

'Tomorrow, at ten sharp, report to organization headquarters at number 26 — Street. You will be sworn in as a member of the Polish Underground Army if you are accepted.'

The acceptance part did not bother him.

'The Polish Army?' he asked, fascinated.

'Yes. We have three armies – the first is in Scotland; the second is in the Near East; the third is here at home.'

His large eyes opened with surprise to amazing dimensions: 'I'll be there at nine – at eight . . .'

'Just make sure to get there at ten,' I said. I put my hand out and Tad put all his strength into our handshake before we parted.

The swearing-in was a simple ceremony. He had to take in one hand a little crucifix, raise the other, and repeat the oath: 'I swear before God, holding in my hand the Cross of His Son, that I shall serve my country, serve for her honor and freedom. To that honor and freedom I shall sacrifice all I have. I shall abide by the orders of my organization authorities and shall keep the secrets confined to me. So help me God.' Having sworn him in, I told him that I was his chief, that he must obey my orders, and that he would be killed if he betrayed us. Then we embraced.

From the very beginning Tad vindicated his mother's high opinion of him. The knockabout life he had been leading on the streets of Warsaw in all kinds of company had added an element of shrewdness and mental agility to his native brightness that made him meet all emergencies with quick, adroit responses. Altogether, these were excellent qualities for a liaison boy. His first mission, which he accepted with as much anxious solemnity as if the fate of all Poland depended on it, was to deliver an envelope to a house in the outskirts of the town of Nowy Sacz. The envelope contained a cutting from a German newspaper.

I warned him that in Nowy Sacz there was a great prison and that the Gestapo men stationed in it were exceptionally vigilant in their scrutiny of strangers. The suburb to which he was going was the habitat of the German troops who protected the city against guerrilla warfare. I admonished him to be discreet, discretion being more important in our work than bravery. When I told him that he would not be able to get a permit to travel by train, he grinned as though anything that made the mission more difficult pleased him.

To our men in Nowy Sacz, I sent an advance notification of the fact that a new messenger was arriving and requested an estimate of his ability and intelligence. Tad accomplished the mission with dispatch and promptness, portentously bringing back to me an envelope which contained nothing more than a favorable estimation of his merits. During this period, Mrs Lisowski, whom I met frequently, informed me that his habits had undergone a marked change. He had become neat, more disciplined, and rather quiet. He walked about with an air of mystery and importance that amused her greatly. This stage in the development of Tad was, however, only short-lived.

Despite his eagerness and willingness to work hard, it was not long before his recklessness and love of gaiety became quite a problem. Frequently, his imprudence enraged me. One day I had an appointment with him at the Kierbedz Bridge, which was guarded by German soldiers at all hours. We were to arrive from opposite directions. When I approached him, two sentinels passed the spot where he waited. I found Tad leaning over the parapet reading a copy of the underground *Information Bulletin* in utter absorption.

I leaned over the parapet myself, at some distance away from the calm Tad, my heart in my throat. The guards passed by the thin, innocuous-looking lad as though he were not there. I shook my fist at him surreptitiously and walked over to deliver a fearful tongue-lashing. Tad looked up at me with round eyes and pressed his fingers to his lips.

'Shhh,' he said, pointing with his other hand to the sentinels who were still within earshot.

A few days later Tad pulled a stunt which so exasperated me that I could have strangled him. He had apparently become acquainted with three other liaison boys of approximately the same age and had prodded them into a mad wager. They were to take copies of the four largest underground papers and stand in the middle of a trolley car, openly – and dangerously – reading them. The first one who lost his nerve would be the loser with some sort of evil penalty attached. They read the papers flagrantly and successfully all the way to the end of the line and decided that there was no loser. For some strange reason they decided not to repeat the performance on the way back. Two of the boys were so elated at their own bravado that they gave a detailed report of the events to their superiors. The next day I received two sharply worded notes to the effect that Tad was demoralizing the other liaison boys.

The minute I saw Tad, I exploded violently.

'You little idiot! I've got a good mind to kick you out of here altogether,' I raged. 'It's not bad enough that you go about risking your own silly neck for no reason but you have to encourage the others to do the same.'

He hung his head in a display of penitence. I toned down my

voice a bit, and muttered a series of incomprehensible threats, and finally lapsed into silence altogether.

'I'm sorry, Witold,' he said humbly, 'I would rather die than endanger you. It's hard for me to stop taking chances, but I promise you I won't do it again.'

Tad had a way about him that was hard to resist. His penitence always seemed sincere and heartfelt, and I believe that it was, for the moment. I let myself be mollified.

'All right,' I said, 'but one more time . . .'

He grinned up at me, relieved. 'Would you like to hear a story?' he asked me.

I was doubtful. The thawing process should not be too quick.

'If it is something important, go ahead,' I finally grumbled. In reality the stories of Tad generally amused me no end. He picked up every current joke and bit of gossip that floated about. He was a mine of all news items and rumors.

'Well,' began Tad earnestly, 'it seems that Adolf Hitler came to Heaven one day and presented himself to Saint Peter. "I am Adolf Hitler," he said, "and I want to live here." Saint Peter was puzzled by his arrogance and went off to consult God. "There is a man outside the gate who demands admittance. He acts very important and says that his name is Adolf Hitler." The Lord frowned severely. "And you kept him waiting? Saint Peter, Saint Peter, won't you ever learn about diplomacy and politics? Hurry back and bring him in – but watch him." Saint Peter rushed out and after a few minutes returned to the Lord, looking very worried. "Now what has happened?" inquired the Lord angrily. "Where is Hitler?" Saint Peter shook his head sadly and wailed, "He has done everything, everything." "What do you mean – everything?" thundered the Lord. "Everything, everything. He skinned the Great Bear, stole the Big Dipper, and sheared the Ram. Then he used a cream separator on the Milky Way and locked up all your best prophets in a ghetto!"'

I laughed and then became solemn again. 'It's no use to talk to you, you little imp. Go to the devil, but be back here tomorrow at nine sharp.'

Tad waved flippantly at me and strolled away.

After a while it became apparent that his position as messenger boy was beginning to lose its charm for Tad. The lack of excitement and overt danger bored him and the apparent triviality and routine nature of his assignment chafed at his pride and desire for adventure. Besides, like an artist, he needed scope for his highly developed talents for conniving and for nimble thinking. I could see that he was bursting with the desire to explain his needs to me, but was afraid to offend me or appear remiss in his allegiance to the movement. I broached the subject myself.

'Tad,' I said to him, 'you are pretty tired of your job here, aren't you?'

'No, no,' he protested feebly, 'I like it.'

'But you would like something a little more important, a little more exciting, wouldn't you?'

He looked at me gratefully and explained his dissatisfaction.

'You see,' he said, 'I know everything we do here hurts the Germans, but I can't see it with my own eyes. I just run here and there without any idea of what is happening. I would like to work in a place where I could do damage directly and see the results. Do you understand?'

'Of course, Tad,' I said, smiling. 'I'll see what I can do for you.'

I sent to my superiors and requested that Tad be shifted to what we called 'officers' schools.' I called their attention to his courage and intelligence, although I was worried about the fact that the authorities might be too well-acquainted with his talents for mischief. He was accepted. When the message came through, and I relayed it to Tad, he nearly hit the ceiling with excitement.

The officers' schools were primarily designed to train young boys and girls for work in the Underground. In secret classes, instructions were given on such subjects as street-fighting, sabotage, and diversion. They were familiarized with the use of weapons, tools, and explosives, and grounded in the psychology of terror, mass leadership, and methods of weakening German morale.

After a preliminary period of about five months, the ablest were selected for a post-graduate course with partisan detachments stationed in the woods, mountains, and marshes. Many excellent professionals of conspiracy entered the ranks of the Underground from these schools and were immensely valuable in our struggle.

At the commencement of the training period, neither the pupil nor his parents were informed of the real purpose of his education. Ostensibly, the secret classes, which also met for some academic subjects, were held solely to protect the youngsters from the Nazi demoralization campaign. We did not enjoy this deception but it was necessary to prevent undue alarm, since a great number of the pupils were weeded out in a short time in any case.

Under ordinary circumstances a boy like Tad would never have been accepted as a candidate, for the schools had a high standard of physical and moral excellence. But my personal intervention and his own achievements as an efficient liaison boy gained his admission.

At the same time that Tad was undergoing preliminary training in the officers' school, he was made a member of a group or organization called 'The Little Wolves,' a position that was eminently suited to his unorthodox talents. 'The Little Wolves' was an organization of young boys formed under the leadership of some 'Experts' for the purpose of harassing the Nazis directly, annoying the occupants, poking fun at them, working more sharply on their nerves by diverse stratagems.

The members of this organization were the authors of a large share of the millions of inscriptions that became the most common flower of Warsaw, and bloomed afresh each morning. They painted signs like 'Poland fights on,' or 'The punishment for Oswiecim is near' or 'Hitler Kaputt' with indelible paint on German trucks and automobiles, on German residences, and quite frequently on the backs of the Germans themselves. An epidemic of flat tires on German vehicles resulted from the Little Wolves' thorough and systematic sprinkling of the streets with broken glass, bits of barbed wire, and any other pointed objects on which they could lay their hands.

They festooned the city with caricatures and posters which were constant sources of amusement to the population of Warsaw. The mischievous and diabolically efficient little pack did much to sustain the psychological atmosphere of contempt for the Germans and fostered the spirit of resistance. In the fall of 1942, when the Germans requisitioned all of Poland's furs and wools for the Eastern front, the Little Wolves got up a brilliantly executed series of posters on the topic of the day. A gaunt, gloomy German soldier was depicted swathed in a very feminine mink coat with a silver-fox muff protecting his hands. Underneath were captions on the order of 'Now that I am so warm, dying for our Führer will be a pleasure.'

Naturally, the best cinemas, cafés, and hotels in Warsaw were taken over by the Germans. The most common sign in Poland became 'Nur Für Deutsche' (for Germans only). The Little Wolves stole many of them and prepared a great quantity of duplicates. One morning they were hung on hundreds of Warsaw lamp posts and trees. As it was customary for the Germans to hang Polish offenders on these public gallows, the grisly meaning of the posters was plain to the most stupid.

The Germans had destroyed all the monuments that commemorated Polish heroes or patriotic events. By common consent all Poles made conspicuous detours around the spots where these monuments had been located. Prayers would even be offered up at these spots, to the outrage of the German officials. The Little Wolves used flowers as a symbolic message. They were found in profusion where the monuments had been. They scattered them wherever a member of the Underground had been executed or even arrested, in locations where some particularly heinous German crime had been committed.

Nothing could stop the Little Wolves and their exploits were innumerable, sharp thorns in the sides of the occupants.[1]

When the day came for Tad to leave me he must have felt slightly guilty, because he launched into an effusive display of gratitude for all I had done for him. He concluded with a plea that I keep his mother in ignorance as to his new job and pretend that he was still with me. I growled, but finally conceded.

'I have an important story to tell you,' Tad said, to hide our mutual embarrassment at the leave-taking.

'Another one of your silly jokes? I'll give you exactly one minute.'

Tad launched into a description of the posters they were preparing in response to the German fur requisitions. I was quite delighted by the project. When he was finished, I commented on its crudities with biting sarcasm. Tad hung his head in ludicrous dejection. I flung a wad of paper at him. He jumped nimbly to one side and said:

'Before I go, may I show you something?'

'I suppose so,' I said with a martyred air. 'I have nothing to do all day that is more important than listening to Tad Lisowski.'

Tad pulled a mass of tangled papers out of his pocket.

'What have you got in that pile of junk?'

'This,' Tad answered, waving it in the air, 'is the program of the German Kultur organization. "Days in Poland," it is called. Don't you know about it?'

I most certainly did. A large-scale propaganda campaign had recently been launched by the German General Government to acquaint the Poles with all branches of German achievement, cultural, and industrial progress. I had not yet had an opportunity to scan one of their programs closely, and snatched the papers from Tad's hand. I took one look at the circulars and shot a withering glance at Tad who whistled imperviously at the side of my desk.

The papers were identical duplicates of the German circulars in texture, print, and size, but the contents had been radically altered:

PROGRAM OF EXERCISES

First Day.   Opening of the exhibition called 'The Influence of the German culture on Polish cities' – photographs of cities, villages, and settlements after the September campaign of 1939.

Second Day.   Great spectacle entitled 'The Germans Carry on the Torch of Education' on Hitler Square – public burning on pyres of

Polish schoolbooks and of the works of Henryk Sienkiewicz, Adam Mickiewicz, Stefan Zeromski, Boleslaw Prus, Maria Konopnicka, and others.

Third Day. A lecture in the ruins of the University auditorium, entitled 'Total Culture' – celebration of closing of all schools of higher learning, trade schools, and public schools.

Fourth Day. Freude durch Kraft (Joy through strength) – exhibit of manhunts and arrests at homes combined with an excursion of the Polish intelligentsia to the camps in Oswiecim, Dachau, and Oranienburg.

Fifth Day. A moving picture showing the University of German Culture where Polish university professors are being 'schooled' in concentration camps by the Hitler Youth.

Sixth Day. Visits to German Health Centers in the Parliament Building and in the Aleja Szucha Street, led by the Gestapo. [In the garden attached to the Parliament many Poles were executed. In the Aleja Szucha, the building of the Polish Ministry of Education was changed into the Gestapo headquarters.]

Seventh Day. Opening of a shooting gallery for soldiers and *Volksdeutsche* in Palmiry combined with shooting of Poles standing by the walls or pillars or while running. [Execution spot, where among others Mieczyslaw Niedzialkowski, leader of the Polish Socialist Party, and Maciej Rataj, leader of the Polish Peasant Party, were shot.]

Eighth Day. Ceremony of walling-in of the Jewish district in Warsaw followed by man hunts and shooting within the ghetto.

Ninth Day. Inauguration of a new German District combined with a lightning evacuation of Poles and confiscation of furniture and other possessions.

When I had finished reading this parody of the German document, I looked up to see Tad grinning proudly as he watched my reactions to his handiwork. I joined with him in laughter and then I put my arm around his shoulder.

'I don't know when I shall see you again, Tad,' I said. 'You'll be leaving for the officers' school soon. I know that if I hear of you, the news will be good and that you will always do your duty.'

Tad was touched and confused. I held out my hand and he pumped it as hard as he could and then ran out of the office. That was the last glimpse I ever had of him.

My success with Tad must have stimulated the pedagogue in me, for I also tried to act as mentor to some of the youth in my immediate family, most of whom proved rather disappointing for one reason or another. I tried to get a sallow-faced cousin of mine to emulate Tad, but the effort was a failure. He lacked the nerve and perhaps the physical endowment as well. His sister Zosia, however, compensated handsomely for his failure.

She was a girl of about eighteen, the daughter of an uncle of mine, who had lost his wife in 1940. This uncle was a quiet, retiring sort of man who had worked as a clerk and had always had difficulty in making ends meet. The difficulty had increased in the usual proportion under the occupation with the result that both children were in very poor condition, and suffering severely from malnutrition. Things were even worse before Zosia took the management of the family into her own competent hands, cleaning house, doing the washing, and searching the markets for bargains in food.

She was plain in appearance, built on gawky, angular lines, with straw-colored hair and a pale complexion. Her plucky spirit and her quick intelligence made up amply for her deficiencies. Besides the arduous household labors she performed, she managed to find enough strength and time to attend, and do well in, a secret night school which was run by the Underground.

The Education Department of the Underground had reached in 1942, the year when Zosia was to be graduated, an incredible peak of efficiency.[2] In the Warsaw district alone more than eighty-five thousand children were receiving tutelage through its offices. More than seventeen hundred youths had been graduated from the high schools.

The pupils met secretly in their homes in groups of three or six, for different ostensible reasons, to play chess, for a social visit, to learn a trade. Any common purpose would serve as a pretext. The teacher who came to them underwent a fearful risk. Children are obstinately curious and could scarcely be repressed in their desire to learn the true identity of the teacher, in what school he had taught before the war, where he lived, and other details that it was dangerous to let adults know, let alone children. The safety of these overworked educators depended on the uncertain vagaries of youthful prudence. The unwitting word of a parent or pupil could and sometimes did mean death and bestial torture for these men, a number of whom were caught by the Gestapo in the performance of this invaluable service.

The greatest difficulty that confronted the education authorities was the problem of obtaining a sufficient number of textbooks. After much indecision, it was finally decided to print facsimiles of prewar textbooks so that if they were discovered, they would appear to the Germans as dating before the occupation.

Zosia was due to be graduated in September 1942. For weeks before the day arrived all I heard from her were speculations about her impending examinations. To my astonishment I learned that these examinations were of almost the same standard and specification as before the war. The Polish high-school system had differed from the practices of most countries. To receive a graduation diploma, the applicant had to pass final tests in five subjects, covering the material of a twelve-year course in each. In three of the subjects both oral and written examinations were stipulated. In the remaining two, the kind of examination was elective. Zosia was to have written and oral examinations in Polish, English, and Latin. Physics and mathematics were to be written.

She managed to press me into service as her English tutor. We worked late into the night and sometimes I was compelled to stay over. This, alone, was quite a reward to me. Since no one in the apartment worked in the Underground, it was above suspicion. I could relax completely and enjoy a rare night of tranquil rest. In the morning I would receive from the competent hands of Zosia an equally rare and luxurious breakfast of hot ersatz coffee and bread with marmalade, even from time to time some meat.

The day of the examination rolled around, and Zosia was in a fever of anxiety and anticipation. I was permitted to witness the examination in the subject of Polish since, at that time, it had become known that probably in the near future I was going to England to make a comprehensive report on life in Poland. The examination took place in the office of a director in a firm of movers, whose son was one of the pupils. The site was well-chosen, because many people passed in and out of the building and a few more would not be conspicuous.

Zosia and two boys sat at a large rectangular table, each place being at a considerable distance from the next to prevent cheating. The chairman of the commission sat on the fourth seat. He handed out paper and instructed the pupils to mark on each sheet their number and symbol which in these underground classes always took the place of their name. Then he rose and addressed the three pupils, who were trembling with anxiety:

'My dear young people, ours is a very difficult task. You know that the enemy is striving to destroy the Polish nation by demoralizing and degrading Polish youth. We, the old professors, have devoted our lives to the instruction and improvement of that youth. We are meeting the challenge for your sake, and for Poland. The struggle is not easy. We have suffered many defeats. We are defeated whenever we see one of you entering a German movie house or theater, reading a dirty book, or patronizing one of their gambling houses.

'Today is one of the happiest days of my life, for you, the first graduates of this school, are proof that we are winning this particular war. We realize the hardships connected with your studies and we will take the circumstances into consideration when we grade your papers. Try to do your best, don't be nervous, try to concentrate. For the next three hours, there is no war, no occupation. All you have to think about is your examination.'

He took six cards from his pocket and placed them on the table. 'Select your subject and begin work,' he announced. The students responded with feverish haste.

The professor was a very old man, poorly dressed, and, judging from his tired, gray face, very much overworked. His eyes were red from lack of sleep, his walk heavy and slow. He joined the other members of the commission and myself on the sofa for a moment. I congratulated him on his speech and then whispered:

'Let's go out for a cup of coffee so we won't disturb your pupils by talking.'

The professor glared at me sternly and wagged his finger in rebuke.

'Young man,' he said stiffly, 'do not tempt me into evil ways. I have the greatest confidence in Polish youth, but not on the score of all students' greatest weakness – cheating. From time immemorial youth has cheated, and will continue to cheat, in examinations. I shall have to remain here.'

He returned to the head of the table to keep a sharp eye on his students as he had done for more than twenty years in the great auditorium. After a while, his eyes closed, and he dozed off. The prospect of remaining in this room for three hours bored me, so I scribbled a note to Zosia informing her that I was going to her home and that I should meet her there after the examination. I got up and walked over to Zosia's seat and handed her the note.

Just as she clutched it in her hand, the professor bolted out of his chair as if he had just received an electric shock, flew over to Zosia, and snatched the note out of her hand. Poor Zosia turned pale as a sheet. He scanned the note carefully, turned a reproachful countenance to me, and then said sharply to his students:

'Go on with your work.' He turned to Zosia: 'Miss King' [her symbol], he said, 'your cousin will wait for you tonight at your home.'

Then he glanced significantly at his colleagues as if indicating to them the necessity for constant vigilance during examinations.

I slunk off, red-faced and confused.

When Zosia returned that evening I asked her what her theme had been about.

'Independence in Polish Romantic Literature,' she replied enthusiastically. 'I wrote sixteen pages and I could have written more . . .'

I laughed heartily at this remark while Zosia gazed at me suspiciously. The old rascal had not changed the topic in twenty years. In my time, you could buy leaflets containing essays on a number of examination subjects. One of the leaflets was bound to be on the topic upon which Zosia had probably written so eloquently. I refrained from telling Zosia about this. For her and all the other young people, the topic as well as the graduation had acquired an entirely new significance.

Zosia had done excellently in all her examinations. The diploma she received was merely a calling-card bearing the pseudonym of the chairman of the commission. On the reverse side appeared a few innocent sentences:

Thank you for your charming visit on September 29, 1942. I was most satisfied. You told me such interesting things. Bravo.

Zosia treasured this card above all her possessions. When Poland is reconstituted after the war, thousands of these cards will be exchanged for official diplomas. The moment I saw it, a desire to add it to my collection of underground documents took possession of me. I did my best to cajole and bribe her into letting me have it.

'Zosia, dear,' I said, 'after the war I'll give you ten secret papers of the Government Delegate if you give me this calling-card for my collection. Will you?'

'You are mad,' she answered indignantly.

'Wait, wait. I'll add a few circulars issued by the Commander of the Home Army and a few official announcements of death sentences passed on the Germans by the—'

She interrupted me. 'You are not only mad. You are a pig.'

I have constantly been haunted by the grave problem of the Polish youth who have been deprived of education and have fallen prey to Nazi temptations. For those like Tad and Zosia I have no serious fear. The education they received and their experience in the Underground will make them, if anything, prematurely strong and responsible. As for the mass of Polish, and, indeed, European, youth totally without education for a long period, they are the subject of growing concern. They will constitute one of the crucial problems of postwar Europe.

28

Parliament in Poland

I continued my liaison work for almost three years. During that period, thanks to the strategic vantage point I occupied, I was able to survey the entire structure of the underground movement and to form a detailed picture of the situation as a whole in Poland. The Commander of the Army and the Delegate of the Government decided to use my knowledge in another assignment.

They were sending me to London to visit the Polish Government and to make contact with the Allied authorities, particularly the British and American. I was instructed to convey to them as much as I could of our activities and experiences. The preparations for my departure lasted several weeks. First, I had to obtain proper papers. Going via Hungary was impossible this time, because it would be too difficult to reach England through this route. The simplest thing to do was to try to reach Spain or Portugal. Legally, if possible.

It was not very difficult to find means of securing the proper papers. I managed it myself. Long conspiratorial work had taught me to rely upon myself rather than others and I hit upon a plan which would utilize the presence of the foreign workers among us. In Warsaw alone, some two thousand French workers had been quartered, working for the Germans. This was the result of the politics of collaboration of the French Government, which very willingly 'loaned' its workers to the Third Reich. They were engineers and technicians as well as ordinary workers. One of these French technicians, a man named Tienpont, I had known for some time, having met him at the home of a family of French origin, the Bourdos, which had settled in Warsaw in the nineteenth century. We got along well together. He was a witty, debonair chap, slight in build, very agile and voluble, yet prudent enough to restrain his loquacity at the proper moments. He was extraordinarily greedy, trafficking not only in perfumes and cosmetics smuggled from France but also in cocaine and morphine. His clients were almost exclusively German, although, occasionally, for various reasons, the Underground also bought supplies from him. This strain of greediness and cunning in him I planned to exploit. I had learned from experience that it was easier to twist around one's finger someone who fancied himself a 'smart egg' than a forthright, naïve fellow.

I knew that every three months the Frenchmen working in Poland had the right to two weeks' leave to go back to France to visit their families. After having checked directly that Tienpont was soon to take his leave, I steered the conversation at our friends' to discuss this, and invited him to dine with me at a restaurant the following evening. He accepted at once.

I arrived early so that I could ask the waiter, whom I knew, to make sure that my guest's glass was never left empty.

He understood immediately: 'He has to be well "looked after." You can count on me.'

The Frenchman arrived in an excellent mood, rubbing his hands together in glee. I asked him why he was so happy:

'You look as cheerful as if you'd discovered a gold mine.'

He burst out laughing.

'Not really a "mine," but still! I got a good load of opium today from a colleague in France. The Germans like that. You can always get some money for it.'

'I was going to make you a proposition, but if you're rich now . . .'

'Hold on, hold on! Did I say I was rich? I might be one day. For now, I'm still saving my pennies . . . What were you going to propose?'

'I have to leave Poland for a while to go to Paris. I have friends there . . .'

'And what would that have to do with me?' he asked. 'I don't smuggle people!'

'When you receive your permission for your leave, you'll give me your papers. I'll change the photos so that I can leave. You can have a nice break for two weeks on an estate near Lublin, and when the time was up, you would go back to work and say that your papers were stolen on the trolley. The fine for that is two hundred marks, which we would naturally add to what we'd pay you. What do you say?'

The Frenchman began by pointing out the risks. After hesitating for a while, the deal was agreed for thirty thousand zlotys.

As we were leaving the restaurant, Tienpont took me by the arm, and said: 'I don't want to know why you are going to France and I don't want to know what you plan to do there. It's not any of my business. I can understand that you do not like what I do here. Let's forget about that. Because besides all that, I am a Frenchman. Perhaps a stupid and a bad Frenchman, but . . . well, I accepted your proposal because I hate the Germans. I want to help people like you . . .'

He walked off quickly.

As soon as I had done with Tienpont I informed the organization authorities of my luck. At first my information was greeted with doubt and patent distrust, but as I continued to stress its feasibility and simplicity they accepted my plans.

I was ordered to submit a detailed plan for my trip. The only serious risk my project demanded was to appear as a native Frenchman. All the other hazards were normal perils, the chance of having my papers detected as forged, illegal crossings of frontiers, etc. However, I was prepared to cope with these dangers. I spoke French rather well, but with a marked accent. But in making my way through the territory of the German General Government, and Germany itself, I would have to speak only German. Even though my German was poorer than my French, I felt confident that I could always make myself sufficiently well understood. Of course, any French interpreter would have known immediately that I was not of French origin. At any rate, I resolved to speak as little as possible during the trip and thus avoid exposure. On the score of forging the seal on the new photographs, I had no trepidation. This had become child's play for us. The material I was to gather would be printed on microfilm. Photography was an invaluable element in the Underground.

When I left for England I would carry more than one thousand pages of printed matter for the government on Contax films the size of two or three American matchsticks. This material would be concealed in the handle of a razor, so perfectly soldered that its concealment would be well-nigh undetectable.

I had a feeling of calm security about the journey since all the details were methodically prepared. The underground methods of planning for liaison trips were perfected to a degree which could scarcely be compared with those made for the journeys we undertook at the beginning of our work. The pioneer days when the Gestapo caught me with films exposed so carelessly were gone.

A few days before my departure my liaison girl brought into my office a small piece of thin tissue paper containing some instructions. It stated:

> You are to appear on Wednesday morning at 10.00 a.m. before the Committee of Political Representation of Poland. Grot and Rawicz will be present. Liaison Girl Ira is to take care of all meeting arrangements. Your liaison girl has been contacted by Ira.

Grot was the assumed name of the Commander-in-Chief of the Polish Underground Army.[1] Rawicz was the alias of the Government Delegate.[2]

The following morning, my liaison girl brought Ira to see me. She was a tall, solidly built woman, with a military bearing and the manners of a sergeant-major. Without even greeting me, she barked out:

'Tomorrow morning, at 8 a.m. sharp, you will leave your office. You will meet your liaison officer and another person downstairs. That person will take you to the agreed meeting place. Your identity papers must be in perfect order. You must not be carrying any other compromising documents! The Commander-in-Chief is already too exposed as it is . . .'

I found her very unpleasant and said, sarcastically:

'Thank you very much for the lesson. I never would have thought of it myself.'

She didn't even look at me, just continued:

'I will be waiting at the place to which you will be brought by the liaison officer. As soon as you leave, you will be under constant surveillance. If we are confident that you aren't being followed, I'll take you to the agreed location. Is that clear?'

'Quite clear,' I answered. 'Have you prepared my new legend?'

'Not necessary,' she said curtly. 'The place you are going does not require one.'

She pivoted heavily and trudged out of the office.

The arrangements went off expeditiously and promptly. At 8.00 a.m., on a corner near my home, my liaison girl and an inconspicuous middle-aged woman awaited me. After introducing me to the latter, my liaison girl bade me goodbye and went off. I accompanied the lady, who was pleasant and intelligent, to a modern, imposing-looking apartment house in Zoliborz, changing trolleys twice on the way. We entered the building, climbed five flights, and then rang the bell, according to a simple signal – one short, one long. The door was opened by Ira.

I felt a revival of my distaste for her and did not bother saying 'good morning.' Instead, I indulged my dislike of her in criticism.

'That's a bad business,' I said rather severely. 'The ring is much too obvious. It is clearly a signal and anybody who heard it would recognize it as one.'

'That is none of your business,' she snapped back, nettled. 'You just stick to your own job.'

I did not answer but gazed at her coolly, as if surprised at her ill temper. Her apartment had a feminine daintiness that surprised me. The colorful cushions scattered about, the lace curtains and the prim tablecloth were exquisite, and did not seem to harmonize with her character at all.

Suddenly the telephone rang. She took the receiver from the hook. The conversation was short. I heard her say:

'Yes . . . yes . . . I am so glad she is well. I shall visit you soon . . .'
She put down the receiver.

'Are you ready?' she boomed at me.

I nodded.

'Very well. Let's go. I'll walk in front. You stay about ten paces behind me. If I have any trouble, you are to disappear and ignore me. Is that clear?'

The woman who had brought me to the place went first. Ira followed and then, after a short interval, I walked out. In the street, Ira was turning the corner to the left without glancing behind her or acting in the slightest bit concerned at my fate. I had to hurry in order not to lose her. She walked briskly for about half an hour. Finally she stopped in front of a church, glanced quickly up and down the street, and entered.

I waited across the street for about five minutes and then went inside. She was sitting on a bench in front of the altar. The church was deserted except for two elderly women who were praying, a beggar seeking shelter from the cold, and a beadle busily dusting off one of the side altars. I sat down on a bench at the back of the church and waited. Ira rose after a few minutes, and, passing by me without looking my way, went to a door in the rear of the church, opened it, and disappeared. I got up from my bench and sauntered after her.

The door opened on a long, damp corridor which led into the yard of a private house. At a slight distance in front of me, she entered the house and walked up two flights of stairs. I was close on her heels. She rapped loudly on a door.

It was opened by a young man of medium height. He was well-built, with a fresh, energetic manner.

'You brought Witold?' he asked.

'Yes,' she said, 'this is he.'

'Was there any trouble?' he inquired.

'No,' she answered and added sharply, 'but there may be. You ought to change the meeting place. At this time of the year there are too few people in the church. We were very conspicuous leaving through the back door. And on top of it, that beggar! He was freshly shaven! Who chose such an idiot as a lookout? Far too amateur!'

Her outburst was like machine-gun fire. The young man lowered his head.

He appeared to be a trifle annoyed.

'We have already made plans to have the place changed.'

Ira inclined her head in a manner which could be interpreted as her way of bidding us farewell. The young man grinned as she left the room.

'Tough old chicken, isn't she?'

'They don't come any tougher,' I agreed. 'Where do we go now?'

'Just follow me.'

He led me in and out of a series of small rooms and narrow corridors in the old, rather run-down house. We stopped in the first large room where he asked me to wait. He stepped out and returned after a brief interval, then gestured me into a connecting room.

As I entered, I saw grouped around the table the men who controlled the destiny of Poland, the leaders of the major political parties, the Chief Delegate, the Commander-in-Chief of the Home Army, and the Director of the Office of the Delegate. I knew them all quite well except for the leaders of the National and the Christian Labor Parties. These were new men who had taken the place of two others who had recently been arrested and whom I had known quite well.

The leader of the Socialist Party,[3] whom I had met several times before, and the Commander-in-Chief, approached me with the obvious intention of putting me at ease. The Commander-in-Chief was a tall, courtly, and elderly gentleman who spoke slowly and with grave, graceful gestures. With extreme kindness he put his arm around me and said, 'When do you leave for England, young man?'

I answered respectfully and briefly, 'In about a week, sir.'

'Is everything prepared?' he inquired.

'Yes, sir. I am waiting for a last meeting with the Jewish political leaders and for individual conferences with the leaders of the parties.'

The Commander chuckled.

'You young men! Are you really willing to go? Last time you took a trip we had a devil of a time getting you away from the Gestapo. By the way, how are your hands?'

I held them out. The others gathered around to inspect them.

'I went through a grafting operation a few months ago,' I said, gazing at my hands myself, as if I had suddenly discovered them for the first time. 'Apart from a few small scars, they have healed well. Our doctor did a remarkable job.'

The aged chief of the Socialist Party, who sometimes erred on the side of caution, peered earnestly at my hands. A trifle irritably he remarked:

'To tell the truth, it is not wise for the organization to send you on this trip. Those hands are liable to give you away. As a matter of fact, the Gestapo stressed them in the notices they sent out about you.'

He seemed to ponder awhile and then shrugged his shoulders.

'One cannot tell what is dangerous and what is not. The devil with it all – let's get on with the meeting.'

This called forth some scattered remarks as we seated ourselves around the table. The Delegate, who remained standing, waited until the hum of conversation died down and then proceeded to open the meeting with a formal, ceremonious speech.

'I have the honor to open the thirty-second meeting of the Political Representation of Poland. Owing to the importance of the program, I took the liberty of inviting the Commander of the Home Army, whom I hereby welcome. The purpose of our meeting is to provide material for our courier, Witold, who is going to report to the government-in-exile and to the representatives of the political parties in exile on the situation in Poland and the underground movement. He will also contact the authorities of the Allied nations and inform them about the situation here. Our government is being cabled to this effect.

'Leaders of the individual parties will give Witold material for their representatives in London at separate meetings.'

He turned toward me and added emphatically:

'We believe that he will perform this function impartially and convey material only to the designated persons, without regard for his own opinions and convictions.

'Today,' the Delegate continued, 'at this joint meeting, Witold will be given our official orders, instructions, and our viewpoint on the most important political problems. His mission is concerned only with political matters. Contact in military affairs has been established in another way.'

The men present took turns speaking while the Director of the Delegate's Office made shorthand notes for my use. The stenogram was later transcribed into code and printed on film to be used as the basis of my reports in London. The leaders spoke slowly, making calm, judicious statements. They realized that their words and opinions would be accepted as final and decisive by the men in London. To the men in exile, the message would voice the aspirations and sentiments of occupied Poland.

'Polish unity must be continued and strengthened . . . The government must be an all-inclusive coalition . . . No party has the right to remain aloof and refuse to share the mutual responsibility for the work and policy of the government . . . The continuity of the Polish state must be unimpaired . . .

'The continuity of the state does not mean the continuity of the last Polish regime. The new Poland will be democratic. The old Polish tradition of parliamentarism, which, strangely enough, has been reborn in the Underground, will continue in postwar Poland.

'The political parties are collaborating with each other in the fight against the occupant and in the support of the government. But they certainly differ in their programs – and they want to differ. Once liberated from the enemy, we shall organize a general election to the Parliament which will decide the political and social structure of Poland and will show the relative strength of each of the parties.

'The nation's will to resist continues undiminished and we steadfastly remain ready to make sacrifices . . . It is essential to maintain our rigid attitude towards the occupiers, whatever the cost . . . The occupation has not led to Polish Quislings and never will . . . Acts of treason and collaboration are severely punished and remain small in number . . . Traitors are summarily liquidated . . . The government-in-exile must be made aware of the burden borne by the country . . . It must give all support possible and entreat the Allied governments to provide assistance . . . Those in exile must renounce all political ambition and cast aside their rivalries . . . Their fate is neither better nor worse than the fate of the Polish people who have remained in their country . . . The émigrés must help the Allies in their efforts toward victory. After the war, the émigrés returning to our homeland will share with us the knowledge they have acquired in the West.

'The Allies must know that the Polish people are placing their hopes in them . . . Their statements about Poland are taken literally here. When the West declares, "The entire world pays tribute to the Polish people for its unwavering attitude toward the enemy and will never forget it," the Poles accept as a fact that the entire world pays tribute to the Polish people and that they "will never forget Poland . . ."'[4]

The meeting lasted several hours. Grot took the floor to conclude it. The Commander-in-Chief of the Home Army appealed, in a passionate address, for the greatest possible quantity of arms and military equipment to be sent. He gave his assurance that nothing would be wasted – that each rifle, bullet, stick of dynamite, hand grenade would be used to cause the maximum losses to the enemy.

After this, the office director of the Delegation closed his stenographic pad. The meeting was over. The participants left the apartment one after the other, in a pre-determined order.

A coded message was sent by short-wave to the government in London and to our organization in France:

Karski leaving soon. Goes through Germany, Belgium, France, Spain. Two-week stay in France; two weeks in Spain. Inform all 'transfer cells' in France, also all Allied representatives in Spain. Password: 'Coming to see Aunt Sophie.' Announce him as Karski.

29

The Ghetto

Before I was due to leave Poland a meeting was arranged for me – on the order of the Delegate of the Polish Government in London and of the Commander of the Underground Army – with two men who, formerly eminent in the Jewish community, were now directing the work of the Jewish Underground. One was the head of the Zionist organization, the other was the leader of the Jewish Socialist Alliance, the Bund.[1] The latter also had the dangerous and arduous task of directing the work of a special department of the Delegate of the Polish Government which organized relief for the Jewish population and attempted to smuggle the most valuable inhabitants out of the ghetto.

We met at twilight in a huge, empty, and half-ruined house in the suburbs. The fact that they were both present at the same time was significant. It meant that the material I was to be given to transmit to the Polish and Allied governments contained nothing of a political nature and was not limited to either group. It constituted the expression and contained the information, sentiments, requests, and instructions of the entire Jewish population of Poland as a unit, a population that was at the moment dying as a unit.

What I learned at the meetings we held in that house and later, when I was taken to see the facts for myself, was horrible beyond description. I know history. I have learned a great deal about the evolution of nations, political systems, social doctrines, methods of conquest, persecution, and extermination, and I know, too, that never in the history of mankind, never anywhere in the realm of human relations did anything occur to compare with what was inflicted on the Jewish population of Poland.

The two men were unforgettable, less like men than incarnations of mass suffering and nerves strained in hopeless effort. Both lived outside the ghetto but were able, by secret means, to enter and leave it as they pleased (I myself was to find out that this wasn't all that difficult). In the ghetto, they could be themselves and didn't stand out amongst the other inhabitants. On the 'Aryan' side, they had to completely transform themselves so as to not arouse any suspicions. They dressed differently and behaved differently. They became other people. They were like actors who were playing two rôles that were mutually exclusive. They were forced constantly to be on their guard so as not to make the slightest slips in their language, gestures, or behavior. The smallest mistakes could cost them their lives. The Bund leader in particular, with his distinguished gray hair and whiskers, ruddy complexion, erect carriage, and general air of good health, elegance, and refinement, passed easily as a Polish 'nobleman.' He was about sixty years old.

Before the war he had been a well-known lawyer with an excellent reputation as an expert in criminal law. Now he appeared before the German authorities as the owner of a large store, prosperous, dignified, and unruffled.[2] How great an effort of will this pose must have necessitated I realized later when he accompanied me to the ghetto. The air of well-being and savoir-faire seemed to vanish instantly. The well-groomed Polish merchant underwent a sudden transformation and became a Jew, one of the thousands of wretched, exhausted, starving Jews that the pitiless Nazis tormented and hunted with inhuman vindictiveness.

The other one was just over forty. He had Jewish features that must have been difficult for him to disguise. He gave the impression that he had suffered terribly and seemed to have great trouble in controlling his nerves.[3]

The first thing that became clear to me as I sat there talking to them in the silence of the darkening Warsaw suburbs was the complete hopelessness of their predicament. For them, for the suffering Polish Jews, this was the end of the world. There was no possible escape for them or their fellows. This, too, was only part of the tragedy, only partially the cause of their despair and agony. They were not afraid of death itself, and, indeed, accepted it as something almost inevitable. Added to this realization was the bitter knowledge that in this war, for them, there could be no hope of any victory whatsoever, none of the satisfaction which sometimes softens the prospect of death. The Zionist leader made this clear to me at once.

'You other Poles are fortunate,' he began. 'You are suffering, too. Many of you will die, but at least your nation goes on living. After the war Poland will be resurrected. Your cities will be rebuilt and your wounds will slowly heal. From this ocean of tears, pain, rage, and humiliation your country will emerge again but the Polish Jews will no longer exist. We will be dead. Hitler will lose his war against the human, the just, and the good, but he will win his war against the Polish Jews. No – it will not be a victory; the Jewish people will be murdered.'[4]

It was an evening of nightmare, but with a painful, oppressive kind of reality that no nightmare ever had. I sat in an old, rickety armchair that had two bricks stacked one on top of the other in place of one leg. I didn't move for fearing of falling, or – I don't know – perhaps because what I was hearing had frozen me to the spot in terror. They paced the floor violently, their shadows dancing weirdly in the dim light cast by the single candle we could allow ourselves. It was as though they were unable even to think of their dying people and remain seated.

After we had talked a while, after they had tried for a while to convey to me some idea of what their plight was like, the Zionist leader, holding his head between his hands and crying like a whipped child, burst out:

'What's the good of talking? What reason do I have to go on living? I ought to go to the Germans and tell them who I am. If all the Jews are killed they won't need any leaders . . . But it's no use telling you all this. No one in the outside world can possibly understand. You don't understand. Even I don't understand, for my people are dying and I am alive.'

The older man tried to calm him, laying one hand on his shoulder while the other clenched and unclenched nervously at his side.

'We have work to do,' he said, 'and very little time to do it. We have to talk to the point.'

There was a pause while the Zionist leader struggled to regain his self-control. 'Forgive me . . .' he murmured.

I did my best to stay calm.

'I understand what you're feeling . . . I will do everything I can to help you as much as possible. I am going to London on a mission for the Polish Underground. I will very likely have the opportunity of giving my report to the representatives of the Allied Powers.'

'Will you really?' The Zionist leader interjected hopefully. 'Do you think you will get to see Roosevelt and Churchill?'

'Perhaps. Or if not, then certainly someone close to them. I am going on an official mission. I will be accredited by the Polish Government in London. My status will be official and you must give me your official message to the outside world. You are the leaders of the Jewish Underground. What do you want me to say?'

They hesitated for a moment as if to consider all that they had to say and to select the phrases that were closest to their true feelings, that expressed their plight and their desires most significantly. The Bund leader spoke first, resting his hands on the table as though it helped him to concentrate on what he was about to say.

'We want you to tell the Polish and Allied governments and the great leaders of the Allies that we are helpless in the face of the German criminals. We cannot defend ourselves and no one in Poland can defend us. The Polish underground authorities can save some of us but they cannot save masses. The Germans are not trying to enslave us as they have other people; we are being systematically murdered. That is the difference.'

'That is what people do not understand. That is what is so difficult to make clear. Over in London, Washington, or New York, they undoubtedly believe that the Jews are exaggerating, that they're hysterical,' the Zionist added nervously.

I nodded my assent. The Bund leader continued:

'Our entire people will be destroyed. A few may be saved, perhaps, but three million Polish Jews are doomed. As well as others, brought in from all over Europe. The Polish Underground is in no position to prevent this, and the Jewish Underground even less so. The Allied Powers must bear the responsibility. Only from outside the country can effective help for the Jews be brought.'

This was the solemn message I carried to the world. They impressed it upon me so that it could not be forgotten. They added to it, for they saw their position with the clarity of despair. At this time more than 1,850,000 Jews had been murdered. These two men refused to delude themselves and foresaw how the United Nations might react to this information. The truth might not be believed. It might be said that this figure was exaggerated, not authentic. I was to argue, convince, do anything I could, use every available proof and testimonial, shout the truth till it could not be denied.

They had prepared me an exact statistical account of the Jewish mortality in Poland. I needed some particulars.

'Could you give me,' I asked, 'the approximate figures of the murders of the ghetto population?'

'The exact figure can be very nearly computed from the German deportation orders,' the Zionist leader informed me.

'You mean that every one of those who were presumably deported was actually killed?'

'Every single one,' the Bund leader asserted. 'Of course, the Germans kept up a pretense that this was not so. Even now, when there can be no doubt, letters are received from people whom we know to be dead, cheerful letters in which they inform their families and friends that they are healthy, working, and living on meat and white bread. But we know the truth and we can put you in a position to confirm it with your own eyes.'

'When did these deportations begin?'

'The first deportation order came in July. The German authorities demanded five thousand persons a day. They were supposed to be sent out of Warsaw to work. They were sent directly to the execution camps. It was then raised to six, seven, and finally to ten thousand a day. When Czerniakow, an engineer who was chairman of the Jewish Community, received the Germans' demand for ten thousand people daily to report for "work," he committed suicide.[5] He knew what it meant.'

'How many were "deported" altogether?'

'Over three hundred thousand. More than one hundred thousand are left and the deportations are still going on.'[6]

I turned pale. It was now the beginning of October 1942. In two and a half months, in one district in Poland, the Nazis had committed three hundred thousand murders. It was, indeed, the report of an unprecedented species of criminality that I had to bring to the outside world. But my report was not merely to be based on their uncorroborated word-of-mouth stories.

They offered to take me to the Warsaw ghetto so that I could literally see the spectacle of a people expiring, breathing its last before my eyes. They would take me into one of the many death camps where Jews were tortured and murdered by the thousands. As an eyewitness I would be much more convincing than a mere mouthpiece. At the same time they warned me that if I accepted their offer I would have to risk my life to carry it out. They told me, too, that as long as I lived I would be haunted by the memory of the ghastly scenes I would witness.

I told them that I had to see these things for myself. Soon I hoped to reach the other side of the barricade and to have an opportunity to convince what was left of the civilized world of the facts. Unless I had first-hand acquaintance with what I had to report I did not feel equal to the task.

It was settled, then, that, as soon as possible, arrangements should be made for these visits to take place. We would continue our discussions of how I could most effectively present their case to the rest of the world. I left them still standing in the nebulous, wavering light, two dejected shadows that wished me goodnight with a feeble warmth that denoted a trust in my person rather than any confidence in our enterprise.

Our second meeting was held in the same place. Their persons had altered as little as the circumstances they described. No more fitting place for our conversation could have been imagined – the desolate ruin of a house, the dismal silence interrupted only by our voices and the moaning wind that seemed constantly on the verge of extinguishing the candle that cast wan, irregular patches of light into the blackness.

For a while we discussed my forthcoming trip to the ghetto, disposing mechanically of details like my attire and behavior as though we were pushing them out of the way of more important topics. Finally I asked them what they wanted me to say to the British and American authorities if they asked me how they could help. The answer I got was bitter and realistic. They talked like men who knew that most of the proposals they had to make could not be put into execution, who did not even hope they would be executed, but who had to offer them as the only possible means of putting an end to the suffering of their people.

The Zionist leader spoke first:

'Germany can be impressed only by power and violence. The cities of Germany ought to be bombed mercilessly and with every bombing, leaflets should be dropped informing the Germans fully of the fate of the Polish Jews, and we ought to threaten the entire German nation with a similar fate both during and after the war. We do not believe in and do not aim at a slaughter of the German people but such a threat is the only possible way to check the German atrocities. Such a warning backed up by force might frighten the German people into putting enough pressure on their leaders to make them change their practices. Nothing else will.'

'We know,' the Bund leader added, 'that possibly this plan cannot be carried out, that it cannot fit into Allied military strategy, but we can't help that. The Jews and those who wish to help them cannot afford to approach this war from a purely military standpoint. Tell the Allied governments, if they want to help us, to issue official declarations to the German Government and people telling them that the consequences of continued persecution will be mass reprisals, the systematic destruction of the entire German nation.'

'I understand,' I said. 'I will do my best to tell them and make them understand what you have told me.'

'We demand still more,' said the Zionist leader. 'Hitler has said that all Germans, wherever they live or whatever they think, are one compact racial group. He has united them into a single army with the purpose of dominating the world. He is conducting a total war against civilization and his avowed purpose is to destroy the Jews completely. It is an unprecedented situation in history and can be dealt with only by unprecedented methods. Let the Allied governments, wherever their hand can reach, in America, England, and Africa, begin public executions of Germans, any they can get hold of. That is what we demand.'

'But that is utterly preposterous,' I said. 'A demand like that will only confuse and horrify all those who are sympathetic with you.'

'Of course,' the Zionist answered. 'Do you think I don't know it? We ask it because it is the only rebuttal to what is being done to us. We do not dream of its being fulfilled, but nevertheless we demand it. We demand it so people will know how we feel about what is being done to us, how helpless we are, how desperate our plight is, how little we stand to gain from an Allied victory as things are now, because if it comes in a year, in two or three years . . . we will have ceased to exist!'

They paused for a moment as if to let the knowledge of their true condition sink into me. I felt tired and feverish. More and more these two frantic figures pacing the floor in the shadowy room, their steps echoing in the hollow silence, seemed like apparitions, their glances filled with a burden of despair, pain, and hopelessness they could never completely express. Their voices were pitched very low, they hissed, they whispered, and yet I continually had the illusion that they were roaring. It seemed to me that I was listening to an earthquake, that I was hearing cracking, tearing sounds of the earth opening to swallow a portion of humanity. One could hear the cries and shouts of the frantic people falling into the chasm. I kept quiet, for fear of saying something that might be considered inappropriate, given the enormity of the problem they were sharing with me.

'It is impossible,' they hissed, raising their fists as if threatening all those who were on the other side of the barricade. 'The democracies cannot calmly put up with the assertion that the Jewish people in Europe cannot be saved. If American and British citizens can be saved, why can't evacuation of even the Jewish children be arranged on a large scale, of Jewish women, of the sick, the old? Offer the Germans an exchange. Offer them money. Why can't the lives of a few thousand Polish Jews be bought by the Allies?'

'How? How can this be done?' I asked, bewildered by these turbulent, desperate suggestions. 'It is opposed to all war strategy. Can we give our enemies money, can we give them back their soldiers to use against us in the front line?'

'That's just it. That's what we're up against. Everybody tells us, "This is contrary to the strategy of this war," but strategy can be changed, strategy can be adjusted. Let's adjust it to include the rescue of a fraction of the unhappy Jewish people. Why does the world let us all die? Haven't we contributed our share to culture, to civilization? Haven't we worked and fought and bled? Why do they fight for all the others? Why was it never said that strategy and tactics would be changed to correspond to the methods applied by the Germans to the Jewish population?'

I stood up suddenly.

'What plan of action do you want me to suggest to the Jewish leaders in England and America? They have something to say about the course of this war. They can act for you.'

The Bund leader came up to me in silence. He gripped my arm with such violence that it ached. I looked into his wild, staring eyes with awe, moved by the deep, unbearable pain in them.

'Tell the Jewish leaders that this is no case for politics or tactics. Tell them that the earth must be shaken to its foundations, the world must be aroused. Perhaps then it will wake up, understand, perceive. Tell them that they must find the strength and courage to make sacrifices no other statesmen have ever had to make, sacrifices as painful as the fate of my dying people, and as unique. This is what they do not understand. German aims and methods are without precedent in history. The democracies must react in a way that is also without precedent, choose unheard-of methods as an answer. If not, their victory will be only partial, only a military victory. Their methods will not preserve what the enemy includes in his program of destruction. Their methods will not preserve us.'

He paused and for the first time released my arm from his grip. He paced about for a moment nervously and then came to a halt in front of me. He spoke slowly and with great deliberation as though each word were costing him an effort.

'You ask me what plan of action I suggest to the Jewish leaders. Tell them to go to all the important English and American offices and agencies. Tell them not to leave until they have obtained guarantees that a way has been decided upon to save the Jews. Let them accept no food or drink, let them die a slow death while the world is looking on. Let them die. This may shake the conscience of the world.'

I sank into my armchair. My whole body felt chilled and sore. I was shivering and I felt the pulses in my temples pounding. I rose to go.

'One moment more,' the Zionist leader said, 'this we did not intend to tell you, but I want you to know it. We do not demand such sacrifices from our leaders abroad out of cruelty. We expect to make them here ourselves. The ghetto is going to go up in flames. We are not going to die in slow torment, but fighting. We will declare war on Germany – the most hopeless declaration of war that has ever been made.'

The Bund leader suddenly got up, as if surprised by his colleague's statement – the Zionist had obviously said something he shouldn't have. But then he whispered:

'We are organizing a defense of the ghetto' – the words trickled slowly from his pursed lips – 'not because we think it can be defended, but to let the world see the hopelessness of our battle – as a demonstration and a reproach. We are even now negotiating with your commander for the arms we need. If we get them, then, one of these days, the deportation squad is going to get a bloody surprise.'

'We shall see,' the Zionist concluded, 'whether we Jews can still obtain the right to die fighting and not – as Hitler has ordered – to die suffering.'

Two days later I went to the Warsaw ghetto with the Bund leader and another of the Jewish Underground. The Germans had, of course, designated the poorest district in Warsaw as the site of the ghetto. The houses were all old and shabby, and no more than two or three stories high. The streets were narrow and without more than a semblance of a pavement or sidewalk. Great gaps had been torn in this collection of hovels by the German bombardment and no repairs had ever been attempted – the heaps of rubble remained as they had fallen. A brick wall about eight feet high had been built around the entire, desolate area, from which all the 'Aryans' had been evacuated and into which more than four hundred thousand Jews had been forced.

I wore an old, shabby suit and a cap pulled down over my eyes. I tried to make myself look very small and thin. At my sides walked two typical inhabitants of the ghetto, wretched-looking, dressed in rags, scrawny and half-starved. We had reached the ghetto by a secret passage that must have been obvious to anyone who scrutinized the district at all carefully.

Adjoining the wall on the outside was a large open court that likewise surrounded nearly the entire ghetto. One of the buildings on this court was so constructed that its front door opened into the Aryan district, while an exit from its cellar led directly into the ghetto. This building gave many Jews the opportunity of contact with the outer world. With bribery, circumspection, a willingness to take the risk of being caught, and a thorough knowledge of the confusing cellars, the passage was comparatively easy. Indeed, at that time, the building had become like a modern version of the River Styx which connected the world of the living with the world of the dead. Now that the Warsaw ghetto no longer even exists, destroyed in the heroic 'defense' my friends had promised, I can mention the building and its cellars with impunity. Now the friendly building can no more help the unfortunate Polish Jews than I can harm them by revealing its secret.

Is it still necessary to describe the Warsaw ghetto? So much has already been written about it, there have been so many accounts by unimpeachable witnesses. A cemetery? No, for these bodies were still moving, were indeed often violently agitated. These were still living people, if you could call them such. For apart from their skin, eyes, and voice there was nothing human left in these palpitating figures. Everywhere there was hunger, misery, the atrocious stench of decomposing bodies, the pitiful moans of dying children, the desperate cries and gasps of a people struggling for life against impossible odds.

To pass that wall was to enter into a new world utterly unlike anything that had ever been imagined. The entire population of the ghetto seemed to be living in the street. There was hardly a square yard of empty space. As we picked our way across the mud and rubble, the shadows of what had once been men or women flitted by us in pursuit of someone or something, their eyes blazing with some insane hunger or greed.

Everyone and everything seemed to vibrate with unnatural intensity, to be in constant motion, enveloped in a haze of disease and death through which their bodies appeared to be throbbing in disintegration. We passed an old man standing against a wall staring lugubriously and with glassy eyes into space, and although he barely moved from his spot, he, too, seemed to be strangely animated, his body tormented by a force that made his skin twitch in little areas.

As we walked everything became increasingly unreal. The names of streets, shops, and buildings had been printed in the old Hebrew characters. My guides informed me that an edict had been issued forbidding the use of German or Polish for any inscriptions in the ghetto. As a result many of the inhabitants could not read the names at all. From time to time we passed a well-fed German policeman who looked abnormally bloated by contrast with the meagerness of those who surrounded him. Each time one approached we hastened our steps or crossed to the other side as though we had been contaminated.

We passed a miserable replica of a park – a little square of comparatively clear ground in which a half-dozen nearly leafless trees and a patch of grass had somehow managed to survive. It was fearfully crowded. Mothers huddled close together on benches nursing withered infants. Children, every bone in their skeletons showing through their taut skins, played in heaps and swarms.

'They play before they die,' I heard my companion on the left say, his voice breaking with emotion.

Without thinking – the words escaping even before the thought had crystallized – I said:

'But these children are not playing – they only make believe it is play.'

We heard the sound of a large number of footsteps rising and falling in unison. A group of about a hundred young men were approaching us. They marched in formation in the middle of the street and were accompanied by policemen. Their clothes were torn and dirty like the rest but they were obviously stronger, betternourished. The reason was apparent. As they passed us I noticed that each carried a ragged bundle from which protruded the end of a loaf of bread and some green vegetable tips.

Their physical condition was indubitably better than that of their neighbors. But there was something uncanny, robotlike, about their appearance. They walked stiffly. The muscles on their faces seemed to have set rigidly into a mold of habitual, unbroken fatigue. Their eyes were glazed and blank and focused straight ahead as though nothing could distract their attention.

'Those are fortunate,' the Bund leader informed me. 'The Germans still find them useful. They can work repairing roads and tracks. They are protected as long as their hands last and their muscles move. Everyone in the ghetto envies them. We supply as many people as we can with forged documents proving that they hold similar jobs. Otherwise they would be murdered. We have saved thousands of lives this way. But this cannot work much longer.'

Frequently we passed by corpses lying naked in the streets.

'What does it mean?' I asked my guide. 'Why are they lying there naked?'

'When a Jew dies,' he answered, 'his family removes his clothing and throws his body in the street. If not, they have to pay the Germans to have the body buried. They have instituted a burial tax which practically no one here can afford. Besides, this saves clothing. Here, every rag counts.'

I shuddered. A phrase came to my mind which I had heard often and thought I had never fully comprehended till that moment: *Ecce homo* – behold the man.

I saw an old, feeble man staggering along, lurching against the walls of the houses to keep from falling.

'I don't see many old people,' I said. 'Do they stay inside all day?'

The answer came in a voice that seemed to issue from the grave.

'No. Don't you understand the German system yet? Those whose muscles are still capable of any effort are used for forced labor. The others are murdered by quota. First come the sick and aged, then the unemployed, then those whose work is not directly connected with the German war needs, finally those who work on roads, in trains, in factories. Ultimately, they intend to kill us all.'

Suddenly my companions seized my arms. I saw nothing, did not know what was happening. I became frightened, thought I had been recognized. They rushed me through the nearest entrance.

'Hurry, hurry, you must see this. This is something for you to tell the world about. Hurry!'

We reached the top floor. I heard the sound of a shot from somewhere. They knocked at a door. It opened halfway to disclose a white, emaciated face.

'Do your windows face the street?' the leader asked.

'No, the courtyard. What do you want?'

The Bund leader slammed the door shut furiously. He rushed to the opposite door and battered upon it. It opened. He pushed aside a young boy, who ran back into the room with frightened cries. They urged me to the window, pulled down the shade, and told me to look through the slit at the side.

'Now you'll see something. The hunt. You would never believe it if you did not see it for yourself.'

I looked through the opening. In the middle of the street two boys, dressed in the uniform of the Hitlerjugend, were standing. They wore no caps and their blond hair shone in the sun. With their round, rosy-cheeked faces and their blue eyes they were like images of health and life. They chattered, laughed, pushed each other in spasms of merriment. At that moment, the younger one pulled a gun out of his hip pocket and then I first realized what I was witnessing. His eyes roamed about, seeking something. A target. He was looking for a target with the casual, gay absorption of a boy at a carnival.

I followed his glance. For the first time I noticed that all the pavements about them were absolutely deserted. Nowhere within the scope of those blue eyes, in no place from which those cheerful, healthy faces could be seen was there a single human being. The gaze of the boy with the gun came to rest on a spot out of my line of vision. He raised his arm and took careful aim. The shot rang out, followed by the noise of breaking glass and then the terrible cry of a man in agony.

The boy who had fired the shot shouted with joy. The other clapped him on the shoulder and said something to him, obviously complimentary. They smiled at each other and stood there for a moment, gay and insolent, as though aware of their invisible audience. Then they linked their arms and walked off gracefully toward the exit of the ghetto, chatting cheerfully as if they were returning from a sporting event.

I stood there, my face glued to the window. In the room behind me there was a complete silence. No one even stirred. I remained where I was, afraid to change the position of my body, to move my hand or relax my cramped legs. I was seized with such panic that I could not make the effort of will to take a single step or force a word out of my throat. It seemed to me that if I made the slightest movement, if a single muscle in my body so much as trembled, I might precipitate another scene such as I had just witnessed.

I do not know how long I remained there. Any interval could have passed, I was so completely unconscious of time. At length I felt someone's hand on my shoulder. Repressing a nervous start, I turned around. A woman, the tenant of the apartment, was standing there, her gaunt face the color of chalk in the dim light. She gestured at me.

'You came to see us? It won't do any good. Go back, run away. Don't torture yourself any more.'

My two guides were sitting motionlessly on a dilapidated couch, their heads between their hands. I approached them.

'Let's go,' I said, stammering. 'Take me out of here . . . I am very tired. I must go immediately. I will come back some other time . . .'

They rose quickly and silently and placed themselves at my sides. We clattered hurriedly down the broken staircase without saying a word. In the streets I almost broke into a run while they kept up with me as best they could. I kept going this way, at a half-run, through the door and cellars of the secret building until we reached the door that led to the other side.

It is hard to explain why I ran. There was no occasion for speed and, if anything, our haste could have aroused suspicion. But I ran, I think, simply to get a breath of clean air and a drink of water. Everything there seemed polluted by death, the stench of rotting corpses, filth, and decay. I was careful to avoid touching a wall or a human being. I would have refused a drink of water in that city of death if I had been dying of thirst. I believe I even held my breath as much as I could in order to breathe in less of the contaminated air.

Two days later I repeated my visit to the ghetto, to memorize more vividly my visual impressions. With my two guides I walked again for three hours through the streets of this inferno, the better to testify the truth before the leading men and women of the free countries of the world. I reported my experiences to prominent members of the British and American governments, and to the Jewish leaders of both continents. I told what I had seen in the ghetto to some of the world's great writers – to H. G. Wells, Arthur Koestler, members of the PEN Club – as they could describe it with greater force and talent than I. I told it to others, too, less well-known and to one, in particular, who will never be heard from again.

In London, five weeks later, a meeting was arranged for me. To me, it was one of innumerable such meetings and not the most important. Since my arrival in London I had been swamped with literally hundreds of conferences, conversations, contacts, and reports. I had been involved in them from 9.00 a.m. to midnight every day, with hardly a respite or an intermission except for absolute necessities. This time I expected one of the leaders of the Jewish Bund. His name was Szmul Zygelbojm.[7] He had been in Poland until 1940, had worked in the Jewish Underground, had been a member of the Council of the Warsaw ghetto, and had, I believe, even been held for a time as a hostage by the Nazis. He had then made it to London, sent as a delegate by the Bund to represent the Jewish Socialists in the Polish government-in-exile.

Our meeting was set for 2 December 1942 at Stratton House, near Piccadilly, at the headquarters of the Polish Minister of the Interior. It was an enormous building; when I finally managed to find the number of the correct office on the fourth floor, Zygelbojm was already there, waiting for me, sitting behind a small desk. He appeared tired. He looked like a type of man I had often encountered among Jewish leaders, with the mistrustful, piercing eyes of a proletarian who had worked his way to the top of the power hierarchy. His early life had surely been very hard.

'What do you want to hear about?' I asked.

'About Jews, my dear man. I am a Jew. Tell me what you know about the Jews in Poland.'

'Are you entitled to see the material I received at the joint conferences with the leaders of the Jewish Bund and the Zionists?'

'Yes, I am. I represent the Jewish Bund in the Polish National Council and I was one of the leaders of the Bund in Poland.'

I began my story in a cut-and-dried fashion. I had finally, after much experience, mastered a kind of formula for these situations. I had found that, on the whole, the most effective way of getting my material across was not to soften or interpret it, but to convey it as directly as possible, reproducing not merely ideas and instructions but the language, gestures, and nuances of those from whom the material came. That has been my job – faithful, concrete reproduction.

Zygelbojm listened intently, thirstily, with an avid desire for information it was impossible to satisfy. He sat rigidly with his legs far apart and braced, his body inclined forward, a hand on each knee. His dark, wide-open eyes were staring fixedly at a point on the ceiling far behind me. They never blinked. The expression on his face hardly varied, not a muscle of it moving, except for the occasional contortion of his cheek in a nervous tic.

'Conditions are horrible. The people in the ghetto live in constant agony, a lingering, tormenting death,' I was reciting almost by rote. 'The instructions their leaders gave me cannot be carried out for political and tactical reasons. I spoke to the British authorities. The answer was the one your leaders in Poland told me to expect: "No, it is impossible, it can't be done."'

Zygelbojm rose abruptly and advanced a step or two toward me. His eyes snapped with anger and contempt. He dismissed what I had just told him with a sharp wave of his hand that made me feel as though I had been slapped in rebuke.

'Listen,' he almost shouted. 'I didn't come here to talk to you about what is happening here. Don't tell me what is said and done here. I know that myself. I came to you to hear about what is happening *there*, what *they* want *there*, what they say *there*!'

I answered with brutal simplicity and directness.

'Very well, then. This is what *they* want from their leaders in the free countries of the world, this is what *they* told me to say: "Let them go to all the important English and American offices and agencies. Tell them not to leave until they have obtained guarantees that a way has been decided upon to save the Jews. Let them accept no food or drink, let them die a slow death while the world looks on. Let them die. This may shake the conscience of the world."'

Zygelbojm started as though he had been bitten and began to pace around the room agitatedly, almost breaking into a run. Worried lines formed between his contracted eyebrows and he held one hand to his head as though it ached.

'It is impossible,' he finally said, 'utterly impossible. You know what would happen. They would simply bring in two policemen and have me dragged away to an institution. Do you think they will let me die a slow, lingering death? Never . . . they would never let me.'

We talked at great length. I gave him all the details of my instructions. I told him all I knew about the Jews in Poland and all I had seen. He asked innumerable questions, wanted more and more concrete and even trivial details. Possibly he felt that if the picture I gave him was clear and minute enough, he could suffer together with them, be united with them. He asked me what the houses looked like, what the children looked like, what were the exact words of the woman who put her hands on my shoulder while I was watching the 'hunt.' What was my impression of the Bund leader, what did he wear, how did he talk, was he nervous? He asked me what the corpses of the dead Jews on the ghetto streets looked like and did I remember the words of the child dying in the street.

He shrugged his shoulders.

'Ah, I forget. You can't talk Yiddish, you are not a Jew.'

I did my best to satisfy his thirst for facts and details, emptying my memory of everything that it had stored up for just such an occasion. At the end of the interview I was utterly fatigued, my powers of response completely sapped. He looked even more tired, his eyes nearly starting out of their sockets, and the tic occurring with increasing frequency. We shook hands, Zygelbojm gazing directly into my eyes, intent and questioning.

'Mr Karski, I'll do everything I can to help them. Everything! I'll do everything they demand – if only I am given a chance. You believe me, don't you?'

My answer was rather cold and impatient. I felt tired, frustrated, strained. So many interviews, so many meetings . . .

'Of course I believe you. I feel certain you will do all you can and all they demand. My God, every single one of us tries to do his best.'

Fundamentally, I think, I felt that Zygelbojm was boasting or, at least, thoughtlessly promising more than he could perform. I felt nettled, harassed. He asked so many needless questions which had no place in the interview. 'Did I believe him?' What difference did it make if I did or did not? I no longer knew what I believed and what I did not believe. He had no right to perplex me further. I had enough of my own troubles . . .

Some weeks later I had all but forgotten Zygelbojm in the endless grind of interviews and meetings. On 13 May 1943 came the epilogue to our meeting. I will remember that day till I die. I was sitting in my room in Dolphin Square during a brief respite, resting, when the telephone rang. I deliberately let it ring three or four times and then picked up the receiver reluctantly. It was an employee of Stratton House.

'Mr Karski, I was told to inform you that Szmul Zygelbojm, a member of the Polish National Council and representative of the Bund in London, committed suicide yesterday. He left some notes, saying that he did all he could to help the Jews in Poland but failed, that all his brothers will perish, and that he is joining them. He turned on the gas in his apartment.'

I hung up.

At first I felt nothing at all, then a wave of mingled shock, grief, and guilt. I felt as though I had personally handed Zygelbojm his death warrant, even though I had been only the instrument. Painfully, it occurred to me that he might have found my answer to his last question cold and unsympathetic. I had become, I thought to myself, so cynical, so quick and harsh in my judgment, that I could no longer estimate the degree of self-sacrifice possible to a man like Zygelbojm. For days afterwards I felt all my confidence in myself and in my work vanishing and I deliberately forced myself to work twice as hard in order to avoid these intolerable reflections.

Since then I have often thought about Szmul Zygelbojm, one of the most tragic victims of this war and its horrors. For Zygelbojm's death did not have a shadow of consolation. It was self-imposed and utterly hopeless. I wonder now how many people can understand what it means to die as he did for a cause that would be victorious, yet with the certain knowledge that victory would not stave off the sacrifice of his people, the annihilation of all that was most meaningful to him. Of all the deaths that have taken place in this war, surely Zygelbojm's is one of the most frightening, the sharpest revelation of the extent to which the world has become cold and unfriendly, nations and individuals separated by immense gulfs of indifference, selfishness, and convenience. All too plainly, it marks the fact that the domination of mutual suspicion, estrangement, and lack of sympathy has progressed so far that even those who wish and strive for a remedy by every possible means are powerless and able to accomplish pitifully little.

30

'To Die in Agony . . .'

A few days after my second visit to the Warsaw ghetto, the Bund leader was to arrange an opportunity for me to see a Jewish death camp.

The camp was located near the town of Belzec,[1] about one hundred miles east of Warsaw, and was well-known all over Poland from the tales of horror that were circulated about it. The common report was that every Jew who reached it, without exception, was doomed to death. That was the only reason to be sent there. The Bund leader had never been in it but had the most detailed information in its operations, which he had had principally from the Polish railroad workers.[2]

I was to go on a day when executions were scheduled. The information was easy to obtain because many of the Estonian, Latvian, and Ukrainian attendants who worked there under Gestapo supervision were in the service of Jewish organizations. Not from any humane or political consideration, but for money. I was to wear the uniform of one of the Estonians who would stay home while I went in with his papers.[3] I was assured that chaos, corruption, and panic prevailed in the camp to such an extent that there was no chance of my disguise being penetrated. Moreover, the whole expedition was perfectly organized in advance. I would go through a door habitually guarded only by Germans and Ukrainians, for an Estonian might sense a stranger in me. The Estonian uniform, itself, constituted a pass, so that my papers would probably not be inspected. To make the camouflage more foolproof, still another bribed Estonian militia man would accompany me. Since I knew German, I could talk with the German guards if it became necessary and they, too, could be bribed.

The plan seemed simple and flawless. I agreed without any hesitation and without the slightest fear of being caught.

Early in the morning of the day we had selected, I left Warsaw in the company of a Jew who worked outside the ghetto in the Jewish underground movement. We took the train to Lublin. A hay cart was waiting for us there. We took the dirt tracks because the farmer who was transporting us wanted to avoid the busy Zamosc road. We arrived in Belzec shortly after midday and went directly to the place where the Estonian was supposed to be waiting to give me his uniform.[4] It was a little grocery store that had once belonged to a Jew. The Jew had been killed and since then it was being run, with the permission of the Gestapo, by a local farmer who was, of course, a member of the Underground.

My Estonian uniform was there waiting for me but the man to whom it belonged had evidently decided it was more prudent to remain away. Knowing what was in the air, he had decided it was safer not to have his face seen by me since, for all he knew, I might take it into my head to betray him later. However, he had left me in good order a complete outfit: trousers, long boots, a belt, a tie, and a cap. The idea of letting his personal papers be used had apparently given him qualms, too. Instead he had left me the papers of one of his colleagues who had probably returned to his native Estonia a long time ago and had taken the opportunity to sell his papers. I was not surprised. Selling papers was an established business in Poland, not at all frowned upon. The uniform and the shoes fitted me remarkably well but the cap came down to my ears. I stuffed it with papers and squeezed it about till it fitted. Then I asked my companion how I looked. He said I looked like a model Estonian militia man.

An hour or two later the Estonian who was to accompany me arrived. He spoke German so we had no difficulty in understanding each other. My program had not been changed. We would enter through the eastern gate, as planned. After we entered, my guide would take me to a place suited for observation. He confirmed the Bund leader's assurance that the camp was so disorganized, chaotic, and indifferently managed that I could stroll about in perfect freedom. I was to stick to the place assigned me throughout the executions and in that way I would miss nothing. After the executions all the guards would be leaving the camp. I was to join them, mingling with the mob of mixed attendants but avoiding the Estonians. He reiterated the latter precaution solemnly, warning me that if I had any close contact with them, it would be easy for them to recognize me as not 'their man.'

He gave me a brief, dissatisfied, critical scrutiny and then began to order me about like a martinet. I was told to polish my boots, fix my tie, and tighten my belt. He even informed me that my posture was too relaxed and undignified. I said nothing and did as I was told but with a slightly grudging air, striking a pose of exaggerated military stiffness. He relented a little and excused himself on the grounds that the Germans were very severe about such matters and did not like to see 'their Latvians, Estonians, and Ukrainians negligently dressed.'

The camp was about a mile and a half from the store. We started walking rapidly, taking a side lane to avoid meeting people and possibly having to endure an inspection. It took about twenty minutes to get to the camp but we became aware of its presence in less than half that time. About a mile away from the camp we began to hear shouts, shots, and screams. The noise increased steadily as we approached.

'What's happening?' I asked. 'What's the meaning of all that noise?'

'The Jews are getting hot,' he said, grinning as though he had said something witty.

I must have glared at him for he changed his tone abruptly.

'What could it be?' He shrugged. 'They are bringing in a "batch" today.'

I knew what he meant and did not inquire further. We walked on while the noise increased alarmingly. From time to time a series of long screams or a particularly inhuman groan would set the hair on my scalp bristling.

'What are the chances of anyone escaping?' I asked my companion, hoping to hear an optimistic answer.

'None at all, sir,' he answered, dashing my hopes to the ground. 'Once they get this far, their goose is cooked.'

'You mean there isn't a single chance of anybody escaping from the camp?

'Ha! Maybe . . . but we'd need help,' he replied cautiously.

'From whom?'

'One of the guards. Perhaps a guard who looks like me. But it's an insane risk to take. If any guard were caught trying to help a Jew, they'd both be shot in the head at once!'

But I had caught his interest all the same because, as we were walking, he was watching me out of the corner of his eye. I pretended not to notice. He didn't persist but added craftily:

'Of course, if a Jew pays well – very well – it can be done. But it is very risky, it has got to be handled right . . .'

'How can they pay? They don't have any money on them, do they?'

'And who's asking *them* for money? It's payable in advance. With them' – he nodded toward the camp – 'no one would make a deal. You can only do business with people from the outside. People like you. If someone came to see me and said that such-and-such a Jew would be in the transport tomorrow, then I could do something. But on one condition: cash up front.'

'Have you saved many Jews so far?'

'Not as many as I'd like, but a few, anyhow.'

'Are there many more good men like you there who are so willing to save the Jews?'

'Save them? Say, who wants to save them?' He looked at me in bewilderment as though I were talking unheard-of nonsense. 'But if they pay, that's a different story. We can all use some money.'

I did not venture to disagree. It would have been hopeless to try to persuade him of anything different. I looked at his heavy, rather good-natured face and wondered how the war had come to develop such cruel habits in him. From what I had seen he seemed to be a simple, average man, not particularly good or bad. His hands were the calloused but supple hands of a good farmer. In normal times that was what he probably had been, and a good father, a family man, and a church-goer. Now, under the pressure of the Gestapo and the cajoleries of the Nazis, with everyone about him engaged in a greedy competition that knew no limits, he had been changed into a professional butcher of human beings. He had caught onto his trade well and discussed its niceties, used its professional jargon as coolly as a carpenter discussing his craft.

'And what are you here for?' The question was at once shrewd and innocent.

'Well, you see, it's this way. I'd like to "save" some Jews, too,' I said with an air of sly conspiracy, 'with your help, of course. That's why I've come to the camp to see how everything works.'

'Well, don't you go trying to do anything without us,' he warned me. The prospect of competition seemed to upset him. I hastened to reassure him.

'Don't be silly. Why should I work without you? We both want to make money and we can both help each other. We would be foolish to work against each other.'

He was now highly interested.

'How will your people pay you – a flat rate or for each Jew separately?'

'Now, that's just what I've been wondering about. Which do you think I ought to ask for, which pays more in the long run?'

He paused to deliberate.

'If I were you,' he said, 'I'd make my rates per Jew. You lose too many opportunities of making a haul if you work on a flat rate for a group. You never know who you might get hold of, or how you might be able to pump him for cash. If someone really wants to get someone out of here, he won't haggle. You have to have "*Kiepele*," brains, as they say. Without that, you get nothing.'

'You are perfectly right. I guess that's the way I'll work.'

'You'll be better off,' he said. 'But remember – fifty-fifty. Don't try any tricks.'

I hastened to reassure him, telling that it would be harmful to my work for me to attempt cheating him. Besides, weren't we both honest men, was it likely that we should try to cheat each other?

This satisfied him completely. I now had the status of a younger colleague. He wondered if I was going to stay permanently in the business of 'Jew dealing.' 'You're from Warsaw. It's better there. It's closer to the ghetto. It's easier to "save" people from there,' he said, winking knowingly.

I retorted that, on the other hand, that was bringing down the 'price,' but he complained about how difficult life was. A dreadful smell seemed to be all around us. We were getting closer. I thought with relief that soon I wouldn't have to listen to him any more.

When did I think the Germans would win? He wondered. I proceeded to doubt if the Germans would win at all. This struck him as utterly ridiculous. There was no room for doubt. Look at what had happened so far. Hitler was a fiend, a demon, a magician. Nobody had a chance against him.

As we approached to within a few hundred yards of the camp, the shouts, cries, and shots cut off further conversation. I again noticed, or thought I noticed, an unpleasant stench that seemed to have come from decomposing bodies mixed with horse manure. This may have been an illusion. The Estonian was, in any case, completely impervious to it. He even began to hum some sort of folk-tune to himself. We passed through a small grove of decrepit-looking trees and emerged directly in front of the loud, sobbing, reeking camp of death.

It was on a large, flat plain and occupied about a square mile. It was surrounded on all sides by a formidable barbed-wire fence, nearly two yards in height and in good repair. Inside the fence, at intervals of about fifteen yards, guards were standing, holding rifles with fixed bayonets ready for use. Around the outside of the fence, militia men circulated on constant patrol. The camp itself contained a few small sheds or barracks. The rest of the area was completely covered by a dense, pulsating, throbbing, noisy human mass. Starved, stinking, gesticulating, insane human beings in constant, agitated motion. Through them, forcing paths if necessary with their rifle butts, walked the German police and the militia men. They walked in silence, their faces bored and indifferent. They looked like shepherds bringing a flock to the market or pig-dealers among their pigs. They had the tired, vaguely disgusted appearance of men doing a routine, tedious job.

Into the fence a few passages had been cut, and gates made of poles tied together with barbed wire swung back, allowing entrance. Each gate was guarded by two men who slouched about carelessly. We stopped for a moment to collect ourselves. To my left I noticed the railroad tracks which passed about a hundred yards from the camp. From the camp to the track a sort of raised passage had been built from old boards. On the track a dusty freight train waited, motionless. It had at least thirty cars, all filthy.

The Estonian followed my gaze with the interest of a person seeing what kind of an impression his home made on a visitor. He proceeded eagerly to enlighten me. 'That's the train they'll load them on. You'll see it all.'

We came to a gate. Two German non-coms were standing there talking. I could hear snatches of their conversation. They seemed to be talking about a night they had spent in a nearby town. I hung back a bit. The Estonian seemed to think I was losing my nerve.

'Go ahead,' he whispered impatiently into my ear. 'Don't be afraid. They won't even inspect your papers. They don't care about the likes of you.'

We walked up to the gate and saluted the non-coms vigorously. They returned the salute indifferently and we passed through, entering the camp, and mingled unnoticed with the crowd.

'Follow me,' he said quite loudly. 'I'll take you to a good spot.'

We passed an old Jew, a man of about sixty, sitting on the ground without a stitch of clothing on him. I was not sure whether his clothes had been torn off or whether he, himself, had thrown them away in a fit of madness. Silent, motionless, he sat on the ground, no one paying him the slightest attention. Not a muscle or fiber in his whole body moved. He might have been dead or petrified except for his preternaturally animated eyes, which blinked rapidly and incessantly. Not far from him a small child, clad in a few rags, was lying on the ground. He was all alone and crouched quivering on the ground, staring up with the large, frightened eyes of a rabbit. No one paid any attention to him, either.

The Jewish mass vibrated, trembled, and moved to and fro as if united in a single, insane, rhythmic trance. They waved their hands, shouted, quarreled, cursed, and spat at each other. Hunger, thirst, fear, and exhaustion had driven them all insane. I had been told that they were usually left in the camp for three or four days without a drop of water or food.[5]

They were all former inhabitants of the Warsaw ghetto. When they had been rounded up they were given permission to take about ten pounds of baggage. Most of them took food, clothes, bedding, and, if they had any, money and jewelry. On the train, the Germans who accompanied them stripped them of everything that had the slightest value, even snatching away any article of clothing to which they took a fancy. They were left a few rags for apparel, bedding, and a few scraps of food. Those who left the train without any food starved continuously from the moment they set foot in the camp.

There was no organization or order of any kind. None of them could possibly help or share with each other and they soon lost any self-control or any sense whatsoever except the barest instinct of self-preservation. They had become, at this stage, completely dehumanized. It was, moreover, typical autumn weather, cold, raw, and rainy. The sheds could not accommodate more than two to three thousand people and every 'batch' included more than five thousand. This meant that there were always two to three thousand men, women, and children scattered about in the open, suffering exposure as well as everything else.

The chaos, the squalor, the hideousness of it all was simply indescribable. There was a suffocating stench of sweat, filth, decay, damp straw, and excrement. To get to my post we had to squeeze our way through this mob. It was a ghastly ordeal. I had to push foot by foot through the crowd and step over the limbs of those who were lying prone. It was like forcing my way through a mass of sheer death and decomposition made even more horrible by its agonized pulsations. My companion had the skill of long practice, evading the bodies on the ground and winding his way through the mass with the ease of a contortionist. Distracted and clumsy, I would brush against people or step on a figure that reacted like an animal, quickly, often with a moan or a yelp. Each time this occurred I would be seized by a fit of nausea and come to a stop. But my guide kept urging and hustling me along.

In this way we crossed the entire camp and finally stopped about twenty yards from the gate which opened on the passage leading to the train. It was a comparatively uncrowded spot. I felt immeasurably relieved at having finished my stumbling, sweating journey. The guide was standing at my side, saying something, giving me advice. I hardly heard him, my thoughts were elsewhere. He tapped me on the shoulder. I turned toward him mechanically, seeing him with difficulty. He raised his voice.

'Look here. You are going to stay here. I'll walk on a little further. You know what you are supposed to do. Remember to keep away from Estonians. Don't forget, if there's any trouble, you don't know me and I don't know you.'

I nodded vaguely at him. He shook his head and walked off.

I remained there perhaps half an hour, watching this spectacle of human misery. At each moment I felt the impulse to run and flee. I had to force myself to remain indifferent, practice stratagems on myself to convince myself that I was not one of the condemned, throbbing multitude, forcing myself to relax as my body seemed to tie itself into knots, or turning away at intervals to gaze into the distance at a line of trees near the horizon. I had to remain on the alert, too, for any Estonian uniform, ducking toward the crowd or behind a nearby shed every time one approached me. The crowd continued to writhe in agony, the guards circulated about, bored and indifferent, occasionally distracting themselves by firing a shot or dealing out a blow. Finally I noticed a change in the motion of the guards. They walked less and they all seemed to be glancing in the same direction – at the passage to the track which was quite close to me.

I turned toward it myself. Two German policemen came to the gate with a tall, bulky SS man. He barked out an order and they began to open the gate with some difficulty. It was very heavy. He shouted at them impatiently. They worked at it frantically and finally whipped it open. They dashed down the passage as though they were afraid the SS man might come after them and took up their positions where the passage ended. The whole system had been worked out with crude effectiveness. The outlet of the passage was blocked off by two cars of the freight train, so that any attempt on the part of one of the Jews to break out of the mob, or to escape if they had had so much presence of mind left, would have been completely impossible. Moreover, it facilitated the job of loading them onto the trains.

The SS man turned to the crowd, planted himself with his feet wide apart and his hands on his hips, and loosed a roar that must have actually hurt his ribs. It could be heard far above the hellish babble that came from the crowd.

'*Ruhe, Ruhe!* Quiet, quiet! All Jews will board this train to be taken to a place where work awaits them. Keep order. Do not push. Anyone who attempts to resist or create a panic will be shot.'

He stopped speaking and looked challengingly at the helpless mob that hardly seemed to know what was happening. Suddenly, accompanying the movement with a loud, hearty laugh, he yanked out his gun and fired three random shots into the crowd. A single, stricken groan answered him. He replaced the gun in his holster, smiled, and set himself for another roar:

'*Alle Jüden, 'raus – 'raus!*'

For a moment the crowd was silent. Those nearest the SS man recoiled from the shots and tried to dodge, panic-stricken, toward the rear. But this was resisted by the mob as a volley of shots from the rear sent the whole mass surging forward madly, screaming in pain and fear. The shots continued without let-up from the rear and now from the sides, too, narrowing the mob down and driving it in a savage scramble onto the passageway. In utter panic, groaning in despair and agony, they rushed down the passageway, trampling it so furiously that it threatened to fall apart.

Here new shots were heard. The two policemen at the entrance to the train were now firing into the oncoming throng corralled in the passageway, in order to slow them down and prevent them from demolishing the flimsy structure. The SS man now added his roar to the deafening bedlam.

'*Ordnung, Ordnung!*' he bellowed like a madman.

'Order, order!' The two policemen echoed him hoarsely, firing straight into the faces of the Jews running to the trains. Impelled and controlled by this ring of fire, they filled the two cars quickly.

And now came the most horrible episode of them all. The Bund leader had warned me that if I lived to be a hundred I would never forget some of the things I saw. He did not exaggerate.

The military rule stipulates that a freight car may carry eight horses or forty soldiers. Without any baggage at all, a maximum of a hundred passengers standing close together and pressing against each other could be crowded into a car. The Germans had simply issued orders to the effect that 120 to 130 Jews had to enter each car. These orders were now being carried out. Alternately swinging and firing with their rifles, the policemen were forcing still more people into the two cars which were already over-full. The shots continued to ring out in the rear and the driven mob surged forward, exerting an irresistible pressure against those nearest the train. These unfortunates, crazed by what they had been through, scourged by the policemen, and shoved forward by the milling mob, then began to climb on the heads and shoulders of those in the trains.

These were helpless since they had the weight of the entire advancing throng against them and responded only with howls of anguish to those who, clutching at their hair and clothes for support, trampling on necks, faces, and shoulders, breaking bones and shouting with insensate fury, attempted to clamber over them. After the cars had already been filled beyond normal capacity, more than another score of human beings, men, women, and children, gained admittance in this fashion. Then the policemen slammed the doors across the hastily withdrawn limbs that still protruded and pushed the iron bars in place.

The two cars were now crammed to bursting with tightly packed human flesh, completely, hermetically filled. All this while the entire camp had reverberated with a tremendous volume of sound in which the hideous groans and screams mingled weirdly with shots, curses, and bellowed commands.

Nor was this all. I know that many people will not believe me, will not be able to believe me, will think I exaggerate or invent. But I saw it and it is not exaggerated or invented. I have no other proofs, no photographs. All I can say is that I saw it and that it is the truth.

The floors of the car had been covered with a thick, white powder. It was quicklime. Quicklime is simply unslaked lime or calcium oxide that has been dehydrated. Anyone who has seen cement being mixed knows what occurs when water is poured on lime. The mixture bubbles and steams as the powder combines with the water, generating a large amount of heat.

Here the lime served a double purpose in the Nazi economy of brutality. The moist flesh coming in contact with the lime is rapidly dehydrated and burned. The occupants of the cars would be literally burned to death before long, the flesh eaten from their bones. Thus, the Jews would 'die in agony,' fulfilling the promise Himmler had issued 'in accord with the will of the Führer,' in Warsaw, in 1942. Secondly, the lime would prevent decomposing bodies from spreading disease. It was efficient and inexpensive – a perfectly chosen agent for their purposes.

It took three hours to fill up the entire train by repetitions of this procedure. It was twilight when all the forty-six (I counted them) cars were packed. It transpired that the train was half as long again than I had first thought. From one end to the other, the train, with its quivering cargo of flesh, seemed to throb, vibrate, rock, and jump as if bewitched. There would be a strangely uniform momentary lull and then, again, the train would begin to moan and sob, wail and howl. Inside the camp a few score dead bodies remained and a few in the final throes of death. German policemen walked around at leisure with smoking guns, pumping bullets into anything that, by a moan or motion, betrayed an excess of vitality. Soon, not a single one was left alive. In the now quiet camp the only sounds were the inhuman screams that were echoes from the moving train. Then these, too, ceased. All that was now left was the stench of excrement and rotting straw and a queer, sickening, acidulous odor which, I thought, may have come from the quantities of blood that had been let, and with which the ground was stained.

As I listened to the dwindling outcries from the train, I thought of the destination toward which it was speeding. My informants had minutely described the entire journey. The train would travel about eighty miles and finally come to a halt in an empty, barren field. Then nothing at all would happen. The train would stand stock-still, patiently waiting while death penetrated into every corner of its interior. This would take from two to four days.

When quicklime, asphyxiation, and injuries had silenced every outcry, a group of men would appear. They would be young, strong Jews, assigned to the task of cleaning out these cars until their own turn to be in them should arrive. Under a strong guard they would unseal the cars and expel the heaps of decomposing bodies. The mounds of flesh that they piled up would then be burned and the remnants buried in a single huge hole. The cleaning, burning, and burial would consume one or two full days.

The entire process of disposal would take, then, from three to six days. During this period the camp would have recruited new victims. The train would return and the whole cycle would be repeated from the beginning.

I was still standing near the gate, gazing after the no longer visible train, when I felt a rough hand on my shoulder. The Estonian was back again. He was frantically trying to rouse my attention and to keep his voice lowered at the same time.

'Wake up, wake up,' he was scolding me hoarsely. 'Don't stand there with your mouth open. Come on, hurry, or we'll both get caught. Follow me and be quick about it.'

he Gestapo, but the most supreme safety, safety in
mund asked me to approach the altar which had
in his room and made me kneel down. He then
y shirt and bare my chest. Surprised, and not at all
was to follow, I obeyed his instructions. He took a
his hands, smiled gently at my confusion, and spoke

authorized by those in whom the authority of the
d, to present you, soldier of Poland, with Christ's
with you on your journey. Wear it throughout your
er approaches, you will be able to swallow it. It will
all evil and harm.'

scapular about my neck. I bent my head and prayed.
knelt beside me and prayed with me. There was a
silence in the room. All I could hear was the faint
beads in someone's rosary.

ought me not only safety but tranquillity throughout
ssed Germany, Belgium, France, and Spain to board
at Gibraltar. The treasure I wore against my chest
de warmth from the day I left Warsaw to the day
d through the noisy streets of London to my first
he Polish Commander-in-Chief and Prime Minister,
ski. It sped me on my journey as if on wings – the
ough all the perilous frontiers of occupied Europe,
any dangers and pitfalls, lasted only twenty-one days.

I followed him at a distance, feeling completely benumbed. When we reached the gate he reported to a German officer and pointed at me. I heard the officer say, '*Sehr gut, gehen Sie,*' and then we passed through the gate. The Estonian and I walked awhile together and then separated. Then I walked to the store as quickly as I could, running when there was no one about to see me. I reached the grocery store so breathless that the owner became alarmed. I reassured him while I threw off my uniform, boots, stockings, and underwear. I ran into the kitchen and locked the door. In a little while my bewildered and worried host called out to me.

'Hey, what are you doing in there?'

'Don't worry. I'll be right out.'

When I came out, he promptly entered the kitchen and called back in despair.

'What the devil have you been doing? The whole kitchen is flooded!'

'I washed myself,' I replied, 'that is all. I was very dirty.'

'You certainly must have been,' was his vexed answer.

I did my best to soothe him and then applied for permission to rest for a while in the garden. He hesitated for a minute as though he were afraid I might flood his garden, too, and then granted it. I wrapped my coat around me and went out into a tiny vegetable garden. I lay down under a tree and with the promptness of utter exhaustion, fell asleep. I awoke with a start, from some nightmare, I think. It was dark, except for a large, brilliant moon. I was stiff with cold and for a moment I could not remember where I was and how I had got there. When I did, I dashed inside the house and found an empty bed. My host was asleep. It was not long before I was, too.

I awoke in the morning. The sunlight, though not strong, was giving me a painful headache. My host stood over me asking if I was ill. I had been talking and twisting restlessly in my sleep. As soon as I got out of bed I was seized with a violent fit of nausea. I rushed outside and began to vomit. Throughout that day and during the next night I continued to vomit at intervals. When all the food had been emptied from my stomach, I threw up a red liquid.

My host was terrified and asked me if the disease I had was conta-gious. I finally succeeded in convincing him that I did not have a disease.

I did not dare get into bed till long after midnight. Before doing so I asked the grocer, who now displayed the utmost solicitude, to try to get me some whisky, a lot of whisky. A few hours later he was back with a bottle. I drank two large glassfuls and fell asleep imme-diately. I slept brokenly for the balance of the day and throughout the following night.

When I awoke again, the sunlight was strong but did not hurt my eyes as much as it had the previous day. The grocer was standing over my bed with a bowl of warm milk in one hand and a piece of bread in the other. I ate the bread and drank the milk, still lying in bed, and then I crawled out carefully, afraid I would fall or stumble and bring on a recurrence of the nausea. I had, however, recovered, but I was still very weak. I managed, with the help of the grocer, to get on the train to Warsaw and arrived there without any further mishap.

The images of what I saw in the death camp are, I am afraid, my permanent possessions. I would like nothing better than to purge my mind of these memories. For one thing, the recollection of those events invariably brings on a recurrence of the nausea. But more than that, I would like simply to be free of them, to obliterate the very thought that such things ever occurred.

Just before I left Warsaw my friends arranged a celebration for me. Early one morning, I was invited to Mass. Many of my friends were devout. Father Edmund, the priest who was to officiate, was one of my best and oldest friends. He had been my confessor for many years. Now he was the chaplain of the Warsaw division of the secret army.

The streets were still sunk in blackness when I set out for the church. It was bitterly cold and the snow that had been falling all the previous day still lay in dark blue heaps on the walks and gutters. I wrapped myself tightly against the cutting wind and walked rapidly

through the empty streets
quently, a German patrol
occupied in keeping thems
leaving Warsaw – and who
how little attention I had p
Eagerly, and walking rapidl
it that I could see, to store i
streets and houses, now qui

When I reached the chu
first gray streaks appearing
in the room of my friend, th
behind the church. When I
were there. Four women had
them was the writer whom w
the Underground.[6] Another w
in Poland. Among the men w
my department. The curtains
the candles cast a pale glow w
the huge room, leaving queer
chill of the morning air, the pr
bled here for me, the mysterio
the whole scene inexpressibly c

We said almost nothing, gre
shakes. It had been arranged so
there before my arrival. The Ma
answered the deep tones of the
nated unhurriedly with no inter
took the Holy Communion. The
the Mass had ended the priest re
did likewise and soon they were
for travelers. I listened in silence,
The prayers were followed by a
secretly been prepared for me. My
my farewell. They were giving m
Not everyday safety, from the club

and the jails of
God. Father Ed
been improvise
bade me open
aware of what
scapular in both
solemnly:

'I have been
Church is vest
Body to carry
journey. If dan
protect you fro

He hung the
Father Edmun
deep reverent
clicking of the

Their gift b
my trip, as I c
a British plan
seemed to ex
when I hurri
reception by
General Siko
entire trip th
through so n

31

Unter Den Linden Revisited

The day to which I had been looking forward for so long arrived. I left Warsaw without any fanfare and with no one to see me off. My papers were in perfect order, the seal on my photograph magnificently faked. The film was excellently concealed in the razor handle. I had plenty of money and was in high spirits.

The train was congested with passengers of every conceivable nationality, a circumstance which made me completely inconspicuous. Nevertheless, I scanned faces, searching for Gestapo agents whom I felt I could recognize at once. When I spotted one or when I was asked to produce my papers, naturally I felt uncomfortable.

However, there was no danger so long as I did not become involved in a conversation in which I might expose myself. To forestall this possibility, I had brought along a bottle of medicine. Seated in the corner of my compartment, I dampened a handkerchief and dabbed my mouth, pretending to suffer untold pain from a toothache. I felt sure that anybody who caught a glimpse of my pain-contorted face would refrain from speaking to me.

The trip to Berlin was slow and monotonous. The compartment was cramped and smelly; the train, one of the antediluvian relics the Germans had left at the disposal of the Poles, rattled and bounced uncomfortably.

Arriving in Berlin, I was possessed of a lively curiosity as to the real situation in Germany. There seemed to be no better way of satisfying it than by paying a visit to an old schoolfriend of mine, Rudolph Strauch. Before the war, when I had attended the Berlin Staats-Bibliothek, I had boarded with the Strauch family, consisting of Rudolph, his young sister, and his mother, the widow of a judge.

In 1937, at my invitation, Rudolph had come for a brief tour of Poland with me.

The Strauch family had always professed deeply liberal and democratic beliefs, and I felt that even now they were probably steadfast and silent opponents of the Hitler regime. I hoped that Rudolph would not be in the army, since he had always been extremely frail. I did not want to miss this opportunity to find out what was taking place in Germany, how it looked, what the people thought. Besides, I liked Rudolph and Berta and wanted to see them again. It did not occur to me that this desire would expose me to an unnecessary risk and that it would give me another adventure. On the whole, the odds seemed highly in favor of a successful visit. Nevertheless, I took the trouble of supplying myself with an adequate legend, which would place me beyond suspicion in case of any unforeseen eventuality. My story would be that I had not taken any part in the war; that at present I was a bookkeeper in a German factory and that I had been granted a vacation which I intended to spend in Paris. The only risk I ran was that someone might, in their presence, ask to see my documents. If this happened, the Strauchs would find out that the name under which I was traveling was different from the name by which they knew me. But I hoped this would not happen. Depending on my reception, I could either imply that I was more or less neutral, bore the Germans no hostility, or was actually collaborating with them and in deep sympathy.

In Berlin my schedule called for me to change within an hour for the train to Paris. The next train that carried workmen would not arrive till the following day. I loitered about till my train had already departed. Then I approached the station master.

'I missed my train and have to wait till tomorrow for another. I would like to see something of Berlin in the meantime. Is it all right if I go out for a while and then stay around the station till my train comes?'

He acquiesced willingly. At the station I checked my suitcase containing the razor with the film, washed up, and walked to the Strauch home.

I had no difficulty in locating their house, which was in a neat but unpretentious lower-middle-class area. I rang the bell and the door was opened by Mrs Strauch who greeted me without much enthusiasm. She then called in her children who received me in much the same way. Rudolph appeared paler and thinner than when I had last seen him. The girl had developed into a well-rounded young woman. She appeared to be competent, sturdy, and rather unimaginative.

They asked me into the study and brought out some brandy and coffee. At first, the atmosphere was rather stiff and constrained, but they relaxed after I had trotted out my legend. They seemed to accept it without any suspicion. As Rudolph was obviously pleased when I said anything that indicated that my sympathies were collaborationist, I emphasized this side of the story, expressing all the standard opinions and beliefs that Goebbels urged upon the Germans and the inhabitants of the occupied countries in endless speeches.

The reserve vanished and Rudolph responded with a passionate monologue on the destiny of Germany. He surprised me by admitting that events on the Eastern front were a bit disappointing. But all his doubts could be stilled in an instant by the invocation of a magical phrase: 'The Führer knows what he is doing.'

When in the course of the ensuing discussion a problem came up for discussion, or an event was mentioned which had unfavorable possibilities for the Reich, the phrase was repeated like the refrain of a popular song. Der Führer would get them out of each and every difficulty that arose. Quite genuinely, this now summarized all the political acumen and beliefs of the erstwhile democratic, liberal, and anti-Nazi Strauchs: 'The Führer knows what he is doing.'

I remained in the house for a few hours and noticed little of significant change. The standard of living was obviously lower, the equipment, clothing, and food around the house of poor quality. The girl worked hard, in a factory, I gathered, though she carefully avoided giving me any details. Rudolph worked in an office, in an *Arbeitsamt*, I believe. Neither was anxious to discuss wages, hours, working conditions, or anything similar. They replied noncommittally to the one or two casual questions I dropped on the subject.

For dinner they asked me to a beerhouse on a sidestreet just off Unter den Linden. It was a 'standardized' meal but ample and fairly cheap, about fifteen marks for the three of us. Discussion at the table centered on the Jews. Rudolph and his sister gave vent to all the common Nazi remarks on the subject. I made an effort to pierce their thick skins by describing in an offhand, neutral fashion the most abominable and revolting of the practices I had witnessed, the death train, the quicklime and chlorine. Their reactions were cool and detached, betraying not the slightest trace of physical, let alone moral, repulsion. Rudolph commented:

'Very efficient. The Jewish corpses will not be allowed to spread disease as they did in life.'

'They must have been warm,' was the response of Berta at the conclusion of my description of the quicklime episode.

During the course of the meal, I detected a note of hostility in Berta's behavior toward me, an odd shade of suspicion and fear. I began to worry and fret. Perhaps I had been exaggeratedly pro-German, or somewhat implausible in my narrative. I might have made a slip somewhere in my facts or contradicted myself. Perhaps the feeling of superiority to a mere Pole was beginning to assert itself. I felt downright alarm when Berta got up from her chair and beckoned Rudolph to follow her.

'Please excuse us,' she said to me with cold formality, 'I have something to discuss in private with my brother.'

They retreated into an alcove a few tables away. The cigarette I was smoking suddenly developed a bitter flavor. What a fool I had been to come, I thought. A glance around the restaurant made it plain to me that if they had gone to inform the police, I did not have a chance of escaping. They returned in a few minutes, Rudolph strained, nervous, and a trifle embarrassed, his sister stubbornly calm and determined.

'They are going to denounce me,' I thought in panic and struggled to control myself and remain outwardly cool and genial.

Rudolph spoke to me in a tense, hoarse whisper.

'Jan,' he said, almost apologetically, 'I hate to say this to you.

Personally, I am very fond of you, but we have to part. All the Poles are the enemies of the Führer and the Third Reich. They try to harm Germany wherever they can and they serve Jewish and British interests. They even help the Russian barbarians. I know that you are different, but what can I do? This is wartime. I will have to break off relations with you.'

My fear subsided, although my anger mounted at this stupid speech, particularly at the silly, official tone of the concluding remark.

'Besides,' Rudolph added, drops of sweat forming on his worried brow as he gazed around the room, 'it is dangerous to be seen talking to foreigners.'

I mastered my anger.

'I am sorry you feel that way,' I said. 'I wanted to be your friend and the friend of Germany. In time, I hope you will change your opinion of me.'

I bowed coolly and got up from the table. Inwardly I seethed with annoyance at the necessity of having to play the hypocrite. What dirty work I was doing. How I envied the lucky fellows that could drop bombs on them. As I strolled to the door, I still felt that possibly he had called the police and I gazed around suspiciously. As I took my coat, I noticed there was a group of men standing around in front of the restaurant. I felt a shiver run along my spine.

'*Entschuldigung*,' I said curtly.

'*Bitte sehr.*'

I was relieved. My first impulse was to dash for safety. Anywhere in Berlin I felt surrounded by enemies, liable to be tapped on the shoulder and questioned at any moment. Realizing that my fears were imaginary, I slowed down and strolled about for a while.

The words of Rudolph filled me with pride. They resounded in my ears: 'All the Poles are the enemies of the Führer and the Third Reich.' 'They try to harm Germans wherever they can . . .' What a tribute!

I returned to the station and lay down to rest in the cold, gloomy waiting room. My mind flashed back to former times when I had been with Rudolph and Berta. They had seemed so kindly and sincere in their affection for me which I reciprocated. They had seemed so warm and spontaneous. Now they were irrevocably, hopelessly spoiled. The problem of whether anything could change and redeem them occupied my thoughts. After the war, what would happen to this country, which for more than a decade had been under a regime that had eliminated every trace of humanity and decency? Could the youth, of which I had seen specimens in the two boys who had indulged their cruel instincts that afternoon in the ghetto, be reformed, be brought back to share in a world based on decency and respect for other people?

I spent the night in the waiting room and left Berlin the following morning.

32

Journey Through France and Spain

On the trip from Berlin to Brussels I continued pretending to suffer from a toothache. This time, I did not go unnoticed. An officious and stout Belgian merchant insisted on clucking his sympathy. My rude monosyllabic responses failed to deter him and when we reached Brussels he insisted on accompanying me to a German Red Cross station. He attached himself to me like a sticking-plaster and there was simply no way of freeing myself without arousing suspicion. Fortunately, he did not notice my accent in French. My toothache saved me.

At the station, my teeth were inspected by a uniformed German non-commissioned officer and a nurse. When they were through the nurse smiled at me and spoke reprovingly.

'You are very careless – your neglect has already cost you many teeth. Now that you are suffering pain you will learn to take care of yourself.'

I had a terrible urge to tell her that what she called neglect had been their Gestapo men.

They insisted on applying antiseptic and administering a sedative. Their solicitousness amused me. That is war, I thought. One group of Germans knocks my teeth out and another swabs the wounds with peroxide.

I did my best to end the incident as quickly as possible. Fortunately, they did not require any papers and I pretended to be unable to talk clearly. On the train to Paris, I dropped the rôle of a man with a toothache and drowsed under the influence of the sedative.

I arrived in conquered Paris at 6.00 a.m. on a cold, rainy morning. It was too early to report to the place arranged by the organization and give the agreed password. I left my suitcase at the check-room and went for a walk.

It was a long stroll from the Gare du Nord to the Champs Élysées. The atmosphere was unbearable. Paris, the city of light, now was melancholy, impoverished, sunk in a seedy lassitude. On the dismal and deserted Champs Élysées I dropped onto a bench. Whenever I had come to Paris I always wanted to stay there for ever. But now my only desire was to get out of the city as rapidly as possible, to get a taste of the wide, free world outside the zone of German occupation and influence.

My reverie was interrupted by the rhythmic tramp of an infantry detachment. A German regiment was marching up the Champs Élysées, the men steel-helmeted, with rifles on their shoulders, and their heads lifted with pride and scorn. The pavement rang under their boots. For the first time since the war began I felt tears running down my cheeks.

I walked back to the Gare du Nord, my mind inflamed by this spectacle of arrogant triumph. I felt like embracing the first French workman I met and saying:

'Have confidence. We will get rid of them. But let us keep on fighting.'

The meeting place was a small confectionery shop near the station. An old lady, whose presence I had expected, was seated behind the counter. I approached her.

'Do you wish to buy cigarettes? I have some for sale.'

'What brand do you carry?' was her correct response.

'Gauloises.'

'How many do you have for sale?'

'As many as there are days since the last storm.'

She smiled at the completion of the stipulated conversation and with great charm and hospitality offered me some coffee and a pastry. She arranged to put me in touch with members of our own underground unit. We still had a Polish military and apolitical branch in France, directed respectively by army officers who had not been able to leave France and by Poles who had settled there a long time ago. It collaborated actively with the French Underground.

Three days after my arrival, a French physician supplied me with my identity papers, which stated that I was a French citizen of Polish origin. I could not be expected to speak French fluently because I had always lived in the Polish surroundings of the Pas de Calais district where I had worked in the coal mines. He also provided me with a German work permit and a French driving license. He informed me that I was to leave Paris as soon as possible.

About ten days later I took the train to Lyons with a French worker, who had been instructed to facilitate my crossing of the Spanish frontier. At the house to which he conducted me in Lyons I was amazed to encounter a captain from the Polish officers' training school which I had attended. As I remained in the house for some time, he had ample opportunity to ply me with questions. Luckily, I was able to supply him with detailed information about his wife, his mother, and daughter, all of whom, I assured him, were healthy and doing as well as could be expected. His wife was supporting his mother and daughter by tilling a suburban garden plot. The daughter had been graduated from a secret high school. He had tears in his eyes when I told him that his wife had not sold a single piece of furniture, not one of his shirts or suits. She had even refused to take boarders lest they ruin the furniture and his easy-chair. When he returned everything would be just as he had left it.

The captain himself had much to tell me. He had been in the Polish Army during the Battle of France, had been captured, escaped from internment and joined the French Underground. Now he was in charge of our Polish section which was busy helping refugees cross the Spanish border.

In Lyons I had a rather pleasant time with my friend. Although Lyons was occupied by the Germans and was one of the centers of anti-Nazi activity, we enjoyed nearly unrestricted freedom to move about.[1] For one thing, the secret organizations operated under much easier conditions than they did in Poland. Contact with England was easier and all the work was simplified by the fact that communication with neutral countries was possible. It occurred to me that Poland did not have a single piece of good fortune to make her lot easier. We were certainly the unluckiest of peoples.

In Lyons I met the most genuine, true-to-form 'war bird' I had yet encountered. He was about forty years old, indestructible in appearance, and a native of a suburb of Warsaw where he had been an artisan. He had been living in France since 1940, as happy in the wartime chaos as a fish in water. He had been a professional ne'er-do-well, farmhand, factory worker, and house painter. He had been in the French Army, in a succession of French jails, and had crossed the country many times from the Channel to the Mediterranean, despite the fact that in all his time of residence he had accumulated only a few words of the French language.

He was an extraordinarily thin and wizened man, as though he had been stripped of all but the elements necessary for his knock-about existence. His face was ridged and weatherbeaten, and was made indescribably droll and appealing by the constant lopsided grin that turned up one corner of his long, straw-colored moustache. His means of transportation and his present mode of existence were equally mysterious.

'How do you travel about by train,' I asked him once, 'without speaking French and without a franc in your pocket?'

He answered in the purest Warsaw rogues' slang.

'Get a peep at this, brother. It's good for any train in France.'

I glanced at the piece of cardboard he handed me. It was a Warsaw trolley-car commutation ticket, plainly dated 1939. I handed it back to him.

'That is a pretty souvenir,' I remarked, 'but you couldn't get a mile away with it.'

'You mean that *you* couldn't,' he replied, grinning shrewdly. 'I know how to use it.'

'How?'

'Well, I just get on any train and ride on it till the conductor comes to collect my ticket. Then I hand him this. When he starts to squawk, I babble at him in six languages, as loud as I can – in French,

German, Spanish, English, Russian, and Polish. I know about ten words in most of them. After a while, he gets deaf from listening to me, goes crazy, and bounces me off at the nearest station. There I start all over again.'

I burst out laughing.

'You mean to tell me that you never got in a jam with your trolley-car ticket?'

'Only once. A dirty "type" of a conductor had the nerve to hand me over to the cops.'

'What happened then?'

'I drove them crazy. I gave them a sob story in all my languages for three days. I didn't let them sleep at night. They finally put me to work in a factory.' The memory of work seemed to affect him with nausea.

'Why don't you learn French?' I asked. 'You would be able to get by much easier.'

'Are you crazy?' he replied indignantly. 'Why the devil should I learn French – to become the successor of Pétain?'

'You know, you will never amount to anything,' I said. 'You ought to do some honest work for a change. You'll get a new slant on life.'

He glanced at me in genuine surprise and horror.

'Who, me? You must be out of your head. Say, I have a good idea. Why don't you drop what you are doing and come with me? We'll get along fine. You aren't bad-looking, you make a nice impression . . . I'll do the thinking for both of us. You won't have to worry a bit.'

My intellectual capacity had never been estimated with such unflattering sincerity.

'Goodbye,' he said, 'I have to keep an appointment.'

'Goodbye. Let me hear from you.'

He winked, tipped his hat gaily, and strolled away. A few days later, I actually did receive a card from him. The spelling was atrocious. I managed to make out that he was doing fine and that I had lost the opportunity of a lifetime by refusing his offer.

The order finally came through for me to get to Southern France on my own. I was to report to Perpignan, to a young Spanish couple who had fought against Franco and had emigrated to France. While waiting to return to their country, they were working with the Underground. I secured a permit to travel by train to Perpignan and located my couple easily enough in a small house on the outskirts of the town, which had been marked off on a diagram that had been given to me. It was up to them to provide me with a guide who would get me across the border and see that I got to Barcelona. There I was to contact some Allied agents who had been notified by radio of my impending arrival.

I had utmost faith in the ability of the young couple to get me through. They were an ardent and enthusiastic pair with a sincere, zealous belief in democracy. After a few days, they apologetically informed me that they were having difficulty. The border was under constant surveillance and I would have to wait until a safe plan was perfected. It was inadvisable for me to leave the house at all.

The next few days were endless. My hosts were out nearly all the time and I could not concentrate on the books I picked up and fingered restively. At last they informed me that arrangements had been completed for my crossing the border. A guide named Fernando would go with me. We would both be on bicycles. He would keep his light turned on. I was to follow, traveling a few yards behind him with my light extinguished. If he stopped and rang his bell, I would know that there was danger and should seek concealment. If he stopped without ringing his bell, it was trivial, and I was to rejoin him in a few minutes.

We started out at nightfall. Fernando, whom I had hardly seen as yet, pedaled on his bicycle about fifty yards in front of me. After we had been going for about fifteen minutes, I heard his bell ring and saw his light stop. I cursed, turned my bicycle around, and went back to the house. Fernando returned shortly afterwards. He explained calmly. It had been a German patrol. I would not have been able to get by. Tomorrow we would try again, using a different system.

The following night Fernando and I walked about four miles out of the village where we met two Frenchmen. They supplied us with our bicycles and we started on the dim, rough road, using now the same system as we had the night before. It was a more successful trip than the previous one, but one of the most upsetting and nerve-racking I have ever taken. His light would constantly disappear around a curve or into an exceptionally dark passage and I would have to pedal furiously to catch sight of it again.

As my own light was extinguished, I had a great deal of difficulty in staying on the barely visible road. The only difference between the road and the terrain surrounding it was that the road was full of ruts and the sides of the road full of ditches. The ruts would cause me to topple frequently into the ditches. The ride became a mad scramble for me as I stumbled, fell, remounted, and dashed frantically after Fernando's feeble light. We had pedaled about forty miles when Fernando stopped and waited for me to catch up.

When I dismounted he took my bicycle and proceeded to hide the two vehicles in some thick shrubbery. He then came over to me and patted me commiseratingly on the shoulder. I would have to wait here until he got in touch with another guide. I sank down on the moist earth under a tree and dozed off.

Fernando returned about two hours later and tugged at my sleeve till I awakened. It was dawn, I noticed, as I rubbed my eyes sleepily. The weather was cold and damp. My limbs felt stiff and rheumatic.

'Did you find the guide?' I asked him.

He shook his head.

'No. You will have to come with me and wait in a fishing boat.'

We trudged along the road which was in somewhat better condition in these parts. It was crowded with early morning traffic of all kinds – wagons, carts. We had to walk quite slowly until we came to a path, onto which Fernando turned. It led to a beach. As it had now become somewhat warmer and was sunnier, I enjoyed the view of the sea. The water was bright blue and dotted with hundreds of vessels – sailboats, launches, and fishing vessels. It was to a decrepit specimen of the last variety that Fernando led me.

'You must stay here,' Fernando told me. 'Don't move till I come back. Lie down and don't let anyone see you.'

'How long will you be gone?'

'A day or two. Here are my sweater and coat. You will need them.'

'No, you'll be cold.'

'Take them. I can get others. Someone will bring you food.'

I crawled into the boat, lay down, covered myself up as well as I could against both the cold and prying eyes, and barely budged for more than sixty hours. At intervals an invisible hand would deposit some food near me and something hot to drink – tea, coffee, and once a bottle of warm wine which I found very comforting. When the cramped condition of my muscles grew unbearable and I wanted to get up and pace about, I quieted myself by repeating two words, 'Remember Slovakia.' Since that day I had determined never to let impatience influence my actions again.

Fernando came back, woke me, and introduced me to my new guide, a short, dark, rugged man with gleaming white teeth. The new guide spoke little French. Fernando asked me if I were ready to go. I assured him that I was if my legs had not turned to stone from the damp and cold. Fernando laughed and murmured something complimentary about my power to endure hardship. We took leave of each other warmly and I continued with my new guide who led me by a side road into the foothills of the Pyrenees.

The hike through the Pyrenees was delightful. The country was wilder than any through which I had ever passed, but also was rich in a vivid green foliage and unusual mountain views. The guide was a cautious man, but very considerate. We could not speak much because he knew only a few words of French and I knew even less Spanish. On the third day, we took refuge in a cave, and it was decided that I was to wait while he went to see a friend in a nearby village who would help him check the location of the various police posts.

He returned in obvious gloom. His friend's brother had informed him that the man had been arrested. It would be impossible to go by train as he had planned. After much reflection, he decided that we would spend the night where we were. The next morning we would go to a village to try to pick up a bicycle or a car. As we were sitting conversing in the dusk we had a scare. Like an apparition, two figures loomed out in plain view, walking toward us. We obviously had been seen. The guide clutched my shoulder but it was too late to take cover.

As they came closer, we saw that they were civilians, apparently unarmed and carrying knapsacks. The guide hailed them.

'Are you coming from France?' he called loudly.

They were more frightened than we were. The older answered in a shaky voice. We invited them over to our cave and they took heart. It developed that the pair were a French officer and his teenage son. They were escaping to join De Gaulle. A few moments of conversation turned us into a harmonious and mutually sympathetic group. They were much worse off than I, for they were attempting to cross the mountains without a guide. I explained the difficulties and hazards to them and invited them to join our party. They accepted the offer gratefully.

In the morning we began the descent of the mountains. The Frenchmen followed behind the guide and myself at a distance of some twenty yards. I attempted a conversation with my guide in pidgin French and Spanish but he was not loquacious. He contented himself with flashing his white teeth at me in a series of brilliant, indulgent smiles. As the path wound through a clump of trees we were startled by a voice addressing us from the side of the road.

A little investigation revealed its owner, an aged Spaniard, who was sitting with his daughter in a little clearing. Between them was a bundle of firewood. A lively conversation ensued between him and my guide.

'Barcelona,' I heard my guide say at one stage of their dialogue.

From a few hearty imprecations, I gathered that the old man was a bitter anti-fascist. He cordially invited us to take shelter in his house and naturally we accepted.

The old man proved to be the most hospitable of hosts. He plied us with the contents of his frugal store of provisions and objected strenuously when we offered him money or appeared to be refusing more food out of politeness. We washed, shaved, tidied up our clothes, and passed a very sociable evening in the rudely furnished parlor. The old man informed us that he had plans for us.

'Your worries are ended,' he told us, the guide interpreting as best he could. 'I will see to it that you get to Barcelona. Sleep well.'

The next morning the old man set out for the village. He returned about noon and we clustered about him with the anxious excitement of a group of schoolboys. The old Spaniard beamed at us confidently and waved his hand reassuringly.

'Everything is taken care of,' he said. 'You have nothing to worry about.'

He disclosed his plan. We would proceed to the railroad station, buy tickets for Barcelona, and get on the train. Once we were on the train, the conductor would take excellent care of us and show us what to do. The conductor would be told all about us by the fireman, who was a bosom friend of the old Spaniard. The only thing we had to do was to be careful, obey instructions, join the army afterwards, and kill all the fascists we could find.

We all thanked him a bit dubiously and held a worried conversation. The scheme did not appeal to me. There were too many friends, and friends of friends, involved to suit my sense of prudence. The Frenchmen apparently felt the same way about it. We consulted the guide, who agreed that there were doubtful elements but thought that, on the whole, we had a reasonable chance of success. Moreover, he pointed out, there seemed to be no other choice.

It was agreed to make the attempt. My guide took leave of us during the night and we set out at dawn of the next day. We walked in single file behind the old man, following the line of the railroad tracks. The dim morning light augmented my uncertainty. The old man walked ahead confidently, never glancing backward until we came in sight of the railroad station. Then he waited near a tree for us to catch up with him.

When we were all together, he collected money from us for the tickets to Barcelona, indicating that we were to wait under the tree till he returned. He came back with the precious tickets, without any mishap. He handed them to us and told us that the train would be there in half an hour. We were to try to obtain seats in the car behind the coal car. He embraced each one of us in turn, told us that we were all fine men who he was sure would fight the fascist dogs bravely, and took leave of us.

We followed his instructions. The car we boarded was empty except for one sleepy-looking individual with a basket in one corner, and two old women in another, engrossed in an animated exchange of gossip. We had not been seated long when the conductor, on whom our fate depended, entered the car. He collected tickets from the other passengers and conspicuously ignored us. This maneuver excited a whispered speculation among the three of us, but we came to the conclusion that it was favorable since he had recognized us.

A few stations later the other three passengers got off the train. The conductor re-entered the car and approached us.

'Tickets?' he inquired negligently.

We produced them slowly and handed them to him. He scrutinized them carefully and then said in a tone of mild surprise:

'Barcelona? You are all going to Barcelona?'

A trifle dismayed we all nodded our heads.

'Yes, we are all going to Barcelona.'

'Good,' he broke into a wide, genial smile. 'From where do you come? France? Belgium? Germany?'

'France,' said my companions.

'Poland,' I replied.

The conductor shook his head violently and broke into an unintelligible flood of voluble Spanish. We did not understand a word of it. He concluded with the word 'Canada.' When he was through we stared at him in bewilderment. He looked at us in frustration and shook his head again.

'From where do you come?' he repeated slowly.

'France.'

'Poland.'

'No, no, no, no. Canada,' he shouted. 'You Canada. You Canada. You Canada.'

He pointed to each of us in succession. Then he stood back and glared at us as if defying us to misunderstand him. I was on the point of doing so and asserting my Polish origin once more when the French officer laid a restraining hand on my arm.

'I understand,' he said. 'He means that we are all to pretend to be Canadians. If a Canadian is arrested in Spain the British authorities can extradite him.'

He turned to the conductor and slapped his chest.

'Canada,' he said triumphantly.

'Canada,' his son echoed.

'Canada,' I added weakly.

'Bravo, bravo!' The conductor beamed at us.

He motioned us to follow him and led us to the coal platform. He opened the door. Six young men, disheveled, stained with grime and coal-dust, stared out at us curiously.

'Canada,' the conductor grinned. 'All Canada.'

We mounted to the platform. The conductor went out and locked the door behind him. We were now committed to his mercy.

In the car the six young men looked at their new companions cautiously.

'Are you French?' the officer with me asked them.

They shook their heads in collective denial.

'We are Canadians,' one of them said.

'From what part of Canada do you come?' I asked in English.

They stared at me in consternation.

'Do you speak English?' I pursued.

'Yes,' one of them answered nonchalantly.

'If you speak English then I am a master of Hindustani,' I replied in French.

The ice was broken. We laughed and exchanged confidences. Like my companions, they were all French and on their way to join De Gaulle. We shared our provisions, ate, and became amiable, standing crowded together on the tiny platform. The ride was long and dusty. Often we speculated on the trustworthiness and reliability of the conductor who, if he had wished, could have delivered us over to the police as easily as if we had been bound, hand and foot.

That important individual finally put in an appearance.

'Next stop, get off,' he said. 'One station before Barcelona.'

He unlocked the door and disappeared, waving farewell. The train ground slowly to a stop. We clambered from the platform, leaped off the train, and scurried away. I and most of my companions apparently knew that in an affair such as this, the only sensible thing to do was to play a lone hand. When out of the corner of my eye I spotted any of the men coming close to me, I ran in a different direction. I half-ran, half-walked, for about twenty minutes and then slowed down to get my bearings.

I was on a little country path cutting through the trees and proceeding parallel to the tracks. Dusk was falling and in the distance I could see the hazy glare of a city – Barcelona, beyond doubt.

The walk to Barcelona lasted several hours and I was tired and hungry when I entered the outskirts. Quite blithely and thoughtlessly, I entered a bistro in a working-class district. I opened the door, marched past two figures seated at a front table, and sat down at a table in the rear. Turning toward the two figures, I saw that they were gendarmes and I began to sweat, as they seemed to be eyeing me suspiciously.

There was a newspaper rack near me. I hastily snatched a paper and pretended a deep absorption, although I could not read a word of it. The waiter approached me and hovered at my elbow, waiting for my order. A single word would have made it obvious I was not a Spaniard and might have meant a disastrous questioning by the gendarmes. I feigned absent-mindedness and said nothing. Luckily the waiter murmured the name of something in a tone of inquiry. I nodded, signifying that whatever he had said was what I wanted. He added something else. I nodded again, signifying that I approved of that, too.

The waiter returned, bringing me coffee and cake. I nibbled at the cake and gulped the coffee, pretending to be completely engrossed in the news. Then I glanced at my wristwatch, scowled like someone who is late for work, heaved myself out of the chair, paid for my snack, and left. When the door slammed behind me, I drew a deep breath and swore to myself, *No more bistros.*

I walked till it was well past dawn, hoping that I might run into my street by chance, not being anxious to try to get information out of anyone whom I did not have an opportunity of first sizing up. When people started to issue from their houses to go to work, I decided to take my chance. I approached an elderly worker and named the street on which was located the contact point that I had been given in Perpignan. He asked me what language I spoke. When I answered, he informed me by means of signs and a few words of French that I was to go seven blocks ahead and ten to the right.

During this war, I have often noticed that simple people are shrewder and quicker to guess the truth than 'experts.' When my guide finished his directions, he looked at me craftily and whispered with a significant smile:

'*De Gaulle, heh?*'

'*De Gaulle,*' I answered.

'*Bien. Bonne chance.*' He waved to me.

'*Merci, monsieur.*' I smiled and continued on my way.

His directions proved accurate and I found quite easily the butcher shop for which I had been told to look. The shutters were drawn. I had been informed that it did not open till noon and I rapped on the shutter with my fist.

'Who is there?' I heard a soft voice from behind the shutters ask in accented French.

I gave him the password.

'I am from Perpignan. Fernando sent me. Honest people will find their hearts.'

The door of the shop opened and a tiny gnome of a man with rosy cheeks stood before me.

'*Entrez, entrez, monsieur,*' he whispered softly.

Inside, the little man asked me to sit down at a highly polished, remarkably well-made oak table. I felt tired, hungry, relaxed, and successful. I was in Barcelona under a friendly roof. He brought me a bottle of wine and some hot, spicy Spanish food which I ate ravenously. He showed not the slightest trace of excitement and apparently was quite used to 'customers' like myself. He did not ask a single question about my trip and talked instead about the war and politics. He launched into a fierce diatribe against the fascists. I asked him if many people in the country shared his opinions. He informed me that everyone did and that the only support the fascist regime had came from the army and the police.

In the afternoon, after having slept for a while on a rude bench in the back of the shop and having made myself as presentable as I could, I went off to the consulate of a friendly country. It was crowded with clients, mostly young men whispering to each other. I went to a desk where a pretty young girl sat.

'What can I do for you?' she asked, not very encouragingly, I thought.

'I would like to have a personal interview with the Consul General.'

She looked closely at me.

'What is your name?'

I gave her the name that had been used in the radio message about me, adding, 'It is extremely urgent.'

She returned in ten minutes to let me know that the Consul General would see me. The room into which she ushered me was spacious and well-furnished. Behind the desk sat an earnest-looking, elderly man. He scrutinized me carefully and then inquired:

'Do you speak Spanish?'

'Unfortunately not.'

'Do you speak English?'

'Yes.'

'Where do you come from?'

'I come to see Aunt Sophie.'

'What is your name?'

I gave him the name. He continued his questioning.

'Have you any identification papers?'

'I was under the impression that my words would be my identification.'

'All's well, Mr Karski. Let me welcome you here, almost on Allied soil. I hope you will feel at home among us. I wish to express my appreciation for not only what you but all your comrades in Poland have contributed toward our victory.'

The conversation that followed was pleasant and frank. We discussed living conditions in occupied Europe, the methods of domination used by the Germans, and the means of resistance used by those they attempted to dominate. He managed the conversation with great tact and finesse, making it as intimate and revealing as possible without intruding on topics that might cause me embarrassment or asking questions that I was not permitted to answer.

He provided me with necessary certificates and papers and turned me over to a clerk who was to help me buy a decent outfit. As I was about to leave I asked him if, in the event of my arrest, they would be able to prove that my stay in this country was legal. His answering smile was subtle and charming.

'Young man,' he said, 'there have been many changes in the last two years. Then, you would probably have been thrown into prison or extradited to the Germans. Now, the worst that can happen to you is that you would be locked up for a day or two until we intervene . . . You know, the closer we are to victory, the greater the friendship of this government for us . . .'

The clerk escorted me to a sleek limousine bearing the initials CD (Corps Diplomatique) on the license plate. We drove for about eight hours and came to a halt in Madrid before a handsome private villa in the diplomatic section. My host was a hospitable, cultured middle-aged man whose general occupation and status I could not determine. He spoke nearly every European language fluently. His wife was very beautiful. After three very pleasant days, during which a message arrived from my government assuring me that they were aware of my movements, my host informed me that I was to leave for Algeciras in the evening. I would have papers and a certificate identifying me as a Spaniard on a visit to his family. Two Spaniards would accompany me.

'On the train,' he cautioned me, 'there will be a police inspection. Pretend that you are asleep and hand him your papers as though you are only half-awake. It is not likely that you will be questioned, but if you are, an arrest will undoubtedly follow. In that case, you are an ally who has escaped from a German concentration camp. If they ask how you came by your papers, give them any French name in any French city you can think of. Don't try to talk with your two bodyguards and don't worry. They will report to us if you are arrested and we will take care of you.'

'It sounds simple enough,' I said.

'It should be child's play after Poland,' he replied.

That night I prepared to leave. One of the bodyguards was introduced to me. He left first and stationed himself on a corner near the house. When I got outside, he started walking and I followed him to a trolley-car station, then sat across the aisle of the trolley from him until he got off at a railroad station. Conspiratorial methods are the same the whole world over. It reminded me of following Ira, the liaison woman, through the streets of Warsaw.

In the train, my guide entered a third-class compartment and I followed. There was only one empty seat, which corresponded with the number on my ticket, and I dropped into it. I pretended to doze off immediately, opening an eye occasionally to glance about and see if I could detect which of the other passengers was the second member of my bodyguard. This keeping of one man in secrecy was also according to the rules. In Poland we called it 'reassurance.'

The inspection passed off easily. Nearly all the passengers handed their cards over rather sleepily and there were no interrogations. Algeciras, though a small city, looks like a typical Mediterranean port. I followed my guide to a modest house in the suburbs. There I was introduced to a thin, dignified old man who had entered the trolley with me and my guide. I had deduced that he was the 'reassurance,' although he must have been sitting in a nearby compartment in the train. I told him that I really needed no introduction to him.

'That's bad,' he said in excellent English, 'I am ashamed of myself. I shouldn't have attracted your attention. How did you recognize me?'

'You need not be ashamed,' I said. 'There were only two other men who got on the trolley – my guide and I. Naturally the third had to be the other man who was assigned to me.'

'Then it really is not my fault,' he replied. 'You should not have been informed that you had two men following you.'

He outlined the plan for the rest of my trip. When night fell we would take an innocent stroll to the seashore through the streets of Algeciras, so quiet, and yet so famous as a center of international intrigue. At the seashore, we would step aboard an unpretentious fishing boat which would transfer me on the high seas to an English motorboat.

Late that evening, in pitch blackness with occasional bursts of rain, we walked to the seashore. We found the fishing boat and the rendezvous at sea was kept with precision. The motorboat signaled us with a powerful light. We drew up close and heaved my suitcase into the English boat. I climbed aboard and was introduced to a Sergeant Arnold. We gazed at the dark, quiet sea until we reached Gibraltar.

Gibraltar loomed impressively out of the grayness. We flashed our signal repeatedly at the English patrol boats. There was something awe-inspiring about this display of power and alertness. Sergeant Arnold must have sensed my feelings.

'It's too bad you weren't here when we invaded North Africa. The sea was nearly solid with ships. What a sight!'[2]

He chatted with me about the wonders of Gibraltar and naval affairs until we docked at the Mediterranean fortress. On shore we were met promptly by a car. Sergeant Arnold took the wheel and whisked me off to an unpretentious two-story building which was an officers' residence. We went through a long, dark hall and emerged into a lounge furnished comfortably in typical English club style. It might have been in the heart of London, to judge from the heavy armchairs, deep rugs, and shelves full of books.

A pleasant hum of conversation issued from the next room, into which we entered. A man disengaged himself from a group of English officers and approached us.

'Good evening,' he said, 'I am Colonel Burgess. We are all very glad that you arrived safely. Tomorrow the Governor will see you and then, in the evening, it's off for London on a bomber.'

He introduced me to the other men and then asked me what I was drinking.

'Whisky and water,' was my request. Colonel Burgess slapped his thigh enthusiastically.

'Behold,' he shouted, 'a man who knows how to drink whisky. Do you know, Mr Karski, that most of my officers desecrate whisky by mixing it with soda water? Where did you learn to drink it with water?'

'I spent about a year in Great Britain. Before the war, of course.'

'Really? Do you know Edinburgh?' he asked, his brows knitted together in humorous ferocity.

'Certainly. I spent a whole week there.'

His eyes lit up with pleasure.

'Did you ever see a more beautiful city?' he asked challengingly.

'Well,' I said diplomatically, 'not in Great Britain.'

'In any other place, then?' he pursued.

'Personally, I prefer Lwow, the Polish city in which I studied.'

'Well I never! He drinks whisky like a Scotsman but prefers Lwow to Edinburgh.'

I had rarely enjoyed such congenial company. We talked for a long time and absorbed quite a number of drinks. By the time I got to bed I was in a hilarious mood.

I woke up in the morning with a sense of luxury. It was so pleasant not to have one's feet turn to ice the minute one exposed them to the air. It was pleasant, too, to look forward to a better breakfast than a piece of black bread mixed with sawdust and a cup of cold ersatz coffee. The meal I was served that morning made the whole trip seem worthwhile.

Late that night we took off for England in a heavy American bomber, a Liberator. The next noon, after a smooth, pleasant eight-hour flight, we coasted onto an English airfield. It took quite a while to route me through the complex English investigation machinery. It was fully two days before I was delivered to the Polish authorities.

My first duty was to report to Stanislaw Mikolajczyk, then the Minister of the Interior in our government. His department had jurisdiction over the activities of the Underground and his main task was to maintain contact with the secret organizations in Poland, to give them financial and military aid, and, if necessary, to help in the work of directing them.

The report I had to make on all sectors of the Underground in Poland and the general situation under the German occupation took a long time. The sense that I was abroad and free lasted only till I began to make my reports. Then I noticed that all my mind and emotions were transported back to Poland. This was true of all my future work. In all the times that my activity consisted of transmitting my knowledge of events inside Poland, I invariably felt as though I relived my experiences and was back again in the Gestapo-haunted, suffering atmosphere of the Underground.

33

My Report to the World

After my preliminary report, I was asked to see Prime Minister
General Sikorski. My admiration and the admiration of our people
in Poland for this man grew tremendously. He was one of the rare
great men who do not crush a nation with their personality. He did
not seek to impose his will upon Poland although his position as
head of the government and Commander-in-Chief of all the armed
forces, including those of the Underground, gave him ample opportunity to exercise unlimited power.

I had a long conversation with him about the plans of the men in
the Underground for the future organization of Poland, the common desire so deeply rooted in all our fighters to make Poland a
genuine, unshakable democracy, one that would assure social justice and freedom to every inhabitant. I told Sikorski that the hopes
of the people centered about him, that the desire of the overwhelming majority was that he carry out our aspirations and lead the
nation during the difficult years to come.

His answer was wistful.

'The people must not forget,' he said softly, 'that old General
Sikorski is more than sixty-two. He is a very tired man. His only
hope and ambition is to be able to contribute to the resurrection of
a free and independent Poland.'

It was quite plain that Sikorski neither wanted to be the leader,
nor would have become a dictator, of Poland. He merely wanted to
serve his nation to the best of his ability.

My schedule at that time called for me to return quickly to
Poland. I asked General Sikorski what his political program during
the war was.

'Above all,' he replied, 'I want to contribute to the maintenance of unity among the United Nations. Only that unity can liberate mankind from Hitler's curse. That unity alone can secure a permanent peace. We must understand that after this war there must be no place for imperialism, isolationism, and nationalism of any kind. There must be active collaboration based upon collective security for all nations.'

I asked him if he thought there was any chance of realizing such a program.

'Why not? Consider the achievements of Anglo–American genius. Can't we all take from them the views and institutions which have not only made them powerful but secured democracy and freedom for hundreds of millions of people? I rely on America and England.'

He was, at that time, immensely confident about the future. He had recently returned from America where his discussions with President Roosevelt had apparently been both important and heartening. In England, similar conversations between him and Mr Churchill had occurred after his return.

I asked him his opinion on the future of Russo-Polish relations.[1] He pondered for a while, then got up and paced the floor. He spoke with care and deliberation.

'No one can foresee developments at this stage. My own policies are firmly based on the necessity of collaboration between all the United Nations. As Prime Minister and as a Pole, I will do everything possible to facilitate such collaboration. Poland wishes to, and will, collaborate with Soviet Russia during and after the war. Not because Russia is powerful, but because such collaboration will be advantageous to all Europe. I mean, of course, the collaboration of a free, independent Poland, governed by her own people and ruled by her own laws, traditions, and culture.'

When I took leave of Sikorski, he said to me:

'Young man, you have worked hard in this war. For what you have done you will be decorated with the Virtuti Militari order. The ceremony will take place the day after tomorrow. But because I like you personally, and have known you through a long and difficult time, because you have honest eyes, because they gaze upon me with friendship, accept this cigarette case from me. It is not a gift from a Prime Minister or a Commander-in-Chief. It is a present from an old gentleman who has suffered a great deal, who has endured many disappointments and many sad hours, who is tired and appreciates friendship. It comes from a man who loves youth, the youth that will build up a new Poland and a new world.'

He went to his desk and drew a silver cigarette case from a drawer. It had his signature engraved on it. He handed it to me with a warm smile. I felt both proud and humble.

After we had shaken hands he smiled and said:

'Now go and get some rest. Don't let all these conferences and reports wear you out. Don't let the Allies do what the Gestapo failed to accomplish. You look thin and pale. I don't like it. I heard you have lost some teeth, too – it's not fitting for a young gentleman and officer. Get them replaced and get them made better than the old ones. We are not so poor as not to be able to reconstruct at least the knocked-out teeth of you, the people from "over there" . . . Oh, yes, and show me your wrists.'

He looked at the cuts that had been made with the razor blade in the Gestapo prison.

'They look nasty,' he said. 'I see that the Gestapo gave you a decoration too. You have things to remember.'

'They don't bother me any longer, General,' I answered, 'but I shall not forget . . . nor will my children and their children.'

'I see,' he said, a little ruefully, I thought; 'you are one of those who do not forgive.'

Three days after I had reported to General Sikorski I had the great honor to be decorated with the Cross of the Virtuti Militari, the highest Polish military order. The ceremony took place in the building of the Polish cabinet at 18 Kensington Palace Gardens. Several members of the government witnessed the act, which was performed by the Commander-in-Chief.

Sikorski came over to me and gave me the official orders:

'Three steps back, stand to attention!'

I was so moved that I could hardly listen. I remember only bits of phrases:

'For merit . . . for loyal service . . . for devotion to your country . . . for courage and sacrifice . . . for your faith in victory . . .'[2]

I had to submit a long report to the President of Poland, Wladyslaw Raczkiewicz. This man was the head of a state that was at a distance from him and had concealed all its offices and institutions. Then I had to make reports to the individual members of the government and the Polish political leaders. It was toilsome, heavy, energy-consuming work.

I also had a meeting with our Minister of Finance.

'I am glad to see you,' he greeted me. 'I presume that you came to inform me about the political situation in Poland.'

'I am very sorry, Mr Minister,' I answered, 'but what brought me here is a different matter indeed. I came to ask the head of the Polish Treasury for a loan. The Gestapo deprived me of my own very good teeth and I am in desperate need of a new set.'

We both laughed heartily.

After a few weeks, I began my second task, that of informing the leaders of the United Nations on the situation in Poland and the condition of the Underground. I was to tell them about our work, our aims, what they could expect from us and what we wanted from them, our mutual efforts for the common cause.

My meeting with Anthony Eden made a vivid impression on me. Although he did not know it, he had been an important influence upon me when I was a student. While I was doing research work in the library of the League of Nations in Geneva, Eden was the ruling idol of my group of friends. His acts, speeches, and manners represented to us the acme of modern statesmanship. He was carefully observed and imitated. I remember how I used to sneak with a group of boys from l'École des Sciences Politiques to watch him play a graceful and urbane set of tennis after having delivered a speech at a meeting of the League Council. I felt like mentioning it to him but refrained.

After I had made my report, Eden said:

'Let's go to the window. I want to have a good look at you.'

And before I left his spacious room in the Foreign Office, he remarked:

'You seem to have been through everything in this war except one: the Germans did not shoot you. I wish you good luck, Mr Karski. I feel honored to have met you.'[3]

I replied, 'I am only one of thousands, Sir, of many thousands.'

And then I started my round of calls on other prominent Englishmen. It did not seem very novel. It was, in fact, very much like the same thing I had been doing in Poland, running from one contact point to another. Of course, here there were limousines and good food. There it was terror and hunger.

Nearly every English political leader was interested in a different aspect of my reports. I cannot fathom how or why it should be so, but no two people had the same interests. Mr Arthur Greenwood, the Labour leader, Lord Selborne, Lord Cranborne, and Dr Dalton, the President of the Board of Trade; Miss Ellen Wilkinson, the fiery Member of Parliament, Mr O'Malley, the British Ambassador to the Polish Government; the American Ambassador, Anthony Drexel Biddle; the Parliamentary Under-Secretary for Foreign Affairs, Richard Law – each and every one of them wanted to hear about something different.

I also appeared before the United Nations War Crimes Commission, which is composed of representatives of the United Nations, and of which Sir Cecil Hurst, the legal advisor of the British Government, is the chairman. I told them what I had seen in the Warsaw ghetto and the Belzec death camp. My testimony was placed on record and I was told that it will be used as evidence in the United Nations' indictment against Germany.[4]

I also gave interviews to the English and Allied press, to Members of Parliament, to literary and intellectual groups. In those memorable days, I had the privilege of meeting the political, cultural, and religious elite of Great Britain.

Poland's contribution to the war effort was a far different thing in a cold, conspiratorial meeting place than the world saw it from remote London. In London, our effort meant some hundreds of thousands of Polish soldiers, a handful of ships, a few thousand Polish aviators who were hailed for their heroic feats in the Battle of Britain but soon became lost in the overwhelming mass of Allied air power. Our efforts meant the brief September campaign and some echoes of obstinate resistance.

In London these things bulked small. London was the hub of a vast military wheel, the spokes of which were made up of billions of dollars, armadas of bombers and ships, and staggering armies that had suffered great losses. Then, too, people asked where did Polish sacrifice rank next to the immeasurable heroism, sacrifice, and suffering of the Russian people? What was the share of Poland in this titanic undertaking? Who were the Poles?

In Warsaw the perspective had been different. There, Polish participation meant accepting the challenge of the most formidable and ruthless war machine that ever existed, while all Europe was passive or compromising. It meant the first resistance to the overwhelming Nazi power – a resistance staged not in defense of Danzig or some corridor but for the moral principles without which nations could not live together. For us in Warsaw, it meant fighting, risking the lives of thousands of underground workers every day. It meant faith until death to the right cause, in spite of the sacrifice of five million lives.

I soon realized that the outside world could not comprehend the two most important principles of Polish resistance. It never could understand or estimate the sacrifice and heroism entailed in our nation-wide refusal to collaborate with the Germans. It could not estimate the fact that our unyielding attitude had prevented a single Quisling from arising, nor imagine what this attitude was like. Nor could the outside world conceive of the Underground in any terms indicative of its real nature. The whole notion of the underground state was often unintelligible to them. In no other country had the Underground attained an analogous triumph. The presence of Quislings, collaboration, and compromise had made it impossible.

The idea that a State – with a parliament, government, judicial branch, and army – could function normally but in secret seemed to them utterly fantastical.

Even many Poles failed to grasp the position of their country in this war. I explained these facts on innumerable occasions to many Polish soldiers and officers. Most of them seemed to harbor a psychological grudge, an odd kind of inferiority complex.

'The Polish Army is not in action,' they would complain, or, 'Aren't we ever going to do anything but train?'

I tried to point out that the Polish Army as a whole, they and we in Poland, suffered greater losses than any of our Western Allies. But every one of them wanted to fight as the Poles in Poland fought, and as soon as possible.

One day I received a sudden call from General Sikorski. I went to his office and he gave me my orders.

'You are going soon to the United States,' he told me abruptly, 'in the same capacity as here. You have no further instructions of any kind. Our Ambassador, Jan Ciechanowski, will put you in touch with prominent Americans. You will tell them what you have seen, what you have been through in Poland, what the Underground has ordered you to tell the United Nations. Remember one thing, under no circumstances are you to make your report dependent on the political situation or the type of people you address. You will tell them the truth and only the truth. Answer all questions that do not endanger your comrades and harm the Underground. Do you understand what I expect from you? Are you aware of how firm my faith is that you will speak impartially?'[5]

'Thank you, sir, yes,' I replied, 'I want to tell you how grateful I am for your confidence and for the way you have treated me.'

When I left this man I had no idea that I would never see him again. It was the greatest of all shocks when a few weeks later the news of his tragic end was flashed around the world. General Sikorski died as a soldier on duty, in an airplane crash near Gibraltar.[6] We Poles had no luck in this war.

A few weeks later, I was watching the Statue of Liberty emerging from the waters of New York Harbor. For me, it was the country not only of Washington and Lincoln but also of Kosciuszko and Pulaski.

Like England, it soon became a place where I relived my experiences in an endless series of conferences, conversations, speeches, introductions, and meetings. Again I heard the same questions from the most prominent men in the country: What can we do for you? What do you expect from us? How can we help?

My reply was:

'The material help you give us is important. But infinitely more important is that your ideals, your way of life, your fairness in public life, your American democracy and honesty in foreign policy be transplanted to Europe. At the same time we Europeans look upon you as the greatest power in the world. So try to apply to the whole world your own principles, expressed in the Four Freedoms and the Atlantic Charter. You will save all Europe and all the world. That is what we want from you.'

Again I satisfied the desire in scores of leading men who wanted to know about my country, men from widely varied spheres – politics, religion, business, the arts. The War Department had to be satisfied through Secretary Stimson and his subordinates, many of whom worked anonymously, as did the Englishmen in the War Office who handled the relations of their country with the rebellious groups in the occupied countries.

I gave information to the State Department through Assistant Secretary Berle and various heads of departments; to the Department of Justice through Attorney General Biddle; to the Supreme Court through Justice Frankfurter. I conveyed my information to Catholic circles through Archbishops Mooney and Stritch; to the Jewish circles through their leaders, Rabbi Wise, Morris Waldman, Nahum Goldmann, among many others whom I met.

I realized then to what an extent the entire world is unified. It seemed to me as though the network of which I was a part performed some function in a single, world-wide organism – an organism from which no member, not even the most powerful, could separate itself.

Finally I came to the most important interview. I was told that the President of the United States wanted to hear from me personally about events in Poland and occupied Europe.[7]

I asked my Ambassador what I should tell him.

'Be exact and brief,' he smiled at me; 'Mr Roosevelt is certainly the busiest man in the world.'

The White House looked to me like a country mansion, new and well-built, surrounded by trees and silence. I missed the superb statues, the ivied walls, the towers, turrets, and the patina of tradition such an edifice is apt to have in my own country. It was typically a country gentleman's house on a large estate. My heart beat rapidly when I entered the White House with my Ambassador, who was to introduce me. This was the very citadel of power. I was to meet the most powerful man in the most powerful nation of the world.

President Roosevelt seemed to have plenty of time and to be incapable of fatigue. He was amazingly well-informed about Poland and wanted still more information. His questions were minute, detailed, and directed squarely at important points. He inquired about our methods of education and our attempts to safeguard the children. He inquired about the organization of the Underground and the losses the Polish nation had suffered. He asked me how I explained the fact that Poland was the only country without a Quisling. He asked me to verify the stories told about the German practices against the Jews. He was anxious to learn the techniques for sabotage, diversion, and partisan activity.

On every topic he demanded precise and accurate information. He wanted to know, to be able to realize, not merely imagine, the very climate and atmosphere of underground work and the minds of the men engaged in it. He impressed me as a man of genuinely broad scope. Like Sikorski, his interests embraced not merely his own country but all humanity. When I left, the President was still smiling and fresh. I felt fatigued.

It was, however, not an ordinary fatigue, but more the satisfied weariness of the workman who has just completed his job with a last blow of his hammer or an artist who signs his name under the completed picture. Something was coming to an end, and all that was left was this weariness, but also the satisfaction of having achieved what I'd set out to do.

The Ambassador wanted to take me back in his car, but I preferred to walk a little. I headed toward La Fayette Square, opposite the White House, on the other side of Pennsylvania Avenue. I knew why I was going there: on one of the corners stands the statue of Kosciuszko with the inscription: 'And Freedom shrieked as Kosciuszko fell.'

I sat down on a bench and watched the people go by. They were well-dressed and looked healthy and complacent. They hardly seemed to be affected by the war. Events passed through my mind in quick, strange fragments.

The exquisite salon of the Portuguese Ambassador in Warsaw and then, abruptly, without any transition, the heat, dust, and smoke of battle and the bitterness of defeat. The endless chaotic march eastward and the futile search for non-existent detachments. Then the whistling winds and the bleak Soviet steppes. The barbed wire of the prison camp. The train. The German concentration camp at Radom and the first glimpse of a brutality that no one had even dreamed of, the filth, the hunger, the degradation. Then the Underground, the secrecy and mystery, the constant, slight trembling of the nerves. The Slovakian mountains and the ski trip, like bursting into the upper world.

Beautiful Paris in wartime . . . Angers full of German spies . . . Then back again over the Carpathian Mountains, back to the land of graves, tears, and sorrow. The Gestapo and the first blow in my sleep . . . then the beatings, the teeth and the ribs, the blood gushing out, filling my eyes, ears, filling the world.

Then the words: 'We were given two orders. The first one was to save you at any price; the other to shoot you in case we did not succeed.'

Then toil in the Underground, humdrum, secretive, and dangerous. The ghetto and the death camp, the memory bringing nausea, the whispered words of the Jews, like the roar of mountains crashing.

Then Unter den Linden – Berta, Rudolph. People I had once loved and whom I now detested. The Pyrenees at night and the Pyrenees by day. The diplomatic world and the conferences. My decoration. And then I saw him, as I can see him now while I write, the weary old gentleman gazing with his fatherly eyes into mine and saying:

'I am not giving you any recommendations or instructions. You are not representing the Polish Government or its policy. The facilities with which we supply you are purely technical. Your task is only to reproduce objectively what you saw, what you experienced, and what you were bidden to tell about those in Poland and the other occupied countries of Europe.'

THE END

Notes

Selected and abridged footnotes have also been translated from the 2010 French publication and added to this edition as endnotes.

Note on the Text

1. Excerpt from the last paragraph of Jan Karski's Introduction to the first Polish edition, dated Washington, 1 September 1999.

Preface

1. This Preface originally appeared as the Postscript to the 1944 American edition.

1. Defeat

1. Before 1918, Oświęcim was located at the extreme south-west of what was then Western Galicia, which was, at that time, part of the Habsburg Empire. Located near the border with Upper Silesia and captured by Frederick II of Prussia during the Silesian Wars, Oświęcim was a garrison town until the eighteenth century, and a railway junction until the middle of the nineteenth century, when it attracted new industry. Once Poland was reunited and became independent once more, Oświęcim again became a city of both Poles and Jews (in 1939, more than 50 percent of its population, about 7,000 people, were Jewish), part of the historical province known as 'Little Poland' (Małopołska). The former Austrian barracks, where the Auschwitz concentration

camp was to be situated from 1940 until its liberation, were occupied in August 1939 by the 5ᵗʰ DAK' (5ᵗʰ division of Artillery) to which Jan Karski belonged. Shortly afterwards the city would become known by its German name, Auschwitz.

2. Marian Kozielewski (1897–1964) was nearly eighteen years older than Jan, who was the youngest boy in his family. As a young man, Marian joined the Legions of Józef Piłsudski in Galicia and served in the 1ˢᵗ Brigade. In July 1917, along with all the other loyal followers of Piłsudski, he refused to swear allegiance to the Central Powers and was jailed until March 1918, when he was released on grounds of ill health. He immediately went back to Łódź and joined their clandestine POW group (Polska Organizacja Wojskowa). Discharged in 1919, he was appointed an officer in the state police force and, in 1931, he was named Chief of the Regional Police Department in Lwów. He brought his mother and brother Jan along with him when he relocated, and Jan studied law and diplomatic relations at the Jan Kazimierz University there. In the autumn of 1934, however, Marshal Piłsudski called Marian back to Warsaw in order to entrust him with the post of Chief of Police of the capital, but, in September 1939, he refused to comply with orders to carry out his duties in the east of the country and remained in post with a small number of his police officers, whom he placed under the command of the Civilian Commissar of Defense of the capital, the Mayor of Warsaw, Stefan Starzyński, an old friend of his from the Legions. He helped Starzyński organize the Civil Guard (Straż Obywatelska), created on 6 September. Marian was decorated with the Medal of Valor for the third time when the military defenders of Warsaw surrendered (28 September). Along with his friend Starzyński, he agreed to remain Chief of the Polish Police in order to put it at the immediate service of the Resistance.

3. The idea of the 'Fifth Column' dates from 1936 and the Spanish Civil War. In 1937–8, the crisis in the Sudetenland and Munich linked the Fifth Column with the German minorities in central Europe, the Volksdeutsche. In the 1931 census, the German minority in Poland numbered 800,000 people – 2.3 percent of the population – mainly concentrated in Pomerania and Upper Silesia. After 30–31 August 1939,

they engaged in acts of sabotage, aided by commandos who were parachuted in. From 1941 onwards, the Polish government-in-exile in London would publish a collection of documents on this subject: *The German Fifth Column in Poland* (London, 1941).

4. At the beginning of 1914, Tarnopol had 33,000 inhabitants, proud of their long-standing multicultural traditions, historical architectural gems, and an intensely active community life, which earned the town the nickname of 'little Lwów'. Tarnopol was returned with Eastern Galicia when Poland was reunited and proclaimed independent, reclaiming its place as a bastion of Polishness on the borders of the USSR.

5. This harangue explained the sudden appearance of the Red Army in Poland. It was broadcast to the Polish soldiers at Tarnopol, who had met an armored division of the 6th Soviet Army at the Ukrainian Front. It reproduced the carefully prepared argument by the 'Propaganda and Direct Action Department of the Red Army'. From 14 September onwards, this same argument was propagated in the ranks of the armed forces of Belarus and the Ukraine, who were responsible for carrying out the dawn offensive on 17 September. The (secret) orders from above instructed the Red Army to 'destroy the Polish Army,' 'tear it to pieces with a lightning strike,' 'advance using grenades and bayonets in the name of the most just of revolutionary wars.' But they were also instructed 'not to appear as the aggressor', as Molotov explained to Ambassador Schulenburg on 10 September. Soviet propaganda also argued that the 'breaking down' and 'disappearance' of the Polish state required the USSR to extend 'fraternal support' for the Belarussian and Ukrainian populations who had been 'abandoned' in the chaos, whom the 'Red Army was coming to liberate from the yoke of Polish capitalists and nobility.' This 'fraternal hand' was also extended to the low-ranking Polish soldiers, in the form of tracts and proclamations written in broken Polish and signed, depending on the target audience, by Komandarm Mikhaïl Kovalov, Commander-in-Chief of the Belarus Front, or by his counterpart, Semyon Timoshenko of the Ukrainian Front. These tracts called upon the soldiers of the Polish Army to 'lay down their arms' or to turn them against the 'blood suckers,' i.e. the 'Polish officers who were members of the nobility.'

2. Prisoner in Russia

1. Following the decision taken at the Politburo the previous day, Lavren-tiy Beria's top secret order no. 001177, issued on 3 October 1939, stated that 'all generals, officers, [and] high-ranking government officials' were to be gathered together in a special camp in Starobelsk (and later also in Kozelsk). All police officers, prison guards, and intelligence agents – 6,192 in total – were placed in the Ostashkov camp in the Tver (formerly Kalinin) region. On 13 April 1943, German radio announced the discovery of a mass grave in the forest of Katyń, near Smolensk; it contained the bodies of 4,123 Polish officers, with whom communica-tions had ceased in the spring of 1940. The Germans blamed this crime on the Soviets, and the government of General Władysław Sikorski requested an inquiry, under the auspices of the International Red Cross. This request, however, gave Stalin an excuse to break off rela-tions with Sikorski and embark on a campaign against this 'ally and agent of Goebbels.' It was not until 14 October 1992 that the then Russian President, Boris Yeltsin, gave the Polish President at that time, Lech Wałesa, the documents and secret files from the archives of the Central Committee of the Communist Party of the Soviet Union that contained a copy of the execution order of 5 March 1940, signed by Stalin and members of the Politburo. Death warrants had been signed for 14,568 prisoners of war from three camps – Starobelsk, Kozelsk, and Ostashkov – as well as 11,000 Polish prisoners from camps in Belarus and the Ukraine: in total, 25,568 victims.

2. In reality, the Ribbentrop–Molotov pact, the 'Treaty of Non-Aggres-sion,' did not include any provisions relating to prisoners, and then, with the second pact of 28 September 1939, the so-called 'Boundary and Friendship Treaty,' the division of the territories agreed in the secret protocol of 23 August was revised and replaced with the proposal for the establishment of a 'definitive border.' This pact, furthermore, specified that the USSR 'would place no obstacles in the way of Reich nationals and other persons of German descent' should they desire to

'emigrate' to Germany. The exchange of Polish prisoners of war was carried out after a separate special agreement had been reached.

3. Exchange and Escape

1. The new German–Soviet border, established on 28 September 1939 by the Boundary and Friendship Treaty, divided the town of Przemyśl on the River San. The historic city center, together with its Jewish quarter, belonged to the USSR. The Zasanie, which means 'on the other bank of the San,' was incorporated into the Reich under the General Government for the Occupied Polish Territories (Generalgouvernement für die besetzten polnischen Gebiete, GG).

2. Cavalry commander Henryk Dobrzański (1896–1940), known as 'Hubal,' was the most famous of all the guerrillas active in the zone occupied by the Germans. He and his comrades held out in the Holy Cross Mountains and the forest of Spała until 30 April 1940, which prompted acts of brutal retaliation against the civilian population for supposedly aiding him and his men.

3. The river in question is the San, which flows into the Vistula.

4. Later on, in 1945, it was revealed that all prisoners of war of Belarussian or Ukrainian nationality – a total of 17,000 – were deported to the Gulag.

5. The declaration of war on Germany by Great Britain on 3 September 1939, followed by that of France, was greeted in Poland with gratitude and renewed hope. It would later be discovered that, when this happened, even Hitler thought his cause was lost. The Anglo-French Supreme War Council met on 12 September in Abbeville and decided not to launch the offensive to the west, but neglected to inform their Polish allies of this decision. There was 'nothing left to do to save Poland,' Chamberlain announced at the time: 'The only way is to win the war.'

4. Devastated Poland

1. Between 11 October and 12 December 1939 the Nazis imposed rationing on the citizens of Warsaw: 250 grams of bread per day per person, and 250 grams of sugar, in addition to 100 grams of rice and 200 grams of salt every two months. The system of ration cards implemented from 15 December 1939 set the lowest intake of calories in all of occupied Europe. Special criteria based on race were drawn up to distinguish between the Poles and the Jews in the distribution of ration cards.

2. This was Paul Moder, SS-Gruppenführer and commander of both the SS and the Warsaw District Police from 14 November 1939 to 4 August 1941.

3. Laura Białobrzeska, born Laura Kozielewska, the sister of the author. She survived the Occupation and died in Poland after the war.

5. The Beginning

1. The man in question was Jerzy Gintowt Dziewałtowski, a young violinist from Lwów, which was where the author befriended him. He actively resisted the invasion and died during the Occupation.

6. Transformation

1. A reference to 'collective responsibility,' a policy established in Poland under Nazi occupation. Jan Karski here cites the massacre of Wawer, a suburb of Warsaw. On 27 December 1939, the Orpo executed 107 male citizens after forcibly pulling them out of their homes. It was an act of retaliation for the murder of two German soldiers in a local restaurant. The practice of taking 'collective responsibility' had been ordered by the Wehrmacht early in the previous September, with the aim of destroying the Polish Resistance still active behind enemy lines.

2. These raids in the summer of 1940 formed a part of the wave of terror called the 'AB-Aktion' that swept across the territory of the whole General Government on the order of Himmler. More than 3,500 political leaders and civilian functionaries were arrested, the majority of whom were quickly executed. In Warsaw, 358 people were shot on 20–21 June 1940 in Palmiry, among them Maciej Rataj, the President of the Sejm, the Socialist Mieczysław Niedziałkowski, the editor-in-chief of *Robotnik*, and Pohoski, the Deputy Mayor of Warsaw. New round-ups took place between 12 August and 19 September 1940; their victims were among the first to be deported to the concentration camps at Auschwitz.

3. On the order of Himmler, Auschwitz I concentration camp was created on 27 April 1940 on the outskirts of Oświęcim, in what had formerly been Austrian barracks. It was initially intended to house Poles from the GG territories and Upper Silesia. On 14 June 1940, the first trans-port, containing 728 Polish political prisoners, arrived there from the Tarnów prison near Kraków. It also contained several Polish Jews. In March 1941, Himmler chose Birkenau, 2½ miles from the camp at Auschwitz, as the site of the new camp, Auschwitz II-Birkenau, which had gas chambers and crematoriums.

4. In May 1940, in the name and on the order of the Polish government-in-exile, Civil Resistance published a call to 'boycott the invaders.' In 1941 this was followed by 'The Code of Civic Morality,' a hand-book for everyday behaviour, forbidding all 'collaboration with the occupiers.'

7. Initiation

1. By decree on 8 October 1939, Hitler annexed the Polish provinces of Pomerania, Poznań, Upper Silesia, the greater part of Łódź (which became Litzmannstadt), the western part of Kraków, Masovia, and Suwałki, with effect from 26 October. Thereafter, Poznań belonged to the newly established Reichsgau Wartheland, governed by Artur Greiser. 'Territories can be made German but people cannot,' wrote

Hitler in *Mein Kampf*. Wartheland as well as Pomerania and Upper Silesia, therefore, underwent the process of Germanization implemented through the expulsion and expropriation of the Polish and Jewish population to the benefit of German settlers: 400,000 expulsions were carried out before the spring of 1940. From 1939 onwards, these measures were accompanied by the introduction of the 'Deutsche Volksliste' in the Poznań region (extended from 3 March 1941 to include all annexed territories): Poles who were able to offer proof of their German ethnicity, and who wished to, could become naturalized German citizens. Soon thereafter, the Nazis compelled the Silesian Poles to enforce this decree as well.

2. The General Government was created by a decree issued by Hitler on 12 October 1939. The territories comprised some 37,000 square miles and 11,863,000 inhabitants: 9,792,000 Poles, 1,457,000 Jews, 526,000 Ukrainians, and 65,000 Germans. Devoid of even a semblance of autonomy or independence (unlike the neighboring Protectorate of Bohemia and Moravia), the region was divided into four districts: Kraków, Warsaw, Lublin, and Radom, and was governed by an administration composed entirely of Germans. Hans Frank (1900–46) headed this administration as Governor-General. Frank was a Nazi lawyer, a high-ranking official of the NSDAP (The National Socialist German Workers' Party, i.e. the Nazi Party). He chose the royal castle and palace of Wawel in Kraków as his residence, and dedicated himself to transforming the GG into a temporary 'reserve supply' of 'sub-human men.' In July 1941, after a victorious attack on the Soviet Union, a fifth district was added to the GG: Galicia, which was comprised of three former Polish regions – Lwów, Tarnopol, and Stanisławów – located between the River San and the Polish-Soviet border established on 1 September 1939. The GG's territory was thus extended to 56,000 square miles, and included 17,600,000 inhabitants, of whom 11,400,000 were Polish, 4,000,000 were Ukrainians, 2,100,000 were Jews, and about 300,000 were Germans, who mainly settled there after 1939.

8. Borecki

1. The official government of the Polish Republic was re-established in Paris on 30 September 1939, in accordance with the Constitution of 1935, which afforded exceptional powers to the president in the event of war. President Ignacy Mościcki, interned in Romania with his government until 18 September 1939, was therefore unable to reach France, and so named as his successor Władysław Raczkiewicz (1885–1947), the former President of the Senate (1930–35), who was already in Paris. Raczkiewicz took the constitutional oath on 30 September 1939 at the Polish Embassy, appointed General Sikorski his Prime Minister, and took over the duties of the interned Polish government. After being housed for a while at the Polish Embassy in Paris, Sikorski's Polish government-in-exile was officially transferred to Angers on 22 November 1939. It was a coalitional government of the four main opposition parties before the defeat of September 1939.

9. Contact Between Cells

1. Jerzy 'Jur,' the pseudonym of Jerzy Lerski (1917–92), was a great friend of Jan Karski at university and during his military service from 1931 to 1934. In 1936, at Jan Kazimierz University in Lwów, Lerski was active in the democratic student movement. He was parachuted into Poland on 20 February 1943 as the political envoy of the Polish government-in-exile.

10. Mission to France

1. Stanisław Kot (1885–1975) was a historian and professor at the Jagiellonian University in Kraków (1920). In 1936, after he became a member of the Executive Committee of the Peasant Party (SL) and a close ally of its very first President, Wincenty Witos, Kot developed an impassioned antagonism toward the 'regime of the colonels.' He grew politically

close to the Front Morges, composed of the opposing centrist political parties, friends of General Sikorski. Having devised a plan with them in September 1939 in Lwów, Kot went first to Bucharest and then to Paris, where, in early October, he rejoined the government of Sikorski that was being reconstituted. He served successively as a Minister without Portfolio, Minister of Internal Affairs (1940–41), Ambassador to the Soviet Union in Moscow (1941–2), and Minister of Information (1943–4) and remained a respected advisor to the head of the government.

2. Kazimierz Sosnkowski (1885–1969), pseudonym 'Godziemba.' Born in Warsaw into a family of the intelligentsia with noble roots, at the age of eighteen he joined the Polish Socialist Party (PPS) and, at the time of the revolution of 1905, joined its military organization (OB-PPS), soon becoming one of its leaders. Remaining loyal to Piłsudski following the schism in the party in 1906, he allied himself with the PPS Revolutionary Faction. As Commander of the Poznań Military District, a post he occupied from 1925, in the wake of the May coup d'état, Sosnkowski was torn between remaining loyal to Piłsudski and his duty to the official government. He attempted suicide and was only saved by an extensive operation, followed by a period of convalescence that lasted a year. He was then Commander of the Southern Front in 1939. After his arrival in Paris, President Władysław Raczkiewicz appointed Sosnkowski to succeed him, in accordance with Article 13 of the Constitution of 1935. On 13 November, General Sikorski named him Commander-in-Chief of the ZWZ, a military resistance organization operating inside Poland. In July 1941 he opposed the terms of the Sikorski–Maiski Agreement, and resigned from the government. After the death of Sikorski on 4 July 1943, Raczkiewicz appointed Sosnkowski Commander-in-Chief of the Polish Armed Forces.

11. *The Underground State*

1. 'Cyna' was the undercover name of Józef Cyrankiewicz. On the order of Cyrankiewicz, the Kraków cell of the PPS organized and financed Karski's escape.

2. Vidkun Quisling (1887–1945) was the founder of the Nationalist Party in the Norwegian government and head of state from 1942 to 1945, becoming, and remaining, the symbol of collaboration with the Nazi occupiers. After the defeat of the Third Reich he was tried and executed by hanging.

3. This was the oath taken by each soldier of the Home Army, the Armia Krajowa (AK), and each member of the Civil Resistance (Delegatura): 'I swear before God Almighty to execute with steadfast loyalty all tasks given to me that lead to the liberation of Poland from the occupiers. I pledge unconditional obedience to my superiors and to never betray the secrets of our organization.' Agents like Karski would also add: 'I swear before God never to reveal to anyone the content of messages, reports, and documents that have been entrusted to me and to loyally deliver them to their destination.' The oath would end with: 'May God be with me!'

12. *Caught by the Gestapo*

1. Franciszek Musiał, pseudonym 'Myszka' (the Mouse), was a member of the ZWZ (later AK). A baker by profession, in 1939 he moved from Tarnów to Piwnicza. He was based in Nowy Sącz, in the region of Kraków and Silesia, and was one of the border crossing guides who took the oath of the Resistance. He had already successfully completed thirty-one crossings to Budapest when he helped Karski. Like Karski, he was imprisoned, tortured, and then deported to various concentration camps, survived the war and died in the late 1970s.

13. *Torture*

1. Prešov is a town in Slovakia, situated between the Polish-Slovakian border and the town of Košice.

2. A Junker was a member of the landed nobility of Prussia.

15. Rescue

1. Krynica (now Krynica-Zdrój) is a thermal spa town situated near Sanok on the River San. It was in the Soviet Zone from 28 September 1939 onwards. Jan Karski names this town instead of Nowy Sącz in order to conceal the true location.
2. 'Stefa Rysińska,' whose real name was Zofia Rysiówna, was not the sister of the guide but the sister of Zbygniew Ryś, a soldier in the ZWZ and head of the Resistance cell in Nowy Sącz, whose mission was to protect the clandestine border crossings to Budapest.
3. The Cross of Valour (Krzyż Walecznych) is a military decoration introduced in 1920 and intended to honor 'deeds of valor and heroism.'
4. Dr Jan Słowikowski (pseudonym 'Dzięcioł,' the Woodpecker) was one of the organizers of Jan Karski's escape and a member of the local cell of the ZWZ. After the war, he headed a children's surgical clinic in Wrocław.
5. The well-built man carrying Karski was Zbygniew Ryś.
6. The Dunajec is a tributary of the River Vistula and has a very strong current.
7. 'Staszek Rosa,' real name Stanisław Rosieński (1919–43), was an activist in the Krakow PPS. He was the co-ordinator in charge of rescuing Jan Karski, ordered by Józef Cyrankiewicz. He was killed in 1943 in Warsaw under unknown circumstances.

16. The 'Gardener'

1. Nowy Sącz.

17. Propaganda from the Country

1. Albert Forster (1902–45), member of the NSDAP from 1923, became the Nazi Party's Gauleiter of the Free City of Danzig (Gdańsk) follow-

ing his election to the Reichstag in 1930. He brutally carried out the Nazi takeover of the city from 1933 onwards. Between September and October 1939 he ordered the massacre of the local Polish elite as well as mass deportations of the civilian population. Extradited to Poland in 1946, he was tried and executed by hanging.

2. In February 1941, General Stefan Rowecki, pseudonym 'Grot' (the Spearhead), Commander-in-Chief of the ZWZ, initiated 'Operation N,' a campaign of counter-propaganda with the aim of demoralizing the soldiers of the Wehrmacht. Written in German, newspapers such as *Der Hammer* and *Der Frontkämpfer* were used to spread anti-Nazi views and the alleged opposition of high-ranking officers to Hitler.

19. The Four Branches of the Underground

1. On 10 October 1939, the German military administration decreed that listening to foreign radio stations was forbidden, on penalty of death. After 15 December 1939, it was forbidden for Poles to even own a radio. Jan Karski was being hidden in the Kraków region by his old Socialist friends, where he again met with 'Cyna,' Józef Cyrankiewicz, who represented the PPS-WRN at the inter-party committee of the local Resistance. As a result of this meeting, Karski agreed to work with the underground publications of the PPS: *Naprzód* (Forward!) and *Wolność'* (Freedom).

2. The author is writing here about the wave of arrests and mass executions during the 'AB-Aktion' carried out between the spring and summer of 1940, timed by the Nazis to coincide with the Blitzkrieg in the West and their victory over France. The names of the victims cited by the author are those of people he knew personally, including civilian officials of the Secret State, such as Rataj and Niedziałkowski, executed in Palmiry on 20–21 June, and Roman Rybarski, a professor of political economy, who was deported to Auschwitz.

3. The decree in question is that of 2 October 1939, issued by the new President of Poland, Władysław Raczkiewicz, who declared 'null and

void all legislative acts of the occupier,' in accordance with Article IV of the International Hague Convention (1907).

4. This military arm of the Resistance, called the ZWZ (Związek Walki Zbrojnej, ZWZ, Association of Armed Struggle) was formed on 13 November 1939 by General Sikorski in his capacity as Prime Minister and Commander-in-Chief of the Armed Forces. His primary command headquarters were located in France, entrusted to the care of General Sosnkowski. The defeat of France and the evacuation of the government-in-exile to London made it difficult to maintain centralized control, however, especially given the long duration of the war. On 30 June 1940 Sosnkowsi issued an 'organizational order' from London, placing the ZWZ entirely in control of the territory as defined by the 1939 borders, under Stefan Rowecki's command. As 'Komendant główny' (Commander-in-Chief), Rowecki was assisted by military staff and had full authority over military operations. On 12 February 1942, the ZWZ received the order to assume the name of Armia Krajowa, AK (the Home Army), as Jan Karski explains. While arrests and mass deportations between 1940 and 1941 in the zones occupied by the Soviets had broken up the ZWZ, paradoxically, Operation Barbarossa (22 June 1941) and the abolition of the German–Soviet border on 28 September 1939 actually made contact between the members of the Polish Resistance easier. 1942 saw the number of partisan units and underground fighters increase, controlled by the AK in the provinces of Wilno, Nowogródek, Grodno, and Białystok (Lithuanian and Belarussian territories), as well as in the Wołyń and Lwów regions. Simultaneously, following Sikorski's orders, conflicting units who held different political convictions within the AK began to unite, with the exception of the two extreme wings, as the far-left Communists did not recognize the legitimacy of the government-in-exile. The AK comprised some 350,000 trained soldiers.

5. These four political parties were: Stronnictwo Ludowe, SL (the Peasant Party); Polska Partia Socjalistyczna–Wolność, Równość, Niepodległość, PPS–WRN (the Polish Socialist Party); Stronnictwo Narodowe, SN (the National Party); and Stronnictwo Pracy, SP (the Christian Democratic Party).

6. The Directorate of Civil Resistance (Kierownictwo Walki Cywilnej or KWC) was established in the autumn of 1940. In late 1940, General Rowecki, Commander of the ZWZ in Warsaw, set out the main rules and 'principles of the civilian fight': 1) boycott of the occupiers; 2) boycott and punishment of all collaborators; 3) organisation of minor acts of sabotage, such as the distribution of leaflets or disrupting theater performances and cinema screenings organized by the occupiers; 4) obligatory assistance to the victims of the occupiers. In April 1941, the management of initiatives within the KWC was entrusted to the lawyer from the Peasant Party, Stefan Korboński. He was given direct access to the government-in-exile in London, thanks to the independent radio transmitter-receiver that the KWC and Korboński had at their disposal. In late 1942, the KWC was entrusted with the organization of the special civilian tribunals, which among other tasks issued warnings to the 'professional blackmailers' who blackmailed or denounced the Jews in hiding in the Aryan part of Warsaw.

21. Assignment in Lublin

1. Marian Kozielewski, prisoner number 6535, was on the first transport to Auschwitz I from Warsaw, which departed on 14 August 1940. He was liberated in May 1941, thanks to measures taken by his wife Jadwiga, née Kzoll (1901–89), a descendant of an old German family that had settled in Poland. The brother of Jan Karski was thus among the first in Warsaw to inform the Polish Resistance about Auschwitz. This information was passed on to London in the summer of 1941 and published by the Polish Minister of Information of the government-in-exile in *The German New Order in Poland* (see Chapter 22 note 1).

2. Food rationing was based on discrimination: citizens of Warsaw received the lowest rations of all the cities of the General Government. From 1940 to 1943, Poles living in Warsaw received on average between 385 and 784 calories per adult per day. In late 1941, the civilian German

population received 2,631 calories per day, Poles 669 on average, and Jews 253. The black market supplied the population with 70–80 percent of essential food products.

3. In February 1940, Hans Frank agreed to the establishment in Warsaw of a legal welfare organization, the Rada Główna Opiekuńcza (RGO), or General Care Council. He insisted that its headquarters be transferred to Kraków in May 1940. The RGO was active over the entire territory of the General Government, including the district of Galicia after 1941. Its forty-four permanent committees had 15,000 volunteers at their disposal. The RGO was funded through charitable donations and it also received grants from the government-in-exile. Though closely watched, the RGO nevertheless managed to act as a front for the civil Resistance. Count Adam Ronikier (1881–1952) was its President from June 1940 to October 1943.

22. Retribution

1. A publication called *The German New Order in Poland* appeared in London from January 1942 onwards; it printed extracts from the Nazi press describing anti-Polish 'incidents' as well as data (places and numbers) pertaining to the massacres carried out between 1939 and 1941, committed both within the territory of the General Government and in all territories incorporated into the Reich.

2. Between 150,000 and 200,000 Polish children were abducted and transported to the Reich, disappearing without trace. Between 28 June 1942 and the summer of 1943, 30,000 children from the Zamość region were deported to concentration camps, becoming the tragic victims of ethnic cleansing.

3. Here Karski describes the Straż Chłopska, set up by the Peasant Party in the autumn of 1940 at the insistence of its youth movement, Wici. In the spring of 1941 these forces took the name of Bataliony Chłopskie, Peasant Battalions. By late 1943 the organization had between 100,000 and 120,000 members, a central command headquarters, combat units, and regional networks.

4. This loan would never be repaid: in 1945, the 'government of Lublin,' set up by the Red Army, would become the official 'government of Warsaw.' It was therefore out of the question that a debt incurred by the 'bandits' of the AK in the name of the 'fascists' in exile in London should ever be settled.

23. *The Secret Press*

1. These two publications were in fact very popular supplements of the official *Rzeczpospolita Polska*.
2. *Pieśń niepodległa* (*The Invincible Song*) was an anthology of poetry secretly published on 30 April 1942, with poems selected by the future Nobel Prize winner Czesław Miłosz. It included works by very young poets in their twenties, the Warsaw school of the 'Generation of Columbuses' (R. Bratny), a generation that tragically perished during war. Among them, Krzysztof Kamil Baczyński (1921–44) remains the poet most loved by the Poles. He was a student at a clandestine university and a soldier in the battalion of Tadeusz Zawadzki (Zośka) in the AK; 'imagine Proust transformed into a soldier,' wrote Miłosz.

26. *Marriage Per Procuram*

1. 'Witek' denotes Witold Bieńkowski, whose pseudonyms included 'Kalski' and 'Wencki.' He was a Catholic publicist and co-editor, together with Zofia Kossak, of the clandestine newspaper *Polska Żyje!* (*Poland Lives!*), published from October 1939 onwards, and co-editor of his own publication, *Prawda* (*Truth*). He was also one of the organizers of the Front for a Reborn Poland, Front Odrodzenia Polski, FOP, in 1941. Having taken an active part in the organization of Żegota, the Council for Aid to Jews (autumn 1942), he was put in charge of the Jewish section founded in February 1943 within the Department of Internal Affairs of the Delegatura, in addition to taking responsibility for the section responsible for aiding prisoners.

2. Zofia Kossak (1890–1968), pseudonyms 'Weronika,' 'Ciotka.' Catholic writer of world renown and granddaughter of the famous painter Juliusz Kossak. In 1941 she co-founded the Catholic organisation FOP, whose underground publication *Prawda* Kossak inspired and directed, as well as publishing numerous brochures. Having taken personal risks in order to shelter Jewish children, she worked with the Socialist Wanda Krahelska to form the Żegota, formally created on 27 September 1942 and recognized by the Delegatura on 4 December 1942. Her name was honored in 1985 when it was inscribed on the list of 'Righteous Among the Nations' in Yad Vashem.

3. *Golgotha*, anonymous clandestine brochure containing forty-six pages, was published by the FOP in Warsaw. It was written by Zofia Kossak.

4. 'Wanda,' code name for Wanda Bieńkowska, née Wilczańska (1913–72). Liaison agent and secretary to Witold Bieńkowski.

5. Jan Karski left Warsaw for London on 1 October 1942. See Chapters 31 and 32 for details of his journey.

6. *Protest*, published on 10 August 1942 with a print run of 5,000 copies and signed by the FOP, is the most well-known text. It was written by Zofia Kossak in the name of Polish Catholics to denounce the mass murder and deportations to concentration camps of the Jews from the Warsaw Ghetto as well as from 'hundreds of towns and villages all over Poland during the past six months.' It was also a protest against the passivity and silence of the international community: 'The Jews are dying in their thousands surrounded by Pontus Pilates who wash their hands of it.' 'The world looks on and says nothing.' 'We can no longer tolerate this silence. We have no right to remain passive in the face of crime. Whoever remains silent after witnessing a murder becomes the murderer's accomplice. These who do not condemn give their consent.' This text was added to the documents preserved on microfilm and entrusted to agent Jan Karski.

27. School – Underground

1. The organization in question is 'Wawer,' with responsibility for 'minor acts of sabotage' and propaganda, formed in November 1939 at the

initiative of the scouts of the Lycée Stefan Batory. The organization's symbolic name was intended to recall the 107 inhabitants of the Wawer district on the outskirts of Warsaw who were executed in December 1939 as part of the system of reprisals known as 'collective responsibility'. Reorganized toward the end of 1940 under the auspices of the former scout leader Aleksander Kamiński and the ZWZ-AK, 50 percent of the organization's members were scouts, Szare Szeregi (the 'Gray Ranks'). In early March 1942, Wawer covered the walls of the town with the anchor, the symbol of hope, made by the interlacing the letters P and W, which stood for *Polska Walczy* (Poland Fights). Many of the fifteen- and sixteen-year-olds who were members of Wawer would join the battalions of Zośka, Parasol, and Kedyw (diversion units) once they reached eighteen.

2. The Nazis closed secondary and higher education establishments in the GG, leaving open only a few technical and professional colleges that corresponded to the first two years of German higher education. The Polish people immediately organized a system of clandestine education. Teachers, professional bodies, and parents drew up a curriculum of underground courses that could be taught all around the country. In Warsaw, out of 103 secondary schools that were closed, 90 had clandestine courses going on, teaching some 25,000 secondary school students (these figures do not include Jewish children). Until 1944, in Warsaw alone, 6,500 Baccalaureates were secretly awarded to secondary school graduates. In Warsaw, there were between 4,200 and 5,000 students attending clandestine higher education courses. Formed in January 1941, the Department of Public Education of the Delegatura run by the Peasant Party and the Socialists began assessing ways to reform education, along with ways of making it more democratic.

28. Parliament in Poland

1. Stefan Rowecki (pseudonyms 'Rakoń,' 'Grabica,' 'Grot,' 'Kalina') (1895–1944). Rowecki was put in charge of the ZWZ in all of the German occupied territories. In May 1940 he was promoted to

Brigadier-General, and on 30 June 1940 was named Commander-in-Chief of the ZWZ (from February 1942 the AK). 'Grot' proved to be an exceptional organizer and leader. His military and political skills, along with his charisma and tact, helped him to unite the rival groups and networks within the AK, with the exception of the extremist groups: the fascists and the Communists. Rowecki remained loyal to Sikorski and expressed his growing mistrust of the 'Soviet ally' to him. Actively hunted by the Gestapo, he was denounced and arrested on 30 June 1943, transferred to Berlin, then to Sachsenhausen, where he was detained for a long time in a bunker cell, tortured, and finally shot sometime between 3 and 7 August 1944.

2. The person in question is Cyryl Ratajski (1875–1942), who received his code names 'Wrzos' and 'Wartski' from General Sikorski, in London, along with his appointment on 3 December 1940. A lawyer from Poznań, he was an active member of Catholic Action and the moderate wing of the National Democrats. A long-standing and popular Mayor of Poznań (1922–4 and 1925–34), he assured the prominence of the Christian Labor Party in the Poznań region. General Sikorski appointed him the 'Head Delegate of the Polish Government for the General Government, resident in Warsaw' with the possibility of extending his mandate to all of the 1939 territories, which he did. Thus, the civilian branch of the Secret State was placed under his supervision. Cyryl Ratajski resigned on 5 August 1942 on the grounds of ill health and was officially replaced by his deputy, Professor Jan Piekałkiewicz, on 17 September 1942. He died in Warsaw on 19 October 1942.

3. Kazimierz Pużak (1883–1950), pseudonyms 'Bazyli' and 'Seret,' was the Secretary-General of the Central Executive Committee of the PPS (1921–39). He was the founder of the secret organization PPS-WRN in October 1939. He represented his party at the PKP (Political Consultative Committee) that he helped found in February 1940 and which was called by Jan Karski the 'secret Parliament.' 'Agent Witold' knew Kazimierz Pużak and met with him several times in May 1940.

4. In March 1942, General Sikorski made his second trip to the United States. His two meetings with Franklin D. Roosevelt gave rise to the radio messages mentioned here; the summer of 1942 marked the

height of the prestige of the leader of the Polish government-in-exile, as well as his hopes and delusions.

29. The Ghetto

1. In 1942, two representatives of the Jewish minority in Poland had seats in the Polish National Council of the government-in-exile in London. One was Ignacy Schwarzbart, a lawyer and a former deputy, who represented the Polish Zionist organizations. He had already participated in the hearings of the Council during their first meeting in Paris in December 1939. The other was Szmuel Zygielbojm from the Bund. It was therefore understandable that the two delegates of the ghetto held the same political affiliations.

2. Leon Feiner (1885–1945), pseudonyms 'Mikołaj' and 'Berezowski,' was the representative and leader of the Bund. Through Karski, he transmitted a report at the end of August 1942 on the implementation of the 'final solution.' He took part in setting up the Żegota, and was its Vice-Chairman from January 1943 to July 1944, a post he took up again following the suppression of the Warsaw uprising, from November 1944 to January 1945.

3. The identity of the Zionist encountered by Karski remains unknown.

4. From autumn 1941, the Warsaw Ghetto was aware of the mass murders carried out by the Einsatzgruppen in Białystok, Pińsk, Brześć and in Wołyń. In February 1942, a survivor of the Chełmno extermination camp managed to get to Warsaw, where he described the mass gassings of the Jews from the cities and provinces incorporated into the Reich to Emanuel Ringelblum. Recorded by Oneg Szabat (the clandestine archives of the ghetto), the information was transmitted to the Jewish section of the Information Bureau of the AK and then passed on to London. Although there were some who refused to believe it and were still uncertain about the meaning of 'Treblinka,' the ghetto 'knew' from 10 August 1942: first David Nowodworski of Harszomer Hacair, having escaped from Treblinka, brought the information, and then a member of the Bund, Zygmunt Frydrych, who confirmed the same

information. The 'knowledge' contained in the reports that Karski transmitted shocked the people to whom he reported it.

5. Engineer Adam Czerniaków (1880–1942) was a native of Warsaw and came from a culturally assimilated Polish-speaking family. In independent Poland, his skills were recognized: he managed the Reconstruction Services of the Public Works Department (1919–21), and then led the Commission for the Reconstruction of the City (1922–8). Elected to the Warsaw Municipal Council, he devoted his energy to the Commission for Urban Development (1927–34) and was elected to the Polish Senate in 1931. In September 1939, he bitterly noted in his *Diary* how the spiritual leaders of the community had fled. Having remained in Warsaw, he was appointed President of the Jewish community by Stefan Starzyński, who was his old friend. On 4 October, the occupiers forced him to organize 'Judenrat' under his presidency. Right until the end, Czerniaków remained honorable through every trial and tribulation; his office displayed the double symbols of patriotism: portraits of the patriotic Rabbi Ber Meisels (1863) and Marshal Piłsudski. Czerniaków certainly knew that the Jews in the ghetto were being sent to their death. But he clung onto the hope of saving as many Jews as he could in Warsaw, and especially the children. On 23 July 1942, on the second day of the mass extermination of Jews known as the 'Grossaktion Warsaw,' he committed suicide after receiving an order from the Nazis to endorse the deportation of children.

6. 'Grossaktion Warsaw,' an operation of mass deportation of the Warsaw Jews, began at 11 a.m. on 22 July 1942 with convoys leaving for the Treblinka extermination camp. Two similar convoys would leave every week for Bełżec. According to German sources, 253,742 Jews were deported during the course of this operation in forty-six days. According to Jewish sources, the population of the ghetto lost 300,000 people, as Karski's information indicated.

7. Szmuel Zygielbojm, pseudonym 'Artur' (1895–1943). One of the leaders of the workers and the leader of the Bund in Warsaw. Secretary of the Trade Union of Jewish Metal Workers in 1920, Szmuel Zygielbojm was elected to the Bund's Central Committee in 1924. He was involved in local politics as a Municipal Councillor, first in Warsaw (1927) and then in Łódź (1936). In September 1939, unlike the majority of the Bund

leaders who fled to the east, he remained in Łódź, and returned to Warsaw on 8 September. There he actively participated in the defense of the capital along with fellow members of the PPS, organising voluntary defense battalions of Jewish workers. Following the fall of Warsaw on 28 September, he volunteered to be one of the twenty hostages demanded by the Germans in exchange for the peaceful entry of the troops into the city. He reluctantly accepted to represent the Bund in the Judenrat, but resigned on 4 November after voicing his strong opposition to the decision to establish a 'closed quarter' in the city. A member of the secret steering committee of the Bund, which he co-organized in October 1939, he left for France at his party's request. On 18 April 1940 he presented the government-in-exile in Paris with a memorandum on the situation in Poland and the first violent reprisals against the Jews. He established a close relationship with Adam Ciołkosz, the leader of the PPS. He then rejoined the steering committee of the Bund in New York upon its order. Chosen by the Polish government-in-exile to take the seat in the newly established National Council, he arrived in London in late March 1942. This position allowed him to have direct access to information arriving from the Resistance. He also received messages sent by Feiner, and his report of 12 May 1942 concerning the scope of the massacres reported the terrifying number of 700,000 victims. Zygielbojm tried to make the British public aware of these facts. The reports brought by Karski about the 'final solution' and a personal letter from Feiner convinced Zygielbojm that it was necessary to send a telegram to Churchill on 15 December 1942. In January 1943 he requested the Bund's permission to act in collaboration with the Zionist Schwarzbart, but in vain. The failure of the Bermuda conference and the tragedy of the suppressed uprising in the Warsaw Ghetto (19 April–16 May 1943), where his wife and son lost their lives, precipitated Zygielbojm's suicide on 12 May 1943. He left a letter addressed to the President of the Polish Republic, Raczkiewicz, and Prime Minister Sikorski in which he denounced the indifference 'of the Allied governments and their people' in the face of the Holocaust: 'My death is an impassioned plea against the passivity with which the world observes and tolerates the total extermination of the Jewish people . . .'

Perhaps through my death, I will succeed in shattering the indifference of those who could still save the Jews of Poland.'

30. 'To Die in Agony . . .'

1. Bełżec was the first of the three extermination camps established in the autumn of 1941 along the River Bug line, as a part of 'Operation Reinhard,' with the aim of exterminating the Jews within the territory of the General Government. Its construction began in 1941, followed by that of the Sobibor extermination camp in March 1942 and Treblinka in May 1942. The operation was overseen via a special headquarters set up in Lublin and led by Odilo Globocnik, the SS General and Chief of Police of Lublin.

2. In fact, Polish rail workers were the first to be informed and called as witnesses.

3. The historic veracity of these facts has since been reaffirmed by scholars, and by Jan Karski himself in 1999, with the publication of the Polish edition of *Story of a Secret State*. It was in fact a Ukrainian (and not Estonian) guard, as all the guards in Bełżec and the neighboring camps were Ukrainian.

4. The camp to which Karski was taken was Izbica Lubelska and not Bełżec. Lesser known of the two, as an annex of Bełżec, Izbica Lubelska nevertheless held an important place in the extermination programme of the thousands of Jews in 'Operation Reinhard.' After a de-lousing operation in Izbica Lubelska, the Jews were either executed in the camp or (the majority) transported to Bełżec, amidst the violence and horrors described by Karski.

5. In Bełżec, as a part of 'Operation Reinhard,' the first Jews were executed from the ghetto of Lublin (30,000 victims were killed between 17 March and 20 April 1942). These were followed by victims from Krákow (a convoy of 5,000 people arrived on 28 May), from Zamość (2,500) and smaller towns and villages, from which citizens were requested to travel 10–20 miles by foot to be placed on trains heading for the extermination camps. Between 10 and 23 August, 50,000 Jews from

the Lwów ghetto were killed in Bełżec. In total, over 550,000 people, Jews and Gypsies, are estimated to have died between May 1942 and April 1943.

6. The person in question here is Zofia Kossak, whom Karski admired greatly and who is described in Chapter 26.

32. *Journey Through France and Spain*

1. Lyon, the most important center of the 'free zone' and second largest city in France, was the 'capital' of French Resistance at the time. Three of the most important Resistance networks were created there: the Franc-Tireur (Snipers), Libération-sud, and Combat. Lyon was also the center of Polish Resistance until 1943, a fact that is not well known.

2. On 8 November 1942, 'Operation Torch' took place: the Allied forces disembarked in North Africa, in Morocco and Algeria. On 11 November the Germans invaded the 'free zone.'

33. *My Report to the World.*

1. Polish-Soviet relations continued to deteriorate. Stalin chose 19 January 1943, the day when Sikorski was leaving New York, to publish a diplomatic note issued to the Ambassador of Poland, Tadeusz Romer, proclaiming the inhabitants of Western Belorussia, the Western Ukraine, and the Wilno region – including native Poles – to be Soviet citizens. These territories were annexed and integrated into the Soviet Federation on 1 November 1939. This ruthless decision thus annulled the right of option agreed on 1 December 1941 that followed a series of meetings between Stalin and Sikorski, effectively forcing thousands of orphans and the deportees to Kazakhstan and Siberia who missed the opportunity of joining the Anders Army in time to remain in the USSR. This declaration made it clear that the border established by the Ribbentrop-Molotov Pact was not fixed, and that Stalin had the clear intention of ratifying the territorial privileges Hitler conceded to him,

with the help of the British and Americans. The Związek Patriotów Polskich, ZPP (Union of Polish Patriots) was officially established on 1 March 1943 in Moscow, which was the Soviets' instrument for defeating and supplanting the legal government-in-exile in London.

2. By a decree of 30 January 1943, issued by General Sikorski, Jan Karski was awarded the Silver Cross of the Order of the Virtuti Militari. Sikorski did not know that the Virtuti Militari Cross had already secretly been conferred on Karski on 2 February 1941 by General Rowecki.

3. In fact, Karski had meetings with Eden on two occasions; Eden questioned him 'in strict confidentiality' on 5 February 1943 about the reactions of the Polish Resistance toward the 'compromise' reached by Sikorski and Stalin on territorial division. During the first meeting, encouraged by Eden's warm reception, Karski requested an interview with Churchill. His request was met with a polite but firm refusal.

4. The United Nations War Crimes Commission was founded on 17 October 1942. On 17 December 1942, a formal declaration by the twelve Allied states and the French Committee of National Liberation condemned the criminal massacres of the Jews in central Europe and called for severe punishment for such crimes.

5. In May 1943 it was decided that Jan Karski should leave for the United States; his departure was prepared with utmost secrecy and he left on 9 June 1943. On 16 June 1943, Karski entered the port of New York.

6. General Sikorski returned to London via Gibraltar after a month-long inspection of the Anders Army based in the Middle East, in Iraq, following his departure from the USSR on 1 September 1942. Shortly after take-off from Gibraltar on the evening of 4 July 1943, the plane carrying him plunged into the sea: only the Czech pilot survived. His daughter and closest collaborator, Zofia Leśniowska, as well as his secretary, Aleksander Kułakowski, died with Sikorski in the crash.

7. On Wednesday 28 July 1943, Franklin D. Roosevelt received Jan Karski with the Ambassador, Jan Ciechanowski; the meeting lasted for an hour and fifteen minutes. The Ambassador's report to the government-in-exile, dated 4 August 1943, as well as a personal 'note' written in Karski's hand, is preserved in the Polish Archives at the Hoover Institution and gives details of this meeting.

Afterword

To have utterly vital information, but to be ignored or disbelieved, must be almost as terrible as to be interrogated for information one doesn't possess. For that was the fate of Jan Karski, hero of the Polish underground resistance, whose Second World War memoir this is. It might read like the screenplay for an incredibly exciting war movie, but it is all true. Yet it was a truth that, tragically, the Western Allies could not bring themselves to believe.

It was Karski (born Jan Kólzielewski – Karski was one of seven wartime aliases) who, in 1942 and 1943, first told the British and American authorities the horrific truth about the Nazi genocide of the Poles, Jews, and others, yet next to nothing came of it. Dismissed as Polish exaggerations, perpetrated for political purposes, it was to be another two years before the West finally recognized the monstrous reality, namely that Karski had been telling the unvarnished truth, that they had not acted upon it, and that, as a result, many thousands of innocents had perished.

Jan Karski was born in Łódź, in central Poland, on 24 June 1914, the youngest of eight children in a Catholic, liberal-minded, middle-class family. After his father died in 1920, Karski's mother moved them all to the predominantly Jewish neighbourhood of Kilinski Street, where he lived until he went to Lwów University in 1931. This meant that much of Karski's youth was spent among Jews, with whom he got on well. He worked hard at his studies in Lwów, hoping to become a diplomat, and, while there, joined the reserve cadets of the Polish horse artillery, graduating top of his class in 1936 and winning the Sword of Honour, which was awarded personally by the President of Poland.

Therefore, Karski was a twenty-five-year-old junior official in the Polish foreign office when his regiment was mobilized on 23 August 1939 and called to its barracks in the then little-known Polish town called Oświęcim (whose German name – Auschwitz – was, six years later, to shake the conscience of the world). When the Wehrmacht proceeded to destroy the Polish army in six weeks of relentless Blitzkrieg warfare, after the outbreak of war on 1 September 1939, Karski's regiment was obliged to retreat eastwards, until, on 17 October, the Soviet Union invaded Poland from the east, blocking their route of escape, and so his regiment was ordered to surrender to the Red Army. A fourth great partition of Poland, as planned by the Nazi foreign minister, Joachim Ribbentrop, and his Soviet counterpart, V. I. Molotov, then took place; a partition which was intended to exterminate that country as a national entity forever.

Forced onto a cattle-truck going further eastwards, Second-Lieutenant Karski was taken to a POW camp and only managed to escape the Katyn Massacre of Poland's officer corps by swapping his uniform and volunteering to be exchanged for the Ukrainian POWs that the Germans had captured. Virtually all his comrades in arms, however, were later taken to the Katyn Forest by the Soviet secret service, the NKVD, where they were shot in the head, one by one, and buried in mass graves among the pine trees.*

On his way back westwards – to an almost equally certain fate at the hands of the SS at Auschwitz – Karski managed to organize yet another lucky escape for himself and a few others, squeezing from the moving train they were on with help from men he had inspired through appeals to Polish patriotism (Karski's breathtaking account of this had me biting my nails in excitement). He then simply walked all the way to Warsaw, ingeniously evading German checkpoints, where he found his sister, Lili, in mourning for her husband, who had been tortured and then shot by the Gestapo. He thereafter made contact with a schoolfriend, who was in the Polish underground

---

* Their tragic story is told with chilling verisimilitude in Andrzej Wajda's haunting 2007 movie, *Katyn*.

army – the 'Secret State' of this book's title – fighting clandestinely against the Nazi occupation with a courage that defies belief, even to this day.

Karski's word-pictures of the heroic resisters at this point of the book are powerfully drawn, such as of the assassin Dziepatowski (pp. 63–5), of Karski's landlady, Mrs Nowak (pp. 70, 80–81), and of the former politician Mr Borecki (pp. 94–6), who nicknamed the cyanide tablet concealed in his ring 'my candy', but who had no chance to swallow it before the Gestapo captured him, broke his arms and legs with iron bars, and shot him (he divulged nothing). This section is as powerful as any memoir of the entire Second World War canon, and, like the rest of *Story of a Secret State*, reminds one of the capacity of mankind for true nobility of spirit, even in its darkest moments.

Karski was meanwhile sent on an expedition to try to make contact with the Polish government-in-exile in Angers, France – once in 1940 and again in 1942 – where he met its leader, General Władysław Sikorski. In a report written for Sikorski in February 1940, Karski explained how he had escaped from the Germans and subsequently 'spent time illegally in Lwów, Łódź, Wilno, Poznań, Lublin, etc,' adding that, although he had volunteered for the Polish army-in-exile, 'I am willing to return and remain in Poland if the government deems that I would be more useful to the country. [. . .] I aspire to serve Poland in the most difficult of conditions.' It took a rare form of courage to make that commitment at that stage in Poland's *via dolorosa*.

The Polish government-in-exile took Karski up on his offer, and thereafter he became their political emissary, returning to Krakow and Warsaw after April 1940, where he quickly impressed the local leaders of the resistance, or 'internal armed forces', as they termed themselves. Using the *nom de guerre* 'Witold', Karski was appointed a subordinate of General Rowecki, commander-in-chief of the ZWZ (Union for Armed Combat), which, in February 1942, was to be renamed the Armia Krajowa.

In further nerve-wracking adventures, he was seized by the

Gestapo in the summer of 1940, with incriminating microfilm in his possession, the bulk of which he managed to dissolve in a barrel of water before capture. He was interrogated and badly beaten, and would undoubtedly have been forced to swallow the suicide pill that he had taped to his perineum had he not sensationally been sprung from the prison hospital at Nowy Sącz by the ZWZ, who afterwards told him that, because he knew so much about the network, they had orders to shoot him if it looked like the escape might fail. This account, and others like it, helps to make *Story of a Secret State* not only a morality tale and a powerfully moving story of one man's struggle to reveal the depths of the depravities of the Third Reich, but also one of the most exciting adventure stories of the war. Furthermore, unlike many personal testimonies published after the war, this has the inestimable advantage of being completely true.

And yet, after his escape from Nowy Sącz, when anyone else would have been forgiven, after all their exertions, if they had lain low for the rest of the war, Karski instead visited the Warsaw Ghetto and the Bełżec extermination camp disguised as an 'Estonian' guard, where he collected much information – though, crucially, it wasn't photographic – about the way the Nazis were conducting the Holocaust. In the course of this incredibly brave and risky project, which required nerves of pre-tensioned steel, Karski witnessed the sickening sight of trainloads of Jews being asphyxiated by what he thought was chlorine, and then buried under quicklime. For these and other acts, in February 1941 General Rowecki awarded him the Virtuti Militari Silver Cross *in absentia*, a fact he only discovered in the late 1990s (Sikorski, by then stationed in London after the fall of France, was to award him the same decoration in January 1943).

In the summer of 1942, having by then adopted the *nom de guerre* Jan Karski, under which he published this book during the war, he was again sent to the West, this time to pass on an important microfilm of the reports detailing the 'major offensive' being carried out by the Nazis against the Warsaw Ghetto, as well as other vital information about the atrocities taking place in the extermination camps of Treblinka, Bełżec and Sobibor. After further adventures, Karski safely got the film through to the Polish government in London on 17 November 1942. He was later extensively debriefed by British Intelligence.

The Poles published the Holocaust information later that year, to a general dearth of global interest. Indeed, the revelations only rated a two-paragraph story on page 18 of the *New York Times*. Nonetheless, Karski conducted meetings with Jewish leaders, and had dinner with Count Edward Ranczyński, the Polish foreign minister and later president of the Polish government-in-exile. Ranczyński – whom I got to know a little in the late 1980s – disseminated Karski's information as widely as possible, including making particular reference to him in his BBC broadcast of 17 December 1942. Ranczyn´ski also facilitated a meeting between Karski and the British foreign secretary Anthony Eden, twice, in February 1943.

In May 1943, Karski was sent to the United States, at precisely the time that Soviet-Polish relations hit their nadir, with the discovery and publicity by the Germans of the mass graves in the Katyn Forest. The Polish ambassador to Washington, Jan Ciechanowski, managed to secure a meeting with President Roosevelt via the good offices of the Jewish Supreme Court Justice and friend of FDR's, Felix Frankfurter. At 11 a.m. on 28 July 1943, Karski met the president in the Oval Office, where, to Karski's and Ciechanowski's dismay, Roosevelt emphasized the importance of compromising with the Soviets. When Karski asked what message he should give the Polish Resistance, the president replied: 'Tell them that we are going to win this war, and tell them that they have a friend in the White House.' In the car on the way back to the Embassy, Ciechanowski accurately summed up the meeting with the deflating words: 'Well, the president didn't say much.'

Both Eden and Roosevelt were naturally disgusted by the Nazi outrages, but the lack of photographic evidence made Karski's claims impossible to deploy as authoritative propaganda. The concentration, during the Great War, of atrocity stories about German soldiers – such as their allegedly bayoneting Belgian babies – much of which later turned out to be untrue, made the British Foreign Office and American State Department wary. Nor did everyone accept that Karski's stories were accurate; as Felix Frankfurter put it: '[. . .] I did not say this young man is lying. I said I am unable to believe him. There is a difference.'

After the war, Karski lived out the rest of his days in the United States, lecturing and writing at Georgetown University, with which he stayed professionally associated in different capacities for more than thirty years (among his students in the 1968 class was the young Bill Clinton). In 1954, Karski became an American citizen; he also made the decision not take back his family name after the war, but kept his *nom de guerre*. That same year, while attending a perform- ance of contemporary dance in a synagogue in Washington, DC, he became reacquainted with Pola Nirenska, whom he had first met in London in 1938, and they married in 1965. Although her parents had managed to escape to Palestine before the war, the rest of Nirenska's family had been murdered in the Holocaust and she had converted to Catholicism. The couple agreed never to speak of the past. She died in 1992.

In October 1981, Karski attended Elie Wiesel's ground-breaking International Liberators Conference, speaking in public about his wartime experiences for the first time since the end of the war, and saying of the Holocaust: 'This sin will haunt humanity until the end of time. This sin haunts me. And I want it to haunt me.' Of his responsibility to speak out, he added: 'God has allowed me to observe and speak of what I have seen, in order to be able to bear witness.' In June 1982, Karski was recognized as Righteous Among Nations by the Yad Vashem Institute in Israel. Three years later, his face covered with tears, Karski appeared in Claude Lanzmann's epic documentary film, *Shoah*.

It was also in 1985 that he published his monumental book, *The Great Powers and Poland 1919–1945: From Versailles to Yalta*, which, not surprisingly, given its subject matter, he described as 'a sad book'. When Poland finally regained its sovereign independence and threw off Communism in 1991, Karski was welcomed back to his homeland, both after the publication of his biography, *Emisariusz Witold* (*Emissary 'Witold'*), by Stanislaw Jankowski in 1991, and then again when the Polish translation of Thomas E. Wood and Jankowski's book, *Karski: How One Man Tried to Stop the Holocaust*, was published in 1995. He was awarded numerous honorary degrees before his death in 2000, and there is a fine statue of him at the intersection of Madison Avenue and 37th Street in New York.

This book, *Story of a Secret State*, sold no fewer than 400,000 copies when it was published in America in 1944, and will hopefully sell even more in this wonderful new edition that you are now holding. Yet Karski himself would gladly have swapped all that success for some more credibility with the British and American decision-makers, especially when it could have made a difference. There can be little doubt, for example, that much greater efforts should have been made to disrupt the railway lines taking victims to the concentration camps, before the exodus of hundreds of thousands of Hungarian Jews to annihilation at Auschwitz in 1944. The might-have-beens of history are never more heart-rending than when applied to the story of this impossibly heroic young Pole, and first-rate literary and historical figure: Jan Karski.

Andrew Roberts
New York City, November 2011

1. Jan Karski. This photograph was taken in Washington at the time of his first mission there (June–September 1943).

2. 1936. On the left, Jan
Kozielewski, the future Jan
Karski, in the uniform of a
student, with his military
brother, Marian
Kozielewski, alongside.

PASZPORT DYPLOMATYCZNY   PASSEPORT DIPLOMATIQUE

*This passport is valid for
travel via Baltic Ethiopia
London, May 29th, 1943
For the Polish Minister for Foreign Affairs
H. Babiński
V. Babiński*

W IMIENIU SPRAW ZAGR.   AU NOM DE LA
RZECZYPOSPOLITEJ POLSKIEJ   RÉPUBLIQUE POLONAISE

Wszystkim, komu o tym wiedzieć należy, wiadomo   A tous ceux qui ces présentes verront faisons savoir
czynimy, iż   que
Pan *Jan Karski*   M *Jan Karski*
Kurier Dyplomatyczny   Courrier Diplomatique

urodzon y w m. *Zgierz*   né à *Zgierz*
dnia *22 marca 1912*   le *22 mars 1912*
udaję się za granicę   se rend à l'étranger

Wobec czego polecamy wszystkim władzom pol-   En raison de quoi nous requérons les autorités
skim cywilnym i wojskowym oraz prosimy odpo-   civiles et militaires polonaises et prions les autorités
wiednie władze zagraniczne aby pozwoliły *mu*   étrangères de vouloir bien *le laisser librement*
swobodnie przejechać i udzieliły pomocy i opieki *w*   passer et de lui accorder aide et protection en cas de
razie potrzeby.   besoin.

Paszport niniejszy ważny jest do *31 maja 1944*   Passeport valable jusqu'au *31 mai 1944*
Londyn, dnia *4 maja 1943*   *Londres*, le *4 mai 1943*

za Ministra Spraw Zagranicznych   Le Ministre des Affaires Étrangères

H. Babiński
V. Babiński

N° *1718 L. 1218*   Podpis właściciel
Signature du porteur   *Jan Karski*

3. Jan Kozielewski's diploma, dated 8 October 1935,
from Jan Kazimierz University in Lwow (now the city
of Lviv, in the Ukraine).

The Jewish Mass Executions

(JAN KARSKI)

ACCOUNT by an **EYE-WITNESS**

News-Talk on European Service of the British Broadcasting Corporation

I was a member of the Polish Underground Movement. It was my duty to keep in touch with all underground parties, including the "Bund"—the Jewish Social-Democratic Organization in Poland, and I left Warsaw in October, 1942, on a mission from the Underground Front to the Polish Government in London.

Among my other duties, I collected matter on the Jewish mass-exterminations carried out by the occupying power. I should perhaps explain why we paid special attention to the Jewish questions. I am not a Jew myself, and before the war I had very little contact with Jews; in fact, I knew practically nothing about them. But, at present, the extermination of the Jews has a special significance. The sufferings of my own Polish compatriots are terrible, and they are, of course, nearer to my heart; but the methods employed by the enemy against Poles and against Jews are different.

Us, the Poles, they try to reduce to a mediaeval race of serfs. They want to deprive us of our cultural standards, of our traditions, of our education, and reduce us to a nation of robots. But the policy towards the Jews is different. It is not a policy of subjugation and oppression, but of cold and systematic extermination. It is the first example in modern history that a whole nation (not 10, 20 or 30, but 100 per cent of them) are meant to disappear from this earth.

The methods of this process are known to a certain extent, but the details are not. The method is, as you know, to collect the Jews from all over Europe, to despatch them to the Ghettos of Warsaw, Lwev and Soon, where they stay for a certain time. From the ghettos they are "taken East" as the official term goes, that is, to the extermination camps, in Belzec, Treblinka and Sobibor. In these camps, they are killed in batches of 1,000 to 6,000, by various methods, including gas, burning, by steam, mass electrocution, and finally, by the method of the so-called "death train".

In the course of my investigation I succeeded in witnessing a mass-execution in the camp of Belzec. With the help of our underground organisation, I gained access to that camp in the disguise of a Latvian special policeman. I was, in fact, one of the executioners. I believe that my course of action was justified. I had no means of preventing the event, but by

9

OVER:

For security reasons – the vo was of Arthur Koestler world known author, hasein strong accent

May 1943

4. (*above*) On 17 December 1942, at 9 a.m., Edward Raczyynski, the Polish government's Minister for Foreign Affairs (1940–43), made the first broadcast on the BBC regarding the 'final solution' that was underway in Europe, based on information provided by Jan Karski in November 1942.

5. (*below*) Text from a broadcast drafted by Jan Karski and read out on the BBC in May 1943. Arthur Koestler read on Karski's behalf, however, as Karski's accent was considered too strong.

MINISTERSTWO
SPRAW ZAGRANICZNYCH

Londyn, dn.9 czerwca, 1943r.

Kochany Janiu,

Polecam Twojej pilnej uwadze a także serdecznej
opiece p.Jana Karskiego który jedzie do Was z Polski
w drodze na Wielką Brytanię. Jego znajomość spraw
polskich jest pierwszorzędna. Wyróżnia się przytym
doskonałą pamięcią i wielką ścisłością. Nie mam
wątpliwości, że będziesz wiedział jak w sposób naj-
właściwszy i najowocniejszy wykorzystać jego wizytę
w Stanach i skontaktować z ludźmi na których nam zależy.

JWPan Jan Ciechanowski,
Ambasador R.P.
w Waszyngtonie.

FEB 28 1944

6. (above) Letter of personal recommendation
from Edward Raczyynski, the Polish Minister
for Foreign Affairs, to the Polish ambassador
in Washington, Jan Ciechanowski. 'London, 9
June 1943. Dear Janiu, I recommend for your
attention, but also for your cordial solicitude,
Jan Karski, who comes to you from Poland,
passing through Great Britain on his way [...]
His knowledge of the Polish business is
excellent. It is characterized, moreover, by his
exceptional memory and great rigor. I am sure
you will be able to use his visit to the United
States in the most suitable and fruitful manner
and will be able to put him in contact with the
people who are important to us. With cordial
friendship, Edward Raczyynski'

7. Ambassador Jan
Ciechanowski (1887–1973),
dedicated to Karski in July
1943 at the time of Karski's
first mission to the
United States.

STORY
of a
SECRET
STATE

By
JAN KARSKI

Houghton Mifflin Company, Boston
The Riverside Press Cambridge
1944

8. (*above*) Jan Karski dictating *Story of a Secret State* to the bilingual secretary-translator Krystyna Sokolowska in a Manhattan hotel room that they used as an office throughout the summer of 1944. Published 28 November 1944 by Houghton Mifflin, the book was a bestseller and sold over 400,000 copies.

9. (*left*) The title page of the 1944 edition of *Story of a Secret State*

Jan Karski (n. Jan Kozielewski) (1914-2000)

Messenger of the Polish People to Their Government in Exile
Messenger of the Jewish People to the World
The Man Who Told of the Annihilation of the Jewish People
While There Was Still Time To Stop It.

Named By the State of Israel,
"A Righteous of the Nations of the World"
A Hero of the Polish People
Professor, Georgetown University (1952-1992)
A Noble Man Walked Amongst Us and Made Us Better By His Presence
A Just Man

10. (*above*) Jan Karski at his home in Chevy Chase, Maryland (USA), 4 April 1995.

11. (*below*) The plaque that appears at the bottom of the statue of Jan Karski, inaugurated on 10 September 2002, in the park of the Georgetown University in Washington, DC, where Karski taught for forty years.